M.J. Simpson

M.J. Simpson is acknowledged as the world's leading authority on the life and career of Douglas Adams, having collected information and material on him for twenty years. When Adams' personal assistant required information on her boss' career, it was Simpson that she phoned. He has been interviewed about Douglas Adams on Channel 4's 'Top Ten TV: Sci-Fi' series and BBC2's 'Reading the Decades', and on many radio stations.

He has interviewed Adams, edited the world's only 'Hitchhiker's Guide' magazine and co-founded Britain's bestselling science fiction magazine SFX.

M.J. SIMPSON

HITCHHIKER

A BIOGRAPHY OF

DOUGLAS ADAMS

Historical Consultant: Kevin Davies

CORONET BOOKS

Hodder & Stoughton

First published in Great Britain in 2003 by Hodder and Stoughton
A division of Hodder Headline

A Coronet paperback

1 3 5 7 9 10 8 6 4 2

A CIP catalogue record for this title is
available from the British Library

ISBN 0 340 82489 1

Typeset in Minion by Palimpsest Book Production Limited,
Polmont, Stirlingshire
Printed and bound in Great Britain by
Clays Ltd, St Ives plc

Hodder and Stoughton
A division of Hodder Headline
338 Euston Road
London NW1 3BH

For my parents, Chris and Pat Simpson.

Contents

PHOTOGRAPHIC ACKNOWLEDGEMENTS

Page 1 (above) courtesy Mrs Jan Thrift/photo Peter Goodwin, (centre) David Wakeling, (below) Hulton Archive/Getty Images. Page 2 courtesy Will Adams. Page 3 ©*Cambridge Evening News*. Page 4 ©BBC. Page 5 (above) Stephen Morley/Original Records from the collection of Terry Platt, (centre) Hulton Archive/Getty Images, (below) Kevin Davies. Page 6 (above) Steve Meretzky, (below) Kevin Davies. Page 7 (above) ©BBC, (below) courtesy John Lloyd. Page 8 (above) Private Collection, (below) ©BBC.

Every reasonable effort has been made to contact the copyright holders, but if there are any errors or omissions, Hodder & Stoughton will be pleased to insert the appropriate acknowledgement in any subsequent printing of this publication.

ACKNOWLEDGEMENTS

This book would not have been possible without the help of many people. In particular the assistance of Sophie Astin, Kevin Davies, Neil Gaiman, Joel Greengrass and Rick Mueller; Simon Jones, Maggie Phillips at Ed Victor Ltd; Andrew Pixley, *Hitchhiker's* collector Terry Platt, Footlights archivist Dr Harry Porter, Michael Willis of Brentwood School and ZZ9 Plural Z Alpha (the Official *Hitchhiker's Guide to the Galaxy* Appreciation Society) has been invaluable.

In addition to the above, Juliana Abell, Will Adams, Mary Allen, Tim Anderson, Eitan Arrusi, Laurence Aston, Eugen Beer, Martin Benson, Abbie Bernstein, Andrea Bolwig, Rayner Bourton, Jody Boyman, Simon Brett, Jonathan Brock, Alan Brooks, Richard Brown, Tim Browse, Ken Campbell, Mark Carwardine, James Casey, Jonathan Cecil, Jack Cohen, Richard Creasey, Mike Cule, Arvind David, Mike Dornbrook, Patrick Dowling, Stephen Durbridge, Sally Emerson, Jill Foster, David Fox, the late Jim Francis, Tom Gardiner, Kathi Goldmark, James Goss, Stephen Grief, Michael Gross, Mickey Hall, Richard Harris, Nigel Hess, Mike Howarth, Mike Jay, Keith Jeffrey, Scott Jennings, the late Peter Jones, Terry Jones, John Joyce, Paddy Kingsland, Brenda Laurel, Alain le Garsmeur, Mark Lewisohn, Sue Limb, John Lloyd, Rod Lord, Jim Lynn, Geoffrey McGivern, Bernard McKenna, Joe Medjuck, Steve Meretzky, Dirk Maggs, Andrew Marshall, Joe Melia, Stephen Moore, John Moore-Bridger, Mark Moxon, Stan Nicholls, Geoffrey Perkins, Philip Pope, Beth

Porter, Christopher Priest, David Prowse, Nigel Rees, Gail Renard, Griff Rhys Jones, Robin Rogers, Nic Rowley, Susan Sheridan, Peter Singer, Martin Smith, Michael Marshall Smith, Robbie Stamp, Charles Thomson, David Wakeling, Max Whitby, Aubrey Woods, Larry Yaeger, Howard Zimmerman and Matt Zimmerman all provided me with valuable memories in interviews or correspondence. Many of the above also supplied useful contacts, informative documents and/or fascinating recordings.

Numerous other people agreed to be interviewed about Douglas but, because of my workload and impending deadline, I was unable to do so. My sincere apologies to them.

Thanks to James Aylett, Mark Ayres, Jess Bennett, Andrew Billen, Simon Bond, Nicolas Botti, Melvyn Bragg, Mary Branscombe, Herman Braunschmidt, Berkeley Breathed, Bridlington, Juliet Brightmore, the British Film Institute, Anthony Brown, Ken Bussanmas, Michael Bywater, Cambridge University Library, John Carnell, Roland Clare and procolharum.com, the *Church Times*, Adam Corres, Mat Coward, Robert X. Cringely, Danny Danziger, Ellen Datlow, Lucy Dixon, Les Eastham and Wiggle FM, Phil Edwards, Ted Elliott, Floor 42, Freddie Francis, friendsreunited.com, Lorraine Garland, Lou Gerring, Jacqui Graham, Richard Gray, Steve Green, Peter Guzzardi, David Haddock, Clayton Hickman, Simon Hodson, David Honigmann, Billie Holiday, Richard Hollis, Sue Hopkins of Brentwood Arts Council, David Howe, Roy Hudd, David Hughes, Eric Idle, Jonathan D. Jones, Jools, Alexander Kahn, Tony Keetch, Jane Killick, Ken Kleinberg, Alois Kronbauer, Dave Langford, Leicester Writers' Club, The Liberal Party, Lisa Lipman at Tech TV, Ian Liston, John McLay, Felicity McNae, Charles Martin, Roger Martin at Video Arts, David Morgan, Alain Nevant, Robert Newman, Jeffrey O'Kelly, Gregg Pearlman, Stephen Peck, Kim Plowright, Jon Preddle, Jenny Preece, John Rainer, Mitch Ratcliffe, Alison Reddihough and Simon Corris, Edward Rice, Frank Ries, Jay Roach, Steve Rogerson, Terry Rossio, Rob Sharp and Ed Hall of *Varsity* magazine, Robert Shaw, Paul Sieveking, Sean D. Sollé, Ian Sorensen, Jocelyn Stevenson, Hans ten Cate, Rachael Thomas, Daniel Thornton, Peter Tootill, Maggie Tree, Keith Turner, Chris Walker, Colin Watkeys, Sarah Whitman at the Great Ape Project, Martin Wiggins, Roger Wilmut, Charles Worth, Su Wright and Takako Yamamura for contacts, suggestions, anecdotes, encouragement and miscellaneous other help. With this number of helpers, I worry that somebody may have slipped through the cracks. If so, my sincere apologies.

Much of the research in this book is drawn from approximately 200 interviews with Douglas Adams – from magazines, fanzines, newspapers, websites, radio and TV – which I have collected over the years (with the assistance of some of the above individuals and many others who provided photocopies or transcripts to the editors of *Mostly Harmless*, the ZZ9 magazine). I am indebted to all the original interviewers and have endeavoured to credit each and every quote. If any have been misattributed, please let me and/or my publisher know so that we can correct future editions.

Enormous thanks for having faith in me and my ability to write this book are due especially to three people: my agent Andrew Lownie, my editor Katy Follain, and my wife Hillary. A special mention also to my parents for their constant support and encouragement, and to my brother Richard for technical support.

Thanks to Jane Belson and Ed Victor for allowing me to write this book. Special thanks to Douglas' sisters, Jane Garnier and Sue Adams, and his mother, Mrs Jan Thrift, for their help and support.

Way back in the mists of time, Neville Hawcock introduced me to *The Hitchhiker's Guide to the Galaxy* when he bought me a copy of the novel for my twelfth birthday, and Jeremy Newsome introduced me to ZZ9 (and hence science fiction fandom) when he rang me to say that he had found the address for a *Hitchhiker's Guide* society in his girlfriend's comic. Belated thanks to both. And finally, thanks to Douglas Adams, a major influence on my life since 1980. Though I only briefly orbited Planet Douglas, the opportunities which that connection offered me have been enormous.

FOREWORD

Douglas Adams was, for several years, my closest friend. He was an extraordinarily gifted, intelligent and funny guy, and I consider myself very lucky to have known him as well as I did. We had an enormous amount of fun – especially in the years before he became famous – and he greatly enriched my life.

Reading M.J. Simpson's painstakingly researched and ineffably sad biography of 'The Big Man', one struggles to draw inferences from such a tumultuous and agonisingly short existence that might be in some way helpful to someone or other.

What I take from it is this. We are all of us trapped in the hidden grid of our upbringing, personality, genetic dispositions and habits. Whether these are caused by nature, or nurture, or a mixture of the two, is neither here nor there. The point is, we find ourselves alive and we must decide what to do about it. Stuff happens. Over most of it, we have very little control. Some of us get rich and famous, some don't – but we can all attempt to do our best under trying circumstances.

The initial conditions with which Douglas was saddled were rather more trying, I suspect, than the author of this book has been able either to discern or to put in print. That Douglas was able so triumphantly to transcend these is a celebration of the human spirit which utterly belies the oft-peddled factoid that we are all 98.7 per cent chimpanzee.

Naturally, I cannot personally vouch for the 'truth' of every statement in this book. Biography is an inexact science – as all science is at its beginnings and at its edges. When even the proportion of DNA we are supposed to share with chimps has recently been revised downward, how can anyone hope to know the whole truth of even a single human life? Many of the facts can never be known, not even by the subject or by those closest to him – perhaps especially not by them. But I can say that Mike Simpson is an honest man who has done his level best to present a balanced picture of what can hardly be described as a balanced life.

Douglas was one of those people to whom anecdotes cling like burrs on a hiking-sock. Watching him trying to learn to ski, to scuba-dive or to play Boggle provided weeks of hilarity for anyone within eyeshot. It was virtually impossible for him to leave any of his vast beds without creating an incident: whether shutting his own leg in his own car door; crashing his brand new Porsche into Hyde Park Corner because he 'forgot' there is about an acre of roundabout at the end of Park Lane; or (famously) putting his back out buttering a slice of bread. He never really learned to drive in the way you and I would understand it – a problem that seems endemic among comic geniuses (Richard Curtis and Ben Elton are both similarly afflicted). His memorable absent-mindedness was consistently endearing, as was his truly gigantic laugh, a vast barking expression of pure merriment as distinctive as a road-drill, frequently ending in a Brobdingnagian cough.

He was born tall and talented, and he became very well-off and very, very bad at delivering anything on time. In all these characteristics, he comfortably outdid me – though in struggling to finish this foreword, I empathise rather painfully with the last.

It is a pleasant game to try to guess the models on whom an author based, or partially based, his most famous characters. There is some such guessing in this book, peppered – as you might expect – with fierce denials from the most likely candidates. My theory is that such speculation is fruitless, because all the best-drawn characters were essentially based on their author.

The largeness, the flamboyance, the love of parties, the ambition, the large fancy vehicles, Douglas shared with his alter-ego, the Galactic President, Zaphod Beeblebrox. Like Marvin, Douglas had a brain the size of a planet, but a tendency to terminal despair, and bits of him hurt a lot of the time. The bafflement, the cups of tea, the basic niceness, these belong to both Arthur Dent and to Douglas Adams, and the Captain of the 'B'-Ark is certainly a self-portrait – as I can personally testify, having once shared a house with him. Douglas remained in the bath for just under a year. Most of all, who else could be the template for Deep Thought, the enormous mind in receipt of the crucial Question which can manage only a meaningless answer.

Meaningless?

Something so funny, so original, so exact, so memorable? Compared to what is the answer '42' meaningless? And it is not beyond possibility that it may even turn out to be correct. There was a delicious moment some years ago when it was announced that the Hubble Constant, the defining parameter of the expanding universe, had been definitely identified as 42. This caused Douglas, as you might imagine, the most fantastical piles of pleasure, which he shovelled JCB-like into every conversation, delighting the rest of us with its ironic synchronicity. Of course, the Hubble Constant, like the Chimp Constant, has turned out to be a hopeless misnomer – its supposed value fluctuates with every passing year – but it was a cracking joke while it lasted.

Douglas is massively missed by his many friends, and by his many millions of fans, but he may also be an even greater loss than we will ever know.

A year or so before he died, he had arranged to have lunch with his old friend, the equally famous writer Richard Curtis. As they strolled up the street towards the restaurant, Richard genially inquired as to what Douglas was working on, and was somewhat taken aback when Douglas announced out that he was particularly excited because he had recently been speculating on the meaning of existence and felt that he had actually come up with the answer.

There was a pause, as Richard took this in. This was a pretty major revelation and, as you might expect, he was as eager as anyone to know the details. On the other hand, he was also looking forward to a jolly, non-working lunch, swapping jokes and gossip. Knowing

Douglas' fondness for expatiating on his latest theories in a manner to which the word 'lengthy' does not really do justice, he realised he was caught on the horns of a doldrum. If he were to say: 'Really? Go on ...' Douglas certainly *would* go on, and those would be the last three words Richard would utter for at least an hour and a half. Alternatively, he could buy time by plumping for a diversionary response, such as: 'And how's Jane ...?'

To his undying shame and to the permanent loss to science and humanity of the actual, definitive answer to Life, the Universe and Everything, Richard made his decision.

Jane, it turned out, was fine – and the lunch, jolly.

Douglas was a tireless exponent of both neo-Darwinism and the virtues of computers. Cursory reading of the literature would suggest that computers are much smarter than people and the great apes very nearly as smart. But such is not the case. Any five-year-old child is incomparably cleverer than the hugest computer in the world, and utterly dwarfs the intellectual capabilities of the wisest orang-utan. Douglas beat all three of them into a cocked hat.

It's true that people faintly resemble gorillas in a physical sense – their skeletons are even more strikingly alike – but in the only way that matters there is simply no comparison.

When we make some headway into discovering what consciousness is, what it's made of, and where it comes from – and there is no discernible progress whatever in this field so far – things may get a little more interesting. Perhaps then we will be able to shake off the dispiriting reductionism that infects almost all of modern science. Death, whether of oneself or one's friends, is the hardest trial a human being has to face, and the prospect is not even slightly improved by a belief, however well-argued, in the pointlessness of an indifferent cosmos.

To those of us who cling to the notion that the universe is meaningful, it seems very unfair that Douglas should have had such a short life. Fortunately, he didn't believe life was meaningful, so he probably wouldn't agree.

I sincerely hope that he is in for a pleasant (if intellectually embarrassing) surprise, because – if the theologians are correct about the nature of eternity – there can be no deadlines in Heaven.

John Lloyd
Oxfordshire 2002

John Lloyd co-wrote *The Meaning of Liff* and *The Deeper Meaning of Liff* with Douglas, and co-wrote two episodes of the original radio series of *The Hitchhiker's Guide to the Galaxy*. He also produced *Not the Nine O'Clock News*, *Spitting Image* and *Blackadder*.

HITCHHIKER: A Biography of Douglas Adams

PRELUDE - **FORBIDDEN PLANET**

SATURDAY 13 OCTOBER 1979 was a pleasant if undistinguished autumn day in London. Douglas Noël Adams, a twenty-seven-year-old scriptwriter, was on his way to Forbidden Planet, a small shop specialising in science fiction, fantasy and horror books and ephemera. Tucked away down a side street, the dark, cramped shop was a haven for those SF fans who had discovered it and who could browse through shelves of rare American paperbacks or boxes of dog-eared film stills. Douglas had accepted an invitation from the management to sign some copies of his first novel, *The Hitchhiker's Guide to the Galaxy*, published the previous day and adapted from his own surprisingly successful radio scripts.

A couple of streets away from Forbidden Planet, Douglas' taxi slowed, then stopped. Crowds of people were milling about; it was some sort of demonstration. Douglas paid the driver and continued on foot, threading his way through the good-natured crowd.

As he came into Denmark Street, he found the crowd narrowing and forming into a line, which snaked along the pavement then made a sharp turn into the front door of Forbidden Planet, where a small poster announced: 'Douglas Adams signing copies of *The Hitchhiker's Guide to the Galaxy* here today.' It wasn't a demonstration, it was a queue for a signing session. His signing session. These people blocking the roads were all fans of *The Hitchhiker's Guide to the Galaxy*; they were here to buy his book and have him autograph it.

The next day, *The Hitchhiker's Guide to the Galaxy* was number one in the *Sunday Times* paperback bestsellers list. Douglas Adams, twenty-seven-year-old scriptwriter, was officially a bestselling author. He later described the events of the weekend as, 'like having an orgasm with no foreplay',[1] or, in more polite company, 'like being helicoptered to the top of Mount Everest'.[2]

The story of the crowds who milled around inside and outside the little science fiction shop, patiently awaiting their new hero, so numerous that they held up the traffic and almost kept him away from his own signing session, is enshrined in the extraordinary history of Douglas Adams' extraordinary life. Douglas told the anecdote many times in many interviews. His friends repeated it to interviewers in the wake of his death. Nicholas Wroe used it as the opening hook for a profile of Adams in the *Guardian*, reprinted as the prologue to the posthumous collection *The Salmon of Doubt*.

It's a wonderful story, the sort of rags-to-riches moment that every struggling writer dreams of. It would be even better if it was true.

To be fair, parts of the story undoubtedly are true. Douglas did sign an awful lot of books that day, nearly a thousand. And certainly the novel went straight into the bestseller list, but that was the following weekend, after it had been on sale a full week. As for having to battle through a crowd big enough to stop the traffic – that certainly didn't happen, not at that first signing.

'The signing, which began nail-bitingly with a trickle of punters, was hit by a deluge about twenty minutes in,'[3] recalls shop manager Stan Nicholls, now a successful SF/fantasy author himself. 'Most signings start slow and then you get a bit of momentum building up. Quite often the psychology of customers is, "I won't get there too early because I'll have to stand in line." It was enormously successful but there wasn't a question of crowds and police and traffic, I'm afraid.'[4]

Robert Newman, then a student but later a civil servant and President of the *Hitchhiker's Guide to the Galaxy* Appreciation Society, is more specific: 'I was about fifth in the queue of ten or so people. I got Douglas to sign my book, chatted to him and hung around in the shop for a while before leaving. Certainly no more than twenty people turned up to see him while I was there.'[5]

That makes sense. This wasn't a famous author making a public appearance at a big bookstore to sign a hyped new novel. It was an unknown first novelist signing a barely publicised paperback at an obscure specialist shop. Nicholls' attempts to get the event mentioned in the media had come to naught. Why on earth would anybody turn up before the announced time? Instead, they all turned up twenty minutes into the session, ironically assuming that by then any initial queue would have safely dissipated.

'It could have been about 1,500 people in all, which for a signing is quite phenomenal,' estimates Nicholls. 'We had a Pan rep there who had brought a couple of spare packs of books in the boot of his car and we said, "Don't bother bringing them in. We probably won't need them." Because most signings aren't very well attended, even for some big names. But not only did he have to bring them in, he had to go and get some more! I remember also sending one of the lads who worked in the shop over to Foyle's to see whether they could let us have some copies. We got through a hell of a lot.'[6]

So it was undoubtedly a massive success – Douglas signed for four hours in the end, and nobody went home disappointed – but this only happened after it gathered momentum. The problem with Douglas' version of events is that it became embellished and exaggerated, and possibly confused with the signing for *The Restaurant at the End of the Universe* one year later at the same shop.

'By the time the *Restaurant* signing was supposed to start the queue went round the block and was probably over a thousand strong,' remembers Robert Newman. 'After an hour of shuffling forwards a stoned hippy behind us said, "Hey man, why's everyone queuing to get in the music shop?" We told him we were queuing for Forbidden Planet and he said, "Shit! Shit! Shit!" but then stayed in the queue for another ten minutes until we reached the shop he wanted to visit.'[7]

So Douglas did have a hugely successful signing at Forbidden Planet the Saturday after his first book was published, and he did have hundreds of people queuing in advance of a Forbidden Planet signing – although the traffic-stopping bit still sounds dubious – but they were two different events. Each remarkable in its own way, but twelve months apart.

Therein lies the problem with researching Douglas Adams' life. He was a great raconteur and had an ever-expanding repertoire of stories which he told in hundreds of interviews around the world. But as a successful writer, and more pointedly as a frustrated writer-performer, he couldn't help embellishing the stories, honing them at each successive interview, as a stand-up comedian will hone a routine. A word here, a date there, all to make the story pithier, sharper, funnier.

The situation is not helped by Douglas' memory, which was not good to start with and had to cope with many, many more interesting and exciting people, places, events and things than happen in most people's lives. (Douglas said on more than one occasion: 'I can't remember anything that happened between last weekend and when the Beatles split up.'[8]) Consequently it tended to play tricks on him, as above. He admitted this himself in his introduction to *The Hitchhiker's Guide to the Galaxy: The Original Radio Scripts*, which begins with the ubiquitous story of how he came up with the title: 'lying drunk in a field in Innsbruck . . . copy of *The Hitchhiker's Guide to Europe* with me . . . occurred to me that someone ought to write . . .'[9]

After three paragraphs of this, Douglas admits: 'Now, this may well be true. It sounds plausible. It certainly has a familiar kind of ring to it. Unfortunately I've only got my own word for it now, because the constant need to repeat the story has now completely obliterated my memory of the actual event.'[10] This was in 1985; he continued to tell it, usually without the above caveat, for the rest of his life.

Douglas Adams wasn't a liar. But when you lead a life as fascinating as his, bits of it will become muddled. And when you tell enough interviewers about those bits, you will start to believe the muddled version, especially if it has a good punchline about orgasms or Mount Everest.

Which is really just a cautious warning that some of the details – sometimes significant details – of stories that you may have come across regarding Douglas Adams will be modified in this book.

But this shouldn't detract from the fact that, despite an almost complete lack of publicity, *The Hitchhiker's Guide to the Galaxy* sold phenomenally well from the moment it first appeared in bookshops. Douglas had certainly arrived, and at an enviably early point in his career, which nicely balanced the fact that, later on that same Saturday, he arrived late for a dinner party at Terry Jones' house in Camberwell.

'I remember Douglas arriving late and saying how sorry he was but he'd been at his first book-signing,' says the former Python. 'It was for the paperback of *Hitchhiker* and he'd signed a thousand books! He looked absolutely stunned. I think it was the first time he had any real indication of just how popular he was going to become.'[11]

CHAPTER 1

CAMBRIDGE HAD MANY significant roles in Douglas Adams' life. He went up to university there in 1971 and came down again three years later with a degree, a portfolio of comedy sketches and John Cleese' telephone number. He returned to the town in 1976 to direct a Footlights revue. One of his *Doctor Who* stories was filmed in Cambridge, and when ideas from that story were reworked into a novel, that too was set in a dusty old college on the banks of the Cam. The *Hitchhiker's Guide to the Galaxy* computer game was developed in Cambridge (although, to be fair, it was the one in Massachusetts) and one of Douglas' last great triumphs, his extemporaneous speech 'Is There an Artificial God?', was given at the Digital Biota 2 conference on artificial life – in Cambridge (the one in Cambridgeshire).

'I liked Cambridge a lot,' he once said. 'I always felt a special affinity with the place.'[1]

And it was in Cambridge that Douglas Noël Adams was born, to Christopher and Jan Adams, in Mill Road Maternity Hospital on 11 March 1952. Later that same day, his comedy career began: 'According to my mother I was such a gangling baby the nurses brought me into the maternity ward with a nappy on and said, "Look, Gandhi!" I was quite a neurotic child, twitchy, inclined to live in a world of my own. I didn't learn to speak until I was almost four. My parents were so concerned they had me tested for being either deaf or educationally subnormal.'[2]

Jan Adams was a nurse: 'My mother's a great lady, she is somebody who is always at her best dealing with anybody else's problems – and can never deal with any of her own.'[3] Christopher Adams was studying for a postgraduate degree in theology with a view to taking holy orders: 'He became a teacher for a few years, then suddenly he became a probation officer. After that he became a lecturer in probationary group therapy techniques, then astonished everybody by suddenly becoming a management consultant. He has a sideline as a computer salesman. I expect there is some rationale behind my father's life.'[4]

Douglas had Irish, Scottish and German blood in him: 'My maternal grandfather was a Donovan from Cork. He was, like many Irish living in England, more Irish than the Irish. On his sixty-fifth birthday – the day he retired – he came home from work and said, "That's it, I've done my bit, I'm going to bed." He did so, and stayed there till his death seven years later.'[5] Douglas' most notable ancestor was his great-grandfather, a German actor-director with the unlikely name of Benjamin Franklin Wedekind (1864–1918) who predated the theatre of the absurd with his use of distorted scenes, broken dialogue and caricature. His paternal grandfather – also called Douglas Adams – was an ear, nose and throat specialist in Glasgow, and Douglas was surprised to find in later life that the name Adams carries much weight in the history of Scottish medicine (for a detailed breakdown of the Adams family genealogy, see Nick Webb's book *Wish You Were Here*). Douglas' own brief thoughts of becoming a GP were immediately discounted because of his tendency to faint during medical scenes in movies.

Douglas rarely spoke about his early childhood and claimed to have few memories before the age of five when his parents divorced: 'I think it's blocked. Both my parents remarried pretty quickly and each had more children. So as well as having one whole sister, I have a whole bunch of half-brothers and sisters.'[6]

Susan Adams was born three years after Douglas in March 1955. Christopher Adams remarried in July 1960 – to a wealthy widow called Judith Stewart, née Robertson – giving Douglas and Sue two stepsisters, Rosemary and Karena (Kena), and a half-sister Heather born in July 1962. Jan Adams married a Dorset vet, Ron Thrift, in July 1964, providing two more half-siblings, Jane and James, in August 1966 and June 1968 respectively. Until their mother remarried, Douglas and Sue lived a curiously bifurcated existence, shuttling between their parents who were separated by only ten miles geographically but to a much greater extent socially. Jan lived with her parents in a small, crowded house in the Essex town of Brentwood. Grandpa Donovan was, as has been noted, voluntarily bedridden, while Grandmama Donovan was a local character known throughout the town as 'the RSPCA lady'. A lover of animals beyond the call of duty, she was occasionally seen cycling one-handed along Brentwood High Street, her other arm wrapped around a slightly damaged swan. Consequently the house was packed with injured and unwell animals of all kinds, which played havoc with Douglas' asthma for five days every week.

Then at weekends Sue and her brother slipped into another universe. Christopher Adams and his new family lived just outside Brentwood in the little village of Stondon Massey, in an enormous mock-Tudor edifice named 'Derry'. There were huge gardens, a tennis court, two stepsisters to play with, hair-raising trips round the Essex countryside in their father's Aston Martin, even a couple of elderly domestic servants – a far cry from the fur- and feather-strewn chaos of the Donovan household. Jan and Christopher were not on speaking terms, so handovers were carried out between grand-mother and stepmother, to avoid any chance of the acrimoniously divorced couple coming accidentally face to face.

The relationship between Douglas and his father was somewhat fraught and continued to be so for the rest of Christopher Adams' life; it was not something which Douglas ever discussed in public. Indeed, the scarcity of his recorded memories of childhood probably reflects more on a desire for privacy than his notoriously bad memory.

'My childhood holidays were pretty modest,' recalled Douglas, on one of the few occasions when the subject was raised. 'The highlight was a fortnight in the Isle of Wight when I was about six. I remember catching what I was convinced was a plaice, though it was only the size of a postage stamp and promptly died when I tried to keep it as a pet.'[7]

After a couple of uneventful years at Primrose Hill Primary School, in September 1959 Douglas became one of just over a thousand boys at Brentwood School, the exorbitant fees paid for by his wealthy stepmother. With a long, distinguished history dating back 400 years, it seemed to have changed little since the turn of the century, still enjoying such dubious activities as 'fagging' and the appointment of senior boys as 'praepostors' who technically had the ability to hand out corporal punishment (though this was rare). Notable 'Old Brentwoods' include fashion designer Hardy Amies, interviewer Robin Day, historian David Irving, disc jockey Noel Edmonds, Foreign Secretary Jack Straw and comedian Griff Rhys Jones, who was a year below Douglas and distinguished himself with numerous prizes.

Douglas was at Brentwood for just over eleven years, eventually leaving in December 1970 (in *The Salmon of Doubt*, he mistakenly refers to 'twelve whole years'). The Brentwood academic year was divided into Michaelmas, Lent and Trinity terms, and lessons were Monday to Saturday, with Wednesday and Saturday afternoons devoted to sport and slightly longer holidays to compensate.

Douglas spent his first four years in the Preparatory School or 'Prep' (not to be confused with 'prep' which meant homework) before taking his eleven-plus. There were about 200 boys in the Prep, which was divided into four Houses. As a seven-year-old new boy, Douglas started in the Fourth Form, progressing annually through the Third Remove and Second Remove to the First Form, then to Junior Remove B.

'Douglas and I started off together in the Prep School in 1959,' remembers David Wakeling, one of Douglas' twenty Form IV classmates and now a teacher himself. 'We went right the way through the Prep School together. We were both in the same day-boy house, Heseltine, and then we became boarders at the same time as well. Apart from one year, we remained in the same boarding house throughout. Initially he was one of those people who, at the age of seven, was tall and completely uncoordinated. He had great difficulty fitting in with things like games of football. In the playground, he was more likely to be in the corner with other like-minded, non-sporting people, creating stories and ideas and inventing new games, rather than actually joining in with the physical crowd.'[8]

Douglas was immediately marked out from the crowd by virtue of being extraordinarily tall: 'I was different from other kids in one major regard in that I was *so* much taller than them and they could scarcely see me, so I lived a rather isolated life.'[9]

Prizes were awarded at Prep, Junior and Senior Speech Days every July and in his second year Douglas distinguished himself by winning the Junior Prize for Reading. To be honest, there were a very large number of prizes awarded, and D.N. Adams only rarely featured in the list of prizewinners, but this does indicate a literary bent and generated his first mention in *The Brentwoodian*, the thrice-yearly school magazine (there was also an intermittent literary magazine, *Greenwood*).

Flushed with success, Douglas moved up to Remove II in 1961, where he met Form Master Frank Halford, who was to have a profound influence on him. Halford had joined the school the same year as Douglas and would remain there until his retirement in 1991. He taught French and English to D.N. Adams and twenty-three other ten-year-olds. In 1998 Adams and Halford were both interviewed for a newspaper feature on famous people and the teachers who had inspired them.

'Hundreds of boys have passed through the school but Douglas Adams really stood out from the crowd – literally,' remembered Halford. 'He was unnaturally tall and in his short trousers he looked a trifle self-conscious. Yet it was his ability to write first-class stories that really made him shine. I remember him as being friendly and intelligent, and from the first it was obvious that he had a flair for English. There was a definite sparkle in his style and he showed a flair for original thought.'[10]

'I immediately warmed to his friendly, enthusiastic manner and I instinctively trusted him,' said Douglas of his mentor. 'He had such a profound influence on me that I can still remember where his lesson fell in the timetable – between break and lunchtime on Thursday mornings.'[11]

On 7 March 1962, D.N. Adams became the first and only boy ever – in thirty-two years of teaching – to receive ten out of ten from Frank Halford, who thought that Douglas' adventure yarn about hidden treasure, 'was technically and creatively perfect; a remarkable piece of work for a boy of that age.'[12] The mark was a touchstone for Douglas which he never forgot. 'Even now, when I have a dark night of the soul as a writer and think that I can't do this any more, the thing that I reach for is not the fact that I have had bestsellers or huge advances. It is the fact that Frank Halford once gave me ten out of ten, and at some fundamental level I must be able to do it.'[13]

For many years afterwards, pupils at Brentwood who queried why their superlative work received only nine out of ten from Mr Halford were told of the incident: 'When they complained that I never gave them full marks, I said, "Oh, I did once. I gave a boy called Douglas Adams ten out of ten."'[14]

Other teachers, however, weren't quite so supportive and Douglas was frequently chided for putting jokes in his history essays. His absurd height also made him an easy target for teachers seeking to exercise their authority. 'Towards the end of the Prep School, our geography teacher was a guy called called David Curtis,' recalls David Wakeling. 'Douglas was taller than Curtis and so Curtis picked on him a bit. On one occasion we were studying Canada and he said to Douglas, "You know, Adams, you and Canada have a lot in common. You're both a great lumbering region."'[15]

Douglas became involved in school societies, including the Prep School Photographic Society, an early blossoming of what would later become a passion for gadgets of all kinds. Douglas had a lifelong amateur interest in photography, though it was later eclipsed by his fondness for cars, guitars and computers. However, when his success allowed him to indulge his passions, Douglas was rarely without a top-of-the-range camera, most notably during his *Last Chance to See* expeditions.

So it was that in issue 215 of *The Brentwoodian*, in September 1962, the brief report on the Trinity Term activities of the Prep School Photographic Society carried the by-line 'D.N.A'. Ever since the publication of Neil Gaiman's book *Don't Panic* in 1988 it has been believed that Douglas' first published works were his two letters which appeared in *Eagle* comic in 1965, but the discovery of the Photographic Society report brings his first publication forward by three years. It's hardly the most exciting piece of reportage but it's interesting for what and when it is – and for its use of humour. Here, for the first time in more than four decades, is Douglas Adams' literary debut:

Photography Club
This term we were taught about developing the film to make negatives, and from that stage went down to the cellar in pairs to print them. Some of the results were hilarious, such as Buckley's attempt, which turned green!

We were going to go for a 'snap-shot' session and then develop any finished film, but we didn't have time.

As usual, we owe thanks to Mr Bull for many enjoyable hours.

D.N.A.

For anyone with a literary or journalistic interest, that first published piece, the stamp of approval by an editor, the chance to be read by people who don't actually know you, is a major, major step. Young D. N. Adams must have been pretty chuffed, especially as it was unlikely he would ever see his name in the sporting pages of the magazine.

'There was a strong emphasis on sport,' says Charles Thomson, a Brentwood contemporary who is now a poet and artist. 'The Head Teacher, Richard Sale, and the School Bursar had both been county cricketers.'[16]

'Douglas wasn't particularly bad at sport, he just wasn't particularly competent, and I don't think really he could see the point,' recalls David Wakeling. 'He was certainly not competitive in that way. He would turn out, if needed, for the House Second XV rugby team; he would never shirk the sporting thing. But certainly in the Prep School, playing cricket was not his idea of fun. He would more often than not be talking to the trees on the boundary, rather than concentrating on the ball. He found it quite difficult to get involved with the team games and really showed no interest in individual sports at all.'[17]

Douglas' own comment on the matter was that his school cricket career, 'was a sort of microcosm of Ian Botham's. At one stage I'd been playing fairly well: I was made Captain of the House Junior Second XI. It was a great moment for me – and I turned in a succession of ducks – this is where I suggest the parallel with Ian Botham. So I was relieved of the captaincy. Unfortunately, there the parallel broke down because I continued to do very badly.'[18] He also showed some proficiency at swimming.

Douglas was now in Form I and preparing to take his eleven-plus, which would determine the rest of his school career. He was also developing his dramatic ambitions as a member of the Prep School Play Club who performed for masters, parents and pupils on Speech Day in July 1963. The play was called *Five Who Pass While the Lentils Boil* and *The Brentwoodian* noted that, 'Sutton and Adams and others made vigorous appearances'. In his fourth year at Brentwood, Douglas had made his literary and dramatic debuts; he was well on his way to becoming a writer-performer.

CHAPTER 2

ACADEMIC YEAR 1963–64 was a curious transition year which exemplified the complexities of the Brentwood system. Douglas was in Junior Remove B which was for some purposes classified as part of the Junior School although technically he was still at the Prep. New boys had joined his form at the start of each Michaelmas Term, as others had departed, but progress to 'JRB' saw the influx of numerous new schoolmates. Among them was a name which would have far-reaching consequences: P.N.M. Johnstone.

In the original radio series of *Hitchhiker* (and on the first pressing of the LPs), 'Paul Neil Milne Johnstone' is cited as the worst poet in the universe, worse even than the Vogons or the Azgoths of Kria. Forty years on, David Wakeling remembers Johnstone. 'In a very unpleasant way, we were awful to Paul Neil Milne Johnstone. He was a ginger-headed, freckled, bespectacled, little boy and he became the butt of a lot of bullying actually. I myself was guilty of a lot of that and feel quite ashamed for it, but it happened. Paul Johnstone did produce odd stuff in terms of poetry. And the more obscure it was, the better he liked it. Douglas could see right through it. So he deserved the mention!

'When you look at the first *Hitchhiker* book there are quite a few references in there to people who were around the school at the time. The Vogon guard humming Beethoven's Fifth – that I'm certain is me. I used to do it around the boarding house, at lights- out time. It was the only piece of classical music I'd ever appreciated at the age of fourteen or fifteen.'[1]

Meanwhile, Douglas' dramatic career continued. In that year's Lent Term, on 13 March 1964, the Prep School Play Society presented three historical plays, including one about Drake entitled *On the Golden Hind*. 'D.G. Mann, C.C. Rowe and D.N. Adams carried particular conviction as military gentlemen,' noted *The Brentwoodian*, while 'P.N.M. Johnstone wore his beard with pride.'

One of Douglas' rare forays into trouble occurred one week later: 'The worst damage I ever did to my knees was on the morning of Friday, 20 March 1964. The Beatles' 'Can't Buy Me Love'/'You Can't Do That' was released that day so, quite reasonably, I think, I broke out of school, ran a mile to Radiogram in the High Street, bought a copy, ran back, climbed into Matron's sitting-room window, taking a lot of skin off my knees in the process, hunkered down bleeding profusely in front of her record player, and managed to play both sides about three times before I was caught, bandaged, and slippered. I didn't care – it was the Beatles.'[2]

The Fab Four had an enormous effect on Douglas Adams. Ever after he cited his two biggest influences as the Beatles and Monty Python – 'Both were messages out of the void saying there are people out there who know what it's like to be you.'[3] – and the incredible thing was that within five years of leaving school he would have worked with members of both groups. 'The Beatles planted a seed in my head that made it explode. Every nine months there'd be a new album which would be an earth-shattering development from where they were before. We were so obsessed by them that when "Penny Lane" came out and we hadn't heard it on the radio we beat up this boy who had heard it until he hummed the tune to us.'[4]

This love of the Beatles tied in with Douglas' growing interest in the guitar which he learnt from the age of twelve and which, though he retained his piano skills, was to be his instrument of choice for the rest of his life: 'Because I'm left-handed, which is a problem when you're a guitarist, I could never play anybody else's guitar, and only had a very, very cheap, boxy, little guitar as a kid – that was the only thing I could ever play.'[5]

'Douglas would try to get the Beatles genre of music into

everything he did,' remembers David Wakeling. 'For example, he managed to persuade The Powers That Be that it would be a good idea for him to sing a Beatles song in chapel. That was unheard of, when all that was sung in chapel were *Hymns Ancient and Modern* and the occasional anthem. But he did manage to do that; he played his guitar and sang "Blackbird" from *The White Album* – in chapel – which in those days was revolutionary, and frowned upon by many, many people, but he got away with it.'[6] That was in Michaelmas Term 1969, after earlier attempts at introducing 'Eleanor Rigby' to the chapel repertoire had been ousted by a performance of the *Messiah*.

However, his initial musical aspirations were fuelled not by Lennon and McCartney but by Hank Marvin: 'The first time I ever became excited by the guitar was listening to the Shadows when I was a kid. I listened to the Shadows obsessively before the Beatles came out, and I used to walk around the whole time playing air guitar and walking into lamp-posts.'[7] (The 'walking into lamp-posts with eyes open' story was a favourite of Douglas'; it's in *Don't Panic* and numerous other interviews. Only on this occasion, when he was a guest on *Desert Island Discs*, did he qualify it with the air guitar connection. To walk into a lamp-post in broad daylight under normal circumstances suggests a boy totally wrapped up in his own thoughts, which makes for a far better anecdote than a boy simply trying to remember the chords to 'Apache'.)

And so to the Main (Junior) School, Michaelmas 1964. Douglas, having passed his eleven-plus with flying colours, was assigned to Form Upper II along with numerous of his former classmates and a few new boys (including the gloriously named C. StQ. Playford). The Main School had about 800 boys, of whom a quarter were boarders.

Up to this point Douglas had been a day-boy, still living with his grandmother, Mrs Donovan, and her constantly changing RSPCA menagerie. 'She was an extremely well-taught, self-taught person, and you met her in every sphere of life in Brentwood,'[8] recalls School Chaplain Tom Gardiner.

When Douglas became a boarder he joined Barnards, a small house of fourteen boys overseen by House Master Alan Brooks who recalls, 'Douglas was always happy to entertain others. In Barnards he invented a ghost to add variety to his nightly dormitory stories.'[9]

'He kept most people awake most nights by telling stories and unravelling great long yarns about the ghosts that were creeping around the place: the white lady of this and the grey lady of that,' confirms David Wakeling. 'Half the dormitory was trying to get to sleep, just ignoring him or telling him to shut up, and the rest of them were in tears through fear! He played on that of course, that was fodder for him.'[10]

'Whenever I left school at four in the afternoon I always used to look at what the boarders were doing rather wistfully,' reminisced Douglas about this transition. 'They seemed to be having a good time and, in fact, I thoroughly enjoyed boarding. There is a piece of me that likes to fondly imagine my maverick and rebellious nature. But more accurately I like to have a nice and cosy institution that I can rub up against a little bit. There is nothing better than a few constraints you can comfortably kick against.'[11]

'The boarding system at Brentwood School was very protective,' remembers Wakeling. 'To my way of thinking, it was one of the pluses of the school. The house masters, the house tutors, matrons, etc. were very protective; they had a good pastoral sense and looked after people well. One's life was full of activities so it was very difficult to have the time to become homesick. I think Douglas dealt well with it. He certainly was more gregarious within the boarding house situation than he was around the rest of the school.'[12]

Nevertheless there was one 'constraint' which apparently distressed Douglas greatly. During his four years at the Prep School, his legs had stuck out alarmingly from his shorts, but with passage to the Main School came the chance to finally wear long trousers. As recounted in his contribution to *The Best of Days? Memories of Brentwood School*, Douglas discovered that the school shop simply did not have trousers of the extraordinary length which he required, and were unable to provide bespoke trousers until four weeks into the term: 'Four weeks of the greatest humiliation and embarrassment known to man or, rather, to that most easily humiliated and embarrassed of all creatures, the overgrown twelve-year-old boy.

We've all experienced those painful dreams in which we suddenly discover we are stark naked in the middle of the High Street. Believe me, this was worse, and it wasn't a dream. I still carry the scars inside, and though I try my best to bestride the world like a Colossus, writing best-selling books, and ... (well, that's about it really, I suppose), if I ever come across as a maladjusted, socially isolated, sad, hunched emotional cripple (I'm thinking mainly of Sunday mornings in February, here) then it's those four weeks of having to wear short trousers in September 1964 that are to blame.'[13]

'I don't actually remember him being embarrassed by it,' says Wakeling. 'Once they realised that they had to make trousers long enough for him, those trousers were provided at two pairs a year or whatever it was, and the problem was overcome. I think the embarrassment side of it was a good story but it was no more than that. He always had grazed knees as a kid of course, but we all had that.'[14]

It was at Barnards that Douglas first showed an interest in *Doctor Who*, writing a comedy sketch called 'Doctor Which': 'It was a parody of *Doctor Who* with the idea of Daleks being powered by Rice Krispies or something! Very embarrassing!'[15] Frank Halford later remembered, '... how impressed I was by the sketch he wrote for the boarders' Christmas party in 1963. Little did I realise that the eleven-year-old boy who wrote it would go on to be a scriptwriter and editor for *Doctor Who*.'[16] (The sketch was actually written for Christmas 1964.)

As well as weekly adventures with *Doctor Who*, Douglas was a voracious reader of juvenile science fiction. Among his favourites were the *Kemlo* novels by E.C. Eliott, about the first generation of adolescents born and raised in space, and the adventures of 'Tiger' Clinton as chronicled by Captain W.E. Johns, better known as the creator of Biggles. But Douglas' biggest thrill was his weekly date with Dan Dare in that most iconic of British comics, the *Eagle*.

'It was brilliantly drawn and had really good stories and he was seminal throughout the whole generation of kids,' enthused Adams. 'The Mekon was just the most wonderful, exotic villain ever. I used to spend ages just drawing the Mekon.'[17]

A (very) short story by Douglas, entitled 'Suspense', was published on the letters page of *Eagle and Boys' World* in the issue dated 23 January 1965 (reprinted thirty-seven years later in *The Salmon of Doubt*). This success was announced in assembly, to polite applause. 'It certainly boosted sales of the *Eagle* that week!' says David Wakeling. 'Dan Dare and the stories in the *Eagle* were really bread and butter for Douglas. He was one of the very few people who read that particular comic. Everybody else was reading *Dandy* and *Beano* and *Valiant* and things, but Douglas started off with *Swift*, then went on at a very early age to *Eagle*.'[18]

Douglas received the princely sum of ten shillings for his letter ('You could practically buy a yacht for ten shillings then'[19]) and followed it with another five weeks later (reprinted in *Don't Panic*).

Trinity Term 1965 saw two landmark achievements for thirteen-year-old Adams. He starred as 'The Tramp' in *The Insect Play* and he passed Grade I piano. 'He was active in theatricals, and was always ready to entertain with piano or as a southpaw guitar player,' recalls Alan Brooks. 'Once on stage he was difficult to dislodge.'[20]

The Insect Play by Josef and Karel Čapek (who famously coined the term 'robot') is a three-act allegory of human society in which a deceased tramp witnesses the follies of butterflies, beetles and ants. 'The cast, and in particular the Tramp, played by D. N. Adams, played it by ear, perhaps to the detriment of the meaning and artistic unity of the play but to the benefit of interest and enjoyment,' was *The Brentwoodian*'s view, adding: 'Congratulations to the Tramp, ably played by Adams, for throughout the play he identifies himself with the audience, as observers of the insect world. His death takes him into this world and the audience follows him, Tramp and audience becoming involved in a new relationship with the play as participants rather than mere spectators. Adams's portrayal was adequately sympathetic for the audience to realise their involvement, no easy task.' Also in the cast, playing an ant, was a boy named Robert Benton, who would later make a significant decision which would affect Douglas' career considerably.

CHAPTER 3

OVER THE SUMMER, there was a slight reorganisation as Barnards and Old Houses ceased to exist. Douglas was reassigned to Otway House, joining fifty other boys, with Alan Brooks still House Master.

'One of our teachers told us that our school was the cream and that our class was the cream of the cream, so we weren't lacking in confidence boosting,' recalls Charles Thomson. 'Brentwood was a very civilised school. Although it was a public school, there was a certain liberal air about it. For example, the French teacher, when we did general studies, played us Bob Dylan.'[1]

A burgeoning folk scene in Brentwood saw the establishment of a folk club, providing for performers and audiences from all three of the town's schools. Occasionally, external performers were booked and some time during Michaelmas Term 1965, more than 300 people crowded into the Memorial Hall to hear, as *The Brentwoodian* put it, 'Paul Simon, a folk singer from America'. Simon was all but unknown at this point, so it was more the novelty of an international act than his name value which attracted such an audience. Douglas immediately became a huge fan. (Many years later in New York, Douglas tried to arrange a meeting with Paul Simon. It looked feasible until Simon's PA enquired how tall he was. On learning that Douglas was six foot five, the meeting suddenly became far less likely. Paul Simon is about five foot three and even in 1965 Douglas would have towered over him.)

'When I learnt to play the guitar, I was taught by Paul Simon. He doesn't know this,' said Douglas. 'When I was a kid I would sit and play the same record over and over and over again, dropping the needle in the groove, then bringing it back and dropping it in the same groove over and over and over again, until I'd worked out every single note and every finger position and so on.'[2] The Paul Simon gig in Brentwood is listed as 4 December 1964 in reference works, but it was certainly 1965, as it was reported (with a photograph) in the January 1966 *Brentwoodian*. Another nascent pop legend visited Brentwood that same month, when the School Christmas Dance on 13 December enjoyed music by 'Dave Bowie and the Lower Third'.

'In the school the main thing was this hippy thing and the issue of long hair,' remembers Charles Thomson. 'I was definitely in the rebel camp, I used to sell *Oz* and *International Times* round the school. Douglas definitely was not in the rebel camp, although you wouldn't have thought of him as being a square or a wimp or anything like that. I would have seen him as being urbane, quite self-possessed, very much an individual, quite restrained – he wasn't a flamboyant character at all, he was very solid – perhaps slightly aloof if anything, though that could have been a self-defensive tack.

'There was never a sense of him being one of what the Head Teacher called "the long-hairs". Although there was one very amusing incident where the Head Teacher once accused Douglas of being a rebel. Richard Sale went, "Oh yes, you're one of these rebels, aren't you, Adams?" Douglas just stood there, looking completely bemused, because he wasn't. I don't know what on Earth he did to deserve that; he probably questioned something.'[3]

However, schoolmaster Mickey Hall recalls: 'Douglas was always trying it on with the system, without trying to buck the system. That was his style. He became very popular, particularly with the younger boys who saw him as a character. He was known affectionately as "Bernie" after Bernie Winters.'[4]

The highlight of the Brentwood dramatic year was the Winter Theatrical, a Shakespeare play at the end of Michaelmas Term. In December 1965, Douglas made his main stage debut in a small role and *The Brentwoodian* reported that, 'A. Dolezal and D. Adams played their parts in *Romeo and Juliet* very well.' Come Trinity Term and it was time for another Junior School play, *The Boy with a Cart*, 'in which D. Adams, J. Greaves and R. Raikes appeared.'

Another opportunity for Douglas to perform before an audience was the Junior School Debating Society. On 9 December 1965 the society held a 'Pros and Cons' debate, at which Douglas was one of the speakers. He also took part in the 'Hat Night' on 20 February 1966, which was a chance for any member to speak on any subject of their choice. The assembled members then voted for the speaker whom they felt to have been most persuasive, and Douglas came joint second. However, the most interesting debate was held on 14 October 1965. What ideas were lodged in the young Adams brain when the motion proposed was, 'This House thinks that the Brentwood by-pass will not benefit the people of Brentwood'?

Speech Day 1966 saw Douglas receive a Special Prize for Service in Chapel. A mixture of religious devotion and passion for choral music kept Douglas very involved with the school chapel through-out his Brentwood years. 'It was expected of boarders that they would attend chapel every Sunday,' recalls David Wakeling, 'and Douglas did so and was a leading light in that. He hadn't begun to question faith at all at that stage, or if he had, he was coming down on the side of believing and being an active member.'[5]

Michaelmas Term saw Douglas step up into Upper IV, the Senior School and another new house, confusingly called School; Mickey Hall was the House Master. The January 1967 *Brentwoodian* noted that, 'Benton and Adams displayed their talents in the Winter Theatricals', which that year was *The Tempest*.

'Douglas brought a new quality to when we had our house suppers,' remembers Hall. 'We invited guests in and the boys put on dormitory plays and sketches. Douglas' scripts were a bit long-winded and complicated as you might expect. I remember at one house supper, with our VIP guests – probably just the Headmaster and the Bursar – he produced a quite outrageous sketch about Lennon and Yoko Ono in the sack – literally in a sack! Highly amusing but it takes some explaining away to your boss!'[6]

One area of inter-house rivalry in which the resolutely non-sporting Adams could contribute was the annual House Music Competition, specifically the Unison Song section. School, which had a history of losing dismally, entered the competition in 1966 with a rendition of the National Anthem, an off-beat choice which earned them second to last place. There was a bright spot in Trinity Term, however, when the house acquired a television set, which was 'invaluable for Wimbledon and *The Frost Report*' according to the school mag.

The first series of *The Frost Report* started on 10 March 1966 and provided the first significant TV exposure for John Cleese, indeed for any of that generation of Footlights alumni. Douglas was an avid viewer and decided there and then that he would become a writer-performer of comedy, like Cleese. (Prior to this, he had no clear ambition: 'At one point when I was at school, rather reluctantly I thought, "Well, maybe I could go and work for Pilkington's Glass. Maybe glass is interesting." Then I thought, "The BBC is an interesting place to go," but there seemed little chance of getting into the BBC.'[7])

One of the more archaic aspects of Brentwood life, which Douglas and his schoolmates suffered through their Fourth and Fifth Forms, was the Combined Cadet Force. 'School finished a bit earlier one afternoon a week for those in the CCF, which was mandatory for two years,' recalls Charles Thomson. 'We would don uniforms, do drill, read maps and use the .22 rifle range. There was a whole armoury, with Lee Enfields, bazookas and Bren guns, all presumably left over from the war, and a 25-pounder field gun. I joined the medical section which is where you went if you didn't want to lug a bazooka around.'[8]

Douglas never mentioned his two years as a part-time army cadet, but given his generally pacific nature and the overall lack of coordination in his gangly limbs, it was probably an unpleasant experience for him and a dangerous one for everyone else.

On 21 October 1967, with Douglas firmly ensconced in Upper V, something absolutely unprecedented happened to School House: they won the the Unison Song section of the House Music Competition. The winning performance was a stirring rendition of 'On

Ilkley Moor B'Aht 'At', and though the musical director was a boy named Hargreaves, Douglas was certainly involved in the competition. To the boys of School House, and to their amazed masters, it was a famous victory.

Douglas was once again in the Winter Theatrical; Mickey Hall recalls: 'There was much fun in the house when he was in *Macbeth*. It was a fairly small part but of course he got murdered every night.'[9] But the most significant event for Douglas in Michaelmas Term was his appointment to an official position within the school chapel. As Sacristan – the post was also called Chapel Praepostor – he assisted the Chaplain, Rev. T.A. Gardiner, with general duties and looked after chapel property. Douglas was Sacristan for approximately eighteen months, until Easter 1969.

'He was my Chapel Prae, and he was very good,' recalls Tom Gardiner. 'He was using my vestry to work in because they didn't have many facilities at School House, and I welcomed him to it: "If you want to work, use my office. It's warm, it's dry." I've always said that to every Chapel Prae. But it became very obvious that he wasn't doing any work, he was just using my room to interview people, using it as his office, and I'm afraid I got rather fed up with this and I got rid of him as Chapel Prae. We had a bit of tension. We fell out over that and also over the revue thing.'[10]

'The revue thing' was a Sixth Form entertainment organised by Gardiner. Douglas was keen to help but wanted to do something more than a traditional revue of songs and sketches and eventually took no part: 'It was fairly obvious that he had his own ideas about what should go into the revue but he couldn't really explain them properly. We never actually saw anything on paper and I think this is because he was still finding his way to the things that he wanted to do.'[11]

Such extracurricular activities did not distract Douglas from his studies – he took ten O-levels and passed them all except Greek. 'He was good at anything he wanted to be good at, he was a very bright person,' recalls David Wakeling. 'He was good at science but he wasn't particularly keen on it. He saw that he needed to do science to get a spread of O-levels to progress to A-levels and progress to Cambridge, but he didn't see it as being as important as the arts subjects.'[12]

Douglas moved into the Sixth Form, Lower VI Arts, in 1968, while remaining in School House which, against all the odds, retained the Unison Song Cup. At A-level, he studied Mediaeval History, Modern History and English, a decision which he ever after regretted, not so much for the path he chose but because he had to choose at all: 'It was that decision you have to make when you're fifteen or sixteen about which A-levels you're going to do. It always haunts me – did I take the right decision? It's a great flaw in our educational system – you divide into these two cultures from that age on: the arts on the one side, the sciences on the other, regarding each other with a mixture of contempt and loathing.'[13]

Interestingly, in 1979 he claimed, 'I've always been interested in science – I very nearly did science A-levels – I was very hot on physics as a child.'[14]

One of Douglas' duties as Sacristan was to write the Chapel Report for *The Brentwoodian*, which he did in issues 233 and 234, which also featured a lengthy review of his highest profile performance yet, in the title role of the 1968 Winter Theatrical, *Julius Caesar*. 'Douglas Adams as Caesar accorded with the note in the programme,' reported the magazine, 'and dwarfing most of the other characters, prescribed a suitably dictatorial and impressive figure, although he was too keen to place his hands on his hips as if to reassure himself of his superiority.'

Having passed on the mantle of Sacristan, Douglas became Secretary of the Chapel Choir, working alongside Choir Master John Moore-Bridger. 'He was a keen member of the choir, a keen member of the chapel generally,' recalls Moore-Bridger. 'He was always one of the reliable types if you gave him a solo.'[15] The academic year finished with the Lower VI Prize for English awarded jointly to two outstanding pupils: D.N. Adams and ... P.N.M. Johnstone.

As well as starring roles on stage, comedy influences and religious responsibilities, the Sixth Form brought something else into Douglas' life: a steady girlfriend. Helen Cutler was a pupil at the nearby Ursuline Convent School, and David Wakeling recalls that she and Douglas had a fairly strong relationship: 'It was a bit tempestuous and I believe it carried on after schooldays, on and off. It was an interesting relationship, because not many boarders had girlfriends. I suppose he was seen as a leader in that field.'[16]

For the 1969–70 academic year, the Sixth Form forms were renamed and Douglas was now in Upper VI (5). While completing his A-levels, he found plenty of time to indulge in non-academic pursuits, writing a Chapel Choir Report for the September 1969 *Brentwoodian*, and joining the Senior School Debating Society. One of the motions proposed in Michaelmas Term was 'This House would shave its head' and the school magazine reported that, 'Mr Douglas Adams attempted to link what he described as "the Skinhead Philosophy" with the Rule of St Benedict.'

'Thanks to D.N. Adams' multifarious talents,' boasted the School House report in the January 1970 *Brentwoodian*, 'we won the Unison Song Competition for the third year in succession.' There is also a photograph of Douglas conducting the House Team from the piano.

And so we come to 20 January 1970, when Douglas N. Adams, along with six other people, was initiated into an exclusive society called Candlesticks, whose members gathered to read plays by candlelight. Admission was by invitation only – a letter from the Headmaster – following which the initiate was required to write a poem about a candle. Hence Douglas' 'Candle Power' which was published in the Lent Term's issue of *Greenwood*. (This was Douglas' one and only contribution to the magazine: 'Each time I meant to write something in *Greenwood*, I missed the deadline by two weeks.'[17])

Issue 238 of *The Brentwoodian* (June 1970) carried no fewer than three Adams pieces: reports on behalf of the History Society and the Chapel Choir (Douglas apologised for the lack of Chapel Choir Report in issue 237 – he had missed the deadline), plus a lengthy article/review about a performance group of students who called themselves Paris Green, an early incarnation of which had actually included Douglas. Artsphere, a broad arts-based club of which Paul Neil Milne Johnstone was an active member, announced plans for a School Arts Festival at the end of June, to include a special edition of the Artsphere magazine *Broadsheet* with 'a satirical supplement to be written under the auspices of Mr Meredith and Douglas Adams'.

Nearly a decade after he discovered the Beatles, Douglas' other great influence had appeared on 5 October 1969 when the first episode of *Monty Python's Flying Circus* was broadcast: '*Monty Python* started when I was seventeen. Right from the word "go" it had just a huge impact on me. Those of us who wanted to watch *Python* would congregate in the television room, just to make sure everybody agreed that we were going to watch *Python*.'[18] But on 15 December 1970, towards the end of the second series, a problem arose . . .

'There was a football match, and it gradually became clear that the rest of the room was not going to watch *Python*, it was going to watch the football, and there was a bunch of about four of us who suddenly went into a full panic at that point because we were going to miss *Python*! My grandmother lived about two miles away, so we just leapt out of school, broke out and ran, covered the distance to my grandmother's house in record-breaking time, burst in upon the poor frightened grandmother, and said, "Excuse me, we're going to watch *Python*."'[19]

'*Python* was a big thing,' confirms Charles Thomson. 'I didn't even have a TV but people would come in and talk about the latest *Python* thing. They would rehearse it, go over it. It was funny, it was wacky and there was this sense of doing something that was outside the system.'[20]

Those Brentwood boys who were destined for Oxbridge stayed on an extra Michaelmas term as Form VII. Douglas won an Exhibition in English to St John's College, Cambridge (chosen because his father went there); so did Paul Neil Milne Johnstone, in his case to Emmanuel College. The January 1971 *Brentwoodian* contained a History Society Report by Douglas N. Adams. Also included, as with every issue, was the list of school-leavers and their achievements, which proclaimed: 'Valete, D.N. Adams: Civics Prize, Elocution Prize, Debating Soc. Sec., History Soc. Sec., House Music Captain, Chapel Choir Sec., Winter Theatricals 1965–69, Candlesticks.'

On page 21 were Chapel Choir Notes by Douglas, once again apologising for the two-term gap since the last report. Not yet eighteen, he already had a reputation for repeatedly missing deadlines.

INTERLUDE - **EUROPE**

DOUGLAS LEFT BRENTWOOD School at the end of Michaelmas Term 1970 and went up to Cambridge in October 1971, giving him a good ten months to find something to do. He had what is now known as a gap year.

He took a few menial jobs, including a stint as a 'chicken-shed cleaner' and another as a porter in the X-ray Department of Yeovil General Hospital. He also went hitchhiking around Europe: 'I went to Austria, Italy, Yugoslavia and Turkey, staying in youth hostels and campsites, and supplemented my diet by going on free tours round breweries. Istanbul was particularly wonderful, but I ended up with terrible food poisoning and had to return to England by train, sleeping in the corridor just next to the loo. Ah, magical times . . .'[1]

It was in Austria that Douglas had the first germ of an idea about *The Hitchhiker's Guide to the Galaxy*. Which is to say, it was there that he thought up the title. Or at least, as explained in his introduction to the radio scripts, it was there that he said he thought up the title in early interviews, and who was he to argue?

Douglas gave literally hundreds of interviews over the years and the vast majority of them started off by asking where he got the idea, leading Douglas to trot out the same old 'I was hitchhiking around Europe . . .' story and to his credit he never sounded weary of telling it, though he undoubtedly was. Very occasionally, Douglas broke from the version which he – and all his fans – knew by rote and waxed more poetic, as in this 1997 interview: 'In the year I took off between high school and college, I travelled. I had a copy of a book called *The Hitchhiker's Guide to Europe,* which I got from someone and still have, and which probably counts as stolen by now. I was lying in a field in Innsbruck, Austria, and the stars came out, and I thought, "Oh, it looks much more interesting up there." A title fell out of the sky: *The Hitchhiker's Guide to the Galaxy.* It seemed like a book that somebody ought to write, but it didn't occur to me that I should be the one to do it.'[2]

This grand European hitchhike had an enormous effect on Douglas. Having never travelled further abroad than the Isle of Wight, it inspired in him a tremendous love of travel and exploration, it opened his eyes to exotic new cultures, and most importantly he discovered his freedom.

They say you can't go home again. Douglas continued to explore Europe, with friends, during his undergraduate years. But once his usual mode of travel had become the first-class cabin of an airliner, there was no going back to the carefree days of his youth: 'I returned to Istanbul once. I was flying back from Australia and arbitrarily decided to stop off in Istanbul on the way back. But getting a taxi in from the airport and staying in a nice hotel instead of getting a ride in on the back of a truck and sleeping in the back room of a cheap boarding house somehow robbed it of its magic. I wandered around for a couple of days trying to avoid carpet sellers and then gave up.'[3]

CHAPTER 4

'**WHEN I WENT** up to Cambridge it was great because I suddenly found a lot of other people who I felt I could actually get on with. And also the other great thing about going up to university was that it suddenly didn't matter if you were good at games.'[1]

Douglas went to Cambridge University for one reason only: to become a writer-performer in the most famous, most exclusive undergraduate comedy society in the world – Footlights: 'I wanted to be a writer or performer in the same way the Pythons are and therefore desperately wanted to go to Cambridge and get into the Footlights.'[2] Technically, however, he was there to study English Literature, something about which he subsequently felt slightly guilty, in light of his burgeoning interest in science: 'I did have something of a guilt thing about reading English. I thought I should have done something useful and challenging. But while I was whingeing I also relished the chance not to do very much. If I had known then what I know now I would have done biology or zoology.'[3]

'The chance not to do very much' is a telling phrase. 'I'm a perpetual essay-crisis person,' said Douglas. 'In three years I only ever managed to complete about three essays.'[4]

One of the first friends he made was a young history student from Northern Ireland, Keith Jeffrey (now a university professor), who found him, 'very tall, very witty, with a comparative zest for life, an occasional gloomy side, but a life enhancer, no question about that. We never really talked about work. We just went off and did our supervisions, wrote our essays. I've no real sense of him toiling heavily over the books, though I dare say we shared that. There was too much else to do actually. We were not taking life too seriously in those days.'[5]

'He must have done some work because he got a degree, although I suspect not very much,' says another of Douglas' Cambridge friends, Jonny Brock. 'He was very bright, but I'm not sure he was terribly interested in English even at that stage. I think he just read English at school and at university because it was the fashionable thing to do in those days. But he was clever enough to busk it.'[6]

One of the core tenets of the Footlights Society is that you cannot apply to become a member. Instead, prospective John Cleeses and Peter Cooks must ingratiate themselves with current Footlights members, letting their comedy aspirations become known. They can then be invited – through an audition process – to perform at 'smoking concerts' or 'smokers', along with established members, in front of the rest of Footlights. If their material is deemed funny enough, the applicant may be permitted to join the club. It is from the material presented at smokers that the sketches and cast for the annual May Week Revue are chosen.

John Lloyd, later to collaborate with Douglas on *The Meaning of Liff* and two episodes of *Hitchhiker's*, explains how a smoker was organised: 'You would plump for a venue, usually a college theatre of some sort or a hall. Then you would leaflet anybody you knew who was in Footlights or who wanted to be, or people who weren't but you thought were very good, and then people would show up for an audition. The rule when I was there was that only writer-performers were allowed in – unless they were girls. Girls were let off, particularly the gorgeous ones! They didn't have to write any jokes. But all the blokes, it absolutely was mandatory that you had to write your own material.'[7]

Douglas was perhaps surprised to find that he could not simply sign up for Footlights: 'My first experience was very off-putting because I found everybody rather grand and aloof, rather cold and unencouraging.'[8] Instead, he joined the Cambridge University

Light Entertainment Society, a far less cliquey organisation which performed mostly for charity. John Cleese had been in CULES (later on, so was Prince Edward); it wasn't Footlights, but it was an outlet for Douglas' writer-performer aspirations and if it was good enough for Cleese, it was good enough for him. Douglas was introduced to the society a few weeks after he arrived at Cambridge when a group of CULES members, styling themselves the Cambridge Cabaret Group, performed a revue entitled *Funny, Bloody Funny* at St John's over 20–22 October 1971.

Keith Jeffrey, who performed with Douglas in the smoker which got them into Footlights, recalls: 'All these things are very snobby. CULES was, as it were, Radio 2 to Footlights' Radio 3. They were always the soft end of the light performing arts, looked on rather snootily by Footlights undoubtedly. But on the other hand, quite good. In those days, Footlights used to have its own rooms, Falcon Yard off Petty Curie, which were amazingly seedy. But they did quite good pub lunches. They were up a flight of stairs above the Cambridge Cruising Club as I recall. Which was always thought to be a witty conjunction.'[9]

'Douglas was a bit discontented with the traditional Footlights clique-ish, closed-shop-ish snobbery,' recalls the writer Sue Limb. 'I remember him mentioning CULES *en passant* and I think Douglas was disappointed that he didn't get elected to Footlights immediately.'[10]

Douglas' only known performance with CULES was a show presented to inmates at Chelmsford Prison: 'We were roundly booed and barracked by the prisoners. When I think of the clever dick material we were probably showing them, I'm not surprised at all!'[11] Footlights auditions were held on 15–16 November 1971 and, after performing in his first smoker, Douglas was elected to membership on 4 February 1972. His champion on the committee, who would become a lifelong friend, was Simon Jones who held the official committee post of 'victualler'.

'I was in charge of that particular smoker,' recalled Jones. 'People, in order to get into Footlights, had to perform a sketch they'd written themselves, and then it would be considered by the committee. Douglas came along with Keith Jeffrey and performed what I thought was a rather amusing sketch, impersonating a hand-pump, which involved spitting. It was funny – at least I thought it was. Nobody else did actually. But I didn't see why he shouldn't do that in a smoker. Douglas always remembers me going out on a limb, virtually challenging the others to a duel over whether he should be allowed to do it. I think he's exaggerating a little, though I certainly did have to justify my choice. They certainly were a bit snotty.'[12]

But Douglas' first stage performance at Cambridge wasn't with Footlights or CULES, it was in a production of Bertolt Brecht's *The Good Person of Szechuan* at the ADC Theatre, directed by Sue Limb. 'I didn't know what I was doing but all these very talented people turned up,' she recalls. 'Because it was my first production it was rather stylised and pretentious and they all had different kinds of black-and-white, clown-like make-up in Brechtian style. I remember using Douglas' immense height to symbolise the crushing of the proletariat. My first impression of him was his immense genial, jovial quality. Even as an undergraduate he was incredibly jovial and endlessly good-natured. He seemed unable to prevent himself from laughing on stage. This is probably why we had this stylised make-up, so that he could look horrid and sneering and brutal, from a distance at least.'[13]

Meanwhile, the Adams-Jeffrey writing partnership was developing new material. 'I think we were working at such an elementary stage, it's hard even to say there was a process,' says Jeffrey. 'If you were to look back at these sketches we did, you'd think they were so fantastically bad. A couple of good ideas but no real talent in putting them together.'[14]

The earliest smoking concert featuring Douglas for which documentation survives was called *Prepare to Drop Them Now* on 5 May 1972, the last event ever staged at Falcon Yard. Curiously, Douglas' contribution was not written by himself; instead, he performed a monologue by Dave Robinson called 'Cyril Fletcher's Last Stand'. Preceding him on the running order was a sketch by Martin Smith and Will Adams. 'Falcon Yard was a marvellous room in an old building in an old part of the town centre,' recalled Will Adams. 'There was a MacFisheries warehouse on the ground floor and

Snoopy's Disco on the floor above. And sandwiched in between was this rather fishy, smoky room with a bar at one end and a stage at the other. And when you went up the old rickety stairs there was a smell of gas and fish, it was tremendously atmospheric.'[15]

John Lloyd recalls Douglas' attitude to Footlights as: 'Pretty enthusiastic, not to say damned dogged. He was an ambitious cove. I suppose we all were, come to think of it. But Douglas didn't seem to possess the normal blocks that prevent many of us fulfilling our potential. Embarrassment, for example. Or self-deprecation. Whatever he did, he did it big, and he was always perfectly certain that whatever it was would come to pass. He wasn't the kind of person who would take, "No. Definitely not. Bugger off," for an answer. He became quite well known in Footlights smokers as the enormous bloke who did enormously long, completely peculiar, unstructured monologues, one of which I seem to remember was about a tree, and which I'm pretty sure he delivered to utter silence. Afterwards he would be in the bar explaining animatedly how well he thought it had gone. As a friend (although not yet a close one in those days) I used to feel a bit sorry for him, because he couldn't seem to find the groove. But with real talent, this is absolutely commonplace.'[16]

Sue Limb remembers that some of the established Footlights people had, 'a rather condescending attitude to Douglas, briefly, at the beginning of his career. It may have been something to do with (a) his extreme good-natured friendliness, and (b) his inability to keep a straight face on stage. I think there was a feeling that Douglas wasn't serious, that he was just having a lark, that his delivery left a lot to be desired. But I always liked him enormously right from the start. He seemed to be so ready for anything and willing to turn his hand to anything. He wasn't prima donna-ish at all like so many of us were. There was a lot of preposterous posturing and prima donna-ing, a lot of us considered ourselves absolutely terrific and put on airs. Douglas never put on airs. Perhaps that was why the Footlights crowd couldn't understand him at first.'[17]

Nevertheless, Douglas made every effort to participate in Footlights affairs and events. On 12 May 1972, one week after *Prepare to Drop Them Now*, there was a Footlights dinner at the Old

Library, preceded by a final farewell drink at Falcon Yard which was demolished on 19 June. Thirty-seven people – about half the membership – attended, including Simon Jones, Martin Smith, Will Adams and Douglas (who swapped seats with a lady named Ann Guerson though it's not clear why).

That year's May Week Revue was *Norman Ruins*, directed by Barry Brown and starring Simon Jones, Sue Limb, John Parry and others. Unusually, there was a film sequence included in the revue, directed and produced by Brown's brother Richard, who recalls: 'The film was a take-off of film adverts of the day mixed up with a Ken Russell spoof. The main sequence was an advert for milk which involved bits of *The Boyfriend* and *The Devils* mixed together.'[18] The film's script was written by Richard Brown and John Parry, although there had been some talk of Douglas collaborating with them which came to nothing. When the revue opened on 5 June 1972 at the Arts Theatre in Cambridge, the *Cambridge Evening News* observed: 'Undoubtedly the funniest thing in the show is a short film owing much to Ken Russell's bizarre style.'

A photograph of Douglas in this film was published in Robert Hewison's excellent book *Footlights! A Hundred Years of Cambridge Comedy* (Eyre Methuen, 1983). A long-haired Douglas, wearing a long dress over a turtle-neck sweater, clutches a copy of *Playboy* to his chest and stares ahead stoically, oblivious to the young lady gazing adoringly up at him.

'Actually he's dressed as Torquemada,' explained Simon Jones. 'I was in that film too and I can't remember who the hell I was. I remember we all got covered from head to foot in white dust because we were filming in the chalk pits in Cherry Hinton because it looked like Greece or something. Funnily enough a few years later we found ourselves down at the china clay pits in St Austell for the planet of Magrathea in the TV series of *Hitchhiker's*. So we were quite used to prancing around with white dust all over us.'[19]

CHAPTER 5

DOUGLAS' SECOND YEAR at Cambridge kicked off with another Sue Limb production at the ADC: Sheridan's *The Rivals*. Once again, Douglas' habit of 'corpsing' (laughing on stage) got him into trouble, and this time there was no black-and-white Brechtian make-up to disguise his grin.

'He was a nightmare to act with,' confides Limb. 'When we were doing *The Rivals* and he played Sir Lucius O'Trigger, he had the most terrible attack of corpsing and giggling. There was a terrible performance at which Douglas started to go and he then infected everybody who came on stage. They all caught this appalling hysteria. Robin Rogers who was playing Jack Absolute had to turn upstage at one point and just hide his face. It was awful. I don't know what it was about Douglas. He was just unable to take anything seriously and of course he was very infectious in his good humour. I don't think acting was really his thing, although he was very good as Sir Lucius O'Trigger with his preposterous Irish attitudes.'[1]

Robin Rogers was another Brentwood boy as were several people on the Cambridge theatrical scene, including that year's Footlights President, Robert Benton. And it was Douglas' Brentwood connections which saved the day when *The Rivals* encountered a casting problem, as Limb recalls: 'I had auditioned at the end of the previous year and we were all going to assemble in October to get *The Rivals* going. And the guy I cast as Fag the manservant was missing because he had some sort of mishap involving a drugs bust on his long vacation. I was a little bit in despair and Douglas said, "There was a chap I was at school with who's just come up and he's very good." And that was Griff Rhys Jones. So Douglas not only auditioned himself, he got Griff Rhys Jones along to audition. I'm proud to say that was Griff's first foray into Cambridge theatre.'[2]

Jonny Brock was also in that production: 'I played Acres, a sort of country bumpkin who fancies himself as a gent, whereas Sir Lucius O'Trigger is a wild, Irish knight, a Falstaff/Quixote-like character. They have a sword fight at some point and then Sir Lucius O'Trigger challenges somebody else, so Douglas had quite a lot of business. He was very tall and angular and John Cleese-like in those days, he was much slimmer. He wasn't a very good actor, he never professed to be, but he was very effective in that part. He wasn't very good at doing the Irish accent but it didn't matter very much. He certainly created that very distinct impression of being all arms and legs and doing funny walks.'[3]

Brock recalls the sword fight between Acres and Sir Lucius O'Trigger as being particularly alarming: 'Douglas had the co-ordination of a mastodon. We did five performances in which the result of the fight depended on whether Douglas could get his weapon out of its scabbard.'[4] 'I don't remember the sword fights – I always closed my eyes,' admits Limb. 'I don't know whether Douglas' coordination was terribly good. Douglas with a sword in his hand and waving his arms around would cover a very big area of a stage.'[5]

That same term, Limb invited Douglas to perform in a smoker which she was co-chairing called *LSO in Flames* (17 November 1972). Douglas and Keith Jeffrey performed two sketches: 'Trees Afoot' (which they co-wrote) and 'Post Offices Prefer Bombs' written by Douglas alone. There was also a solo item for Douglas entitled 'The Serious Sketch'. This seems to have been the end of Jeffrey's partnership with Douglas: 'My sense is that in the end he worked better writing alone. Although he needed a lot of prodding, as we know. But in the end, the main genius was his own. I was less committed to it. He was with people who were keen on doing that sort of thing. It wasn't anything personal I think. But at that stage

I didn't like working with other people, and writing is the sort of thing that actually demands you work with other people.'[6]

Though they were no longer writing together, Adams and Jeffrey remained good friends and shared rooms in this, their second year. Jeffrey was Captain of the Boat Club, as a result of which they were allotted a magnificent two-storey set of rooms in a college lodging house: 'We had a huge sitting room and separate rooms on different floors, this fantastic room with a grand piano, very over the top – which rather tickled us – with turtle shells round the walls and a lot of bits and pieces. Douglas had a room with a desk which in a normal university would have been perfectly adequate for about three people. He was keen on buying books and records and discussing things: "You must try this, and aren't these Bach cantatas wonderful?" That year he got a very snappy Bang and Olufsen hi-fi which I was greatly envious of. We used to play a lot of records and we had dinner parties.'[7]

The room may have had a grand piano, but one thing it lacked was a television, so the weekly date with *Monty Python's Flying Circus* meant a walk across to the Junior Combination Room. 'I saw an immense number of episodes of *Colditz* as I recall,' laughs Jeffrey, 'because it was on just before *Python* and you had to be in about an hour before to get a seat. So there was all this jockeying for position. Of course we could recite all the sketches by heart, but we weren't the only ones in the world to do that.'[8]

I Don't Know – I've Never Looked . . . was a smoker chaired by John Lloyd and future Arts Council Chief Executive Mary Allen on 8 February 1973, at which Douglas performed his own musical composition, 'A Song for Stupid People'. Increasingly, Douglas would use comic songs as a vehicle for his humour. 'He was very instinctive,' recalls Nigel Hess, musical director of that year's May Week Revue. 'The lyrics always came first with Douglas, as you would expect. I think at that time he was still trying to find his way round the guitar, using it to accompany the lyrics, rather than the other way round. The lyrics were always important, rather than the music.'[9]

Meanwhile, Martin Smith and Will Adams were proving very prolific, contributing three or four items to each smoker. 'Douglas wasn't particularly active,' recalled Will. 'Certainly not as much as Martin, who was the leading partner in our partnership. John Lloyd was driving us along. And I think Douglas only performed when he'd got something written down perhaps. I don't think we had an immediate rapport with Douglas any more than with anybody else. In fact I don't think that we really felt on the same wavelength as Douglas at all to start with.'[10]

Nevertheless, some sort of friendship was formed. Martin and Will chaired a smoker on 1 March 1973, *The Heel-Fire Club*, in which Douglas took part purely as a cast member in two of the longer sketches (alongside a long-haired law student named Clive Anderson). Two months later, in *A Burst of Apalsy* (17 May 1973), Martin helped Douglas perform 'Point Taken' (aka 'Pritchard'), the first truly memorable Douglas Adams sketch, though it still owed a hefty debt to *Monty Python*. It involved a British Rail signalman explaining to his boss how he had attempted to demonstrate existentialism by leaving open all the points in the entire Southern Region.

Around this time, Douglas briefly returned once more to debating, at which he had achieved such success while at Brentwood. The Cambridge Union Society broke from their serious discussions for one evening each year to host what was called 'the Funny Debate', which on 5 March 1973 was proposed by Douglas and Keith Jeffrey and opposed by Martin and Will. The motion was, 'This House is sated, saturated but not satisfied', and Benny Green and Jack Trevor-Storey were the guest speakers (Vivian Stanshall had been invited but cancelled at the last moment).

The 1973 May Week Revue was *Every Packet Carries a Government Health Warning*, directed by Stephen Wyatt, starring Mary Allen, Robert Benton, Jon Canter, John Lloyd, Griff Rhys Jones and others. Martin and Will received writing credits for the inclusion of their Leonard Cohen spoof, 'Cohen for a Song', but Douglas did not contribute.

'*Every Packet* . . . was a very, very conservative show, lots of jolly songs and dancing,' recalls John Lloyd, 'with a sort of *I'm Sorry I Haven't a Clue* line in jokes. Puns and stuff. Good ones, mind, but not in the least Douglas' style. He was always quoting John Cleese' legendary Three Rules of Comedy Writing: 1) NO PUNS, 2) NO PUNS and 3) NO PUNS. I don't know if Douglas had submitted any of his own material but it wouldn't have been Stephen Wyatt's kind of thing at all.'[11]

Undeterred by their failure to be included in the revue, Douglas, Martin and Will teamed up to present their own alternative show, *Several Poor Players Strutting and Fretting*. 'Our humour was very different,' said Will. 'Martin and I tended to be perhaps a little bit too structured and logical because that was the way our minds worked. Whereas Douglas had this completely bizarre sense of humour, and there didn't appear to be any common ground to start with.'[12]

Nevertheless, a show was worked out, to be staged at the School of Pythagoras at St John's over 14–16 June 1973 (directly opposite *Every Packet* ...'s run at the ADC). 'The School of Pythagoras was a very ancient building,' recalled Will. 'A real, old, stone-built, I-don't-know-what-century building that had been beautifully converted into a theatre upstairs and a sort of general circulation area downstairs. It may have been because Douglas was at St John's that we got it for free. I think that we were possibly sponsored to some degree and maybe they got their money back from the take. But certainly with the tickets at 30p, or whatever it was, there wasn't a huge cash flow going on. *Several Poor Players* ... was a kind of Not the May Week Revue. And although we didn't have the big production numbers and the big spectacles, I think we scored more of a hit because it was more different. The May Week Revue was just another May Week Revue but this was something completely different – to coin a phrase.'[13]

Many of the sketches, such as 'Post Offices Prefer Bombs', had already been performed to considerable acclaim in smokers. To publicise themselves, Martin, Will and Douglas went out in fancy dress – Douglas was a 6-foot 5-inch turkey – and strolled around Cambridge town centre on 15 May having photographs taken.

Assisted by Stefanie Singer and Rachel Hood in minor female roles, and with additional material by John Parry, Jon Canter and Jeremy Browne, *Several Poor Players* ... proved to be a great success. Will's diary for 14 June records: 'Revue opened in the evening. Great! Full house.'

There was one other credit on the *Several Poor Players* ... programme: John Cleese. Once safely ensconced in Footlights, Douglas had wasted no time in befriending his hero and as a result had permission to perform 'Butterling' (aka 'Zookeeper'), an old *Frost Report* sketch. Memories of how Adams and Cleese met differ. Will Adams said: 'Douglas was always a great one for going up to people and saying, "Hi, I'm Douglas Adams." And one day on Holland Park tube station – if I remember correctly – he saw John Cleese on the platform, went up to him and said, "Hi, I'm Douglas Adams. You haven't heard of me yet," sort of thing. They got chatting and obviously got on okay and became mates. And I can't remember the circumstances of it but we all went down to see John Cleese. I think Douglas must have perhaps sent him some scripts to have a look at and give a view on. This would have been 1973. In fact we subsequently then used to go and see the recordings at Television Centre. And then through John Cleese we got the "Butterling" sketch for the revue.'[14]

And here's Douglas' version: 'One day I was at the Round House going to see some show, and I was at the bar at the interval and the person standing next to me was John Cleese. So seizing the moment, I said, "Excuse me, can I interview you for *Varsity*?" He very graciously said, "Yes, all right", and gave me his number and I went off to interview him a few weeks later.'[15]

Whether it was at the Round House (the theatre in London which often gave Footlights shows a brief West End run) or on a tube station, it's clear that Adams was in no way shy about approaching his childhood hero, and for more than just an autograph. Douglas didn't want to be seen as a fan, but as an equal. Over the years Douglas would take every opportunity to work with Cleese, casting him in *Doctor Who*, *Black Cinderella II Goes East* and *Starship Titanic*. For his part, Cleese always seemed tolerant of, perhaps slightly embarrassed by, Douglas' adulation.

Nevertheless he gave him the script of 'Butterling' and granted him an interview which was published in *Varsity* on 25 November

1972. Unseen for more than thirty years, here is Douglas' introduction to the *Varsity* interview article:

> 'We're out of beer, have some soup,' he said, vaguely trying to find his way round the inside of his fridge. The hard aloof Cleese is a figment of the box; privately he is quiet, unassuming and very friendly, and I was aware of talking to somebody else from Cambridge rather than a television star. He gets a little embarrassed if people expect him to behave like a funny man. 'I tend to over-react against that, I think it's a defence thing, and I immediately become very quiet, polite – as polite as I can screw up the energy to be – but deliberately non-kooky.'
>
> It never occurred to him to make a career in show biz till two BBC radio men turned up at the Footlights revue and later offered him a job as a writer.

The one-page article then continues as a series of Q & A, betraying little of Douglas' journalistic voice. But one can sense even from this brief piece of writing his determination to see himself and Cleese as part of a single peer group, and Cleese' polite – even slightly bemused – tolerance of this extraordinarily confident fan who clearly idolised him. (Douglas often said: 'I wanted to be a writer-performer like the Pythons. In fact I wanted to be John Cleese and it took me some time to realise that the job was taken.'[16]) It was a polite tolerance which Douglas himself would later display to any fans of *Hitchhiker's* who assumed that they could, *ipso facto*, become his friend. Douglas never sought to befriend his fans but he always wanted to befriend his idols and never apparently spotted either the symmetry or the irony.

In the *Varsity* interview, there is one particularly telling exchange which amply demonstrates how Adams modelled himself on Cleese:

> **Q:** To what do you attribute your success?
> **C:** I don't know, no-one's ever asked me that. Obviously I've got the comic way of thinking, but also I'm so frightened of being bad that I work far harder at it than most people. I'm a worrier by

nature, and if you worry at something long enough you nearly always get it right.

Douglas embraced this philosophy utterly. Compare this interview with him, from January 2000:

Q: What's the essence of *Hitchhiker's Guide*'s success?
D: Of course, it's an unanswerable question. If one knew the answer, one could bottle it. The only thing I can say with any degree of certainty is that, however extraordinary its success may have turned out to be, there's a little bit of me that isn't surprised because I actually know how much I put into it. I do find writing terribly, terribly difficult, and I think it's because there's a little bit of me that cannot expect that anything that I've written is going to be any good. So you work at it a bit more and a bit more and you are so determined to pack everything in, so it doesn't surprise me that people have got a lot out of it in the end.'[17]

Jon Canter recalls how surprised Douglas' friends were when this article appeared: 'In the early '70s, if you were at all influenced by hippies and trying to be cool, you weren't ambitious. So I can remember when we were all students, we were absolutely taken aback that Douglas went down to London to interview John Cleese for the university magazine because we saw that as careerism. It was simply Douglas meeting somebody he'd always wanted to meet, but to our way of thinking, it was the thing you didn't do. You never openly said, "I want to get on, I want to make my way in the world." But I think Douglas always had that in him, and I think he was very ready.'[18]

But Douglas' careerism was definitely aimed at writing/performing, not journalism. Certainly his friends in Footlights were suitably impressed by *Several Poor Players Strutting and Fretting* and the trio of Adams-Smith-Adams. 'They seemed to be a perfect combination,' recalls John Lloyd. 'Martin Smith took the kind of David Hatch role, being businesslike and logical and a getter-done. Will Adams was the kindly, lovable Tim Brooke-Taylor-y/Michael

Palin-ish type and Douglas was a kind of lunatic Cleese/Chapman figure I suppose. By working with Martin and Will, Douglas' brilliant aperçus suddenly found a *raison d'être*, a structure and a home. Together, they seemed unstoppable.'[19]

CHAPTER 6

IN HIS THIRD year, Douglas shared rooms with Nick Burton and Johnny Simpson, the latter providing the inspiration for Zaphod Beeblebrox: 'He had that nervous sort of hyper-energetic way of trying to appear relaxed. He was always trying to be so cool and relaxed, but he could never sit still.'[1]

All three of Adams-Smith-Adams found themselves on the Footlights committee: Martin as club secretary, Douglas as PR officer, and Will as 'archivist and falconer'. The trio were a definite fixture in Footlights and '(Adams, Smith, Adams)' was a common writing credit at smoking concerts such as *Duplicator's Revenge* on 25 October 1973. 'How to Plan Countries', the first of their three sketches, concerned a man who finds that his idyllic, rose-covered cottage is to be demolished to make way for a new motorway. (Coincidentally, the 9 October 1973 issue of *Varsity* explained how the construction of the Cambridge bypass threatened the university's new £2 million radio telescope.)

November 1973 was a busy month for Adams-Smith-Adams. On the 8th they contributed three items including 'Song of Tiny Minds' to *Nostalgia's Not What It Was*, and a note at the bottom of the programme read: 'Don't forget the Patter of Adams, Smith, Adams' tiny minds in the School of Pythagoras on November 15th, 16th and 17th.' *The Patter of Tiny Minds* was Adams-Smith-Adams' second revue, with Margaret Thomas taking the female roles and additional material by John Lloyd. It was another rip-roaring success, including Martin's ever-popular 'Cohen for a Song'. On 24 November, Douglas, Martin, Will, Jon Canter, Margaret Thomas, Stefanie Welch, Clive Anderson and Nigel Hess travelled to Bishop's Stortford for a one-off performance simply titled *Cambridge Footlights Revue*. Of thirty-five items in the programme, Douglas wrote or co-wrote twelve and performed in fourteen, including three solo spots – one of which was 'Backdated', a 'self-accompanied talking blues' which never really started:

> *I was walking down the street today,*
> *Or maybe it was yesterday . . .*
> *It may in fact have been last week . . .*
> *Yes . . . it probably was last week . . .*

. . . And so on for five increasingly rambling verses, ending with the stage direction: 'Turns and walks off, frustratedly.' The song was resurrected more than twenty years later, on 12 October 1994, when Douglas performed it live on John Dunn's Radio 2 show.

Rounding out this busy month was *Cinderella*, the Footlights pantomime, from 27 November until 8 December, directed by Crispin Thomas from a script by Jeremy Browne and Jon Canter. Douglas played Prince Charming's father, King Groovy, while Martin and Will appeared throughout the story as a sort of double-act, credited in the programme as 'A mistake' and 'Another mistake'. An audio recording of the pantomime exists, and Douglas' acting is certainly nothing special, even by panto standards. Nevertheless, there's an interesting precursor of Galactic President Zaphod Beeblebrox in the cool ruler that is King Groovy.

Robin Rogers, who played Buttons, remembers: 'With as much leg, body and arms as Douglas had, he was hopeless at the dance routines – we had to be hauled back endlessly to the beginning of each routine in rehearsal because Douglas had found something impossible to coordinate. He was like an 18-hand horse trying to learn dressage. I think his steps in the routines were cut down so that all he had to do was sway from side to side.'[2]

A revised version of *The Patter of Tiny Minds* was performed for one night only (13 January 1974) at the Bush Theatre in

Shepherd's Bush, thus satisfying the trio's desire to perform in London. Mary Allen took the female roles under her stage name of Mary Adams (there was no significance except that she had joined Equity and her agent recommended a name beginning with A). John Lloyd also joined the cast under the pseudonym 'John Smith', hence: Adams-Smith-Adams-Smith-Adams. The trio even considered setting themselves up as a cabaret group called Tiny Minds and had letterheads printed.

'Douglas' material was wonderful to perform,' recalls Mary Allen. 'It was anarchic, it was highly original, it was extremely funny. One of the difficulties sometimes about performing material as a comic that is very funny is to resist the urge to laugh yourself, and I think I probably had more difficulty with that with Douglas' material than any others. Douglas on stage was irrepressible. He always had this great sense of glee, and he was quite difficult to act with in that sense because you always felt that he was about to burst out laughing himself.'[3]

Patter . . . featured Douglas' legendary cat-shaving sketches. The first was an intellectual discussion about the nature of true love, quoting Keats, but concluding with a mention of cat-shaving. Later in the revue, Allen sang a short love song, absolutely straight until the final line: 'Feeling so romantic, think I'll go and shave the cat.' Later still a young couple were discovered canoodling, whispering 'Should we?' 'Dare we?' – then ran off stage hand in hand, followed by the sound of a razor and a feline howl.

Sitting in the audience that night was another up-and-coming comedy writer, Andrew Marshall, who, with his writing partner David Renwick, would create *The Burkiss Way*, a major stepping stone in Douglas' career. Marshall would become good friends with Douglas and work with him in Edinburgh, but in terms of *Hitchhiker's Guide,* his biggest claim to fame is being the inspiration for Marvin the Paranoid Android. 'Douglas, Will and Martin appeared in a small revue at the Bush Theatre with Mary Adams and John Lloyd,' he confirms. 'Douglas played the part of Mr Y-Fronts Silver – "I think that's the least amusing thing in the whole sketch," he said – who had seized a London bus which he was running as a pirate ship, appearing in full pirate's outfit, but conducting an interview on the subject as if it were an intellectual treatise on *Panorama*.'[4]

John Lloyd had come down from Cambridge in 1973 and joined the BBC on 2 January 1974. Up to that point he had been putting together a radio version of *Every Packet Carries a Government Health Warning* and trying to write, as all aspiring comedy writers did, for Radio 4's Friday night topical sketch show *Week Ending*: 'I was sharing a council flat in the city with the Hon. Alex Catto and another banker. There were only two beds in this tiny little flat, and as they were proper bankers who wore suits and I was just a writer, I had to sleep on the floor. And I was absolutely starving. You couldn't really make a living writing radio comedy.

'*Every Packet . . .*, while terribly old-fashioned, was a very entertaining show with a lot of solid set pieces. Footlights had not been up to much for several years and the telly people had stopped coming. But BBC radio showed up in the persons of David Hatch and Simon Brett. We all met them afterwards. They'd really loved the show, so we got on splendidly, and they commissioned a radio version pretty much on the spot. This was a major hit in radio terms. An edited version of the stage show, it was a good deal crisper and very well received. (This despite still being called *Every Packet Carries a Government Health Warning*, arguably the worst title for a comedy programme until *Have I Got News For You?*). A second show with the unutterably pathetic title of *Footlights Successor* was duly ordered and when that also got much praise and excellent ratings, a series was commissioned.

'The BBC didn't want all eight of the original cast of *Every Packet . . .* in a mere half-hour show, so Stephen Wyatt had to nominate who would be in what. He told me I couldn't go to the Edinburgh Festival with *Every Packet . . .* because "you can't act". I started to cry, and he hurriedly told me that I could be in the radio show as a kind of consolation prize. I thought I'd got the short straw there, particularly because obviously I wasn't really crying, but acting all the time! In the end though, I got the best deal. That single conversation in The Baron of Beef, was the real start of my whole career.'[5]

While John Lloyd was finding his feet at the BBC, a smoker on

31 January 1974 called *Litter from America* featured four Adams-Smith-Adams items. On the one hand, this shows how popular and successful the trio were within Footlights; on the other, it suggests a paucity of new talent, and indeed the club had been suffering recruitment problems for some time, a situation not helped by the lack of a permanent home and various administrative/bureaucratic disputes.

A relatively recent innovation had been the introduction of the 'Late Night Revue' in the Lent (Spring) Term, balancing the Christmas pantomime and the May Week Revue at the end of the year (May Week is, of course, in June). In 1974 *Late Night Final* was performed from 26 February to 2 March, directed by Tony Root and Jon Canter. The cast included Douglas, Will, Martin, Clive Anderson and Griff Rhys Jones and there were six Adams-Smith-Adams items in the twenty-six-item programme, with Douglas performing in a couple of other sketches too.

Adams-Smith-Adams' final smoking concert was *In Spite of It All* on 25 April 1974, chaired by Footlights musical maestros Nigel Hess and Nic Rowley. Douglas, Will and Martin performed 'Late Again' and 'The Majority Song' (aka 'No Good Asking Me') of which, incredibly, an audio recording exists. It's an energetic if slightly uncoordinated performance with Martin taking lead vocal in a squeaky voice, Will performing some sort of visual comedy during the instrumental middle eight, and Douglas strumming away furiously on an acoustic guitar:

> *No good asking me, no good asking me,*
> *I don't think party politics is quite my cup of tea,*
> *Labour, Tory, Liberal – they're all the same you see,*
> *The one my father voted for is good enough for me!*

Though the alternative comedy scene was still a few years away, there was a market for occasional student cabaret, especially with a Footlights pedigree, at theatres around the country. For example, *A Room with a Revue* at the Belgrade Theatre, Coventry from 28 March to 6 April 1974 included several Adams-Smith-Adams-scripted items; Martin even travelled to Coventry personally to perform his party piece, 'Cohen for a Song'. (Coincidentally, the Belgrade staged *Hitchhiker's Guide* in 1983, while one of the revue's cast members, Chris Langham, played Arthur Dent on stage in London in 1979.)

It was assumed, and not just by Douglas, Martin and Will, that Adams-Smith-Adams would feature prominently in the 1974 May Week Revue, and indeed they did – as writers. But only one of the trio was in the cast, and his name wasn't Adams.

The show was called *Chox* and was directed by Robert Benton. The cast included Clive Anderson, Jon Canter, Geoff McGivern (later to play Ford Prefect, described in the programme as 'a blunt, stocky Stella Stevens fan ... obsessed with death, art and York City Football Club'), Griff Rhys Jones, Crispin Thomas and Martin Smith ('a member of Adams-Smith-Adams (GB) Ltd'). Benton announced his decision at a meeting in Jon Canter's room on 10 March to which all the cast members were invited, along with Will, Douglas and Nigel Hess (who was also restricted to writing duties). It seems that Will Adams was for some reason unable to attend, as Benton explained his reasoning to him shortly thereafter in a letter:

> *Dear Will,*
>
> *As you know by now I have not been able to cast you in the May Week Revue. Douglas has probably told you the gist of what I said to him and the same really applies to you. I do not think that the big stage show is your metier. The style both you and Douglas have evolved in your own shows is unique and should not be tampered with in the interests of filling an aircraft hangar like the Arts. I also believe, though this is not my business, that your real strength lies in your writing and though I take Douglas' point that he believes a revue should be performed by its writers, I also think there's a strong argument for concentrating on either the writing or performing skill.*

Douglas was gutted. He had come to Cambridge with the specific intent of becoming a writer-performer and had been denied his final chance to tread the boards in a May Week Revue. He had been relegated to the status of writer-not-performer, which was not his ambition: 'The writer-performer was the lynch-pin of all the Python lot when they were at Cambridge. By my time there, it was the director who would decide what to do. To my mind, that always produced very artificial results.'[6]

Friends Mary Allen, John Lloyd and Simon Jones swiftly rallied round with suggestions and support. Will Adams' diary records a briefly considered idea of involving them in another Adams-Smith-Adams review, without Martin and with John Lloyd credited as John Jones to make it Adams-Jones-Adams-Jones-Adams. It was little consolation that Douglas and Will were offered roles as paid 'script consultants' on *Chox*.

'It was a major thing that suddenly Adams-Smith-Adams wasn't involved as an entity,' recalled Will, though he conceded with hindsight: 'I think they were right. Certainly Martin was the best performer of the three of us. But I don't remember getting paid anything at all. I think we were more of a nuisance because all we did was sit there and make comments that they could do without.'[7]

Chox opened on 3 June 1974 at the Arts Theatre, with fourteen of the thirty-nine items on the programme carrying the Adams-Smith-Adams credit, including 'Point Taken', 'Backdated' and a popular ensemble sketch about the AGM of the Paranoid Society, 'Hole in the Wall Club'.

Feelings ran high that summer and it clearly took Douglas a long time to get over the hurt. On 5 June the *Varsity* gossip column even reported: 'at this term's Footlights party Douglas Adams had a slight altercation (punch-up) with Geoff Goldenego McGivern.'

After its regulation fortnight at the Arts, *Chox* played the Nuffield Theatre, Southampton and Oxford Playhouse for a week each with a rearranged programme order and one Adams-Smith-Adams item replaced by another. On 15 July it opened at the Comedy Theatre, London for four weeks with another slight change to the running order, but Douglas and Will could still claim writing credit on more than a third of the show that they were not good enough to perform in. It was in this form, redirected by Crispin Thomas, that it finally transferred to St Mary's Hall, Edinburgh for a month from 16 August.

Reviews were not good. The *Guardian* called the show, 'dismal . . . amateur vaudeville and etiolated whimsy'; the *Financial Times* said it was, 'astonishingly nostalgic'; *The Times* observed that, 'a person or persons called Adams Smith Adams contribute the best and the worst material.'

'There was a huge rush of anticipation behind *Chox*,' recalls John Lloyd, who came to see the revue at the Arts on 11 June accompanied by Con Mahoney (Head of Light Entertainment, Radio) and producer Simon Brett. 'The telly people felt they'd missed a trick with *Every Packet* . . . so they sent their top man, Dennis Main Wilson (Goons, Hancock, etc). He loved it. A telly show was commissioned. A West End transfer was arranged. This thing was going to be massive.'[8]

Even in those days, the difference between exposure on Radio 4 and exposure on BBC 2 was enormous, and Lloyd, still toiling over turning *Every Packet* . . . into a weekly series, knew that an hour on TV was worth more than several weeks on the wireless: 'I didn't think *Chox* was nearly as funny or as likable as *Every Packet* . . ., and I was jealous, bitter and resentful, seeing a glittering future dangled momentarily in front of me and then dashed to the ground and pointed at by jeering mud-larks, while everyone else was carried off shoulder high to be crowned at Westminster. But *Chox* turned out to be made of straw rather than pralines. Where *Every Packet* . . . was unselfconsciously old-fashioned it was also unpretentious and pleasantly silly. *Chox* was studiedly old-fashioned and faintly pervy (I thought so, anyway: all top hats and sheer black tights).'[9]

Douglas agreed: 'It was the height of glam rock and the whole thing was really rather awful in a curious kind of way.'[10]

Chox opened in the West End, with an opening night audience packed with ex-Footlights celebrities, but it was not a hit and closed after a few weeks. Nevertheless, fifty minutes of highlights were broadcast on BBC 2 on 26 August 1974 under the unwieldy title *Cambridge University 1974 Footlights Revue*. Later that week, the *Every Packet* . . . spin-off series debuted on Radio 4 in the *Week Ending* slot where it ran for six weeks. It was called *Oh No It Isn't!* and starred, 'the voices of Mary Adams, Jeremy Browne, Jonathan Canter, John Lloyd, Griffith Rhys Jones . . . the music of Nic Rowley,

Nigel Hess, Tim Brutton, Julian Smedley . . . and the words of John Lloyd, Jeremy Browne, Adams-Smith-Adams and others. Producer Simon Brett.'[11]

Brett had first met Douglas on a visit to Cambridge to check out the 1973 May Week Revue: 'I'd been a producer in radio since 1968, producing lots of comedy stuff. I started *Week Ending*. I was a jobbing Light Entertainment producer, one of the younger ones. They were looking for us to come up with the new bright young shows. In those days there wasn't a comedy circuit as there is now, and so for most comedy talent you would go to Cambridge Footlights or Oxford or Bristol. Or you'd go up to the Edinburgh Festival . . . where it tended to be Oxford or Cambridge or Bristol.'

'Douglas didn't actually work on *Oh No It Isn't!* at all,' clarifies John Lloyd who was effectively script editor on the show. 'I was in *Oh No It Isn't!* and writing it, and I was sort of half-producing it as well, having the inside track of it all. I was sitting in London grinding my teeth, usually on my own, with the occasional state visit from Canter. We probably must have used a small amount of tried and tested stuff from *The Patter of Tiny Minds*. The BBC didn't hate the show, they would have been willing to do another series but I canned it slightly. I didn't think we were really good enough and I had a lot of other things to do. There wasn't really the wind behind it; people didn't make a great deal of effort.'[12]

And so, in the summer of 1974, Douglas came down from Cambridge, having achieved only 50 per cent of his ambition: 'Certainly when I was at Cambridge I wanted to be a writer-performer – I very much had the Pythons in my sights – that's why I wanted to do that kind of stuff. But for some reason the world wasn't that keen on me being a performer. And probably quite rightly.'[13]

CHAPTER 7

'HE WAS GOING to become an accountant,' recalls Keith Jeffrey. 'Just before we graduated, in came Douglas waving a tie which he'd bought, very dramatically, because he was going to go off for an interview to become an accountant. He'd now bought a tie and all was lost and nothing was ever going to be right again.'[1]

Fortunately nothing came of this interview and Douglas resolved to pursue his comedy ambition instead. The first thing he did was to get himself an agent, Jill Foster at Fraser and Dunlop: 'I think he came to me because I looked after some of the Monty Pythons. I was representing Mike Palin, Terry Jones, Graham Chapman and Terry Gilliam. So he probably thought, "She's got four of them. I'll go to her." When he first came to me he was starry-eyed and it was the whole *Python* thing that had set him off. When we take on new clients we always ask them to send us some work and he did send us some sketches that were absolutely wonderful. Then we said that we wanted something more than sketches and he sent a sitcom set on a lighthouse. It was lovely stuff. I think it was the first solo thing he'd written. I was interested enough to say, "Come up and let's meet you."'[2]

On leaving Cambridge, Martin and Douglas moved into a flat in Redcliffe Square, Earls Court, with Will living just round the corner. Foster was invited to come and see *Chox*, with its heavy quotient of Adams-Smith-Adams material, and liked what she saw enough to take on all three writers as a team, although it rapidly became clear that Douglas was much more ambitious than Martin or Will when it came to a writing career. 'The two of them felt it was a good idea to get a day job to support themselves while writing,' he said, 'but I thought if you did that you'd end up doing the day job and not doing the writing, so I simply got the odd office job now and then for a couple of weeks to pay the rent. And they ended up, just as I thought, doing their day jobs, so I went ahead on my own.'[3]

In actual fact, the Adams-Smith-Adams writing team continued working together until the end of 1975, staging two more revues, although these were considerably less successful than *Several . . .* or *Patter . . .* and not just because the titles were worse.

From 6 to 9 November 1974 they took over the Arts Theatre – which *Chox* director Benton had warned them was 'an aircraft hangar' – to perform *Cerberus (The Amazing Three-Headed Revue)*. It was actually a five-headed revue, with additional roles taken by Pam Alexander and Richard Gledhill (replacing Geoff McGivern at the last moment). Disagreements with the stage manager left the trio in a distinctly non-humorous mood on the opening night, which proved to be a disaster. The script was swiftly edited and reorganised for the second performance. Will Adams' diary for 7 November records:

> Tonight was much more successful, but still only a mediocre show. It seems that we've spawned a strange creation here; a revue that is almost a play, which the audience do enjoy but don't laugh much at. It is an intimate show in an unintimate theatre and is badly organised, really. Never before have we felt less enthusiastic for a show. I suppose we've been a bit blasé and haven't worked hard enough.

Nevertheless, the *Cambridge Evening News* was enthusiastic and the audience seemed to enjoy themselves. The opening monologue by Douglas entitled 'Beyond the Infinite' (a reference to *2001: A Space Odyssey*, one of Douglas' favourite films) included a line that would later become familiar to millions of radio listeners: '. . . I can't begin to tell you how far it is – I mean, it's so far! You may think it's a long way down the street to the chemist's, but that's just peanuts to space. Even if you go to the top of the Empire State Building . . .'

By this point, Martin and Douglas were sharing a flat in Fordwych Road, Kilburn with Mary Allen, Nigel Hess, Phil Buscombe (who had played drums for Footlights shows) and actress Judy Treweeke. 'There were only five people at any one time in that flat so how this particular combination worked out I'm not entirely sure,'[4] recalls Allen.

'We had mice in the flat,' remembers Nigel Hess. 'Everybody else was putting down poison for them, but Douglas wanted to encourage them. If we put down a pile of poison, he would make little matchstick tables and chairs and put them round the poison, with little signs pointing towards the poison: "*Haute cuisine* this way." He said if they were going to die, they should die in comfort.'[5]

Adams-Smith-Adams performed a one-off cabaret at Martin's old college, Fitzwilliam, in December 1974, then reunited briefly for their final revue, *So You Think You Feel Haddocky. . .* which they staged at the Little Theatre Club from 6 to 8 November 1975. Unlike previous female collaborators, who were there simply to provide an extra body on stage, Gail Renard became a fully-fledged member of the team: Renard-Adams-Smith-Adams. She was another Jill Foster client, a writer on LWT's *Doctor in the House,* and a protégé of John Cleese who persuaded all six Pythons to see the show. The awful title was Graham Chapman's suggestion (John Lloyd, who was sharing a flat with Douglas at Greencroft Gardens NW6, had suggested *Three Men in a Beaut*).

'They were three wonderful chaps, but each totally different,' recalls Renard. 'Douglas and I were always highly competitive. Douglas, like me, was also highly ambitious; which would feature later in the dissolution of the group. All three chaps were very funny, likable, attractive, charming young men. But we were all poor as church mice, and one of my main memories was dividing up communal food when we worked together. Lunch would consist of two packets of the cheapest soup, which in those days came in small compressed powder blocks. We always had tomato, or to be accurate, tomato-coloured soup! It was vile. We also had a loaf of bread and a lump of cheese and believe me, it was divided into four incredibly equal portions. The boys took it very seriously.'[6]

Adams-Smith-Adams continued to crop up occasionally as a writing credit, as other people used some of their best sketches. John Lloyd was brought in to direct the 1975 May Week Revue, *Paradise Mislaid*, which used some existing Adams-Smith-Adams material, as did *All's Well That Ends*, the 1976 Late Night Revue directed by Chris Keightley. Adams and Keightley were both credited as late as the 1978 May Week Revue (*Stage Fright*), possibly for their 'Kamikaze' sketch. 'Hole in the Wall Club' re-emerged many years later in a *Secret Policeman's Ball*-style comedy gala organised by Rob Buckman in aid of an oncology charity, with Griff Rhys Jones and Michael Palin among the cast.

The very last use of Adams-Smith-Adams as a writing credit was on the LP *An Evening Without . . .*, released in October 1981, some six years after the trio disbanded. This was a recording of a revue which had been staged off and on, in various versions, since February 1977 by ex-Footlighters Rory McGrath, Jimmy Mulville, Martin Bergman, Clive Anderson and Griff Rhys Jones. The LP (on Original Records, which also released the *Hitchhiker's Guide* albums) included 'Hole in the Wall Club' (as 'Committee Meeting'), along with 'Kamikaze'.

'After *Haddocky*, the four of us tried to get the show on elsewhere, and we also tried to get our own telly series,' remembers Renard. 'We stayed together and pushed, to my recollection, for the best part of a year. We always had funny, inspiring comedy-jam sessions, and I loved them!'[7] One possibility which progressed further than others was a children's sketch series, discussed over a series of meetings with Louis Rudd, Head of Children's Programmes at Southern TV, but even that faltered.

While Douglas struggled with ideas for comedy series and sketches, he also worked at becoming a close associate of the Monty Python team. Ironically, although it was John Cleese who had been his first Python contact and, of course, his idol, it was Terry Jones – diametrically opposite Cleese in the group dynamic – with whom he forged the closest friendship. Like everyone, Douglas got on well with Michael Palin (though he wondered if Palin wasn't perhaps slightly too charming) and Terry Gilliam, and he worked closely, if slightly bizarrely, with Graham Chapman. But Cleese and Eric Idle were slightly more distant. Douglas first met Jones when he was an extra in a *Python* sketch in 1975. He recalled this slightly mischievously many years later while publicising his *Starship Titanic* game, for which Jones wrote a tie-in novel. 'Terry was wearing a pink frock and helping to load a nuclear device into the back of a truck. I remember thinking, "When I do my first multimedia CD-ROM, this is the man I want to write the novel of it."'[8]

Like so many of the people who became Douglas' friends and associates in the 1970s, Jones already knew him from his Footlights work: 'I first saw Douglas on stage doing some sketches in a Cambridge revue that had been up in Edinburgh.* I thought the sketch, about a meeting of the Paranoid Society, was funnier than Douglas' performance but I remembered him because of his size. He then started writing with Graham and started coming to Python rehearsals and read-throughs during the last series. Douglas and I started going off to drink real ale together and became good friends.'[9]

In 1974, after thirty-nine BBC programmes, four LPs, two books, two German TV specials, stage tours of Canada and the UK and two films, John Cleese said goodbye to *Monty Python's Flying Circus,* but the other five were persuaded to make one final, six-programme series. The group dynamic within the team had always been two writing duos and two singletons: Cleese/Chapman (both ex-Footlights), Palin/Jones (both Oxford graduates), Idle (also Footlights) and token Yank animator Gilliam. Without Cleese's direct involvement, there was an imbalance in the group, although a certain amount of existing Cleese/Chapman material (some of it left over from early drafts of *Monty Python and the Holy Grail*) was available for use. Chapman found himself writing alone and didn't enjoy it. His style of comedy was at its best when reactive, finding the elements in existing material which could be exaggerated or emphasised to make it truly remarkable. He was

* This was presumably *So You Think You Feel Haddocky . . .* which had not in fact played Edinburgh.

the one who, when John Cleese described a lengthy sketch about returning a faulty toaster, suggested making it a parrot instead.

Chapman had in fact been experimenting with other writing partners as far back as 1969, as can be seen from the writing credits on *Doctor in the House* and its sequels. The very first episode was written by Cleese and Chapman, and Chapman wrote three other episodes in that first series, all with Barry Cryer. Chapman and Bernard McKenna then wrote nine episodes of *Doctor at Large* and twelve episodes of *Doctor in Charge* in its first season. But when that series returned for a second run, McKenna wrote three episodes solo while Chapman contributed just two shows, both co-written with David Sherlock (his lover since 1966). Chapman didn't write at all for *Doctor at Sea* and contributed only one episode of *Doctor on the Go* – co-written with Douglas Adams. One can almost plot Chapman's decline as a writing force on a graph, as he moved from Cleese to Cryer to McKenna to Sherlock and finally to Douglas.

Adams and Chapman first met on 15 July 1974 at the opening night party of the West End run of *Chox*. Chapman was particularly taken with the 'Hole in the Wall Club' sketch. 'We had a few drinks and he said, "Come and have a chat sometime",' recalled Douglas. 'So I went round to see him and had a few more drinks. He was rewriting a sketch that Michael Palin and Terry Jones had written. I think Graham was feeling slightly at a loss, because he always had written with John Cleese in the past. So he had to write a lot by himself, and he didn't take too naturally to that. And he said, "Look, will you help me rewrite the sketch, see if you've got any ideas?" So that was that. I can't remember what it was, actually. I don't think it was the world's greatest sketch.'[10]

The sketch in question was in the last ever *Monty Python* TV episode, broadcast on 5 December 1974. Chapman plays a doctor and Terry Jones is Mr Williams, a man bleeding profusely from a stab wound; while Williams gets weaker and weaker, the doctor tries to make him fill in a form. It's impossible to say what minor piece of rewording Douglas was responsible for – he is credited with 'Silly Word' at the end of the show – but there is one cracking line in it which stands head and shoulders above the rest of the dialogue and could well be Douglas', if only because it's a literary gag. Struggling to write while holding his gaping stomach wound, Williams asks, 'Do I have to answer all the questions, doctor?' 'No, no, no,' says the doctor, 'just fill in as many as you can – no need to go into too much detail. I don't know why we bother with it at all, really, it's such a nuisance. Well, let's see how you've done then . . . Oh dear oh dear . . . that's not very good is it? Look, surely you knew number four! It's from *The Merchant of Venice* – even I know that!'

Douglas' ambition when he left Brentwood School had been to be John Cleese, who at the time was writing comedy sketches for *Monty Python* with Graham Chapman. Less than five years later, Douglas was writing a comedy sketch for *Monty Python* with Graham Chapman. It should have been a dream come true, yet Douglas always played it down. He even seemed embarrassed by questions about his *Python* connection, claiming it was: 'So inconsequential to be hardly worth mentioning. I would certainly not lay claim to being a contributory writer for *Python* because *Python* was those six guys, and my role was quite incidental and coincidental.'[11]

In fact, Douglas not only wrote for *Monty Python*, he appeared on screen too, twice. He was a doctor in the frenetic opening sequence of programme 42 and one of the 'pepperpot' ladies in an establishing shot in programme 43: 'When they went off to do the filming for that fourth series, Graham said, "Look, if you want to come on down and see how it's filmed, then do." So I got in my mother's battered old camper-van, and drove down to Exeter where they were doing it, and I went along for the days they were filming. It was very, very extraordinary to be out with the Pythons filming. You can probably count the number of frames I actually appeared in on the fingers of two hands, but nevertheless a big thrill.'[12]

It was obviously not unheard of for non-Pythons to appear in the background of the show. However, Douglas was one of only two people outside the team to receive a writing credit on the TV series (Neil Innes wrote songs for two shows). All the more amazing, given that when the series started he was a gangly teenage schoolboy, watching the programme on his grandmother's TV.

Douglas also co-wrote a sketch on one of the Python LPs: 'When they were doing the album to *Holy Grail*, and for some Pythonic reason decided they didn't want to do material from the film on the album, there was a sketch I'd written some time before, along with several other people, about a film director wanting to make a new movie with Marilyn Monroe. I rewrote the sketch with Graham, then Terry and Michael rewrote it yet again. By the time it got on the album, I think one of my actual lines still appeared in it.'*[13]

* This was actually an old Adams-Smith-Adams sketch. 'Douglas was the only one mentioned on the album because of some admin error at the Pythons' production office,' explains Martin Smith, who is still somewhat annoyed at the lack of credit: 'Well, a bit . . . even though we did make a (very) few bob from it.'

CHAPTER 8

DOUGLAS AND GRAHAM Chapman worked together for nearly eighteen months on several paid projects, a few of which even got made. 'Douglas started writing very closely with Graham, and that had good things to it and bad things to it,' says Jill Foster. 'People don't like to say it but Graham wasted everybody's time. He was a smashing bloke but there were various people he worked with and he used them and wasted a lot of their time. Douglas was one of them. It didn't do anybody any harm; Douglas loved it and for Graham it was nice because it meant that he could spend more time on the phone or doing whatever else it was he wanted to do.'[1]

Their first post-*Python* collaboration was a sketch show, *Out of the Trees*, one of several projects started by the individual Pythons as the group fragmented. John Cleese, of course, had created *Fawlty Towers* and Douglas was in the audience when the first episode was recorded on 23 December 1974. 'I remember Douglas being bitterly, bitterly disappointed by it,' says Geoffrey Perkins. 'He expected the show to take off from *Python* but instead it seemed to be, as far as he could see, a sitcom on wobbly sets. But he remained a huge fan of John Cleese.'[2]

Meanwhile, Eric Idle was making *Rutland Weekend Television* (Douglas and Martin Smith were offered roles in that show but could not get Equity cards), Terry Gilliam was writing *Jabberwocky*, and Jones and Palin were collaborating on *Ripping Yarns*, the pilot episode of which was broadcast on 7 January 1976. *Out of the Trees* followed three nights later and was the most Pythonesque of all the projects, largely because it consisted of material written for a possible fifth series of *Monty Python*.

'They were still talking about whether they were going to do another series or not,' said Douglas, 'and all the other Pythons were worrying and arguing with each other, and Graham didn't have anything else to do, so he said, "Why don't we start on the next series?" So I said, "Okay, yes, all right!" We started writing a lot of material, whereupon it was eventually decided by all the others they didn't want to do another *Python* series.'[3]

Fawlty Towers went on to become a bona fide classic, *Ripping Yarns* received huge critical acclaim, *Rutland Weekend Television* was a cult hit, *Jabberwocky* launched Gilliam on a stellar directorial career. *Out of the Trees* was never heard from again. In fact, the show doesn't even exist any more in the BBC archives: the video footage was wiped for reuse and only the film was kept, though private off-air copies do exist.

'Graham was quite pleased with the couple of hours' work, whatever it was we'd done, and he wanted to create his own sketch show,' said Douglas, slightly contradicting his memories above. 'John and Graham had pioneered the *Doctor* series on television, and Graham had written one or two others with Bernard McKenna. I was very much the fresh-faced new boy, inexperienced, unknown quantity. On the other hand, I was extremely available. So we worked on that for a while. I think only one ever got made, but we did two or maybe three scripts and it was mostly me and Graham. I wasn't performing at all. It had some good bits but it wasn't really that good.'[4]

Chapman, McKenna and Douglas shared the writing credit on *Out of the Trees*, the cast of which included two future members of the *Hitchhiker*'s cast: Mark Wing-Davey (who had left Cambridge just before Douglas arrived) and Simon Jones. The producer was Bernard Thompson, who later produced a TV version of the 1977 Footlights Revue, *Tag!*. Neil Innes provided the signature tune. Fortunately the script for *Out of the Trees* (working title: *The End of the Road Show*) survives. Unfortunately it's not very good. Chapman has clearly been given his head, Douglas was inexperienced and still slavishly imitating *Python*, and whatever influence the normally stolid McKenna could have was limited. As this is such a rare piece of Adams' work which few if any readers will have seen, it is worth describing. The script begins thus:

> STOCK FILM OF GALAXIES ETC. FOLLOWED BY PLANETS FOLLOWED BY THE EARTH.
> **VOICE-OVER** Than the Universe, a multitude of mighty galaxies, within each galaxy a myriad of mighty star systems, within each star system a multiplicity of mighty planets and in one of these mighty planets the mighty British Rail electric train.
> CAPTION PICTURE: BRITISH RAIL LOCOMOTIVE. ZOOM IN.
> CAPTION: A BRITISH RAIL FILM

... And so on (there is discussion later about how you can't start TV shows with the word 'than'). In a train compartment are two ladies who constantly try to top each other's claims, in a similar way to (but not as funny as) the 'Four Yorkshiremen' sketch. Two characters named Kemp and Michael Edwards discuss television, although they only mention their names once, more than halfway through the programme. The same is true of a bicycle-obsessed scoutmaster, E.W. Clifford-Aldiss in the next compartment. This seems to be Douglas using the same secretary-baiting trick that he would later use on *Hitchhiker's*, when he had the character of Slartibartfast introduced quite some time before the name was actually mentioned in dialogue, just to irritate the lady who typed up the script.

A young man tries to buy a cup of coffee and a sandwich from a British Rail waiter in a scene which is amusing but, like everything in *Out of the Trees*, derivative and sub-*Python*. The train sequence rambles for a while before mixing into a sketch in which Genghis Khan and his soldiers (well, soldier – *Out of the Trees* clearly had the same sort of minuscule budget as *Rutland Weekend Television*) storm into a peasant's tent. The men are slaughtered and the women expect to be raped, but Khan simply wants the peasant's wife to ask him what sort of day he's had. This leads into Khan and his son debating over when they can attack Persia as Khan can't find a suitable gap in his schedule of talks and dinner parties (this was based loosely on John Cleese).

A scene with the railway compartment characters in a waiting room leads into a boardroom sketch, where the Chairman turns out to be Khan again. There's a weak sketch about a cabinet meeting at which all the ministers are firemen, then back to the waiting room again, before the young man and his girlfriend link into the final sketch. She picks a peony from a bush overhanging a garden fence, whereupon two policemen run up and start threatening the young couple. The situation escalates, with more police called in, then the army, until (as Douglas explained), 'Eventually, because this is the part where I was taking over in the sketch, the world blows up.'[5] Two aliens see the global destruction and say, 'Mission has failed. Impossible to effect peony severance prevention.' (Bizarrely, the 'alien spacecraft' is actually the lunar shuttle from the 1969 ITV series *UFO*.) A final sequence is set back in the train compartment.

Out of the Trees has a handful of passable jokes but for the most part it's awful. One can detect Douglas' voice in the young man played by Simon Jones, who could quite easily be Arthur Dent (and in a sense is Arthur, since both roles were written specifically for the actor). 'Look, will you please listen? It's very, very, very simple,' says the young man to the waiter. That's a Douglas Adams line. 'I have been listening, mate. You go and get your own coffee and sandwiches. I've got a job to do, you load of tits,' responds Wing-Davey's waiter. That's a Chapman line, no doubt about it.

The show was recorded in October 1975 and Douglas makes a brief cameo as a thug beating up an old lady in the background of the peony sketch. Chapman, McKenna and Douglas had a couple of meetings about a possible series of *Out of the Trees* in March, but nothing ever happened. 'It was good in parts – it was excellent in parts – it was also dreadful in parts,' was Douglas' opinion. 'No more got made simply because then the Pythons started up all over again with films and this sort of thing and Graham got involved with that.'[6]

In 1986, Douglas adapted the Genghis Khan sketch into a short story, 'The Private Life of Genghis Khan', for *The Utterly Utterly*

Merry Comic Relief Christmas Book. Credited as 'by Douglas Adams (based on an original sketch by Douglas Adams and Graham Chapman)', the dialogue in the story is almost identical to the original script, but Douglas' descriptions of the Mighty Khan's empire and army add considerably to the comic potential, contrasting strongly with the TV version where the 'army' is half a dozen extras in a field.

Next up was *The Ringo Starr Show* (aka *Our Show for Ringo Starr*), a US TV special inspired by the album *Goodnight Vienna*, the sleeve of which shows a scene from *The Day the Earth Stood Still* with Ringo in place of Michael Rennie as the alien emissary Klaatu, alongside the eight-foot robot Gort. Starr had known Chapman since 1969 when they both worked on *The Magic Christian* and had appeared fleetingly as himself in a *Monty Python's Flying Circus* chat-show spoof. When he asked Chapman to write him a script, he got Douglas too.

In terms of his developing idea of science fiction comedy, Douglas saw this as a natural progression from his 'Beyond the Infinite' monologue: 'I'd done a show opening at Cambridge that had science fiction-y elements in the comedy, and doing this just fitted very, very neatly with my particular bent. It didn't get made, but it kind of stuck with me.'[7] And indeed, in the opening narration we find: 'A long time ago in a far, far land. I mean a really long way, I mean you may think it's a long way down the road to the hardware store but that's just peanuts to this sort of distance . . .'

Ringo would have played himself, working as the assistant to an impossibly rich man called Gerald McToothbucket, who rides piggy-back on a black chauffeur. Ringo berates the narrator (which reads as if it was written for John Cleese) for calling him boring and discovers that his life is about to become more interesting. A Gort-style robot crashes through a wall, mistakes Ringo for someone called Rinog Trars and tells him, 'I have been sent by our masters in the galaxy of Smegmon to pass on to you the ancestral powers of your race, the Jenkinsons.' Ringo is given the power to travel through time and space. 'Time is an illusion, it's merely a moving point of focus,' the robot tells him in a line which would later be modified for *Hitchhiker's Guide*. In fact, a whole slew of proto-*Hitchhiker's* ideas are evident here. They meet a large green alien who looks like a prawn and calls people honey, who would become the pink-winged insect receptionist at Megadodo Publications. There's a reference to telephone sanitisers too.

An intergalactic customs man seems to be written for Chapman himself, and a note in the margin shows that a second-hand car salesman was intended as a role for Keith Moon, a friend of Chapman (and hence of Douglas). The salesman tries to convince Ringo that a battered old car is a spaceship in a scene which effectively retreads dead parrot territory. It turns out that the whole garage is actually on a huge spaceship, full of futuristic sarcophagi – and suddenly it's the 'B'-Ark sequence from *Hitchhiker's Guide*.

In fact, Douglas' first use of this idea – a planet divesting itself of the useless third of its population by packing them off in a giant 'ark in space' – had been in a spec *Doctor Who* story which had been rejected by the BBC the previous year. In *Our Show for Ringo Starr*, the 'B'-Ark originates from Earth, not Golgafrincham, but otherwise the scene on the bridge is almost identical, with a sadistic officer wanting to torture the visitors but only being allowed to interrogate them over what they want to drink. The one significant difference is that the Captain is not in the bath but is 'dressed as a very large and very realistic turkey'. Eventually, Rinog Trars (also Ringo) appears and claims his powers. The universe is destroyed at the end.

The one-hour show incorporates musical sequences in which Ringo and his band perform songs from *Goodnight Vienna*, though these are rather arbitrarily inserted into the storyline. The script was for some reason credited to 'Nemona Lethbridge and Vera Hunt (aka Graham Chapman and Douglas Adams)'.

In the late 1980s, Chapman commented: 'The script was never approved by any networks or by cable TV because I think that they thought it a bit rude and because, quite frankly, I don't think they understood it very much. It would have made a very nice show.'[8] Douglas believed that the show, 'was eventually not made, partly through Ringo's various difficulties – he lost interest in it – partly because the deal fell through from one angle or another. It could then have gone on further if he'd wanted to deal with the hassles. He didn't.'[9] In fact the two biggest problems with the script are that it would have been hugely expensive and that there was no apparent market for such sci-fi shenanigans in 1975. Had it been proposed two years later, at the height of *Stars Wars* fever, it would almost certainly have been made.

There is a postscript to all this. In 1999, the script of *Our Show for Ringo Starr* was published in a scrappily edited collection of unseen Chapman scripts entitled *OJRIL: The Completely Incomplete Graham Chapman*. This was compiled by Jim Yoakum, an aspiring American scriptwriter who was Chapman's final writing partner before his death in 1989 and who was consequently appointed literary executor of the Chapman estate. The following year, the script of *Out of the Trees* was posted on a comedy website without permission and, when the webmasters removed it at Yoakum's request, bitter arguments flared up on the site's forum. When the affair was brought to Douglas' attention, he deemed it, 'an awful lot of fuss about a very old and not very good script,' adding: 'I'm no great admirer of Mr Yoakum's.'[10]

Yoakum took exception to Douglas' casual attitude and posted a bitter diatribe on the douglasadams.com forum, complaining about his complacency to what he called 'internet piracy' and accusing Douglas of 'dissing' him. Yoakum alleged that Douglas has asked for an advance on the publication of the Ringo Starr script in *OJRIL* despite deeming it 'juvenile': and 'awful' and asked directly why, if Douglas felt the script to be beneath him, he did not feel that asking for an advance was also beneath him.*

Douglas did not bother to reply (nor did Ed Victor). The unfortunate upshot of all this for fans of both Douglas and Chapman is that, if there are any further collaborations still in Yoakum's files, they are unlikely to be officially published, which is a shame.

---

* The original hardback edition of this book quoted this post verbatim. In accordance with Mr Yoakum's wishes, it has been paraphrased for this edition; the original is available for anyone to see at **www.douglasadams.com/cgi-bin/mboard/info/dnathread.cgi?2107,5**. (The same Mr Yoakum was behind the removal of the short story 'The Private Life of Genghis Khan' from later editions of *The Salmon of Doubt*, though this is again no great inconvenience as the story is available to read at **www.douglasadams.com/dna/980707-07-s.html**.)

INTERLUDE - **BEATLES**

DOUGLAS' TWO GREAT influences were the Pythons and the Beatles. He befriended the former, could he do the same with the latter? We have already seen how he met one Beatle through Graham Chapman in 1975. A decade later, he met another.

'A couple of years ago, I did a job for Paul McCartney,' said Douglas in 1987. 'I was trying very hard not to be utterly awestruck in meeting this guy who helped form the way I thought in the '60s when I was growing up. It didn't really work out, but he said an interesting thing. He did that song with Stevie Wonder called "Ebony and Ivory", and he was saying that for a long time he'd wanted to do something with him but felt very nervous about asking him: "I can't just ring up Stevie Wonder." And his wife, Linda, said, "It's all right, you can actually ring up Stevie Wonder, you are actually Paul McCartney."'[1]

It was Linda McCartney who, having met Douglas, encouraged him to telephone Paul. The mysterious job referred to was in fact a suggestion that Douglas, Terry Jones and John Lloyd could together write the script for McCartney's short animated film *Rupert and the Frog Chorus*.

Two of Douglas' friends, Robbie McIntosh and Paul 'Wix' Wickens, both played in McCartney's band and Douglas can be spotted in the audience in the video of McCartney performing at the Cavern Club in 1999 (Douglas took a couple of photos of the event and posted them on his website). However, to Douglas' disappointment, McCartney never became part of his social circle the way that other musical heroes like David Gilmour and Gary Brooker – and, indeed, George Martin – did. He never attended one of Douglas' parties, though Douglas went to one of McCartney's.

Curiously, despite being equally enamoured of Python and the Beatles, Douglas did not enjoy Eric Idle's spoof *The Rutles*. 'He thought it was a bit mean-spirited, a little bit unkind,' recalls Beatles expert Mark Lewisohn. 'I think that maybe tapped into his unease with Eric Idle's comedy. He liked Neil Innes' music though.'[2]

Douglas' favourite Beatles song was 'Hey Jude', though he considered that 'too obvious' for *Desert Island Discs* and picked 'Drive My Car' instead, and he made a point of listening to at least one Beatles album at least once a week. Against all expectations though, his favourite record *wasn't* by the Beatles: 'For my money the greatest album ever made by anybody under any circumstances is *Plastic Ono Band*.'[3]

CHAPTER 9

CHAPMAN AND ADAMS did one other job for Ringo Starr. In 1973, the ex-Beatle had teamed up with Harry Nilsson to make a spoof horror film called *Son of Dracula*. Nilsson took the title role, a half-vampire character called Count Downe, with Starr as Merlin the Magician, Freddie Jones as Dr Frankenstein and Dennis Price as Van Helsing. The whole sorry mess was directed as work for hire by Freddie Francis who left the project as soon as shooting wrapped – leaving Ringo to supervise the editing – and now politely declines to talk about the film. The script was by actress Jennifer Jayne under the pseudonym 'Jay Fairbank'. Produced by Apple Films, the movie flopped dismally when released in 1974 so Starr had the bizarre idea of completely redubbing the entire film with a new script.

'We had the premiere in Atlanta, the first movie since *Gone with the Wind* to open there, and we had 12,000 kids screaming,' Starr told *Q* magazine, 'but we left town the next day, and so did everyone else. In America, the movie only played in towns that had one cinema, because if it had two, no matter what was on down the road, they'd all go there! It's a bit of a shambles now – we went into a studio with Graham Chapman and revoiced a lot of it, so it makes even less sense now.'[1]

'It had been released very briefly and I think not unsuccessfully,' misremembered Douglas, 'but then they had pulled it back in again because they weren't happy with it. It sat on the shelves at Apple for a year or two, gathering dust, and they thought, "We'd better do something with it – we need to make it funny!" So they set up in Graham's house one of those big Steenbeck things, gave us the film, and said, "Okay, go through the film and write new dialogue for it." We said, "It's not necessary because the movie is not bad, it's actually quite good, and this is the way to really destroy the movie – this is an exercise that can't possibly work." They said, "Well, never mind, here's some money, do it." So we did it, and it didn't work very well, so they said, "Thank you very much," and put it back on the shelves. That's what you get for working with rock stars!'[2]

A copy of the Chapman-Adams script, entitled *Dracula's Little Boy*, apparently still exists in the Apple archives, along with the rerecorded soundtrack (Bernard McKenna recalls providing a voice – Douglas may have done so too). Horror critic Kim Newman calls *Son of Dracula*, 'one of the rarest of all '70s British horror films, never apparently receiving a release of any kind on its home territory and barely seen in America. Once you've seen it, you'll know why.'[3] 'It is not the best film ever made,' admitted Ringo, 'but I've seen worse.'[4]

Curiously for such a huge Beatles fan, Douglas seems to have been unimpressed by Starr. Perhaps to him the Beatles were Lennon and McCartney. Pretty much the only comment Douglas ever made about Ringo was in relation to a conversation which they had about the 'meanings' people found in Beatles songs, something with which Douglas could identify when coincidental 'significances' of 42 were brought to light: 'With this sort of thing going on, you begin to understand all the extraordinary things people used to read into Beatles lyrics. The time I worked for Ringo Starr he said it was ridiculous, they just used to write anything that came into their heads. He said, "the only time we ever put anything consciously naughty into any lyric, nobody noticed it."'[5]

Douglas also contributed to Chapman's surreal memoir, *A Liar's Autobiography* (Eyre Methuen, 1980), the title page of which reads:

A LIAR'S AUTOBIOGRAPHY
VOLUME VII
by GRAHAM CHAPMAN

and David Sherlock
and also Alex Martin
Oh, and David Yallop
and also too by Douglas Adams
(whose autobiography it isn't)

A page of biographies suggests that David A. Yallop murdered one of the other co-authors, then has this to say on Douglas: 'DOUGLAS N. ADAMS. An author not previously mentioned by name, had not in fact been murdered and was merely playing possum under a pile of previously unpublishable manuscripts (see *Hitchhiker's Guide to the Galaxy*). He will probably be shoving a few words in here and there over the next few dozen pages, but only admits this fairly hesitantly because though David A. Yallop is not 6'5", he is extremely fierce.'

In fact, Yallop and Adams are ditched as co-authors in a footnote at the end of the second chapter. It is nearly impossible to spot Douglas' voice in the book, given (a) its autobiographical nature and (b) its rambling, deliberately self-contradictory style. There is a description of a giant spaceship, shaped like a 9.2 km-long filter-tip cigarette, which could conceivably be a Douglas image, but the only thing we know for certain that he wrote was Footnote 2 on page 21. In the main text, Chapman maintains that he was born in Leamington Spa (actually it was Leicester). The footnote says: 'I was in fact born in Stalbridge in Dorset but if you want to send any letters there please note that the correct postal address is Stalbridge, STURMINSTER NEWTON, Dorset.' We can tell that this is by Douglas because the tiny village of Stalbridge was where his mother and stepfather lived. For this, as with *Out of the Trees* (and possibly the Ringo Starr jobs), Douglas was paid directly by Chapman rather than employed as co-author.

'We virtually came to blows about Graham's autobiography,' said Douglas, giving a clue as to the reason for the partnership's demise. 'He actually went through about five co-writers, of which I was the first, and really I didn't think it was going anywhere because I didn't think it was the sort of thing you could do as a pair. I think there's one very bad section which was the bit that he and I co-wrote.'[6]

The working relationship between Douglas and Chapman ended in late 1975; Douglas' anguished final letter (frustratingly undated) was reproduced in the 2003 book *The Pythons Autobiography*. Their last hurrah was the *Doctor on the Go* episode 'For Your Own Good', broadcast on 20 February 1977, in which the father of one of the doctors visits St Swithin's and causes disruption. This took an impossibly long time to come together; script editor Bernard McKenna had a dozen meetings with Douglas and Graham (sometimes together, sometimes singly) between 4 June and 6 November 1975. 'Graham wasn't always available and so I would have meetings with Douglas early in the morning, 9.00 a.m.,' recalls McKenna. 'You could never get Graham before 11.00!'[7] The script was written in August 1975, and possibly the only interesting thing about the completed episode is that it partially inspired the character of the barman in *Hitchhiker's Guide*, who asks Ford whether the end of the world requires people to 'lie down or put a paper bag over our head or something'.

'When I worked for LWT on *Doctor on the Go*, we used to do rehearsals in the barracks in King's Road,' recalled Douglas. 'I remember that there were posters all over the walls telling the soldiers what to do in case of a nuclear attack: (1) Lie down, (2) Close your eyes, put your hands over your ears – and that was it! It also said at the bottom of the notice "Under no circumstances must these details be divulged to any member of the public." The brown paper bag came about because I vaguely remembered that one way of stopping radiation contamination was to use brown paper . . .'[8]

By the time that 'For Your Own Good' was broadcast, Adams and Chapman had gone their separate ways: 'I got to know Graham, and ended up writing with him. I thought, good God, this is fantastic, this is wonderful. But Graham, at that stage, which is fairly well documented so it's not being disloyal, was going through a fairly major drink problem, and at the end of the year an awful lot of good ideas got wasted, and not much had actually been achieved.'[9]

Chapman was getting through a couple of bottles of gin every day, but his twenty-three-year-old protégé was too young, naive and enthralled to question this. Eventually, Douglas found that he could no longer work with Chapman, just as Bernard McKenna,

Barry Cryer and others apparently had before him: 'When we went our separate ways we had a row, I can't quite remember even what it was about, but we were definitely on bad terms for a few weeks or months or something. Though we repaired relations after that, we were never that close again.'[10]

John Lloyd and Douglas were renting Bernard McKenna's flat around this time. ('The other residents in the house didn't like them because they never drew the curtains and played loud music and didn't fit in,'[11] recalls McKenna.) Lloyd has his own view of the Adams-Chapman working relationship: '"Working relationship" is putting it a bit strongly. The "drinking-and-doing-crosswords relationship" was excellent though. Douglas and Graham were not destined to do great things together, being both equally prodigiously disorganised. One of the things Graham liked to do to put off the business of doing any work was go to his local in Highgate at lunchtimes with all the newspapers, and with Douglas. Sometimes people like Bernard McKenna or me would show up and everybody drank a lot of beer and we would do every single crossword together over a ninety-minute lunch. Occasionally, Graham felt moved to take his willy out and put it on the bar.'[12]

What had seemed like the most fantastic break had come to nothing, and hadn't even made Douglas any money: 'I suddenly went through a total crisis of confidence and couldn't write because I was so panicked and didn't have any money and had a huge over-draft paying the £17-a-week rent. So I answered an advertisement in the *Evening Standard* and got a job as a bodyguard to an Arab royal family.'[13]

The job basically involved sitting in a hotel corridor while various young ladies came and went into hotel rooms. It was only when one of them glanced at Douglas, sat quietly with his book, and commented, 'At least you can read on the job', that he realised what was happening. This was also the inspiration for the talking lift in *Hitchhiker's* as Douglas watched empty lifts arrive and depart in the small hours of the morning. When Douglas packed the job in after a few weeks, Griff Rhys Jones took over.

Rhys Jones was Vice-President of Footlights that year and had been at an important committee meeting on 13 January 1976, the minutes of which still exist. President Chris Keightley, Harry Porter, Jimmy Mulville, Nonny Williams and seven others made up the rest of the committee. The task before them was to find a director for the 1976 May Week Revue. External directors, often Footlights alumni themselves, were the order of the day. John Lloyd had directed the 1975 revue (*Monty Python* director Ian McNaughton had also been considered). This year, the minutes noted, Adrian Edwards, Sue Limb and John Parry had all said no. Who could they approach instead?

Four names were listed: Stephen Wyatt, who had directed *Every Packet ... three years earlier; Jon Canter, Footlights President in 1973–74; Martin Smith, former Footlights Secretary; or the seemingly ubiquitous Rhys Jones. Against Griff's name was the parenthetical warning '(exams loom)' and a note that he was in favour of a 'total outsider', with five possibles listed: Rob Buckman, John Stevenson, Chris Langham ('Griff pro' noted the minutes), Crispin Thomas or Graham Chapman. Almost as an afterthought, the note-taker had added: 'Douglas Adams: not interested.' Right at the bottom of the page, in pink ink, was the decisive 'Crispin Thomas the first choice'. Thomas had directed *Cinderella* and the Edinburgh revamp of *Chox* but he didn't direct the 1976 May Week Revue. Douglas Adams did.

The Footlights Committee was meeting only three days after *Out of the Trees* had been broadcast, which probably explains not only Douglas' and Graham's inclusion as possibles, but also why Douglas was too busy. By the time they asked him again, he was recovering from his exhausting year of drunken crossword-solving with Chapman and looking for a fresh challenge.

And so Douglas returned to Cambridge and to Footlights.

'I was riding a bike along the road and I saw this enormous figure loping along the pavement,' remembers Sue Limb. 'I thought, "Surely that must be Douglas. Nobody else is that tall." I skidded to a halt and we had a very genial conversation in which he told me that he'd been asked to direct and I was so thrilled because I thought, "That's more like it." I thought he had a great deal to offer. I certainly got the impression that he was going great guns. I remember being hugely impressed and thinking: How ironic that a few years ago people were saying: "Oh, he's not really Footlights material, not good enough."'[14]

CHAPTER 10

NINETEEN SEVENTY-SIX WAS the year that punk broke, and the poster and title for that year's Cambridge Footlights Revue reflected that. Under the crudely sprayed title *A Kick in the Stalls*, four young men glared menacingly. Tattooed on their threateningly outstretched fists was the angry phrase, 'O H, H O W W E L A R F E D'. The poster is in Robert Hewison's history of Footlights, the air of menace somewhat deflated by the photo below it showing the same quartet in baggy shirts and trousers doing a comedy Cossack dance.

A Kick in the Stalls, like *Paradise Mislaid*, had a loose theme connecting the sketches; in this case, the Russian annexation of a small Eastern European country, Bogoffia. Andrew Greenhalgh, Penelope Johnson, Michael Landymore, Jimmy Mulville, Michael Murray, Charles Shaughnessy, Jeremy Thomas and Nonny Williams made up the cast. Principal writing credits were shared between Mulville, Landymore, Shaughnessy, Chris Keightley, Rory McGrath and the director, with additional material by Williams, Murray, Greenhalgh, Jon Canter, Martin Smith, Will Adams, John Parry, Paul Hudson and Geoff Nicholson. Douglas also gave himself a credit for 'additional music'. As rehearsals progressed, and the publicity machine swung into action, two things became clear: Douglas was keen that the show should be writer-performer led, with all but two of the cast also writing material; and somebody had discovered that Douglas had a peripheral connection with *Monty Python's Flying Circus*.

'If president Chris Keightley and director Douglas Adams promise something different this year,' said the *Cambridge Evening News* on 4 June, 'it is because they and a small team of writers virtually formed a workshop to devise their show. Director Adams is himself a former Footlighter, now entrenched in the challenging ritual of writing *Monty Python* and other television scripts to eke out a living.'

A few months earlier, on 27 February, the paper had run a short interview with Keightley and Adams as they prepared to put the revue together, referring to the newly appointed director as: 'Doug Adams, who came down from Cambridge two years ago to write *Monty Python* scripts':

Doug wondered if in the recent past the club had become too 'show-bizzy' and lost its edge. 'Basically, the Footlights is a writer-performer club.' Doug is in fact the living proof that there could have been little wrong with the club when he left two years ago to become a professional scriptwriter. 'I've been extremely lucky,' he said. 'It's something I've always wanted to do ever since I first saw John Cleese on *The Frost Report* on television years ago.' He has been writing with Graham Chapman most of the time, collaborating on *Monty Python* scripts. 'It's been a fantastic entrée, working in television and film, things one normally wouldn't expect to do so quickly.' At the moment his income if not his ambition is likely to suffer because few BBC television and radio programmes accept contributed sketches.

This was Douglas' first ever interview and already a pattern was developing which would continue unchecked for another twenty-five years and many times that number of interviews. Journalists always latched onto his *Python* connection, especially in the early days when there was little else to write about him: 'It would get to the point where I would say to journalists, "Look, I just want to say before I say anything that I have nothing to do with *Python*." In fact, what made it bad was that I had written about half a dozen lines that appeared here and there in *Python*. They'd say, "What, you mean *MONTY Python*?" "Yes, I didn't write for them."

And they'd say, "What was that like?" I'd then read the account of the interview: "Douglas Adams, one of the major writers on *Monty Python* . . ." And I kept on saying to the Pythons, "I'm sorry, I did not say this."[1]

Nevertheless, the press release for *A Kick in the Stalls* described Douglas as: 'TV scriptwriter and part-time under-assistant spelling mistake corrector to the Monty Python team.' The *Python* connection was brought up again in the brief biography of Douglas printed in the *Kick* . . . programme. It's a tellingly satirical portrait of Douglas as he was in that short period between graduation and *Hitchhiker's Guide*:

> Douglas is larger than the average family and wears two pairs of trousers on each leg. This year's director, he was unable to do the show last year, because he became suddenly tall at the last minute and had to go into hospital to have his clothes burnt off. He is very sensitive about his enormous nose, which the cast refrain from mentioning, even when they are rehearsing it. He has an unending supply of witty stories, which keep everyone amused until long after they've fallen asleep. This doesn't matter however, as he comes round first thing in the morning to tell you what you missed. Recently he worked with members of the Monty Python team, but on the completion of the M62, he has returned to a less demanding job. Always a generous person, he rarely carries money in case he gives it away. Favourite sport: flicking elephants onto their backs and watching them struggle. Possible last words: 'Well, basically I think that the basic basis of this is basically rubbish, actually.'

During the writing and rehearsal period, Douglas stayed with Harry Porter, who had suggested him as director. 'When he stayed here he worked extremely hard, he spent ages on that script,' recalls Dr Porter. 'They all worked very hard on that script, much harder than Footlights usually did. So they got at the end of it a very well-worked-out script. The only trouble was it wasn't very good.'[2]

A Kick in the Stalls had the traditional two-week run at the

Arts from 7 June. The following day, under the headline 'No fun from the Footlights', the *Cambridge Evening News* lambasted the show, calling it 'crushingly unfunny and woefully overlong, lasting two hours forty-five minutes' with 'an almost total lack of originality'. But there was one saving grace: 'One sketch alone shows promise of a good idea, that of a failed Japanese kamikaze pilot who, so far, has flown nineteen missions without success.' Four days later the *Financial Times* said: 'The latest Cambridge Footlights revue suggests that this university format is past its heyday. Too much satire of the media, not enough original inspiration.'

The revue's unwieldy length was heavily cut and, in an attempt to patch things up, *Evening News* critic Deryck Harvey interviewed Andy Greenhalgh and Jeremy Thomas in the 18 June edition. 'We had a couple of radio producers backstage who feel it is crammed with original ideas,' said Thomas, adding that a couple of sketches had actually been filmed for French TV.

Geoffrey Perkins was in that first-night audience: 'It was pure Douglas! It was a very, very Douglas show, full of very good, clever wordplay and some grand ideas that were in many ways utterly impractical. There was this sketch about Simon Stilites on top of a pillar. I can remember an interminable blackout when this great big pillar was manoeuvred on stage and somebody was manoeuvred on top of it, then of course an interminable blackout afterwards to get the thing off. That was pure Douglas, the impracticalities of staging it.'[3]

From the Arts, *Kick* transferred to the Oxford Playhouse for a week, where the *Oxford Mail* said: 'Douglas Adams' direction is rather slack by Footlights standards ... the cast have to work through a fair amount of rubbish in the two-hour show.' The *Abingdon Herald* was more cautious: 'A pleasant evening's entertainment but a noticeable dearth of really funny curtain lines and a tendency to go on milking a comic theme long after it has gone dry.' Douglas and Chris Keightley's 'Kamikaze' sketch was again singled out for special mention.

The revue was at the Nuffield Theatre, Southampton from 29 June where the *Southern Evening Echo*'s reviewer didn't even like

'Kamikaze'. Under the headline 'Footlights joke has fallen flat' he suggested: 'Perhaps Footlights should do the decent thing, like one of their unfunny sketches in the present revue, and commit hari-kari ... Some sketches in the present revue are better than others, but they are all bad.' Playing at the Robin Hood Theatre, Averham for a week, the theatre critic of the *Newark Advertiser* gave it the best revue yet, listing 'Kamikaze' among his favourite sketches: 'There is a lot of talent and originality in this year's revue. The humour is zany; the wit intelligent and often biting.'

Finally, at the end of August, the troupe headed to Edinburgh for a three-week run. Deryck Harvey followed them up there and happily reported to *Evening News* readers that the show was now, 'considerably shorter – half its original length – and brisker', adding that 'Kamikaze' was, 'original and hilarious'. *The Stage* rather grudgingly observed that, 'the predominantly mediocre quality of the material is only rescued by the sheer zest and undoubted talents of the cast', while admitting that 'Kamikaze', 'struck chords of delight'. Other positive Edinburgh reviews came from *The Scotsman* ('reaches the standards of the nostalgic good old days . . . only rarely do they overextend the life of a joke') and the *Edinburgh Evening News*: 'speeds smoothly on its way' – something which it certainly hadn't done at the Arts.

Vindication for Douglas at last? Not quite. The version which played in Edinburgh was, according to the programme, 'redirected by Griff Rhys Jones from Douglas Adams' original production'. This wasn't as soul-destroying as it might seem because such redirection, in the sojourn between the English mini-tour and the Edinburgh residency, was quite common. *Chox*, for example, had been directed by Robert Benton for its initial outing but redirected by Crispin Thomas for the fringe.

'I saw *Kick in the Stalls* in Cambridge and I have the impression it was rather overcomplicated,' says John Lloyd. 'I do remember thinking it was not a good idea to ask Douglas to direct it. Douglas didn't have a single director or producer gene in his whole gigantic genome. I didn't see *Kick in the Stalls* after Griff had tweaked it, but I'm not surprised it was better. He was a superb student director: far and away the best of his generation. On the other hand, comedy writing is one of the very, very few things Griff isn't much cop at.'[4]

On 6 September, the delighted cast of *A Kick in the Stalls* sent a postcard to Harry Porter back in Cambridge: 'The show has had a miraculous renaissance thanks to Mr Rhys Jones. We had a string of excellent reviews from the local papers ... Douglas and John Lloyd have got a show on which is really very funny (tho' one can recognise the Footlights training).' That was *The Unpleasantness at Brodie's Close,* an independent revue by Douglas, John Lloyd, David Renwick and Andrew Marshall.

'*Brodie's Close* was a tremendous experience,' recalls Lloyd. 'Renwick and Marshall are comedy writers of the first water, absolute perfectionists, superb craftsmen. Of the two, Andrew would have been drawn more to Douglas in terms of a similar sense of humour. David's thing is rigorous Cleeseian logic, Andrew is wackier. The four of us got on extremely well, and did a lot of work in a very short time. (This is an emergent pattern of Douglas' life. He found writing utter hell on his own, and immense fun and very easy when working with other people. But . . . he always wanted to work on his own. Go figure, as they say.)

'There were two other people in the group: John Mason, a *Week Ending* writer (who was a bit older than us) and a girl named Becky who may have been John's girlfriend and who was the only one of us to have been to drama school. Douglas and David and Andrew and I were really the engine of the project, although Andrew was just writing. The strength of the show was the material which was really, really good most of the time. That sort of carried the acting – at which we were less obviously good.'[5]

The title was a homage to Dorothy L. Sayers' *The Unpleasantness at the Bellona Club,* while also helping to remind prospective punters where the revue was being staged. John Lloyd and Douglas had T-shirts printed: John's said 'I've been unpleasant at Brodie's Close' while Douglas' said 'So have I'. Douglas received some strange looks when he was on his own . . .

'Brodie's Close is one of those tiny alleys off the Royal Mile with the door to a hall concealed in it, in this case a Masonic hall on the first floor,' explains Lloyd. 'It could not conceivably be called a theatre. There were no wings at all for example. The lighting was a switch on the wall by the door. Costume changes took place on a ledge in a window alcove which abutted the stage, behind an ordinary window-style curtain normally closed to prevent people borne aloft on cherry-pickers peeking in at secret Masonic ceremonies. You had to change entirely standing up, and be careful not to wobble the curtain with your knee.

'I remember Douglas getting terribly upset one night in a bar, because the first couple of nights, though the show generally was going down a storm, every time Douglas spoke, the audience fell respectfully mute. He just wasn't getting any laughs. At the time, Douglas was sporting a huge black piratical beard, and after a few lagers we somehow worked out that this was the problem. Enormous man with very loud voice in tiny cramped hall preceded by this tenebrous efflorescence of follicles. The audience must have felt like Macbeth in a rush-hour tube compartment being told gags by Birnam Wood. Douglas was simply terrifying the audience into silence. That night he shaved off the offending item, and after that everything was fine. He was funny again.'[6]

Andrew Marshall recalls: 'I was going to appear initially, but sadly a teaching job clashed with the dates so I was fated to only write sketches and appear at rehearsals. In one sketch Douglas played my favourite part of his, the overbearing barman, who badgers a customer wanting a quiet drink with constant and irritating references to the customer's "average height": "I bet the women can't keep off you, being 'averagely heighted' like that".'[7]

'We did everything ourselves,' remembers Lloyd. 'Wrote the scripts, performed them, made all the props and graphics, did all the fly-posting and the programmes, and ran our own box office from a tiny collapsible table at the front end of the alley. It was an absolute gas. The show was packed every night. It sat about seventy-five, but we managed to stuff in about ninety people by having them standing at the back in flagrant contempt of fire regulations. By the end of the week, we were scheduling extra performances, and we could have sold out many times over. I think we went home (after expenses) with a tenner each.'[8]

Douglas and John Lloyd worked on several other projects after

Douglas split up with Graham Chapman, some of which developed the idea of science fiction comedy which had begun with *The Ringo Starr Show*. 'Sno 7 and the White Dwarfs was quite a good idea, or at least Douglas and I always thought so,' reflects Lloyd. 'It was about two astrophysicists trapped in a one-room observatory on the top of Everest. One of them was very tidy and the other was very untidy. They realise that the end of the world is about to take place because a superior intelligence has arranged to trigger a sequence of supernovas all over the universe as a promotional advertising slogan spelling out the message 'Things Go Better with Bulp!' Our sun was scheduled to be the full stop underneath the exclamation mark. We did a kind of treatment and sent it to the BBC but were told quite firmly that science fiction was 'very fifties' and there was no market for it whatsoever. This was the year before *Star Wars*.'[9]

Douglas still had hopes for *Sno 7* as late as October 1978, six months after *Hitchhiker's* had been broadcast, telling an interviewer, 'I won't tell you the plot of that actually, because I still might use it.'[10]

The Swasivious Zebu was a radio sketch show: 'Crammed with brilliant, innovative and hilarious material. Can't imagine why it never got made. Probably the "very fifties" title.'[11] *Knight and Day* was a sitcom idea: 'Two guys sharing a flat, one of whom had a day job, and the other of whom worked nights. Didn't get very far. I recently discovered that this is in fact the plot of the Gilbert and Sullivan operetta *Box and Cox*.'[12] Then there was the film adaptation of *The Guinness Book of Records*.

'We were asked by Rae Knight who worked for Beryl Vertue who worked for Robert Stigwood to do a treatment for Mark Forstater who had acquired the film rights to *The Guinness Book of Records*,' remembers Lloyd with commendable accuracy. 'We came up with a treatment that made us laugh a lot about a bunch of aliens (not unlike the Vogons) who were the most competitive race in the universe. They threatened to destroy the Earth unless humanity could beat them in a kind of intergalactic Olympics. They won all the running and fighting prizes, but we had the edge by being much better at eating pickled eggs and walking backwards and so on. Rae and Beryl liked it and we were promised a trip to the West Indies to meet the great Stigwood. At the last minute, though, it all fell through, and the project lapsed.'[13]

The film had originally been offered to Graham Chapman – 'but Graham wasn't really interested'[14] – and had even been briefly considered as an animated musical, leading to an extraordinary meeting on 24 October 1975 attended by Douglas, Chapman, Bernard McKenna, Bob Godfrey and Tim Rice. 'Graham, Douglas and I had been in a pub since noon,' recalls McKenna. 'Later, Douglas couldn't make it to a Who concert that night as he was too "tired and emotional". In the back of the cab on the way back to Graham's house, as Graham comforted him, Douglas told Graham that he loved him and then got annoyed when I burst out laughing.'[15]

'That all went swimmingly for a while,' was Douglas' recollection of the *Guinness Book* project, 'then they eventually dropped it because they said there was no market for science fiction films at the moment.'[16]

CHAPTER 11

ON 27 OCTOBER 1976, the BBC Copyright Department wrote to Fraser and Dunlop with regard to Douglas Adams (the letter was not addressed to Jill Foster, possibly because she was busy establishing her own agency). Douglas was asked to write up to ten minutes of material, at £5 per minute, for the first episode of the second series of *The Burkiss Way*. On 13 December, another letter from the BBC commissioned Douglas to write ten minutes of material for programme six in the same series. By this time the Jill Foster Agency was up and running and Douglas had faithfully followed Jill away from Fraser and Dunlop.

Mostly written by its creators Andrew Marshall and David Renwick, *The Burkiss Way* was a glorious series which never achieved classic status simply because by 1976 radio had become such a minority medium. Sketches melded into one another, using (and often abusing) the medium of radio to its full, with inspired wordplay that showed a real delight in the English language. A popular recurring character, a scuzzy low-life whose name was also his catchphrase, was Eric Pode of Croydon. The show ran for forty-seven editions from August 1976 to November 1980, having developed out of two programmes broadcast in 1975 – on Radio 3 – entitled *The Half-Open University*. Written by Marshall, Renwick and John Mason and produced initially by Simon Brett (later by John Lloyd and David Hatch), the series starred Denise Coffey, Nigel Rees, Chris Emmett and Fred Harris. Coffey and Mason left after the first series; Jo Kendall joined the cast and Brett recruited external writers to replace Mason (from series three onwards all shows would be written by Marshall and Renwick alone).

Though he had seen some of his Adams-Smith-Adams material used in *Oh No It Isn't!* and had written *Out of the Trees* with Chapman and McKenna, this was Douglas' first professional piece of solo writing – and already a deadline problem was developing. Material for the first programme had to be delivered by 5 November, but Douglas eventually handed in a five-minute sketch on 20 December, a parody of Erik Von Daniken – renamed Erik Von Kontrik – which included a rant about how people working in TV looked down on those in radio. (Already Douglas was re-using material as the sketch includes an alien who, like the robot in *The Ringo Starr Show*, comes from 'Your masters in the galaxy of Smegmon'.) This sketch was eventually used in programme seven (12 January), while Douglas was also asked to write some material for programme ten. The ten minutes written for programme six became four minutes of running commentary on a non-happening comedy sketch at 23 Gungadin Crescent, topping and tailing programme eight (2 February), but the ten minutes written for programme ten was not used at all.

Meanwhile, topical Radio 2 comedy show *The News Huddlines* was midway through its third series, and Douglas wrote a 'quickie' (one-joke sketch of thirty seconds or less) for the eleventh programme in the series, broadcast on 19 January 1977, for which he was paid two pounds. On the basis of this success, he was invited to submit further material but no further Adams gags were used in that series. Douglas wrote – and was paid £66 for – twelve minutes of material for *Huddlines* series four, of which two and a half minutes was used.

Douglas made only a very few contributions to comedy sketch shows before creating *Hitchhiker's*. But as Jill Foster recalls, this wasn't for want of trying and what Douglas lacked in broadcast credits he more than made up for in personal contacts, many of whom would stand him in good stead as *Hitchhiker* progressed through the BBC hierarchy: 'Right from the word go Douglas was terribly aware that we needed original ideas from him. He was terrifically good in that once he met someone, he kept in touch with them. He was a dream of a client from that point of view. Douglas was good at selling himself – because he was such a clever writer. He used to ring me at ten o'clock every single morning. You don't do that unless you think you've got your agent something special to offer. It used to drive me mad actually.

'Certainly, right from the start, he was trying to come up with new ideas. The one that sticks in my mind is the very first one, the two men sharing a lighthouse, which was very funny. I couldn't get people interested because he was an unknown but there were certainly signs with that very first script that here was something different, something special.'[1]

Legend says that Douglas contributed to *Week Ending* during this period, but in fact although he tried to write for the show (then produced by Simon Brett), his one and only solo contribution to *Week Ending* was the week after *Hitchhiker's Guide* was first broadcast. (Ironically, Will Adams and Martin Smith were contracted staff writers for *Week Ending* around this time. As a trio Adams-Smith-Adams had sold a few items to the show during John Lloyd's tenure as producer (1974–6), including an early version of the Marilyn Monroe sketch.)

'I don't think there's ever been a worse bit of casting,' said Brett of Douglas' attempts to write for the show. '*Week Ending* is very specific about what is required, and quite dull really. It did a lot of good for a lot of writers, but there are very few for whom it was their natural medium. It was a kind of stepping stone, one of the very few open markets where you could actually get stuff on. But Douglas' mind is very tangential, whereas *Week Ending* needs things to be very focused and short. *The Burkiss Way* was much closer to the way Douglas' mind worked than *Week Ending* ever was.'[2]

'He just couldn't do it,' says John Lloyd. 'He had a go from time to time, but it was quite alien to him. When he did come up with something it was usually wholly unsuitable. He produced a long sketch for *Week Ending* when I was producing it, something thoroughly tasteless and quite, quite mad which had something to do with Lord Lucan's coffin, and which was entirely unusable for about fifteen reasons. But so what if he couldn't write for *Week Ending*? That show used dozens of writers over the years, many of whom got stuff on every week, but who've never been heard of in any other context again. It's a good thing he couldn't slot in because, if he had, he'd have never needed to write *Hitchhiker*, and that would have been an immeasurable loss.'[3]

On 4 February 1977, Simon Brett had a meeting with Douglas, from which sprang two commissions, both dated 3 March. One was for *The Burkiss Way*; specifically Brett wanted to use the 'Kamikaze' sketch from *A Kick in the Stalls* (the commission was for two minutes each from Douglas and Chris Keightley, although for some reason John Lloyd was credited on the programme instead).

'Kamikaze' is a classic sketch with a beautifully simple premise and very clever lines. *The Burkiss Way* version was repeated on *Pick of the Week*, and again a year later in a programme entitled, with typical BBC forced frivolity, *David Jacobs Springs in the Air*. The script was published in both *Don't Panic* in 1988 and *The Utterly Utterly Amusing and Pretty Damn Definitive Comic Relief Revue Book* the following year; Chris Keightley still receives occasional foreign royalty cheques for it.

The other commission was for a half-hour pilot script for 'a science fiction comedy adventure' called *The Hitchhiker's Guide to the Galaxy*, to be broadcast on Radio 4, no date specified. Douglas was offered £165 – half on delivery, half on recording – based on a three-page 'spec' outline, with a page of additional ideas for future episodes, which he had typed up after his meeting with Brett.

Piecing the story together in retrospect, it seems that the 'Kamikaze' sketch may have been commissioned as a bargaining tool. The commission for the *Hitchhiker* pilot was made on 1 March, by which time *The Burkiss Way* programme had been recorded but not broadcast – it went out on 2 March – and the sketch was therefore available as evidence of Douglas' radio writing capabilities. One of the people who greenlit the *Hitchhiker* pilot on Brett's recommendation was Chief Producer John Simmonds, who was known to be a fan of the 'Kamikaze' sketch. Looking at the dates, he must have heard the sketch on a pre-broadcast tape of that particular *Burkiss Way* episode, which he wouldn't have been able to do had Simon Brett gone straight to him a few days after the February meeting with Douglas. The sketch therefore served two purposes: four minutes of proven comedy for *The Burkiss Way*, and clear evidence that Douglas Adams could write extremely funny material for radio. (Did John Simmonds ever realise that it had actually been written a year earlier for the stage and had been singled out for praise by theatre critics from Southampton to Edinburgh?)

'Simon asked me to his office and said, "Have you any ideas for a new radio series?"' recalled Douglas. 'Having at that stage given up on the whole idea of doing comedy science fiction, I came up with various ideas and various permutations of people living in bedsits and this sort of thing, which seemed to be what most situation comedy these days tends to be about. And he said, "Yes, yes, yes, that might work, that might not work." Then after about an hour or so, he said, "You know what I would like to do?" And I said, "No, what would you like to do?" And he said, "I would like to do something which is comedy science fiction." And I fell off my chair at that stage, because it was what I'd been fighting for all these years!'[4]

'I was just aware that there was this huge talent and very original mind, but it certainly wasn't being well-served by BBC Light Entertainment at that stage,' said Brett. 'Then I remember encouraging him to come up with an idea of his own because he clearly wasn't going to fit into anybody else's show. So he came to see me and he had three ideas. One was *The Hitchhiker's Guide to the Galaxy* and neither of us can remember what the other two were! Anyway, I thought *The Hitchhiker's Guide to the Galaxy* sounded the interesting one.'[5]

Given Douglas' passion for recycling it's almost certain that one of his other ideas was the lighthouse sitcom. In fact, the sci-fi comedy pitch which Douglas made wasn't *Hitchhiker's Guide* per se but an anthology series, *The Ends of the Earth*, which would finish each episode with the world being destroyed (week one: world blown up to make way for hyperspace bypass). Douglas always had a slightly scary nihilistic obsession; he contributed the global destruction punchline to the peony sketch in *Out of the Trees* and *The Ringo Starr Show* had finished with the entire universe being destroyed.

Needing an alien character to give the galactic bypass story perspective, and a reason for that character to be on Earth, Douglas plucked from his memory the idea of *The Hitchhiker's Guide to the Galaxy*, the title which he had invented in that field in Innsbruck in 1971 and promptly forgotten about. Or had he?

'I remember Douglas showing up for a writing session after a relaxing holiday where he'd hitchhiked around Greece,' recalls Gail Renard, who certainly didn't know Douglas in 1971. 'He yawned and stretched himself to his full length and said, "I wonder what it would be like to hitchhike around the galaxy?"'[6] We know from Douglas' admission in the radio scripts introduction that he himself had no memory of Innsbruck in 1971. We also know that his first thoughts about combining science fiction and comedy came three years later, when he was writing material for *Cerberus*. There is a very real possibility that even this cornerstone of the Douglas Adams legend was inaccurate and that the actual idea occurred to him in Greece after he went up to Cambridge.

Geoffrey Perkins remembers the *Ends of the Earth* idea as still being extant when he took over production with the second episode, but clearly time is also playing tricks on his memory. By the end of the meeting with Brett, it had definitely been decided that staying with the two characters who escaped the Earth's destruction in the first episode would be better than an anthology series, and Douglas typed out his pitch document for *The Hitchhiker's Guide to the Galaxy*.

'Douglas was terrific at describing things to you,' remembers Jill Foster. 'When he first told me about it – and I think he'd already talked to Simon Brett about it – he just said, "I've got this idea," and started talking about it and made me cry laughing. I have to tell you, I didn't think for a moment it would take off. It was too imaginative and unusual.'[7]

'I suppose I heard about it just after Simon Brett,' says John Lloyd. 'I thought it was great – as did everyone else. No-one at any stage ever felt any other way about *Hitchhiker*. Right from the start it had 'HIT' written all the way through it like the lettering in a stick of rock.'[8]

'In many ways *Hitchhiker* was Douglas' last throw of the dice as a writer,' said Geoffrey Perkins. 'He was considering jacking it all in and perhaps taking a job in Hong Kong.'[9] John Lloyd corroborates this extraordinary idea: 'I remember coming back from work and finding him on his bed in despair, saying that he just wasn't going to make it as a writer and that he was going to become a ship broker in Hong Kong of all bizarre things!'[10] (Martin Smith maintains that the job was in Tokyo; possibly that was a different bout of despair.)

A facsimile of Douglas' *Hitchhiker* pitch document is reproduced in *Don't Panic* and it is very, very close to what became the pilot episode. There are already recognisable phrases ('the minimal research he had done suggested that the name Ford Prefect would be nicely inconspicuous') and there are some interesting differences (the as-yet-unnamed Mr Prosser is more threatening). The outline stops at the revelation that the Earth's entry in the *Hitchhiker's Guide* is 'Mostly harmless' – which, aside from the bit about Vogon poetry, is where the pilot ends. The only significant difference is that the main character is called 'Aleric B' – although this has been crossed out and 'Arthur Dent' written in above it.

On the other hand, the final page of the document ('Some suggestions for future development') bears no relation to any version of the story ever actually written. The suggestion is that each episode will follow the adventures of Ford and Aleric/Arthur as they take odd jobs to help pay their way around the universe, researching for the *Hitchhiker's Guide*. They could even visit 'parallel alternatives of Earth which are more or less the same'. The idea of using extracts from the *Guide* itself as a form of narrator is presented, together with an acknowledgement of the influence of *Gulliver's Travels*.

The thinking behind 'Aleric B' seems to have been to give the audience the mistaken initial impression that the character is alien, an idea which was used instead (not very effectively) for Trillian. However 'Arthur Dent' has an interesting history. Here's the way Douglas told it: 'There are all kinds of odd things about his name. I wanted the name to be, on the one hand, perfectly ordinary, but on the other hand, distinctive. "Arthur" is a name like that – it's not like Dominic or Sebastian or something obviously very odd or even affected. It's a solid, "olde English" name that's perfectly ordinary, but not many people actually have it. There was a character at school called Dent. It just seemed to have the right ring. And also, I suppose, because Arthur was very much somebody to whom things happened – somebody who reacted to things that happened to him, rather than being an instigator himself – he seemed to be a "Dentish" sort of character, and that was partly in my mind, so that's really how the name came about.'[11]

But there is an extraordinary coincidence which has surfaced many times over the years, as Douglas explained: 'I got a letter from a researcher in English literature. He was studying the English Puritan period, with specific reference to John Bunyan and *Pilgrim's Progress*. *Hitchhiker* in many ways borrows its form from one of the oldest forms of literature, the Everyman story – the innocent guy who gets thrown into a strange world – going all the way back to the Everyman plays, the mystery plays, then, slightly further forward, *Gulliver's Travels* and so on.

'So this guy drew these comparisons, and then he came up with this extraordinary thing: there is one book that Bunyan is known to have read called – and you'll see the parallel in the title – *The Plaine Man's Pathway to Heaven*, written by an English Puritan writer called Arthur Dent. And when he stumbled on this, he instantly leapt to the conclusion that I had deliberately made this extraordinary, involved academic joke. He went through *The Plaine Man's Pathway to Heaven* and teased out all the parallels between the two books, and he sent me this long dissertation on this "joke" that he discovered I had "created". I had to write back and say, "I'm sorry, I've never heard of this book".'[12]

It was another of Douglas' great stories. It was often told. Once again, it wasn't entirely true. *The Plaine Man's Pathway to Heaven* by Arthur Dent does exist, but the coincidence of the title is just that; after all, *A Hitchhiker's Guide to Europe* (*sic*) is a much better known book. But Douglas was mistaken when he claimed, 'I've never heard of this book'. In fact, Douglas had seen an original edition of *The Plaine Man's Pathway to Heaven* less than a year before he typed that *Hitchhiker* outline.

In the summer of 1976, while directing *A Kick in the Stalls*, Douglas stayed in Harry Porter's house in Cambridge. 'I used to lecture on seventeenth-century English writers before I retired,' recalls Dr Porter. 'I had in this house about the time Douglas was staying here a book of sermons by a writer called Arthur Dent. It was an original seventeenth-century book, lent to me by Maurice Hussey. I've no idea whether Douglas saw it. It just happened to be lying around here.'[13]

As an English graduate with a love of classical English literature it is inconceivable that Douglas would not have taken a look at this antique book. So was he lying when he said he had never heard of it? No, I think he was just not remembering it. After all, he did have a lot of other things on his mind in the summer of 1976, such as what was he going to do about this extraordinarily long revue, and what were he and John Lloyd going to do in Edinburgh, and why was that man stealing his biscuits.*

Did Douglas use the name as an obscure joke but subsequently forget about it? Or did he forget about *The Plaine Man's Pathway to Heaven* and subconsciously pick the name Arthur Dent without realising the connection? Whatever, it wasn't a coincidence. Despite all that has been said and written over the years denying any connection, the hero of *The Hitchhiker's Guide to the Galaxy* clearly *was* named after the author of *The Plaine Man's Pathway to Heaven*.

The *Hitchhiker's* pilot script was commissioned on 3 March and, incredibly, Douglas wrote it in a month, presenting the finished script to Simon Brett on 4 April. 'Of course, I had the great advantage that no other editor or producer had with Douglas, in that I got the script in on time,' said Brett. 'Because we couldn't make the pilot until we'd got the script so in a sense it almost didn't matter when I got it.'[14]

Brett took the script to the next meeting of the Programme Development Group, who remained largely mystified but agreed to commission a series anyway. Eventually, on 8 June, a recording date for *Hitchhiker's Guide* was pencilled into the BBC schedules. The sound effects would be recorded in a three-hour session on 27 June, and then combined with the actors in an eight-hour recording session the following day. In the meantime, however, *Star Wars* had opened in America and the world had, overnight, gone sci-fi mad.

* See Chapter 26

INTERLUDE - **PRECEDENT**

STAR WARS OPENED in the United States in May 1977. The excitement it generated for anything with a robot, spaceship or alien in it built up in the UK until the film opened in London at the end of December, and across the country in January 1978. *The Hitchhiker's Guide to the Galaxy* started less than six weeks later. The timing was opportune.

It is important to emphasise that *Hitchhiker's Guide* is in no way a spoof or parody of sci-fi, it is humorous science fiction which does what all good science fiction is supposed to do – explores the human condition and man's place in the universe – but does it with humour. 'I never saw myself as actually sending up science fiction,' stressed Douglas. 'There is only one thing that I can think of where I deliberately "sent up" something from the science fiction genre, which was the thing about, "to boldly split infinitives that no-one has split before". It was just one of those things where I thought, "I can't think of anything better – I'll go with that". But otherwise, as far as I was concerned, I wasn't sending up science fiction. I was using science fiction as a vehicle for sending up everything else.'[1]

Was this a completely original idea? That depends on your point of view. There had been plenty of humorous SF stories published in books and magazines over the years but SF literature can be very insular and for the most part these were stories where the humour would only appeal to science fiction fans. Within the mainstream media, science fiction comedy was rare. There was *My Favourite*

Martian and the occasional Disney film such as *The Absent-Minded Professor*, but these were knockabout sitcoms, not comedies of ideas. The only significant attempt to combine thought-provoking SF ideas with sophisticated humour was Woody Allen's *Sleeper*, which was released in 1973 and so could certainly have partially inspired Douglas to pursue the genre.

Douglas went to see *Star Wars* – who didn't? – accompanied by Lisa Braun (later a production assistant on *Hitchhiker's Guide* and later still Mrs Geoffrey Perkins), with John Lloyd and his girlfriend Helen Rhys Jones (Griff's sister). 'The four of us thought it was wonderful,' recalls Lloyd. 'It was certainly the best night I've ever spent in a cinema.'[2]

CHAPTER **12**

THE PILOT EPISODE of *Hitchhiker's Guide* was recorded on 28 June 1977, at which point Douglas was paid the second half of his writer's fee. But before that happened, there was the little matter of casting. 'I don't think I've ever worked with a writer who was so clear about what he wanted and how it should be,'[1] observed Simon Brett. Douglas asked for, and got, Simon Jones as Arthur Dent and Geoffrey McGivern as Ford Prefect, which was convenient as the characters had been written with those two actors in mind.

'The script wasn't written, but I know that he did call and ask if I was interested in playing myself in a radio pilot he was doing,' recalled Simon Jones. 'What was interesting as far as I was concerned was for me to find out exactly what Douglas thought about me. I wasn't altogether flattered! I didn't think I was the sort who went wandering about trying to find a decent cup of tea. But who knows? He's probably right.'[2]

'Arthur Dent was never meant to be Simon,' stressed Douglas, 'although it was written with Simon in mind as an actor. Let's make that distinction quite clear. It is by no means a portrait of Simon Jones in any way at all. It's written to his strengths as an actor which is a very different thing. Nor, by the same token, is it autobiographical.'[3]

Zaphod, Trillian and Marvin were not in the pilot; the only other characters were Mr Prosser, Prostetnic Vogon Jeltz, Lady Cynthia Fitzmelton and the Barman. Jo Kendall played Lady Cynthia, an unnecessary character who was dropped from all subsequent versions of the story apart from one or two stage productions. 'She was being so high-handedly oblivious of the wreckage she was causing and was talking about it in this terribly condescending way because she was a stockholder in the construction company that wanted to demolish Dent's house,' explained Douglas, 'but that got lost and she didn't really work.'[4]

Kendall had been in the 1963 Footlights Revue *A Clump of Plinths* (aka *Cambridge Circus*) which became *I'm Sorry, I'll Read That Again*, while David Gooderson (the Barman) had been in 1964's *Stuff What Dreams Are Made Of*. The original actor booked to play Prosser and Jeltz (the one is of course the intergalactic equivalent of the other) fell ill anyway and Bill Wallis was called in at a day's notice to replace him. Wallis had appeared in *Springs to Mind* in 1958, thus completing an all-Footlights cast. Apart, that is, from the narrator.

'In my first term at Cambridge I went along to a charity auction,' explained Douglas, 'and the auctioneer was Peter Jones. I was terribly impressed with him. I'd seen him on television and heard him on the radio, but he'd never made a particular impression on me. He has this very amiable, slightly lost persona, but it was extraordinary, seeing him work an audience for about three hours off the top of his head, and continually giving the appearance of being just slightly out of control and slightly uncertain of what was going on, but obviously being an absolute professional as far as what he was doing.

'After I'd written the first episode and I was talking to Simon Brett about how to cast the narrator, I didn't really have any clear ideas but for some reason I kept on thinking it ought to be a sort of Peter Jones-y voice. We thought, "Well, who can do a Peter Jones-y voice?" And we thought of all sorts of people who could do a Peter Jones-y voice, and for some reason it took us an awfully long time to think, "Well, Peter Jones could do quite a good Peter Jones-y voice, couldn't he?" And he was absolutely perfect, and a delightful man to work with actually.'[5]

'I was in Cornwall doing a bit of work, writing,' recalled Jones. 'A script arrived in the post from the BBC and they asked me to read it, said they were thinking of doing a pilot and was I interested? I read it and I must say I was fascinated. It was such a very different style to anything I'd been asked to do before, so I told them I would be very interested.'6

The recording at the Paris Studio, Lower Regent Street, home to legendary series such as *The Goon Show*, went without a hitch. There had been some concern among BBC suits about recording a comedy series without an audience, but Simon Brett had successfully argued that an audience was not only unnecessary but impractical, since *Hitchhiker's* would be recorded more like a drama than a sitcom. One could not expect the public to sit still for several hours watching actors read lines in different parts of the stage, sometimes in separate booths, with narration recorded separately and the whole thing requiring subsequent sound effects and mixing.

A rough edit of the show was sent to Paddy Kingsland at the BBC Radiophonic Workshop, and on 6 July he got together with Simon Brett and Douglas to assemble the finished show, after which the three repaired to the Dover Castle pub for a drink. There was still one level of BBC bureaucracy to pass before a full series was commissioned, and once again Simon Brett's track record proved decisive: 'Once we had edited the recording, I went back to my Heads of Department and played them this tape. They sat around in total silence for half an hour. And at the end, my boss said to me, "Simon, is it funny?" And I said, "It is." And he said, "Oh well, that's good enough for me, we will put it up to the next level of authority," and it was put up there and accepted and then a series was commissioned.'7

The memo giving permission to commission a further five episodes came through on 31 August, and the following day a formal commission was sent to Douglas, but not by Simon Brett. He had landed a job in television and was working out his notice, so the task of producing *Hitchhiker's Guide* fell to his protégé Geoffrey Perkins. Perkins knew Douglas slightly already, having first met him when the Oxford Revue was sharing a theatre in Edinburgh with *A Kick in the Stalls*, although, as with so many people, he knew the name 'Douglas Adams' even before meeting the man, through a mutual friend who had hitchhiked around Europe with Douglas in his student days.

The commission of 1 September offered Douglas £180 per script for five episodes. This was welcome money indeed as by now he had a huge overdraft and was sleeping on his friends' sofas. It was more than a year since he had returned from Edinburgh and in all that time his total income from writing had been no more than about £500.

There was just one problem: *Doctor Who.*

Douglas had twice sent ideas for stories 'on spec' to the *Doctor Who* production office. The one in 1974 had included the 'B'-Ark sequence that was subsequently reused for *The Ringo Starr Show* and *Hitchhiker's Guide*, but otherwise remains a mystery, especially with regard to the identity of the 'friend' who wrote it with him. A couple of years later he had submitted a story in which the Doctor battled a race of cricket-playing robots, which was rejected as 'too silly' (but which would eventually be used in a quite different context). Script editor Robert Holmes thought that Douglas had talent, however, and indicated that he would consider commissioning a *Doctor Who* script if he could see some example of Douglas' scriptwriting ability. (Or as Douglas put it: 'It was sent back rather curtly with a note saying, "We'd like to see more evidence of talent than this."'[8])

By July 1977, Douglas had a thirty-minute script on his desk which was confirmed as good enough for BBC radio. Since it looked like nothing would happen for a long time, he decided to send Robert Holmes the *Hitchhiker* pilot script as a writing sample. But by this time Holmes was being replaced by Anthony Read, so the reply, and an offer of a meeting, came from producer Graham Williams. In mid-July Williams commissioned Douglas to write a four-part outline entitled 'The Pirate Planet' to be delivered by 31 August. In a startling move never repeated, Douglas actually submitted this outline nine days *before* his deadline on 22 August.

Legend tells that Graham Williams' commission to write 'The Pirate Planet' and Geoffrey Perkins' commission to write Episodes Two to Five of *Hitchhiker* were made within a week of each other. This is largely because Douglas said things like: 'The commission to write the scripts for *Hitchhiker* and for four episodes of *Doctor*

Who came through in the same week. The one was meant to be a stop-gap for the other.'[9] In fact, the BBC Copyright Department files show that Williams' formal BBC commission paperwork is dated 20 October 1977; his letter to Douglas confirming that this was happening would have been a few days earlier, a good six or seven weeks after Perkins', whose commission is dated 1 September. But like many of Douglas' anecdotes it was a good story and the essence is there: he certainly did find himself writing two hours of *Doctor Who* and two and a half hours of *Hitchhiker's Guide* simultaneously.

Douglas' original ideas for what would become 'The Pirate Planet' involved a world hollowed out by millennia of the Time Lords mining it for a unique element and with a machine which drained the natives' aggression. A Time Lord engineer sent to dismantle the mining apparatus becomes trapped in the machine, absorbs the pent-up aggression, and determines to take revenge on his own race by jumping the planet through space and materialising it around the Time Lords' home planet of Gallifrey.

'The actual script was much too long – on paper it was twice as long as it should have been,' recalled Douglas. 'It started out as quite a simple story but it had to arch its back to get round several problems and weave past a couple of things that were in the pipeline. The whole script actually did make sense from beginning to end – in fact they were astonished that it did. But by the time it had been cut to the proper length, large holes had begun to appear.

'The whole plot eventually hinged on eternal life, which actually is a bit dull, but originally it had involved a drug-pushing analogy. I had envisaged a fly-by-night company which went around looking for those people that were most afraid of dying and sold them "time-dams" which would hold up time, making it go slower and slower, until the people were into the last few seconds of their lives. The company would also sell them the energy needed to power the dams, so that the clients don't realise they are going to need a lot more energy at much higher prices.'[10]

As he worked on the script, the eternal life storyline faded away and the space-hopping planet story came to the fore. Douglas also had to fit his episodes into an 'arc story' which had been conceived for the entire season. The Doctor and his new companion Romana were searching for the six scattered, disguised components of the 'Key to Time' in order to prevent the Black Guardian from conquering the universe. (For such a heavily researched series, it is curious that no *Doctor Who* historian has ever commented on the coincidental parallels between this premise and that of Douglas' 1976 submission, 'The Krikkitmen', in which the Doctor and his companion were searching for the five scattered, disguised components of the 'Wickit Key' in order to prevent the Krikkit Warriors from conquering the universe.)

The four *Doctor Who* scripts were due by 1 January 1978 and the first one landed on Graham Williams' desk on 18 November 1977. On 1 November a production schedule had been drawn up for *Hitchhiker's Guide*, on the assumption that the six-episode run would be broadcast at 10.30 p.m. on Tuesdays, starting on 7 February: recording episodes on 9 and 23 November, 13 and 20 December and 17 January. Two effects recording sessions were also scheduled at the Paris Studio in November.

Douglas was staying with his mother and stepfather in Dorset, feverishly swapping between *Doctor Who* and *Hitchhiker's*. The second radio episode was delivered in October, with 'The Pirate Planet' Part One in November, and then *Hitchhiker's* Episodes Three and Four following on 14 and 22 December. (The episodes were not, at this stage, called 'Fits' – that Lewis Carroll-inspired suggestion was made by Geoffrey Perkins much later.)

'Oddly enough, I found *Doctor Who* quite liberating to do,' recalled Douglas. 'At one point I was writing both *Hitchhiker* and *Doctor Who* simultaneously, and in many ways, even though people assume there was some cross-fertilisation, in fact they inhabit such entirely different universes, there really wasn't. But I did notice one odd thing which was: I was writing episodes of *Hitchhiker* which all seemed to happen in corridors, and writing episodes of *Doctor Who* which called for huge, enormous, impossibly elaborate sets. I thought, "I've got this the wrong way round."'[11]

Parts Two to Four of 'The Pirate Planet' were finally delivered on 26 January; Part One was formally accepted on 19 February and the remainder of the scripts nine days later. Although not without some reservations on the part of Graham Williams: 'I think it sent Graham off into several epileptic fits because it turned into such a complicated script with so many effects and so many things I was asking for: aircars and inertia-less corridors and planets which ate other planets. I remember when I was reading the final synopsis to Graham and Tony, and Graham was sinking lower and lower in his seat. There was a deadly silence when I'd finished, and I said, "Well, do you like it?" And Graham said, "Now I know how Kubrick felt."'[12]

Graeme McDonald (Head of Serials) actually wanted to reject Douglas' scripts but was dissuaded by Read and director Pennant Roberts. 'It needed a lot of whipping into shape but all the elements were there,' said Read. 'Douglas had some marvellous creations but his weakness was getting the structure right.'[13]

'I've always wished that the story could have been a six-parter,' said Douglas. 'In the end I'd written such full scripts that there was easily enough for three hours of it rather than two. I felt that there were all sorts of sudden truncations at the end and I think it was probably the best worked-out plot I'd ever done, but unfortunately it's not apparent on screen.'[14]

'The Pirate Planet' was shot on location in May and June 1978 and broadcast from 30 September. The story runs something like this: The Doctor, Romana and K-9 locate the second segment of the Key to Time on the desolate planet Calufrax, but when the TARDIS materialises it ends up on the considerably more pleasant planet Zanak, ruled by the Captain, a semi-robotic tyrant with a robot parrot or 'Polyphase Avatron' on his shoulder. The Captain's fortress-like 'bridge' has a burnt-out 'macromat field integrator' which allows the entire hollow planet to jump through space and materialise around other planets before mining them of all their resources and crushing them into super-dense spheres. Repairing the device requires quartz, of which the nearest supply is on . . . Earth. K-9 fights the Polyphase Avatron and the Doctor uses the TARDIS to block Zanak's attempt at materialising around Earth; the engine rooms are destroyed and all the bad guys die. The Doctor restores the planet Calufrax to normal, having realised that the whole planet is the second Key to Time segment.

'The Pirate Planet' was well-received by *Doctor Who* fans and garnered reasonable viewing figures, although Douglas himself was never terribly happy with the finished product: '"The Pirate Planet" actually shouldn't have been so overtly funny or joky as it was. I wrote it with a lot of humour in it, but the point is, when you do that it very often gets played to the hilt. I felt there was too much feeling of: "Oh, the script's got humour in it. Therefore we've got to wheel out the funny voices and the silly walks," which I don't think does it a service.'[15]

Meanwhile, Douglas had hit some pretty major problems with *Hitchhiker's* and had, in desperation, called on an old friend to help him.

CHAPTER **13**

'**AFTER LONG PERIODS** of intense inactivity, I was suddenly going out of my mind with too much work to do,' said Douglas. 'I sat down and wrote four episodes of *Hitchhiker* just like that, four at once, and then took a break off to write four episodes of 'Pirate Planet'. Then because I was in a bit of a state by that stage, co-wrote the last two episodes of *Hitchhiker* with John Lloyd. How did I come to write it? I don't know, I suppose I just got drunk a lot!'[1] Which mention of alcohol contrasts interestingly with an interview given exactly one month later: 'Writing is sitting at your desk all day long banging your head against sharp objects, drinking lots of cups of tea and keeping the whisky bottle firmly locked away.'[2]

Of course, Douglas didn't write 'four episodes of *Hitchhiker* just like that' as the first episode was already complete. That interview is from October 1978, less than a year later, and already he is getting confused about details. But that is understandable: it was a pretty confusing year: 'When writing the radio series, I would basically make it up as I went along, and had no idea what was going to be in next week's episode. I was just in a bit of a panic as to how I would make this week's episode make sense.'[3]

Episode Two introduced Zaphod Beeblebrox, played by Mark Wing-Davey, who had appeared in the 1970 revue *The Footlights Comic Annual* and had achieved some notoriety within Footlights for his long hair and bright blue dinner jackets. The episodic nature of Douglas' writing meant that Zaphod was not expected to be a regular character. 'Someone rang up and said would I play this part in two episodes of *Hitchhiker's Guide to the Galaxy*, of which they'd done a pilot,' Wing-Davey recalled. 'I read the script and I'd heard that Peter Jones was going to be in it, who I knew and I like a lot. So I rang him up and I said, "Look, I've been asked to do this *Hitchhiker's Guide*. You did the pilot – what's it like?" He said, "I don't understand it frankly, but it's all right I suppose." So I said, "Okay, it'll be a laugh." '4

Even Douglas had no idea where the character's name came from: 'The name was a product of a thing that happens quite often, which is when you're sitting, struggling away, writing something. You have a little notebook by the side of whatever you're working on, so any little stray thought that occurs to you, you jot down there. At the end of the day, you very often find that the little stray thoughts you've put in the notebook are very much more interesting than what you've been writing. The name "Zaphod Beeblebrox" turned up in the notebook at the end of the day. I couldn't even remember having written it down.'5

Susan Sheridan was cast as Trillian, a character loosely based on one of Douglas' ex-girlfriends, and variously named Goophic and Smoodle in earlier drafts. Sheridan was also unsure at first: 'Like most of the cast, I suspect, I read the script and didn't understand a word of it.'6 And then there was Marvin. The Paranoid Android himself. Douglas repeated, *ad infinitum*, the story about where Marvin came from. Here is the fairly definitive version: 'Marvin was based on an old friend of mine called Andrew Marshall, who is also a comedy writer – we're a morose lot, aren't we? It used to be that you'd be terribly nervous about introducing Andrew to everybody. You'd be with a bunch of people in the pub and Andrew would come up and you'd say, "Andrew meet John, meet Susan . . ." Everybody would make introductions, and Andrew would stand there. And once everybody else had come to a finish in whatever they were saying, Andrew would then say something so astoundingly rude that it would completely take everybody's breath away. In the silence that was to follow, he would then stalk off to a corner of the pub and sit there, nursing a pint. I would go over to him and say, "Andrew, what on Earth was the point of saying that?" And he would say, "What would be the point of not saying it? What's the point of anything?"[7]

Marshall defends himself thus: 'Despite my own physical appearance of a WWF wrestler forced into retirement due to an unspecified groin injury, I am in fact, and always have been, an intensely shy and reflective person. I was, at the time, a truly innocent boy from a small fishing port quite unprepared for the extraordinary people around me who had benefited from a public school education and a stint at Oxbridge. Struggling to find a suitable way to react to the utterly dazzling talent and overwhelming levels of self-confidence and importance proved painfully difficult for me at the time, and that is likely the source of Douglas' well-known remarks that I tended to be rude to people he introduced me to. From my point of view I was just trying to find something amusing to say. Or indeed anything to say at all.

'I remember being in the Captain's Cabin, round the corner from the Paris Studio, when he handed me some pages of script to read, asking for my opinion. This was the first appearance of the Paranoid Android. I remember reading it and being entirely knocked out by how good it was. "What do you think?" he asked me. And, to my great credit, my word of honour, I actually replied, "I think you should prepare to be famous." With the benefit of hindsight, I imagine he was trying to see if I recognised anything in the characterisation, but I have to tell you that I didn't.'[8]

The role of Marvin went to Stephen Moore: 'I didn't turn up till the second episode when things had started getting a little bit smoother. Actually, I think in effect they'd got a little bit worse. We were literally given bits of paper as we walked in, saying, "This is what you say. Go into that cupboard and we'll treat your voice." So I didn't meet any of the cast for several hours on the first day – because I was locked in a cupboard.'[9]

'When I was doing the radio programme Geoffrey Perkins and I worked in close collaboration on casting,' recalled Douglas. 'We argued an awful lot but had a lot of fun together and it was a very good working relationship, even though we couldn't stand each other from time to time. Certainly I was responsible for the casting of Simon, and Geoffrey McGivern, oh and Mark, actually. Stephen Moore was Geoffrey Perkins' idea.'[10]

As with Zaphod, Marvin was only expected to appear in one or two episodes. 'Douglas was writing it episode by episode, without any clear idea where he was going,' remembered Perkins, 'but that meant that if something was good, we could bring it back. Marvin, for example, I said we should keep but Douglas thought he had used up the idea. I said, "No, look. The whole world of this series keeps changing all the time. We've got to keep some core characters."'[11] The episode was recorded on 23 November, with Dick Mills and Harry Parker taking over radiophonic duties from Paddy Kingsland. The recordings were by now running one episode behind schedule, with Episode Three following on 13 December, the date originally booked for Episode Four.

'The radio series was where it originated; that's where the seed grew,' said Douglas. 'Also, that's where I felt that myself and the other people working on it all created something that really felt groundbreaking at the time. Or rather, it felt like we were completely mad at the time. I can remember sitting in the subterranean studio auditioning the sound of a whale hitting the ground at 300 miles an hour for hours on end, just trying to find ways of tweaking the sound. After hours of that, day after day, you do begin to doubt your sanity. Of course, you have no idea if anybody's going to listen to this stuff, but there was a real sense that nobody had done this before. And that was great; there's a great charge that comes with that.'[12]

On 10 January 1978, with Douglas still beavering away on 'The Pirate Planet', only one week to go till the final *Hitchhiker's* recording day, and two episodes still to put in the can, a revised schedule emerged from the BBC. Episode Five would be recorded on 21 February and Episode Six one week later, with separate recording sessions for Peter Jones. However, it wasn't taping the actors which was slowing down production, it was the sheer unprecedented volume of post-production work.

'When we made the series, we didn't have any of the technology,' recalled Geoffrey Perkins. 'We had one eight-track machine. A lot of it was mixed live, and a lot of it was loops of tape going round the studio. Actually, a lot of what we did in *Hitchhiker's* would be incredibly easy now. We were on the cusp of the technology. I remember doing the first sound effects for the series, and at the end of the day I had finished all the effects for the first three minutes of my first episode.'[13]

'Having grown up with *Sergeant Pepper* and *The Dark Side of the Moon* it seemed to me that radio production was lagging behind all the things that could be done with sound,' said Douglas, 'apart from a few sonic experiments that were conducted on Radio 3 which nobody listened to very much. I wanted the thing to sound like a rock album, to do everything I could to convey the idea that you actually were on a spaceship or an alien planet – that sense of a huge aural landscape.'[14]

Consequently, the unprecedented step was taken of assigning six full days of Paris Studio time – 24 and 31 January, 14, 16 and 23 February, and 3 March – to production work on *Hitchhiker's*. Douglas was heavily involved in the production, far more than might be expected from a writer, especially one who was supposed to be completing a *Doctor Who* script. Eventually he simply ran out of ideas with two episodes of *Hitchhiker's* still to be written. It wasn't writer's block, it was exhaustion. Geoffrey Perkins recalls the moment when Douglas finally admitted defeat: 'I can still remember, having done Episode Three which was fine but starting to get slightly thin, then Episode Four came in and Douglas was saying, "I'm not sure I can make it to the end of the series."'[15]

'My writing muscles were so tired that even though I had a rough idea of what was supposed to be happening in the last two episodes, I had quite simply run out of words,' said Douglas. 'Since John Lloyd nearly always beat me at Scrabble I reckoned he must know lots more words than me and asked him if he would collaborate with me on the last couple of scripts.'[16]

'Douglas had got stuck at the beginning of Episode Five, and was pretty stressed about it,' remembers Lloyd, who wrote one third of Episode Five and half of Episode Six. 'He'd simply run dry of ideas. He said to me that he felt that he'd proved to his own satisfaction that he'd done something completely original on his own, but he wasn't enjoying the process any more. The deal Douglas offered was that if I would help him out finishing the series then, if there was a second or subsequent series, we'd do it together. After all, we'd been working together on almost everything else. It was a natural realignment.'[17]

Like Douglas, Lloyd had been promoting for some time the idea of combining science fiction with comedy ('That was what we did pretty much all the time. We just couldn't understand why no-one else appeared to share our enthusiasm.'[18]) and had been working on a novel entitled *Gigax*, which he now plundered for ideas: '*Gigax* was a half-written (and no doubt dreadfully callow) comedy science fiction novel that I was working on. In the book, a "gigax" is the largest area encompassable by the human imagination. The obligatory "Empire" in the story is several hundred "gigaxy" in extent. Douglas thought there were far too many adjectives in it. However, there were also a great number of ideas. When Douglas asked me to help him out with *Hitchhiker's*, I dumped the whole manuscript on his desk and said, "Have what you want."

'The first four episodes had taken Douglas almost ten months to write. Five and Six took us just three weeks. We wrote together, sitting in the converted garage of a house I shared with Alex Catto in William Mews, Knightsbridge. It was his parents' place. I generally did the typing and Douglas the pacing about. Quite often we would start with a bit of *Gigax*, which Douglas would immediately spin into something a great deal sharper and funnier.'[19]

The final two episodes were recorded on 21 and 28 February as planned. Roy Hudd played Max Quordlepleen, compère of Milliways ('I didn't understand a word of it and adlibbed most of the compère's speech. Nobody seemed to mind.'[20]); Jonathan Cecil was the polite Golgrafrinchan First Officer ('We weren't given a script, just the pages of our own scenes, so we didn't really know what was happening. Geoffrey has an apparently very gentle manner, but he gets whatever he wants.'[21]); and Aubrey Woods was the aggressive Second Officer ('I remember entering the BBC Club and downing copious quantities of hock and seltzer trying to get my voice back.'[22]) The Captain of the 'B'-Ark was David Jason, long before he was Del-Boy Trotter or Inspector Frost.

'The guy Douglas most resembled,' said John Lloyd once, 'is the

Captain of the "B"-Ark.'[23] This was because they both spent vast amounts of time in the bath, and the idea is borne out by the *Ringo Starr Show* version of the scene, when the Captain was dressed as a turkey. 'Douglas liked dressing up as a turkey,' recalled Martin Smith. 'He did it several times.'[24] (Once to publicise *Several Poor Players ...*, once in the *Norman Ruins* film, in a parody of the scene in *The Devils* when Huguenots were dressed as blackbirds.) Though friends compared Douglas to Arthur or Ford or Marvin, there seems little doubt that he himself identified most strongly with the Captain of the 'B'-Ark, knowing that as a comedy writer he was neither a great achiever ('A'-Ark) nor someone who actually made things ('C'-Ark) and therefore part of the 'useless third' of the planet's population. It was an interesting visualisation of Douglas' self-doubt.

The final mixing and effects session on Episode Six was completed on 3 March, with five days to go before the series debuted. It was a year to the day since Douglas had been commissioned to write the pilot episode and he had earned a grand total of £1,065: 'There seemed to be quite a long way to go before I broke even.'[25]

INTERLUDE - **ANSWER**

IT WAS ON 29 March 1978 that Radio 4 listeners first discovered the Answer to the Great Question of Life, the Universe and Everything. From then on, Douglas was plagued by people pointing out meaningless coincidences or simply failing to understand the bathos of the joke. When pressed, he gave various explanations of how that particular number was arrived at – which, it should be stressed, are not explanations of what it means. It doesn't *mean* anything.

'If you're a comedy writer working in numbers you use a number that's funny, like 17¾ or whatever,' said Douglas. 'But I thought to myself that, if the major joke is the answer to life, the universe and everything and it turns out to be a number, that has got to be a strong joke. If you put a weak joke in the middle of it by saying not only is it a number but it's 17¾, it slightly undermines it. I think the point is to have complete faith in the strong joke and put the least funny number you can think of in the middle of it. What is the most ordinary, workaday number you can find? I don't want fractions on the end of it. I don't even want it to be a prime number. And I guess it mustn't even be an odd number. There is something slightly more reassuring about even numbers. So I just wanted an ordinary, workaday number, and chose 42. It's an unfrightening number. It's a number you could take home and show to your parents.'[1]

Other times he was not so loquacious: 'It was a joke. It had to be a number, an ordinary, smallish number, and I chose that one. I sat at my desk, stared into the garden and thought, "42 will do." I typed it out. End of story.'[2] (This story is slightly belied by the fact that

Douglas was already using the number; for example his second *Burkiss Way* sketch includes the address '42 Logical Positivism Avenue'.)

Very occasionally, Douglas let slip that there was a history to the number, involving John Cleese. In one of his last ever interviews, he revealed that Procol Harum also played their part: 'There's a story on one Procol Harum track of someone going off to find enlightenment and there's a bathetic answer. So it occurred to me that you take the question and build it and build it and build it and then the answer is a number – completely banal. It should be a number of no significance, part of the joke. I remember working as a prop-borrower on a Video Arts training film and John Cleese was playing a negligent bank teller adding up a column of numbers who pays no attention to a customer who goes off to a good bank teller. And as he passes John again on the way out John comes up with the figure he had been adding up. There had been a lot of discussion at lunchtime as to what that should be and I seem to remember the most ordinary number was thought to be 42.'[3]

There are still further layers to this story. In a posthumous collection of Graham Chapman material, *Graham Crackers*, it was claimed that Chapman, who was not on that Video Arts shoot, had suggested 42 to Douglas as the answer to life, the universe and everything. In fact several short stories have circulated ascribing the idea directly or indirectly to Chapman, none of which are at all verifiable of course, with both parties being (a) notoriously inaccurate raconteurs and (b) deceased.

When asked about Chapman's claim, Douglas replied flatly: 'It's completely untrue.'[4] But after Douglas' death, when John Cleese was asked to verify the Video Arts anecdote, he claimed that he and Chapman had originally come up with 42 as the funniest number when they were first writing together in the 1960s.

Perhaps it's true, as Douglas often claimed that 42 is simply the funniest two-digit number. 'The funniest three-digit number,' he once pointed out, 'being 359.*'[5]

---

* Douglas found great humour in the significance of telephone numbers, so it is probably no coincidence that 359 was the dialling code for his home in Islington.

CHAPTER 14

THE VERY FIRST episode of *The Hitchhiker's Guide to the Galaxy* was broadcast on Radio 4 at 10.30 p.m. on Wednesday 8 March 1978. 'Much to Douglas' annoyance, the BBC decided they were going to put it out on Wednesday nights at 10.30 p.m.,' said Simon Jones, 'which they subsequently claimed was their tried and true tack of turning something into a cult hit: putting it on when nobody would listen.'[1]

The response was astounding. Over the course of six weeks listenership built at an exponential rate, purely through word of mouth. In the history of radio comedy, it was quite unprecedented. A couple of days after that first episode, Simon Brett bumped into Douglas: 'He said, "Have there been any press reviews?" and I said to him, rather patronisingly, "Oh Douglas, come on. This is a radio programme. You know how much coverage radio gets. Maybe at the end of the series there'll be a round-up in one of the papers saying: 'of the current comedies, this one was mildly amusing'." But he was absolutely right. That Sunday, at least two of the Sunday papers picked up on it.'[2] (One factor in the show's success, which has not been considered until now, is that there was simply nothing else on between 10.30 p.m. and 11.00 p.m. that evening. Radio 2 had a forgettable sitcom called *Malcolm*; BBC2 had a dramatisation of the Windscale Enquiry; BBC1 had a preview of the World Figure Skating Championships; Radio 3 had a documentary about the discovery of hepatitis B.)

'Halfway through the first run we got an audience figure in,' recalled Geoffrey Perkins, 'and it was 0.0, which meant that theoretically, no-one was listening to it. But I was getting twenty to thirty letters a day, maybe more. We really knew it was a hit when we got a letter which had just been addressed to "Megadodo Publications, Megadodo House, Ursa Minor", and somebody had written in the corner "Try BBC". I thought if the Post Office had heard of us, we must have made it.'[3]

The first episode of *Hitchhiker's* was featured in *Pick of the Week* and, in a cruel irony, Douglas finally sold a quickie to *Week Ending* in the week that 'Fit the Second' was broadcast. Because the audience had grown so quickly, many of those who heard the second half of the series had missed the first half and the letters clamouring for a repeat persuaded Radio 4 to rebroadcast the entire series from 23 April, only two weeks after the final episode had been broadcast. Then again six months after that. *The Hitchhiker's Guide to the Galaxy* was officially a hit.

In May 1978, desperate for a regular income, Douglas finally got himself a job – as a BBC radio producer. *Week Ending* was the BBC's proving ground for new producers as well as budding writers; unfortunately, Douglas was no better at producing the programme than he had been at writing for it. 'Well, *everybody's* produced *Week Ending*,' commented Douglas. 'I've produced it, John Lloyd's produced it, Geoffrey Perkins has produced it, Griff Rhys Jones has produced it – I mean everybody has. The Queen hasn't produced *Week Ending*, I know that. Not that she hasn't been asked, of course, but she was busy.'[4]

Douglas took over production from Griff Rhys Jones with the programme broadcast on 19 May 1978. Griff was back in the chair the next week, then Douglas took over for the five programmes broadcast 2 to 30 June, before handing back to Griff and never troubling the series again. The billed cast were David Jason, David Tate, Bill Wallis (all of whom had been in *Hitchhiker's*) and Sheila Steafel (who would make her own unique contribution to *Hitchhiker's* later). Chris Emmett from *The News Huddlines* and *The Burkiss Way* replaced Jason in a couple of the shows at the last moment because of TV commitments.

'There was a very curious period after we'd done the first series of *Hitchhiker's*, with Douglas having a hiatus as far as writing went,' remembers Geoffrey Perkins, 'and he was offered a job as a radio producer for a year. Just temperamentally, I'm not sure that's quite what Douglas was suitable for. I can remember being asked to go down to *Week Ending* when Douglas was doing it because there had been rumblings from the cast about how they weren't putting up with this for much longer. So I went down there to see what he was doing and it was like a mini object lesson in how not to direct actors. He would say to people, "Hmm, I'm not sure about that. Could you do it a bit more like John Cleese would do it?" I remember him talking away to the cast, a great, long speech with the talkback button down and you could see the actors trying to speak. I said, "Douglas, take your finger off the talkback button. You can't hear them talking to you."'[5]

Despite this, Douglas recalled his time on *Week Ending* as 'quite fun'.[6] His other producing jobs – if there were any – remain largely mysterious, although he cited a programme on the history of practical jokes for which he interviewed Max Bygraves and Des O'Connor. (John Lloyd: 'I did one of those. He might have done it with me.'[7]) Douglas contributed a sketch to a show called *Not Now, I'm Listening* (21 May 1978) and devised questions for two John Lloyd-produced editions of *The News Quiz* (26 August and 2 September 1978).

'I expect Danny Greenstone, the other producer, was away on leave,' says Lloyd, 'and I thought I'd give Douglas a go on the grounds that he was (a) brilliant, (b) my best friend, (c) we were great collaborators. It wasn't that it needed a lot of extra people, it was just more fun and much quicker to come up with the questions with somebody else. Trouble was Douglas was never any good at all with anyone else's formats. He could only do his stuff. He really, really wanted to be able to write one-liners for *The Two Ronnies* or sketches for *Week Ending* or whatever, but he just could not do it. You might as well have asked him to write thank-you letters in Korean. None of it made the slightest sense to him.'[8]

It was while Douglas and John Lloyd were both working for BBC radio that they chalked up one of the oddest credits of either career:

two episodes of a cartoon series called *Doctor Snuggles*. 'I listened to *The Hitchhiker's Guide to the Galaxy* and I thought it was wonderful,' recalls series creator Jeffrey O'Kelly. 'I told the producer that that's the kind of imagination I'd like to connect with my own. I think their agents had put them forward, and so John Lloyd and Douglas weighed in on *Doctor Snuggles* with me.'[9]

'I don't remember how the contract came our way, but I can say that, like every other collaboration we embarked on, it was immense fun,' remembers Lloyd. 'By that time we had adjoining offices in BBC Light Entertainment Radio, round the back of Broadcasting House, and we'd sit in one or other of the two offices and moonlight in the evenings. We got (I think) £500 for each script, one of which was called "Doctor Snuggles and the Nervous River". It was a fortune for us, when you consider that our BBC salaries would have been between £2,000 and £3,000 per annum. We loved writing animation because the only limits were our own imaginations. We also loved the fact that the Dutch producer was called Joop Visch, pronounced "Yoop Fish", his assistant was a young man called Wim Oops, and his secretary was called Veronica Plinck.'[10]

Douglas resigned his job in October to work on *Doctor Who*, but he left Radio 4 with one final legacy, *Black Cinderella II Goes East*, broadcast on Christmas Day 1978. This was a pantomime – a fairly straightforward version of *Cinderella*, despite the title – cast entirely from ex-Footlights personnel. Rob Buckman was Prince Charming and Peter Cook his brother Prince Disgusting, Richard Baker narrated, Tim Brooke-Taylor and Graeme Garden were the ugly sisters and John Pardoe MP, Deputy Leader of the Liberal Party, was the Liberal Prime Minister (something you would only find in a fairy tale). Music was by Nigel Hess and Nic Rowley with lyrics by Jeremy Browne: the team who had provided songs for the 1973 Footlights pantomime when Douglas had played King Groovy. The slightly vague writing/producing credit was: 'Script by Rory McGrath and Clive Anderson, with the assistance of the producer Douglas Adams and John Lloyd.' The biggest coup for Douglas was persuading John Cleese to appear (albeit on tape) as the Fairy Godperson, four years after he had sworn never again to work for BBC Radio (following a dispute over a banned sketch).

'I think the title was Douglas',' remembers Lloyd. 'He certainly had a huge amount of say over everything – casting, scripting etc. – except for doing the actual work. Producing wasn't Douglas' bag, to be perfectly frank, so I went along to the recording and helped him out a bit with the boring nuts and bolts. What made Douglas such a remarkable writer is that he would worry and worry away at a concept. Long after anybody else would have thought, "This is good enough," he would be still perfecting the lines and making them just that little bit extra. Which is why I think *Hitchhiker* lasts, the depth of thought that's gone into it.

'But at the kind of pressure we used to work with in radio, you have to know when to stop. You have to say, "All right, it's not perfect but that'll do. We'll sort that out later." Douglas was not capable of doing that. So with *Black Cinderella II*, it became pretty obvious that if Douglas was left in sole charge it wasn't going to happen. You couldn't have left it just with Douglas sitting there worrying in his genial way: "Maybe we should do this . . ." People would be drumming their fingers and chewing the carpet, wanting to get on with things.'[11]

Nevertheless, Douglas claimed, 'I was largely responsible for the project. John Lloyd helped on that one.'[12]

'I can remember Douglas being in the box, but it was John who I remember as the producer,' says Nic Rowley. 'It was really quite a hurry because of all those people being busy: rehearse and record in one day. My memory is of John being the technical organiser, with Douglas coming down the stairs from the room where the writers used to sit. I think probably what must have been happening was that John was technically directing and Douglas was working on any changes to the material at that time. But I don't remember Douglas being technically involved.'[13]

It was while Douglas was an actual BBC employee that he was commissioned, on 2 August 1978, to write a *Hitchhiker's Guide to the Galaxy* 'Christmas Special' and also a second series of the show, at a greatly improved fee of £345 per episode. Series Two was initially seven programmes, then six and it settled at five. The 'Christmas Special' (aka 'Fit the Seventh') was recorded on 20 November 1978 and broadcast on Christmas Eve.

'The Christmas episode was, to be honest, one of the traditions of BBC Radio: "Oh, the show has been a hit. Why don't you do a Christmas episode?",' explains Geoffrey Perkins. 'Clearly doing a Christmas episode of *Hitchhiker's* was a ludicrous idea. There was this original idea of actually basing it on the Nativity in which the guiding star turns out to be Marvin falling through the atmosphere. We did toy with that but we thought no, so we did it as an in-between episode.'[14]

By now, Perkins was familiar with Douglas' inability to deliver scripts on time and initiated the practice which would later become standard: 'I had to move in with Douglas for a few days while he worked on the script. I think I was one of the first people to do this.'[15] Despite this pressure, the script still wasn't finished when it came to recording and Douglas was forced to sit in an office at the Paris Studio typing on carbon paper booklets (called 'snappies') to produce multiple copies of his work which could be instantly distributed to the cast. Sometimes these last-minute pages contained surprising new events, or even new characters.

'A bit appeared with this character called Roosta,' remembers Perkins. 'He'd just written it in. I put the talkback button down and said, "Douglas seems to have written a character in called Roosta. Does anybody know any actors who they think are good who live near here?" Alan Ford got cast because he was a friend of Mark Wing-Davey.'[16]

The script saw Zaphod and Marvin arriving inexplicably at the offices of the *Hitchhiker's Guide*'s publishers, Megadodo Publications, a gigantic double skyscraper linked by a bridge halfway up ('The decadence and cool of the *Guide*'s offices was a sort of dig at *Time Out*,'[17] confided Douglas). One of the episode's highlights was a confrontation between Marvin and a giant Frogstar Robot Class D, on the bridge linking the towers, ending with the Frogstar Robot so enraged at the way Marvin has been treated that he shoots out the floor in frustration and plummets to his doom, many floors below. This scene was one of Douglas' favourites and reappeared in most, if not all, of the film drafts which he wrote over the years.

CHAPTER **15**

WHEN DOUGLAS WAS offered the post of *Doctor Who* script editor by Graham Williams on Anthony Read's departure, it was the last thing he expected: 'I was a bit stunned by that actually. Graham just phoned me up and said, "Do you want the job?" and I was, well, startled. It was straight out of the blue.'[1] (In actual fact, Williams proposed the idea to Douglas in the bar at Television Centre.) Douglas handed in his notice with BBC Radio and moved into the *Doctor Who* production office, just as Read was moving out: 'We tried to get an overlap period but the BBC wouldn't wear it because there isn't enough money to employ two script editors simultaneously. I chatted to him, we had a few drinks together, that's about it.'[2]

Not only was the handover perfunctory but it happened before the end of season 16, meaning that Douglas' first job was to work with Williams on an uncredited rewrite of the final scene of Bob Baker and Dave Martin's 'The Armageddon Factor', the culmination of the 'Key to Time' arc story, with the Doctor confounding the Black Guardian's plans.

This was a busy period for Douglas. A couple of weeks after taking on the *Doctor Who* job at the end of October, he described how packed his schedule had suddenly become: 'It's funny actually, because I'm trying desperately to write the second series of *Hitchhiker* at the moment, and in the meantime it's turning into a sort of mini-industry because I'm doing a book version for Pan

Books, which is going to be out late next year, assuming I manage to finish the bloody thing. It's supposedly being edited down into a double album, though the record company who are doing it are having financial difficulties at the moment, so what the future of that project is I don't know at the moment. And BBC TV are talking about turning it into an animated version as well. Plus of course *Doctor Who*, which makes for a very hectic workload!'[3] (Nothing else about the mooted animated series was ever mentioned but Douglas referred to 'the cartoon' later in the same interview, indicating that it wasn't just a slip of the tongue.)

Although 'The Pirate Planet' had been well received, Douglas had been criticised by some fans for injecting too much comedy into the show, something which he defended, saying that he intended that script to be played straighter than the actors and director had done: '"The Pirate Planet" trod a narrow dividing line between being outright funny and being dramatic. I always think this is the most interesting area to operate in, because humour is obviously an important part of *Doctor Who*, but it must never undercut the drama, it must always reinforce it. If *Doctor Who* starts getting too many gags in it, or just jokes, then that just completely throws everything out of the window.'[4]

'I wrote a treatment for a four-part adventure called "The Doomsday Contract" which I was extremely proud of,' recalls John Lloyd. 'I remember I had to work pretty hard on it because *Doctor Who* had hundreds of rules as to what you could or couldn't do. I don't know how close it got to being commissioned as a full script because almost immediately on delivery, I moved to BBC TV to produce *Not the Nine O'Clock News* and Douglas left *Doctor Who* to become full-time Douglas.'[5]

Douglas made a conscious effort to try and recruit established science fiction writers onto the programme, including novelists John Brunner and Christopher Priest: 'Douglas phoned me out of the blue,' recalls Priest. 'I had heard some of the first *Hitchhiker* series, although to be completely honest I didn't think it was nearly as funny or original as most other people seem to think. To me it wasn't as funny as some of the other Radio 4 comedy shows, nor was it at all original as science fiction. But it was okay and it had made a sufficient impression on me that I had noted the writer's name. When Douglas phoned I knew at once who he was. He said nothing about *Hitchhiker* but asked me if I'd ever thought of writing for *Doctor Who*.

'I said, "No thanks," and added some sort of rude and ribald comment. (You couldn't exactly describe me as a fan of *Doctor Who*: it has always seemed embarrassingly third-rate to me.) Douglas laughed and said, "Okay, fair enough." But they were making a genuine attempt to improve things. He mentioned a couple of other book writers he was approaching at the same time and said the BBC had given them a bigger budget, were prepared to work with the writers to get things right, they were paying top-whack writers' fees . . . and anyway why didn't I come in one day and have a lunch at the BBC's expense? The upshot of that was a four-part story, "Sealed Orders," which I wrote and was paid for, but by the time I delivered it Douglas had moved on and the series was back in its bad old ways.'[6]

Douglas commissioned numerous stories from various writers; the five which made it to the screen in some form were: 'Destiny of the Daleks' by Terry Nation, 'Nightmare of Eden' by Bob Baker, 'The Horns of Nimon' by Anthony Read, and 'The Gamble with Time' and 'The Creature from the Pit' by David Fisher. The final six-parter Douglas kept for himself.

'The best definition of my job is that until the time when the writer finishes the scripts I represent the BBC to the writer,' he explained, 'because I know what sort of shape the script has to have in the end – so I have to help the writer to mould his particular ideas into the way that *Doctor Who* works. Some writers latch onto it very quickly and others don't, one has to guide them.

'Then, once the scripts are finished and accepted, I change sides, because you are then representing the writer to the BBC, to the actors and director. It's a difficult job to define in more detail than that because there are grey areas that overlap with the producer's job. There's a slight friendly rivalry between me and Graham: we have to achieve a balance between us, because although I tend to have fairly outlandish ideas, and I do guide the writers quite a lot, responsibility eventually comes down to the producer and I can't take a decision that he doesn't agree with.'[7]

Douglas and Williams hit two big problems during the year they worked together. The first was David Fisher's 'The Gamble with Time', a Bulldog Drummond pastiche set in 1920s Monte Carlo. Williams requested some changes, including relocating the story to present-day Paris, but Fisher was unable to comply for personal reasons. 'He turned out to have been having terrible family problems, and he was in a real turmoil,' remembered Douglas. 'He'd done his best, but he didn't have a script that was going to work, and we were in deep trouble. This was Friday, and the producer came to me and said, "We've got a director coming on Monday, we have to have a new four-episode show by Monday!" So he took me back to his place, locked me in his study and hosed me down with whisky and black coffee for a few days, and there was the script.'[8]

The script which Douglas and Graham Williams wrote over 16–19 March 1979, based on Fisher's story, was credited to the pseudonymous David Agnew and retitled 'City of Death'. In May the cast and crew went to Paris for the series' first-ever overseas location work. Douglas tagged along but was sent back to London after a lengthy pub crawl with 'Destiny of the Daleks' director Ken Grieve. Studio recordings followed, during which Douglas discovered that John Cleese was available to make a cameo appearance. A scene was swiftly added in which two art connoisseurs (Cleese and Eleanor Bron) find the TARDIS in a gallery and sing its praises as a piece of modern art, although Douglas was never happy with the way the sequence was filmed.

'City of Death' found the Doctor and Romana on holiday in contemporary Paris, where they spot that something is up with time. Teaming up with a private detective called Duggan, they investigate the mysterious Count Scarlioni who turns out to be a hideous alien called Scaroth. The last of his race, his spaceship had exploded when he was orbiting Earth millions of years ago, somehow sending twelve different Scaroths to points in time, where they have been working to develop human technology to the point where time travel is possible. Scarlioni plans to raise funds for this project by selling six genuine *Mona Lisa*s which an earlier version of himself persuaded Leonardo da Vinci to paint, then use the completed time machine to travel back to primeval Earth and prevent the destruction of his spaceship. The Doctor, Romana and Duggan work together to prevent this happening after the Doctor realises that it was the destruction of Scaroth's ship which caused the creation of life on Earth in the first place.

The story was broadcast from 28 September 1979 and achieved, in its final week, the highest ratings ever for a *Doctor Who* episode. It remains a firm favourite with fans and is generally regarded as one of the fourth Doctor's finest adventures.

And then there was 'Shada'.

'I'll tell you the history of that programme,' said Douglas. 'I was down to write the six-parter at the end of that season. I had in mind a story that I wanted to do and the producer said, "No, that's over the top. I don't want to do that story. Come up with something else." I so much liked my story that I kept on and on about it, thinking that eventually he'd run out of time and have to accept that story because it would be ready to go. Well, he still wouldn't accept it. Finally, about three days before his director was due to join, I had to sit down and write something else. So I wrote "Shada" which was a last-minute panic thing to do. Didn't particularly like it. I thought it was rather thin – at most a mediocre four-parter stretched out over six parts.'[9]

Douglas' rejected idea involved the Doctor becoming fed up with constantly battling evil. He would attempt to retire, but would be called on to save the universe once more when it was threatened by a race of cricket-playing robots – it was another attempt at 'The Krikkitmen'. Tom Baker liked the idea but Williams saw it as too much of a send-up. Douglas wondered how you could send up a programme about a man who flies around the universe in a police box with a bag of jelly babies and a robot dog.

The story Douglas wrote instead, initially entitled 'Sunburst', saw the Doctor and Romana visiting Cambridge University and an elderly don named Professor Chronotis, in reality a retired Time Lord who has been at the same college for 300 years without anybody noticing. He wants the Doctor to return an important book which he borrowed from the main library on Gallifrey, but the book has accidentally fallen into the hands of a student, Chris Parsons. An evil alien named Skagra, in collaboration with a crystalline race called the Krargs, needs the book in order to locate the prison planet Shada and the exiled Time Lord criminal Salyavin. After the usual cliffhangers and escapes, the Doctor defeats Skagra and normality is restored. (Of course, Douglas couldn't resist a few Cambridge in-jokes. Chris Parsons has a friend named Clare Keightley, a reference to former Footlights President Chris Keightley.)

Location work was done in Cambridge in October, with Emmanuel College as the fictional St Cedd's, Douglas' *alma mater* of St John's having refused permission to film there. ('Douglas was disappointed that John's wouldn't play ball,' says Keith Jeffrey. 'Those were the bad old days when colleges had principles and wouldn't sell their soul for the sight of some commissioning editor.'[10]) However, studio recording in November fell victim to strike action by BBC technicians and when the dispute was cleared up, *Doctor Who* was judged to be a lower priority than other strike-hit shows and the production, due for broadcast from 19 January 1980, was formally abandoned in December.

'Shada' was the final *Doctor Who* story for both Douglas and Graham Williams, for whom a joint farewell party was held at Television Centre on 14 December. Douglas had decided to resign in August and the cancellation was a blessing in disguise, allowing him more time to work on his remaining *Hitchhiker's* radio scripts and the pilot script for the TV series. Incoming producer John Nathan-Turner made an attempt to remount and complete the production the following year, asking Douglas to rewrite the story into a four-parter, but this eventually came to nothing and in June 1980 the existing footage was consigned to the BBC archives. '"Shada" wasn't that great,' said Douglas. 'It's only acquired a notoriety because it wasn't made. It's much more alive in people's imaginations because of that.'[11]

But 'Shada' refused to die. In 1983, *Doctor Who* celebrated twenty years with 'The Five Doctors' in which Tom Baker declined to appear, so footage from 'Shada' was incorporated into the programme. And in 1987 Douglas reworked ideas from 'Shada' and 'City of Death' into *Dirk Gently's Holistic Detective Agency*. Then in 1992 'Shada' was announced for video release – and no-one was more surprised than Douglas. 'It was one of those things that somehow or other had got though the net,' he said. 'I tend to get sent lots of stuff to sign and assume that it all has been okayed. So I don't have to look too closely, I just sign stuff. And whoever it was had forgotten that I wanted "Shada" sat on.'[12]

Douglas requested that his name be taken off the video sleeve, then decided to donate his royalties to Comic Relief, which meant that it made sense to put his name back on the sleeves, but by then they had been printed, so a sticker was added. Tom Baker filmed some linking material to cover the missing scenes, and a facsimile of the rehearsal script was included.

Reference books will tell you that Douglas wrote/co-wrote three *Doctor Who* stories: 'Shada', 'The Pirate Planet' and 'City of Death'. In fact, Douglas contributed to the scripts of four *Doctor Who*s – five if you include 'The Armageddon Factor'. 'When I was working as a writer, I assumed it was the writer's job to write and the editor's job to edit,' he said, 'but I discovered when I became script editor that most writers thought it was the other way round! There was one particular writer who shall remain nameless who actually gave us a script which was basically a series of jotted notes with a few explosions in it, so one had to write that almost from the ground up.'[13]

Douglas judiciously declined to specify the script in question, but did offer the following comments: 'I'm not sure how much I should say about this as I wasn't involved in the writing, officially speaking. When you did a Dalek script it had to be done by Terry Nation – a canny fellow, and very charming. He had to get paid for the script, but the script he brought forward was a couple of explosions and a couple of people running up a corridor. So you had to turn that lot into a story.'[14]

With both parties deceased, it is a matter of conjecture how much work Douglas had to do on Nation's script. 'Jotted notes with a few explosions' is clearly an exaggeration, but by the same token it seems clear that Douglas' involvement was more than a normal script editor's role. His touch was most evident in the nearest thing to a *Hitchhiker/Who* crossover, when the Doctor glanced briefly at a book by Oolon Colluphid (an off-screen *Hitchhiker's* character based on John Allegro, author of religious conspiracy texts).

'*Doctor Who* at that point was quite literally driving me mad,' said Douglas. 'I had far more work to do on the scripts than I expected, and it was hurting my radio stuff, which put a lot of pressure on me. I've never liked pressure.'[15] That may sound an odd comment from a man who took on radio scripts, TV scripts and a novel simultaneously, but it is also significant. It was not the only time Douglas referred to being 'driven mad' by work, clearly meaning actual psychological problems and not just annoyance.

'I eventually did go mad at one point when I was living in a flat in Roehampton,' he admitted in one particularly candid interview (this would have been while working with Chapman). 'I can remember spending an entire day crouched behind the sofa crying. I mean, it was that extreme. I think that was probably about the closest I ever came to killing myself. I then moved in with my mother and stepfather. My mother was terrific. I must have been hellish to be with at that stage, because I was completely immobile, and just overwhelmed with depression. But my mother was very, very supportive, and I have always been very grateful for that.

'Because I had got rather fat and unwell, I started to make myself run round the country lanes. Outside the house was a hill, and I remember the first time I tried it, I managed just about 100 yards up the hill, and thought, "This is absolutely going to kill me," which made me feel even more depressed. But I stuck at it, and after a while I was running five miles two or three times a week. And that eventually played a very, very major part in the psychological battle to get myself up and functioning.'[16]

Running round the country lanes was feasible in Stalbridge but was not an option in Islington or Los Angeles. Ever after, Douglas would combat work-related stress with strenuous physical exercise in the gym . . .

Among the lasting legacies of Douglas' time on *Doctor Who* were two friendships: with Tom Baker, who worked again with Douglas on *Hyperland** ('I was always disappointed that Douglas didn't

---

* See Chapter 34.

ask me to do *Hitchhiker*,'[17] he once said) and who was occasionally let loose to run the bar at Douglas' parties; and with Lalla Ward (Romana) who subsequently met her future husband, biologist Richard Dawkins, through Douglas.

Overall, Douglas enjoyed his time on *Doctor Who*: 'I had been a fan when I was at school. It was fun to do for a year, but that was quite enough.'[18] Except that it wasn't enough. Douglas and Tom Baker also attempted to interest people in the 'Krikkitmen' idea as a film treatment in April 1978 (partially reprinted in *Don't Panic*). Douglas then became involved with another abortive *Doctor Who* film project for Paramount in 1980. Most frustratingly of all, in the few weeks between the BBC's acquisition of *h2g2* and Douglas' death, he was in talks with Alan Yentob about ... something to do with *Doctor Who*. Might this have been a follow-up to the web-based serial 'Death Comes to Time', guest-starring his friend Stephen Fry? Or a follow-up to the Comic Relief special 'The Curse of Fatal Death' starring his friend Rowan Atkinson? Or something new, perhaps a fortieth anniversary special for 2003? We may never know.*

---

* In November 2002 came the unexpected announcement that BBCi had recorded 'Shada' as an internet audio serial for 'webcast' in Spring 2003. According to the publicity, 'Shada' is a 'lost classic', the recording of which is a fine tribute to Douglas Adams. This, as we have seen, does not exactly square with Douglas' own comments on the story ...

CHAPTER 16

'A PUBLISHER CAME and asked me to write a book,' said Douglas, 'which is a very good way of breaking into publishing.'[1]

'I was the commissioning editor of Pan Books in 1978,' says Nick Webb, 'and I heard *Hitchhiker's Guide* on the radio. I was immediately won over by it so I beat a path to his agent's door. We haggled and I bought the rights. I wasn't the only publisher to be interested; one or two other people had also heard it and thought it was wonderful. I bought the rights and then, showing my normal gift for timing, promptly left before the book became an enormous bestseller.'[2]

'Don't let Nick Webb take too much credit for it,' cautions Jill Foster. 'I felt he always took too much credit for Douglas and I just wanted to scream: "No, actually Douglas came up with this idea, and Douglas wrote it." But I mustn't be nasty. Nick certainly was a moving spirit in getting the book published. There were a mass of publishers to whom we could have sold it, but you have to choose one in the end, don't you?'[3]

'There was a brilliant letter,' remembers Geoffrey Perkins, 'from the oxymoronic BBC Enterprises, turning down the book and the record of *Hitchhiker's*. It said, "Thank you very much for asking us. Unfortunately we can't do this. In our experience, books and records of radio shows don't sell." Apart from the belated irony of the books of *Hitchhiker's*, actually if you look at the top ten bestseller lists around the time that *Hitchhiker's* came out, it was chock-a-block full of books that had big radio tie-ins: *Adrian Mole* and books of *Quote . . . Unquote*. The overlap between the Radio 4 audience and the book-buying audience is huge. Years later, Douglas and I had a lunch with some people from BBC Enterprises where this guy said, "We've made a bit of a cock-up and frankly we'd like to have some of the merchandising rights back." Douglas, in a rather magnanimous mood, gave them quite a lot of these rights and to the best of my knowledge they never did anything with them at all.'[4]

The contract with Pan for a paperback novel based on the radio scripts was signed on 18 August 1978. (Hardback rights were sold to Arthur Barker Ltd, who published the book a few months after Pan in February 1980, aimed largely at libraries and therefore now very rare indeed.) Having bought the book, Webb then had to persuade his bosses that it was a good idea: 'We all sat around the table in this airless room in the middle of Pan Books. The editorial director was there, Sonny Mehta, and the sales director and all my editorial colleagues. I think I was the only person who had actually heard the radio programme, and there was a certain amount of cynical disbelief. But I had bought the book by then anyway, which was naughty of me, because I was quite junior, I didn't really have the power to spend the company's money without getting the say-so from The Powers That Be. I think they all looked at it a little bit as Nick's indulgence.'[5]

Douglas was absolutely delighted at the chance to write a novel: 'I thought it was an enormous opportunity because obviously most people have a horrendous amount of difficulty writing a novel on spec and then trying to get anybody interested in it. And I knew that I suddenly had a chance here to pole-vault through all of that.'

The one slight problem was that, of the three hours of *Hitchhiker*, twenty-five minutes had been written by John Lloyd: 'While the series was still going out on air, Douglas and I were lunched by (I think) six different publishers. We easily liked Nick Webb the best, and agreed to do the book with him for an advance of £3,000 between us. We booked a villa on the wrong side of Corfu for a month in order to write it on the strength of that.'[7] Between booking the holiday and actually leaving for Greece, however, Douglas had a change of heart and wrote to Lloyd, explaining that he had decided to write the novel alone.

'I asked John how he would feel about collaborating on the book because I felt very nervous at that point,' recalled Douglas. 'Then I thought about it a bit more and thought, "No, actually I can do it myself." I didn't handle it very well so John was very disappointed. Johnny and I are very good friends and so we're incredibly good at rubbing each other up the wrong way from time to time. I rashly talked about maybe we should think about collaborating and then changed my mind and that was perfectly within my rights. On the other hand, I should have handled it a bit better.'[8]

'I was very hurt and very angry, to be honest,' says Lloyd. 'It was a dreadful shock – particularly as I don't think Douglas had ever written me a letter of any variety before. But Douglas' letter provided the impetus for me to go and ask for a job in television, so I owe him a favour really. It means we can both, after all, point to work that we can truly claim to be our own. With hindsight, I think there's some truth in the idea that Douglas needed to keep his vision pure, and I have to say I've never, ever resented the situation after those first few weeks of disappointment.

'I went and got an agent in order to secure my half-share of the advance (which, poor as we both were, I had already spent in anticipation). I had to work hard to dissuade him from what he wanted to do – which was demand ten per cent of everything with the name *Hitchhiker* on it in perpetuity! I didn't want anything like that. I couldn't possibly have lived with myself. And I have to say that I have never, ever resented Douglas' success (still less the money) which was hard-won and thoroughly deserved.'[9]

Having booked the villa, Lloyd saw no reason why he should not at least enjoy the holiday while Douglas slaved over his typewriter. Keeping him company was Mary Allen, who has terrible memories of the location: 'When Douglas was asked by Pan to write a book, he decided that what he needed was some time to himself. So he and John Lloyd booked a villa on the west coast of Corfu. Just before they went out, they began to get a hint that this wasn't a particularly attractive part of Corfu because Simon Brett had just been to that very village, and came back and said, "For Heaven's sake, whatever you do, rent a car. You've got to be able to get out of it." I actually wasn't told this when Douglas said, "Mary, we're going on holiday: me, Johnny, Corfu, could be good. Why don't you come too?"

'It was September, the weather was atrocious, it was very windy. There were two rooms in this villa, and John Lloyd was writing in one of those rooms and Douglas was writing in the other room. So anyone who wanted to do anything else had to sit outside, which meant wrapping yourself up in a blanket, and if you were trying to read a book, having a pair of pegs so that you could actually keep the pages down.

'Douglas is a writer who needs to test his material against anyone he can find. So every so often you would hear: "Mary, can you just hear the last few pages?" And Douglas would then come out and read you his pages and would receive comments. It was very, very funny, but of course, once you'd heard it about fifteen times, it wasn't quite so funny. It was a terrible holiday, absolutely ghastly. This place was just as unpleasant as Simon Brett had predicted.'[10]

Pan Books had set publication for October 1979. They hadn't exactly hyped the book, but they had done some advertising, and had commissioned two covers: the familiar psychedelic one that was used and an earlier abandoned design showing an astronaut thumbing a lift to Alpha Centauri. By the end of the holiday, Douglas had written about twenty pages.

'Douglas was very keen to turn *Hitchhiker's* into a book, he really was,' recalls Jill Foster. 'It was only after a while that he discovered what hard work it was writing a book! And I don't think he entirely got over that. I'm not knocking him, he's like masses of writers. You know what it's like: the fear is wonderful, but the sitting down and writing it – they're all stars at displacement activities, aren't they? There's no doubt, he did find it very hard work. And sometimes, even with radio, we had to do quite a bit of bullying, I seem to remember. No agent is worth their salt unless they're good at the bullying, and frightening their clients into meeting delivery dates. Or not too long afterwards.'[11]

'The first book ends somewhat suddenly,' explained Douglas, 'and the reason for this was because: this was the first book and the publishers were already getting fed up with waiting for me to finish it – and after a while somebody phoned me up and said, "Look, for Heaven's sake, finish the page you're on and let us have it!" So I did! Which is why I have to write the second one. Everybody's been too polite to mention how abruptly it finishes.'[12]

This is another oft-repeated story, but once again it may not be completely true. There are some smoking guns here, not least that Douglas' then editor, Caroline Upcher, has no memory of any such request. In contemporary interviews Douglas said that the book covered only the first four radio episodes because he didn't want to use any co-written material and, 'I also wanted to keep those last two episodes for the end of the second book.'[13] The first *Hitchhiker's* album, scripted simultaneously, also only covers 'Fits the First to Fourth', where 'finish the page you're on' clearly doesn't apply, and the simple truth is that the book actually ends in *just the right place*.

With the characters escaping the galactic cops thanks to Marvin's destruction of their spaceship, there is a narrative conclusion and Arthur as hero has completed his emotional journey from naive Earthman to galactic traveller, browsing the electronic *Guide* to discover more about the universe he now calls home. The story does *not* stop suddenly, and Douglas had no more radio scripts left to adapt, so 'finish the page you're on' sounds like another exaggeration. (The most likely truth is that he was *re-writing* the novel and asked to finish working on whatever page he was on; that makes sense and fits the known facts.)

'True, I don't know. Credible, certainly,' is John Lloyd's opinion. 'Douglas never realised just how much grief he would cause by not delivering on time. That's why you get all those great jokes about the Pan executive saying, "Finish the page you're on." Because obviously most book editors don't go around saying things like that, but the extremity of the situation with Douglas always forced people to behave in an uncharacteristically bonkers way.'[14]

And so, the day of publication approached.

'One evening, Douglas and I met in Leicester Square for a few drinks and a meal,' recalls Christopher Priest. 'As we walked down to the nearest pub we passed a bookshop. Douglas suddenly noticed they had copies of *Hitchhiker* on sale: "My God, it's out already!"

He wanted to walk by, but I persuaded him to go in and have a look. Inside the shop we discovered that all the shelves along one entire wall had been stocked with copies. Douglas was, to say the least, amazed. I introduced him to the man standing by the till, who practically passed out with surprise. He was Douglas' first fan, I think. Douglas blushed bright red: I had never seen anyone look so discomfited and pleased at the same time.'[15]

A few days later came that legendary signing session at Forbidden Planet: 'Initially *Hitchhiker's* didn't make much penetration, it seemed to me, into the science fiction field,' recalls Stan Nicholls. 'But there I am in the shop, and suddenly word of mouth started to come up, it started to get a bit of a buzz. People would come in and say, "Are you taping it too?" I remember also having conversations with Nick Webb who could see the publishing potential in it. I said to my boss, Nick Landau, "Let's do a signing with Douglas Adams," and he said, "Who?" Which is not a criticism of Nick, it's just that most people hadn't heard of it. So we went to Pan and said, "Let's do this." We set it up and we did a flier, basically taking a bit of a gamble on it. We knew it was popular on the radio but we didn't know if a book would work. As indeed Pan didn't know a book would work.[16]

'We needn't have worried. Books evaporated like pan-galactic gargleblasters in a drought. It was the best signing the shop had ever had, and was only surpassed when the second book came out. Years went by before anybody else came near to matching it. Douglas was obviously dumbfounded by this zoo. People presented him with poems and crayon sketches of his characters, and in extreme cases sang at him – but he handled it brilliantly. When we finally ushered out the last straggler and bolted the doors, long after the signing was supposed to have finished, the adrenaline was still flowing.'[17]

The legend that later sprang up around this signing was not helped by subsequent press coverage: 'The diary section of the *Evening Standard* carried an item on it and was rather critical of Douglas. I think the publicist at Pan Books had rung the *Standard* and said, "Douglas Adams has just had this wonderful signing." So they rang him, and Douglas said that he had signed more than 1,500 books an hour. The *Standard* had worked it out and said, "This is not possible. You couldn't do that. Are you really saying you signed 6,000 books?" Not for the first time I have to say – and I'm not being critical of Douglas – there was an element of exaggeration.'[18]

There was also an element of exaggeration in Douglas' claim that the book, 'went to number one in the bestseller list in the first week of publication and stayed there,'[19] which was faithfully repeated by many journalists, not least Nicholas Wroe in the *Salmon of Doubt* prologue: 'Next day his publisher called to say he was number one in the *Sunday Times* bestseller list.'[20] Like the tale of the crowds outside the shop, this story was accepted without question and nobody ever thought to check the bestseller lists to see if it was true.

For one thing, a book published on Friday 12 October could not possibly make the bestseller list on Sunday 14; sales for its first week would appear in the *Sunday Times* on 21 October. However, no *Sunday Times* bestseller list was published on that date (or any Sunday that month) as industrial action prevented the paper from being printed throughout October 1979. Bestseller lists were still published, however, in the trade magazine *The Bookseller* and the issue dated 27 October 1979 (hence on sale from Saturday 20) lists *The Hitchhiker's Guide to the Galaxy*'s debut in the paperback charts – at number nine. It was number one in its second and third week, was replaced by a Graham Greene novel and then a Giles annual, then topped the list for another week before dropping again. By anybody's standards, this is an exceptional success for a debut novel – it's just not quite as exceptional as the version which Douglas, for some reason, believed. He must have known the truth at some point, but once again his memory became corrupted.

'Feelings of wonder and joy,' is what Jill Foster remembers from this time. 'My husband, who represents Gareth Edwards, and I were going to buy some curtain material and we walked past W.H. Smith in Sloane Square. There were two windows: one was taken up with *Hitchhiker* and the other with Gareth Edwards' autobiography. We stood there and smirked at these windows; we just thought it was wonderful!

'And Douglas loved it, he absolutely loved it. He went out and he bought his Porsche and I think he adored that. I remember we went to Wales to see the *Hitchhiker's* play and he broke the speed limit all the way there and only half the way back because I said, "Douglas, please, it would be awfully nice if we're still alive when we get home." He was very young, he thought it was wonderful. He made problems of it later and I don't know why, I don't know what went on in his head. I know a lot of writers who can't meet delivery dates. But certainly in those initial years he had a wonderful time. He was a young man with lots of money, lots of recognition, his fast car, and undoubtedly his girls – though his agent obviously didn't know that side of things!'[21]

INTERLUDE - GENRE

THOUGH *THE HITCHHIKER'S* Guide to the Galaxy was a hit on radio and a bestseller when it was published, reception among the science fiction community was mixed. Douglas had not emerged from, and didn't seem to embrace, science fiction fandom, and there was concern that he was receiving acclaim for breaking new ground which had already been well explored. There was no doubt that Douglas was well read, but how well read was he when it came to science fiction?

Nick Webb recalls, 'We talked mainly about science fiction and the people that we had read. Robert Sheckley, we talked about, and Bob Shaw. We just enthused about science fiction.'[1]

'Douglas shared with me an interest in comedy and science fiction,' remembers Andrew Marshall. 'I recall once staying up literally all night talking with him about various books including Robert Sheckley's *Dimension of Miracles* which was always one of my favourites, and the works of Philip K. Dick and Robert Silverberg.'[2]

'On that first occasion he just hung out with us in the Forbidden Planet basement after the signing,' recalls Stan Nicholls. 'We started talking about science fiction and that ended up with me going round the shelves of the shop with him following me with a box. "Have you read this?" "No." "You've got to read this. Have you read that?" I certainly got the impression that Douglas hadn't actually read much SF. He seemed to be a bit lost.'[3]

'Douglas had almost nothing to say about science fiction (or not that I can remember),' says Christopher Priest. 'I know on one occasion I asked him in a tentative sort of way if he'd ever read Robert Sheckley or Fredric Brown or William Tenn. My impression always was that the existence of an established SF genre had come as a bit of a surprise to him, and that although he had read a few SF books (mine among them) it wasn't the source of inspiration many people would like to think it was.'[4]

Nevertheless, Douglas occasionally offered comments on other SF authors: J.G. Ballard – 'I do have a liking for his early work'[5]; Iain Banks (who incorporated Douglas' books into the plot of *Walking on Glass*) – 'I've never been able to get around to finishing one of his stories'[6]; H.G. Wells – 'I've read *The War of the Worlds* and *The Time Machine* but I can't remember them making a great impression on me'[7]; Isaac Asimov – 'I wouldn't employ him to write junk mail'[8]; Arthur C. Clarke – 'His writing is a little dull perhaps'[9]; Walter M. Miller Jr – '*A Canticle for Leibowitz* is a wonderful book'[10]; A.E. Van Vogt – 'Before you actually get to the story, you have to wade through pages and pages of Vogt telling you how brilliant he is and then how brilliant the story you are about to read is. Unfortunately this is a claim which isn't usually borne out by the story when you eventually read it.'[11]

The only two SF writers whom Douglas constantly cited as inspiration were Kurt Vonnegut ('I derive a great deal of pleasure reading anything by him,'[12] he said, later qualifying this by saying that he only liked three early Vonnegut novels) and Robert Sheckley, to whom he was often compared: 'People kept saying, "If you write this stuff, do you know the work of Sheckley?" So I finally sat down and read *Dimension of Miracles*, and it was quite creepy. There are coincidences, and though they're very tempting to people there are after all only a small number of ideas. I got to meet Sheckley and had lunch with him in New York.'[13]

It's all very contradictory. Douglas' friends recall him being an SF reader, while SF professionals who knew him found him largely unread in the genre, yet he could offer an opinion on numerous writers, from Van Vogt to Vonnegut. The answer to the mystery perhaps lies in Douglas' answer to the question, 'Are you actually interested in science fiction?': 'Yes and no. I always thought I was until I discovered this enormous subculture and met people and found I knew nothing about it whatsoever.'[14]

CHAPTER 17

WHEN THE PAPERBACK of *Hitchhiker's Guide* was published, there was an advert on the back page: 'Don't Panic! *The Hitchhiker's Guide to the Galaxy* double LP can be yours for only £6.99. Megadodo Publications in association with Original Records brings you the unreal thing itself.' The story behind the LPs of *Hitchhiker's Guide* and *Restaurant* . . . (advertised in the back of the second book under the headline 'Panic Now!') is complex and messy and told here for the first time.

Original Records was an independent record label established in 1977 by Laurence Aston, former Deputy MD of Transatlantic Records, primarily to release the works of jazz composer Mike Westbrook, whom he managed. A handful of other avant-garde/jazz recordings had also been released on the label when Aston heard *Hitchhiker's* on its first or second repeat in 1978 and realised that it was something special: 'The production made you want to hear each episode again to capture all the details, characters and references. "Aha!" I thought. "This would make a brilliant LP with a ready-made audience." So I contacted Geoffrey Perkins to see whether the BBC was planning an album version and, if not, who had the rights. He offered to investigate, but it took several weeks of persistent calls, running eventually into six months, before I got an answer.'[1]

BBC Enterprises had of course turned down the offer of a record along with the book, and had only ever bought the broadcast rights to Douglas' scripts, so recording rights were up for grabs. Aston got in touch with Jill Foster: 'Jill and Douglas seemed open to the idea of me handling the record rights and they asked me to make them an offer. The deal I proposed was relatively simple. An advance of £500 against a modest "artist" royalty for Douglas. Original Records would pay all recording and manufacturing costs and royalties would be payable to Douglas when those were recouped. Jill would help to secure a page in the back of the paperback.'[2]

(Foster's memories of this contract are not good ones: 'I don't like to talk about it – it was a disaster. It was the first and only time I've trusted a lawyer to help me through something I wasn't that familiar with. I should have listened to my own instincts.'[3])

'In 1978 the "audiobook" market was in its infancy,' explains Aston. 'The record industry was going through one of its regular periods of turmoil and the economy was generally in very poor shape. I knew from my years at Transatlantic that a specialist spoken word album could not be sold conventionally. There were not enough record shops with spoken word departments or racks, and those that did have them were poorly managed.'[4] (Although spoken word comedy albums sold well in the seventies, *Hitchhiker's* was seen as a dramatisation rather than comedy.) 'I knew there was a sizable audience for *Hitchhiker's* on LP and tape and my idea was to turn the conventional marketing strategy on its head and make the album available only through one source – the ad in the book – allowing buyers to feel they were members of a unique, almost secret club. Also, each copy sold would deliver a higher profit margin, enabling Original Records to recover the recording and manufacturing costs over a smaller number of units.'[5]

With the first album roughly equivalent to the first four radio episodes, a second LP was under consideration, to be launched alongside the second novel which Pan had optioned, and/or the second radio series. Unlike the book rights, when Nick Webb had had to compete with other interested publishers, nobody else seemed keen to re-record *Hitchhiker*, or even to distribute Original Records' albums. (Although Geoffrey Perkins recalls one previous approach from a now-forgotten company: 'We agreed to do a record with these people who were very sneaky. I can remember them getting us to sign some contract while watching a hardcore porn movie that was going on in the corner, and of course having never really seen hardcore porn it was a bit distracting. I think we signed it and then they just disappeared.'[6])

As well as Douglas' 'artist' royalty, Aston helpfully suggested an industry wrinkle which could earn Douglas more money: performing and mechanical rights were assigned to Original Music (Original Records' sister company), which could then register them with the Performing Rights Society and the Mechanical Copyright Protection Society. Douglas thereby received a second £500 advance and a second revenue stream which he otherwise would have missed out on.

With Geoffrey Perkins' help, Douglas condensed the first four radio scripts into four LP sides. Most of the original radio cast were retained, although Trillian was recast, as Susan Sheridan was working on a Disney cartoon. Respected avant-garde composer Tim Souster, who was managed by Aston, provided new music and recorded a new version of the signature tune 'Journey of the Sorcerer': 'I could see why the thing became a cult when I played my music to Douglas Adams,' he commented. 'He'd say, "Wonderful, Tim – but can you make it more concave?"'[7]

'As a whole production set-up I was quite pleased with the records,' recalls Perkins. 'It was nice to do something just slightly more high-tech than we'd done at the BBC. There were certainly some additions that were written for the records which remained for the television show and the books; Douglas had a bit more time, although you never have enough time.'[8]

Original Records, which had been a one-man operation (Aston had taken out a personal loan to cover *Hitchhiker's* recording costs) took on Don Mousseau, who garnered some useful PR for the album. Records and tapes sold through the advert in the book and a few magazine ads, and an exclusive deal for retail sales was signed with the Virgin Megastore in Oxford Street, who paid upfront for a large order of albums. With the book riding high in the bestseller charts, the radio series repeated again, and positive reviews in the music and sci-fi press, things were looking good by Christmas 1979.

A company called Stage One then approached Original Records and signed a deal to distribute the album to shops around the UK. Stage One had just installed a new computer system to handle their sales and accounting, and there lay the start of the problem. The computer became operational in January 1980 while Aston was in Cannes at a trade fair; when he called Stage One for sales figures he was pleased to find, after a few teething troubles, that they had sold 2,000 units on the first day. Aston called again the next day and was told that a further 2,300 units had been sold, with another 2,500 units the day after.

'I checked with Stage One to make sure this was a daily figure, not a cumulative one, and they confirmed it was daily, calculated by the new computer on the basis of orders received,' remembers Aston, recalling a classic ely.* 'We had a stock of 10,000 albums in the warehouse and no spare sleeves. At this rate we would exhaust the stock in one week and need to re-press immediately. I waited till the fourth day and the figure was over 2,600 units, so I pushed the button to re-press sufficient stock to cover a chart album for a month: 20,000 additional units and another 10,000 sleeves to cope with the next re-pressing. However, it was only when we got back to London the following week that Stage One admitted they had made an elementary error, blaming the computer: they had given us the cumulative sales figure as if it was daily. We were facing a classic cock-up: we could not stop the re-pressing order by this time, the sales were not there to pay for the re-pressing and we would be lumbered with enough stock for a year, instead of just a month. The storage cost alone was to be a millstone around our necks.'⁹

A consequence of this overstock was that Original Records were owed a considerable VAT rebate – just as the staff of Customs and Excise went on strike. Firing an incompetent accountant, hiring a new one and then explaining the situation to the Inland Revenue cost more money and generated more stress. To top it all, a complaint from Douglas' former schoolmate Paul Neil Milne Johnstone had required a re-edit of the master-tape to remove

* See Chapter 24

his name from the recording. However, by paying themselves no salaries or fees and personally guaranteeing an overdraft, Aston and Mousseau were able to pay Douglas' royalties (including his share of an advance from an Australian distributor) and some of their overheads.

But there was a light at the end of the tunnel. The *Hitchhiker's* TV series, scheduled for January 1981, was expected to boost interest in the album; Geoffrey Perkins had introduced Aston and Mousseau to pop parodists the HeeBeeGeeBees, who had chart potential; and the bank was prepared to arrange their finances so that they had enough capital to record the album of *The Restaurant at the End of the Universe.*

The second LP, using the Disaster Area storyline rather than the Haggunenon one from the radio series, was recorded in summer 1980 and the cast, who had been on flat fees for the first album, signed royalty agreements, expecting it to match that success. In total, the *Hitchhiker's* album sold about 30,000 copies mail order and the same number retail over its eighteen months of release. The *Restaurant . . .* album was heavily promoted, widely distributed and supported by a single of Souster's theme music – and also sold about 60,000 copies before being deleted after six months.

'We spent a fortune on display advertising in the pop and national press, in-store display material, radio promotion of the single, and editorial tie-ins with the launch of the TV series,' recalls Aston. 'With the bigger more visible campaign of Album Two and the TV programme running, we expected to at least double the figures of Album One. Could it be that there were in fact only 60,000 people in the UK, out of the one million who bought the book, that were prepared to part with more money to buy the albums?'[10]

In retrospect, it is completely logical that *The Hitchhiker's Guide to the Galaxy Part Two – The Restaurant at the End of the Universe* would only sell to people who already owned Part One (although to be fair, the paperback of *Restaurant . . .* apparently outsold that of *Hitchhiker's* and the *Life . . .* paperback outsold both – for which there is no logical explanation). Another problem for Original Records was that they were unable to orchestrate a hoped-for US licensing deal, negotiations with Arista having broken down over the small print. Furthermore, it became clear that a second TV series, which would have supported a possible third album, was not going to happen. And the HeeBeeGeeBees had failed to make the charts, their album only just covering its costs.

Douglas, meanwhile, claimed that the second album should not have been released without further editing: 'Geoffrey Perkins and I were annoyed about that. We did a rough tape but it was far too long and a bit woolly, and we decided to leave it for a few days and come back and edit it with a fresh mind. Meanwhile, unbeknownst to us, the record company had taken the rough tape and put it out. Which is why that record is (a) very long on both sides and (b) full of blah.'[11] (Aston is sure that the released album, though undoubtedly overlong, was not a rough tape.)

'Even though *Restaurant* was a top 50 album for a brief period in the autumn of 1980,' recalls Aston, 'the revenue was not enough to repay everyone in the production, as well as the cost of marketing, sales commission and manufacture, and we were forced to slow down the outflow of cash to avoid exceeding our borrowing at the bank. It was altogether a disheartening and difficult period. Eventually the tap ran dry and we had to cut back severely to keep afloat. This meant, among other things, holding back royalties until we could trade our way out of debt.'[12]

By this time, Original Records had a new distributor, RCA, but Douglas had a new agent, Ed Victor, altogether a tougher negotiator than Jill Foster. For all that she worked well with Douglas, Foster was primarily a TV and radio agent. Victor was in America when Douglas first tried to contact him but returned the call immediately on his return: 'He said he wanted to talk about having an agent. So I said, "I'd love to see you," and he said, "When would you like to do that?" and I said, "How about now?" So he said, "Fine." So he came around to my office, I mean literally he was there in a half an hour, and we spoke for two and a half hours without stop. At the end of which he said, "I like you. I'd like you to be my agent." I said, "You don't want to think this over?" He said, "No, I don't want to think it over." So we became pals and agents in that minute.'[13]

'We attempted to discuss the situation openly with Ed Victor,' remembers Aston, 'who refused to help in any way and threatened to wind up the company unless we paid off the overdue royalties. It was all the more galling because Douglas had just received a very large advance from Pan for future books and an option on the script from a Hollywood producer. Although we owed Douglas money, it seemed like a drop in the ocean; and compared with Pan or the BBC, Original Records was a tiny company whose principal capital was ingenuity rather than cash. But Douglas, through Ed Victor, was now treating us as if we were a major corporation.'[14]

'Original Records was originally just a little two-man outfit working out of a small studio,' said Douglas in September 1982. 'Then they put out the *Hitchhiker* albums and they are now in a suite of offices with secretaries and everything. I walked into their office and said, "Heh, heh, heh, you're spending my royalties, aren't you?" To which they replied "Heh, heh, heh, of course we're not." I'm currently in the middle of a lawsuit with them.'[15]

In fact, by that point Aston and Mousseau had laid off their only secretary, moved out of their London office and were running Original Records from their homes: 'Under threat of legal action by Ed Victor, on behalf of Douglas, we eventually agreed to give Douglas back his master rights and mechanical copyrights, provided we continued to pay royalties. This was a humiliating experience. The lawyers essentially asset-stripped Original Records.'[16] This was particularly galling for Aston in light of his having originally set up the mechanical copyright deal to help Douglas when he was using his £1,500 advance from Pan to pay off his overdraft.

Throughout 1982, the bank steadily reduced Original Records' overdraft and back-dated corporation tax had to take precedence over royalties. The HeeBeeGeeBees' rights were returned in lieu of royalties, leaving Aston and Mousseau with nothing except a warehouse full of unsold LPs: 'Ironically, our balance sheet still looked good because we continued to show the value of our massive overstock at trade rather than cost price, but in reality selling the stock of *Hitchhiker* LPs was a slow and frustrating process. Our only option seemed to be to cut everything to the bone, to keep going and trade our way out of debt.'[17]

Meanwhile, nobody involved with the recordings was seeing any income from the second album (beyond a small advance) because they were all on royalty contracts. 'I was being managed for a brief period by Harvey Goldsmith,' recalls Geoffrey Perkins, 'and I put Harvey onto them, saying, "I can't get any money out of them. Can you see what you can do?" He came back about a month later and said, "I can't fucking get any fucking money out of them. I think you've fucking had it." You've got to worry, haven't you, if Harvey Goldsmith can't get any money?'[18] But of course Goldsmith couldn't get any money. There was no money to be had because it was all tied up in a huge stock of unsold records, resulting from Stage One's inability to understand their computer (in the case of the first album) and Aston and Mousseau's naive belief that Part Two of a story could outsell Part One if you advertised it enough.

'At this point we alerted Douglas, through Ed, that there would be no further royalties until trading improved,' recalls Aston, 'and that, in the event of his winding up the company, the Inland Revenue and the bank had first and second call on our assets and that there would be nothing left for creditors, including Douglas.

'But that is exactly what Ed did. Whether or not Douglas actually understood the implications, I will never know, as he did not speak directly to me at the time, using Ed's lawyers as his preferred means of communication. A writ arrived from them to put Original Records and Original Music into compulsory liquidation. The winding-up order was approved by the court and, as predicted, the Revenue took its money, the bank recovered some but not all of its loan and overdraft, calling in a personal guarantee from one of our original backers, and that was that. Not a penny was paid to trade creditors, first among whom was Douglas.'[19]

Douglas and Ed licensed the recordings to Hannibal Records in the USA, and subsequently to Simon and Schuster, but they have been unavailable since 1988 and the current ownership of the rights and location of the master tapes is unknown.

'As you can imagine, I was bitter and disillusioned after Original Records went out of business,' reflects Aston. 'In more philosophical moments, I remember thinking that we were paying the price for being ahead of the game. But then I also remember thinking: how could someone with Douglas' sense of humour, irony and goodwill be so avaricious that he would re-acquire the masters and rights and put out of business the very people who had created them with him, when not even the BBC had been interested? Yes, we made mistakes, though more out of an excess of enthusiasm and a lack of financial acumen than any ill-will towards Douglas or a desire to deprive him of his just rewards. But then I think that acquiring a lot of money in a short space of time does strange things to people. Perhaps the Douglas I met in 1979 was not the same person I said goodbye to – and no thanks for all the fish – in 1982.'[20]

CHAPTER 18

WHILE ALL THE fuss was going on over novels and records – and *Doctor Who* – Douglas was also supposed to be writing a second radio series of *Hitchhiker's Guide*. Not only that, but on 29 May 1979 the Head of Light Entertainment, John Howard Davies, commissioned a pilot script for a TV series from Douglas. The initial offer was £1,100 for the pilot and £1,250 for a possible further five or six scripts, but Jill Foster successfully negotiated both figures up to £1,450. The pilot script was due for delivery by 1 August, which would have been hopelessly optimistic even if Douglas hadn't had all those other irons in the fire.

One of the problems which he immediately encountered was that it was no longer original or different to consider SF as mainstream entertainment: 'It's very difficult because the first series was written just before the big science fiction boom took off, and immediately everyone's accusing you of jumping on the bandwagon, when you've been trying and fighting for it for years. But now, since all that has happened, one is suddenly going back into an area where you feel you broke new ground, and suddenly there are multi-storey car parks and office blocks. It's very difficult going back into it, thinking, "What do I do now?"[1]

Nevertheless, a script for 'Fit the Eighth' was written and the show was recorded on 19 May (in fact, *Radio Times* called the episodes 'Fit the First to Fifth' and they were only later numbered sequentially with the first series). Douglas being Douglas, it wasn't a complete script, so the rest of the episode was recorded a few weeks later. Douglas still being Douglas, he hadn't actually finished the script by that date either, so a third session was booked. Recording for 'Fit the Ninth' was set for 11 July (but eventually happened on 14 November, and even then required another recording session nine days later); by 19 July, the TV pilot deadline was revised to 30 November and Douglas finally delivered it in December.

'The second series started painfully coming out,' recalls Geoffrey Perkins. 'Some time around October, we'd done one episode and we'd agreed in principle that the show could go out from the end of January, thinking: "Well, that's another five weeks, which takes you into March. Yes, we can do it by then." I went on holiday and came back to discover some horrible Faustian pact had happened, whereby we'd been given the cover of the *Radio Times* – which for a radio show was unheard of – as long as the show could go out across a single week in January. And by that point we'd recorded one show. That was incredibly hectic!'[2]

At least the novel was out of the way by then, and Douglas' scripts for 'Shada' were formally accepted on 11 October, but there was still the TV pilot script distracting him. 'Fit the Tenth' was committed to tape on 3 December, with John Le Mesurier, the original choice for Slartibartfast, as the Wise Old Bird. (Perkins: 'To be honest, I think it was just me and him. I'm not sure there was even anybody around doing his lines for him.'[3] Le Mesurier: 'Oh, I had a terrible time. They made me sit in a corridor, in a draft, all afternoon.'[4])

'Fit the Eleventh' was taped on 3 January 1980, with the series now locked in for 21–25 January, and 'Fit the Twelfth' followed on 13 January. This was so close to transmission that the *Radio Times* had already gone to print, hence the Man in the Shack – who actually rules the universe – was credited to the anagramatical 'Ron Hate'. 'Jonathan Pryce got asked to play the ruler of the universe but we had to apologise because it hadn't been written yet,'[5] recalls Perkins. Pryce was cast instead as Zarniwoop and the Autopilot, and Stephen Moore was the Man in the Shack.

Perkins remembers Ken Campbell (Poodoo) as, 'one of the oddest bits of casting. It seemed to be easier to say to Douglas, "Think of somebody you know, write for them, and even if we can't get them that person's got a character." Because Douglas could write completely interchangeable lines between characters. So we got Ken Campbell in, because Douglas knew Ken, to play a character, and it was quite hard to get Ken Campbell to sound like Ken Campbell. We had to do impressions of Ken Campbell back to him.'6 'That often happens,' muses Campbell. 'I'm not really all that good, that's the problem. I can do me if I know me, but people's notions of me, I don't know what bit they mean.'7

Of course only the actors were recorded on those dates; there was still a vast amount of post-production work to be done, even more so than before as Paddy Kingsland was now writing original music, whereas the 1978 series had used Douglas' record collection.

'The second series was made in the space of a week and nearly killed us,' recalls Kingsland. 'The first thing I got was the Peter Jones sections, a week or two before, because the music was largely to cover those. I think Douglas had actually written all of those in a block so that they could be recorded in one go, rather than having to get Peter back in several times. Then, the week before transmission, bits and pieces of Episode One, maybe the whole of Episode One, was available. Then it got worse and worse and worse. Geoffrey was down in the Paris Studio, recording the voices. Douglas was in the narrator's booth, passing bits of paper through, actually writing bits and pieces while the actors were there.'8

'I can remember David Hatch phoning me up in the middle of the week,' says Perkins. 'He said, "I'm just calling to check: we are going to make it, aren't we?" But what could anybody do? Once you'd actually recorded all the voices, then yes, somehow or other you were going to do it. The last episode took three days, with Paddy Kingsland having to go home about lunchtime on the Friday because he was hallucinating! My girlfriend, Lisa Braun, turned up with a bottle of champagne to celebrate the end of the show and started to take over the editing of it.'9

Somehow, against all the odds, the series was finished in time, but it was a close-run thing. In his notes to the published radio scripts, Perkins remembers that the final episode was, 'completed some twenty minutes before it was due to go out and then spirited in a fast car down the Edgware Road, the three miles to BBC

Broadcasting House, where it arrived just a few minutes before transmission.'[10] In respect of the frantic way in which the series had been assembled, some of the final scenes were remixed for subsequent repeats.

And Douglas' opinion on all this? 'It was a big mistake. The first series was simply something that was there and people found. The second series had all this hoopla around it. But the speed with which we had to make it was unconscionable. It was so complicated it created nightmares. But a couple of years ago I was looking something up in the book of scripts and began to think, "This is like a disowned child." I've actually been unfair to it because all I remember is the hell of making it.'[11]

Meanwhile, other people were approaching Douglas with projects for which they thought his unique approach might be suitable. Schools producer Mike Howarth was developing a ten-part series called *Exploration Earth: More Machines.* For £30 (according to BBC files), Douglas was to provide 'suggestions for development of a serial, from his extensive experience in science fiction writing.' 'I remember the meeting very well,' says Howarth. 'He was very busy and couldn't do any writing but wanted to help me design a sci-fi series (of course I was jumping on the bandwagon). We had a beer in the Langham and he outlined to me the basic structural elements so I could use them.'[12]

Around the same time, TV producer Patrick Dowling approached Douglas about writing for a new children's series called *The Adventure Game,* 'a collection of lateral thinking problems in a Lewis Carroll sort of world derived from a mixture of the original *Adventure* on mainframe computers and the cooperative role-playing of *Dungeons and Dragons.*'[13] In this fondly remembered programme, a team of celebrities were transported each week to the planet Argond and challenged by shape-shifting aliens to solve puzzles through a mixture of logic and intuition, with only the eventual winner allowed back to Earth. It was a Pythonesque sci-fi concept which was to game shows what *Hitchhiker's Guide* was to sitcoms. Dowling set up a meeting at Television Centre and Douglas turned up on time, having sat next to Quentin Crisp on the bus.

'I didn't research Douglas before the meeting at all, so I supposed he was more established as a writer at that point than later became evident,' says Dowling. 'What I wanted chiefly was not so much scripts, for they were vestigial, as to knock ideas back and forth. In retrospect, if I'd had a clearer idea of what I wanted, I think I could have persuaded Douglas to join in. We could probably even have worked over the phone without need for him to put pen to paper. As it was, he was concerned about the amount of work he had already agreed to do and I was still uncertain of how I was going to develop my production.'[14]

In 1979 the World Science Fiction Convention (Worldcon) came to Britain: Seacon '79 in Brighton over 23–27 August. Pan Books sent Douglas along to give a talk entitled 'Across the Galaxy with TARDIS and Thumb' and several programme slots were set aside for fans to listen to *Hitchhiker's*, which was nominated in the Best Dramatic Presentation category of the World Science Fiction Awards or 'Hugos'. Unfortunately, the heavy American presence at the convention meant that not enough people had heard the show and it came second to *Superman*.

'Surprise guests at Seacon included Tom Baker, who arrived over an hour late,' observed Steve Green in his fanzine *Omega*, 'and Christopher Reeve, who accepted the Hugo Award on behalf of the *Superman* team, accompanied by a few hisses from *Hitchhiker's* fans. He joked, "I'd just like to say to the producers of *Hitchhiker's Guide to the Galaxy* – it was fixed." An admirable reaction.'

CHAPTER **19**

THE EARLY IDEA of adapting *Hitchhiker's* to television in animated form never came to anything. But in September 1979, with the novel due out imminently and the second radio series in disarray, John Lloyd sent a memo to John Howard Davies suggesting a television adaptation of *Hitchhiker* and a chain of events was set in motion. Douglas signed the contract to write the TV pilot script in June 1979, a rather rash agreement since he was working on 'City of Death' at the time, as well as script-editing the rest of that *Doctor Who* season, and supposedly writing five more radio episodes of *Hitchhiker's*. The script was eventually handed in five days before Christmas, but would probably have been even later had 'Shada' not been abandoned.

'Within certain groups of people *Hitchhiker* is now very well known, but it isn't well known in England as a whole,' said Douglas, just before the series aired. 'So one of the reasons for doing it is for all those people who don't listen to the radio and can't read. To be arrogant – this is an appallingly arrogant thing to say – television may or may not be good for *Hitchhiker* but *Hitchhiker* will be good for television. Television situation comedy has got to a dire state.'[1]

John Lloyd was announced as series producer, but *Not the Nine O'Clock News* – which had been abandoned after a single, untransmitted programme in April 1979 because of an impending general election – was reinstated in the schedules for six weeks from 16 October. Lloyd was therefore unavailable for *Hitchhiker* and was given a token credit of Executive Producer, later changed to Associate Producer.

The job went instead to Alan J.W. Bell, who also directed the series. Largely unfamiliar with *Hitchhiker's Guide*, he had heard a repeat of 'Fit the Seventh' which mystified him completely. Douglas had no say in Bell's appointment and would have preferred to work with Lloyd. Nevertheless he was tremendously excited about the prospects of bringing *Hitchhiker's Guide* into the visual medium: 'If it turns out the way I'm beginning to visualise it, I think it will actually look very extraordinary. What you can do just with computer diagrams and computer graphics is immensely exciting.'[2]

Exciting and costly. It had been decided to match Peter Jones' narration with computer graphics depicting whatever he was talking about, but when the BBC Graphics Department put together a budget it left their bosses scratching their heads in despair. The problem was solved thanks to a young animator named Kevin Davies, working for a company called Pearce Studios. Davies was a passionate *Hitchhiker's Guide* fan who was also active in *Doctor Who* fandom and had already interviewed Douglas in November 1978 for the fanzine *Tardis*. ('Douglas was on fine form,' recalls Davies, 'and was surprised at our initial interest in *Hitchhiker's* – "Ah, you know about that!" – and at the amount of questions concerning the same: "Is this interview meant to be about *Doctor Who* or *Hitchhiker's*?"'[3])

Pearce Studios were based in a building in west London, parts of which were also rented by the BBC. On 11 January 1980, Davies heard the distinctive sound of R2-D2 coming from one of the other rooms and with teenage confidence went to see what was happening. He found Alan Bell editing a *Jim'll Fix It* sequence in which a *Star Wars* fan visited the set of *The Empire Strikes Back*. Spotting that Davies was a keen and knowledgeable SF fan, Bell asked him if he was familiar with something called *The Hitchhiker's Guide to the Galaxy*. Davies enthused wildly about the show and, on learning that Bell had been offered the TV production but was unsure about how to provide graphic images under the narration, dragged the startled producer along the corridor to meet his boss, Rod Lord. Lord politely showed Bell a few examples of the company's work and expected to hear no more, but eleven days later, Bell was back with an offer.

'It was interesting to meet Alan and show him the show-reel,' says Lord. 'But I never really, truly expected anything to come of it. I thought that Alan was being polite. So I was actually very, very surprised when he came back not very long afterwards and he was obviously serious. We ended up doing the first half of the Babel Fish as a trial piece.'[4]

What this meant was that all the animated sequences in the TV series of *Hitchhiker's Guide* were done by Pearce Studios using traditional cel animation techniques. Not one computer was used anywhere in the series' production. Yet many people, apparently forgetting how incredibly crude and blocky computer graphics were in 1980, remain convinced that the *Guide* graphics were done that way. Over the years, lazy journalism in poorly researched books has promoted this myth.

'The first time I met Douglas was when he came with Alan to have a look at the rushes of the Babel Fish sequence,' recalls Lord. 'I remember taking him up to the theatre and running it, and Douglas saying straight away, "Right, that's it. Got that cracked then." And that was pretty much it – we all went to the pub. Douglas came to the studio one other time, which was when we were having problems coming up with something for the currency sequence. There were big holes in the script description which basically just said, "More of the same." It was becoming difficult to come up with anything that would fill the screen, so we did get Douglas in. I remember him striding up and down the middle of the studio, waving his arms about, coming up with some pretty crazy things.'[5]

'These graphics sequences are digressions really,' said Douglas. 'They're commentaries on the plot, or more often on something that isn't in the plot but which is there in order to distract your attention from what's happening in the plot if it's getting boring at that point.'[6]

When it came to casting, Douglas was keen to retain as many

of the radio cast as possible, while Bell was hoping to start from scratch. In the end a compromise was reached. Jones and Wing-Davey returned as Arthur and Zaphod, while Sandra Dickinson and David Dixon were cast as the new Trillian and Ford. However, for the pilot episode, the only cast required were Jones, Dixon, Joe Melia as Mr Prosser, and Martin Benson, under layers of prosthetic make-up, as Prostetnic Vogon Jeltz ('I thought that Douglas Adams must have – how shall I put this? – a very odd mind. I found it amusing in the same way that wearing odd shoes would be amusing'[7]), plus a number of extras. And of course, Peter Jones: 'I rather thought they would probably ask me to narrate it as I did on the radio. In fact I thought at the time: why didn't they just use that? But there was probably some contractual problem about that.'[8]

The very first footage filmed, on 26 March 1980, was the Vogon Constructor Fleet's view of London, shot from the top of what was then the NatWest Tower and is now improbably known as Tower 42. Location filming with the cast began on 8 May in London and then moved to Sussex, with Douglas in tow, to film Arthur's house and his local pub. Joe Melia, another former Footlighter who had actually been in the same revue as Bill Wallis, the radio Prosser, recalled, 'It was very enjoyable. We all gathered round a television in the hotel to watch a friendly between England and Argentina. I remember Douglas taking some of us out to a very posh restaurant in Sussex called Gravetye Manor, and that was the first time I had ever seen a jeroboam of champagne. That was very generous of Douglas – he was obviously feeling pretty happy about things.'[9]

Douglas was for the most part content to sit around reading Bruce Chatwin's *In Patagonia*, but did appear in the background of the pub scene. This was the first of several Adams cameos in both the live-action and animated sequences of the series (for more information on these, check the DVD production notes). The studio session for the pilot episode was on 7 June and post-production was wrapped up later that month. There was still no firm commitment to a full series. A screening was organised at the National Film Theatre on 5 July, to record the audience's laughter and prove to BBC executives that the show was actually funny. Davies suggested recruiting hardcore SF fans from the monthly meetings held in the One Tun pub in London, where he and Bell were surprised to find someone else handing out *Hitchhiker's* related material – fliers promoting a new stage version at the Rainbow Theatre. *Hitchhiker's Guide* was about to suffer its first fall . . .

CHAPTER **20**

AFTER THE RADIO series and before the TV series, *The Hitch-hiker's Guide to the Galaxy* had been a play, staged at the Institute for Contemporary Arts (ICA) in London by Ken Campbell's Science Fiction Theatre of Liverpool in May 1979. Campbell already had a reputation as a maverick in British theatre and was prompted to consider adapting *Hitchhiker's Guide* by his friend Gerry Webb, a leading light of the British Interplanetary Society.

'Gerry said, "You've got to do *The Hitchhiker's Guide to the Galaxy* because the fans all love it. It's got to go on",' says Campbell. 'It was then, as a result of that, that I looked into it. I'd only heard a couple of episodes when it went out so I wasn't myself a fan of it then. But I got recordings. Myself and John Joyce, we listened to these tapes again and again then we got the scripts from the BBC. We reckoned it would not make a successful theatre piece, or not one that we'd be confident in. It worked very well in its way, in its half-hour episode form, but it's got no structure really that holds it together in any regular way.'[1]

Joyce ran the SF Theatre of Liverpool with Campbell and recalls their meeting with Douglas: 'It was made clear that we could have the theatre rights because Douglas didn't think it could be done in the theatre, so it wouldn't be too much of a bother to give us those.'[2] 'But what it had got was the fact that people loved it,' enthuses Campbell. 'We reckoned that we'd only have confidence in it if it could be done as a ride, like a ghost train or something of that sort. Then, enquiring further how this could be done, it turned out there was a company called Rolair who had just come up with the notion of airpods.'[3]

Airpods operate like hovercraft, lifting themselves, and whatever is on them, a fraction of an inch off the floor. They required a completely flat, smooth surface, and fortunately the ICA had recently installed a new floor in its main theatre space, with removable seating. Rolair agreed to lend Campbell some airpods in return for the publicity and a special performance for potential clients. However, this method did restrict the audience to eighty people.

'We got this bloke, Mike Hirst; he's a theatrical genius, I've used him on everything,' recalls Campbell. 'He built an auditorium which would go on top of these pods and then they got pushed by the strongest people who were in the returns queue. We would walk up the returns queue every performance, see who was strongest, and inform them they'd got no chance of getting in unless they pushed the auditorium. They used to love that. We used to buy them a drink and they were heroes of the evening.'[4]

Douglas gave Campbell free rein to adapt the radio scripts how he saw fit: 'We didn't really rewrite anything, it's just that we didn't do it all because that would be what, three hours' worth. I think we did an hour and a half. It began in the bar, then when the world blew up we saved everybody who was in the bar by getting them quickly into their places and then – whoo-poom! – the auditorium took off.'[5]

The very first rumblings about a feature film version started around this time too. A British producer – name long forgotten – contacted Douglas about the film rights. 'She offered us something like a thousand pounds for the rights to the film,' remembers Geoffrey Perkins. 'Douglas thought, "Wow!" and he said yes, then he thought about it overnight and he phoned his agent up and said, "No, actually. I won't take it. Can you send her her cheque back?" Later, when serious conversations started going on about films and it got into the press, this woman wrote to Douglas, saying, "Just to let you know, I'm sure you remember, I actually own the film rights." Douglas phoned his agent up, with a rather cold feeling in his stomach, and said, "You remember ages ago when that woman wanted the film rights and we said yes then we said no. You did send the cheque back to her, didn't you?" His agent said, "I'm sure I did. Let me look." It had been forgotten, and this woman was paid off quite a lot of money.'[6]

The ICA version of *Hitchhiker's Guide* had been followed by a very successful production by Theatr Clwyd which toured Wales in early 1980. Adapted by Jonathan Petherbridge, it featured an incredible inflatable Haggunenon which was later loaned out to other stage productions. This was the play that Douglas took Jill Foster to see in his Porsche.

The third, and most famous, stage version – fliers for which were being handed out at the One Tun – was at the Rainbow Theatre, an aging rock venue in London, from 15 July 1980, and was an infamous failure. 'I saw the productions at the ICA, Clwyd and the Rainbow,' recalled Perkins. 'The ICA had the incredible hovercraft which to a certain extent covered up the details of the show which were a little rough. The Rainbow production of course was a disaster, which lost all the detail of Douglas' writing.'[7]

'Now that was based on greed,' says Ken Campbell, bluntly. 'The thinking was: "This is just going to go." We did it as well as possible but it seemed that the blight of our original thinking was on it. We had various quite expensive technical things. It was at a time when laser lighting was relatively new and unseen, and we had laser experts all signed up to be part of it but they were on a deferred payment. So once it looked dubious as to whether the show was going to attract an audience, some of the guys, for example the laser people, fled from it. So it made a show that was moot mooter.'[8]

It wasn't Campbell's fault. He remained convinced that, the Theatr Clwyd production notwithstanding, *Hitchhiker's Guide* in the flesh worked best as a ride. At the ICA he had been a major creative force in the production; at the Rainbow he was a director for hire: 'I purposely kept myself out of any of the production side of it and the financing of it – mainly because I'd said, "Don't do it." At all the meetings – "Shall we do it? Shall we not do it?" – I said, "No, don't do it. Let's leave things like they were. I don't think this is a good idea."

'But others who'd been involved at the ICA all said, "No, fuck it – this is our chance when we could get rich! We'd be insane to say no! The Rainbow's there, Douglas wants to go with it. If we get it all set up, would you agree to direct it?" Well, the answer was yes. It would have been a good idea to say no. Then it would still have been a failure but it wouldn't have been my fault. There wasn't sufficient backing to do it. Some dodgy money got borrowed, people were hunting one of the geezers who'd borrowed the money and he had to go in hiding. It was one of those things that had got to work otherwise there's trouble. But I wasn't involved in the finance of it, I would only have seen any money had it been a hit.'[9]

Initially the prospects looked good. *Hitchhiker's* had been a critical hit at the ICA and that was before the book was published. Now it was an established bestseller, with news of the impending TV series in the press. It could attract a thousand people to an obscure bookshop and it could even draw crowds in provincial Welsh theatres. Surely a big, spectacular stage show would be a smash hit, especially with some of the ICA team behind it. The radio show had been made to sound like a rock album so why not present the stage show like a rock concert?

'Douglas revelled in the delight that everyone had at the ICA,' recalls Campbell, 'which is what led him to suppose that things would be okay at the Rainbow. He liked the idea that our team and our enthusiasm were going to be doing the big Rainbow one, but as a matter of fact we fucked it completely for him.'[10] 'I should have known better,' said Douglas, years later, 'but I had so many problems to contend with at that time I really wasn't thinking clearly. The thing at the Rainbow was a fiasco.'[11]

'There will never be another first night like it,' recalled Mike Cule who played various roles including Deep Thought and the Dish of the Day. 'The huge 1930s auditorium of the Rainbow was full, with 2,000 or more people who knew *Guide* better than us. Backstage was a little chaotic. They were still making my Vogon costume when I put it on, and the second half hadn't had a technical rehearsal. In the second half, the universe ended . . .'[12]

Like the first night of *A Kick in the Stalls*, the Rainbow production proved to be way, way too long. 'Eleven o'clock rolled around and the audience headed for the last tube trains,' recounted Cule. 'And we went on and on till way past midnight . . .'[13] Though the show's length was cut drastically after the opening night – just as *Kick*'s had been – the critics panned the ill-thought-out production and audiences deserted it in droves. The play closed early, having played out its last few performances to mere handfuls of people. 'The atmosphere backstage was hilariously amateurish and unreal, due in part to the amount of drugs consumed by the crew,' remembers Kevin Davies, who sculpted and operated props for the play. 'Ken Campbell has an "anything goes" attitude to theatre which really only works on small-scale productions.'[14]

'I was obviously the right chap for the ICA ride version and the wrong person for the Rainbow,' agrees the director. 'I think it needed a very strong, outside person who would have put on something that everybody would undoubtedly have liked. Except for people who loved the original, who'd complain. We felt bizarrely that we were putting on something that was: "Well, I suppose the fans are going to like this because all the stuff's there." On the other hand, it may well be that there's only certain things that would work at the Rainbow. We were doing it with a big degree of enthusiasm, but it was repertory-ish, it was too stuck in the usual mould, however exotic and quirky. It was like setting off a sparkler at the Albert Hall.'[15]

Ironically, Douglas was actually more involved with this production than either of the previous two. He sat in on rehearsals and it was his idea to swap the actors in the two leading roles, with only days to go. He also brought in an old friend to help ease Campbell's burden. 'Douglas asked me in, really at the last minute, to do a little bit of work with the actors,' recalls Sue Limb, 'because Ken Campbell had a huge amount of work on his plate already with trying to get all the multimedia things sorted. I think Douglas just invited me to stroke the actors' egos. I enjoyed that very much indeed and I was very appreciative of Douglas' generosity, creating a little job for me.'[16]

Geoffrey Perkins was less appreciative, and not just because Douglas rang him up at two o'clock in the morning: 'He said, "I've just realised that what the Rainbow show needs is somebody who knows the script, who can talk to actors and can help change things. So I thought I must phone you up and ask: have you got Sue Limb's telephone number?" I said, "Douglas, it's two o'clock in the morning. You've just phoned me up, have basically described somebody who you want for the show who I thought for one moment sounded a bit like me, then asked me for somebody else's telephone number." He went, "Oh God, no, obviously, no, if you, I hadn't thought you'd be interested . . ." It was very Douglas.'[17]

CHAPTER 21

THE *HITCHHIKER'S* PILOT was well-received by both BBC executives and critics who saw it at the Edinburgh Television Festival in August 1980, and the following month the go-ahead was given for five more episodes, to be screened in the New Year. Douglas was well advanced on the remaining scripts and had already delivered Episode Two as early as April. Without *Doctor Who* to worry about, the TV series was clearly going to be a lot easier than the second radio series.

Location filming took cast and crew – and Douglas – down to Cornwall where the actor contracted to play Naked Man Walking Into Sea Throwing Money Away failed to show and Douglas was persuaded to take the role. Douglas' blue Golf GTI – he had sold the Porsche after crashing it into Hyde Park Corner – led a convoy of vehicles to a different local restaurant each evening. Studio recording started on 8 November, with Douglas on set most days, reading Eddie the computer's lines, which would later be dubbed by David Tate.

The first episode was broadcast on 5 January 1981, and shooting on episode six was wrapped the following day with the last few pieces of animation following shortly afterwards. A wrap party was held that night and then another one at Douglas' flat the following Monday, with cast and crew gathered around the TV to watch the first broadcast of Episode Two.

The *Guide* graphics generated a lot of interest as they were quite unlike anything seen before, and many people assumed that the BBC had access to state of the art computer equipment, especially as the images had been clearly seen on the prop in Simon Jones' hand. (This was done using a 16mm projector and a series of strategically positioned mirrors on an extendible frame concealed behind the sleeve of Jones' dressing gown.)

'After the first episode went out on air, I got a call at the studio from some computer magazine,' remembers Rod Lord. 'This guy wanted to know whether we'd used what he referred to as "the new Sinclair flat-screen". I said, "How do you mean?" He said, "Well, you must have been able to do it so that the graphics could be held in the book." I just said, "I'm ever so sorry to disappoint you but there wasn't an ounce of anything in there that wasn't traditional animation." He said, "No, I don't believe it. We've had this discussion going on since last night in the office here."'[1]

'The television show was . . . good in parts,' said Douglas diplomatically. 'But the parts in which it was good were all the "computer graphics". The great thing about those was they were so packed with information – all of which was actually relevant but went by too fast. So you could keep on watching it and get more and more stuff out of it. We see lots of movies these days with tons of computer graphics, but they're more or less there just to look good. They're set-dressing and none of it bears examination. The great thing I always thought about the graphics in *Hitchhiker* was that it was actually an integral part of what was happening.'[2]

But Douglas was never happy with the TV series, and as the years went by he became less and less diplomatic, laying the blame for the show's perceived failings squarely with Alan Bell.

Douglas in 1985: 'I didn't like the TV series so much as the radio. I think we could have done quite a bit better, but there were various people pulling in different directions. We'd had a very good time doing the radio show, and it wasn't the same.'[3]

Douglas in 1991: 'Basically I didn't have a happy experience with television. The producer and I were at constant loggerheads, and there was quite a lot of casting there that I actually thought was plain wrong. There was one particular instance of an extremely good actor being cast in a role that he had simply no idea how to do. And he knew that he had no idea how to do it, and we all had to go off in a huddle with him in another room where the producer couldn't see us and try to coach him to get it right.'[4]

And Douglas in 1998, responding to the question, 'What's your opinion of the TV adaptation of *Hitchhiker's Guide*?' 'Low.'[5]

Nevertheless, the series was a big hit with both audiences and critics and created many new fans of *Hitchhiker's Guide*. It was widely assumed that a second series would follow a year or so later, and hints about the story starting and ending at a cricket match suggested that the plot would have been adapted from the still unused 'Krikkitmen' idea.

'I had a great deal of say in the TV series, but the producer didn't have a great deal of listen, unfortunately,' bemoaned Douglas. 'I found it deeply frustrating, I must say, because it could have been something absolutely wonderful. I had a definite set of ideas about how to make it unlike anything that had been on television before. The producer wasn't interested in that. I was rather aggrieved and, to be honest, by the end of the first six episodes it became a bit of a stand-off. I didn't want to carry on doing it if we had the same producer and the BBC wouldn't change him.

'We agreed that we intended to do another series, but I kept delaying signing the contract or writing the scripts because I wanted to resolve this problem. It went further and further down the road until I eventually said, "Look, if I can't have what I want I'm out of here." So I went off and wrote another book. It's sad. It was a perfectly good television series, but the radio series was a really ground-breaking radio series, and it could have been a really ground-breaking television series.'[6]

'The television people did want to do a second series of *Hitch-hiker* but Douglas decided he didn't want to do it,' recalls Jill Foster. 'We were on the verge of signing a contract when Douglas left me to go to Ed Victor, then rang and said, "I don't really want to do that." So I had the sad job of getting him out of the contract.'[7]

'There was going to be a second series, it was all commissioned,' confirmed Bell. 'I made sure we had more money – about fifty per cent more – and the actors were told the dates, though Peter Jones was the only actor booked. During that time, Douglas went past his script deadline and time was running out. We needed to have information because otherwise, six weeks before production, what can you do? We needed sets built. We gave him another three weeks and the meetings were going on and then that was it, it had to be cancelled.

'Douglas is very strange, he believed that the radio was the ultimate series and that TV let him down. I don't know, maybe it did. We got on quite well, but I thought he was a hindrance. We used to tell him that the dubbing dates were in three weeks' time when we'd done it the day before, just because if he came along he interfered all the time, and I have to say, not necessarily for the better.'[8]

Among Douglas' less than practical ideas were that the mice should be actors in mouse costumes and that Marvin should be a leotard-clad actor sprayed gold. 'That impasse went to the head of department,'[9] recalled Bell. The only ideas for Series Two actually discussed with Douglas were the opening sequence at a cricket match and a planet where the population were permanently miserable because if they became happy they exploded.

The design of Marvin was a cause of great contention on the series: 'Curiously enough I never had a very clear picture in my mind of what Marvin looked like and I still don't,' admitted Douglas subsequently. 'I don't think the TV one quite got it.'[10] Visual Effects Designer Jim Francis agreed that Douglas' lack of visual ideas was the chief stumbling block: 'One of the hardest people to please was Douglas. He'd never quite realised what the Heart of Gold or Marvin or anything looked like. When you put something in front of him he'd just go, "No, it's not like that. That's not how I see it." Marvin was a classic example. I had three weeks – he'd chucked every other design out.'[11] Stephen Moore remained unhappy with the finished design: 'I said, "I'll do the voice, but that's not how I imagine Marvin." He should be a robot, a brilliantly technical robot, and that looked more like a Japanese doll.'[12] Douglas later commented on how he envisaged Marvin in the film: 'I think the colour is important. He's not silver any more, he's the colour of a metallic black Saab Turbo.'[13]

In 1981 Douglas travelled to New York to meet with executives at

ABC about a possible American series: 'It was like every horror story you've ever heard. They weren't really interested in how good it was going to be – they wanted to do a lot of special effects. They also wanted not to have to pay for them. Somehow they were managing to budget the first episode without knowing what was in it. There were terrible stories coming back after meetings with executives. There were remarks like, "Would an alien be green?" Eventually, everything got abandoned because the first episode's budget came to $2.2 million. It would have been the most expensive 22-minute TV show ever made.

'The script was terrible – I wasn't writing it. At the time, I had so much to do and they didn't seriously consider me. I was in America anyway and they asked me to come and hang around the production office for a week. It gives you an idea of the crazy proportion of this thing: they paid me for that one week four times as much as I was originally paid to write the whole series for radio. One very good thing came out of it. I met Ron Cobb who was going to be designing the series. I would like to get Ron to work with me on the film which is very much a live project.'[14]

Though it has always been believed that the US TV series got no further than meetings, in fact Cobb did sketch up some designs, including a version of Marvin which Douglas liked: 'It had the stooping quality which he needs. You can see on the one hand he's been designed to be dynamic and streamlined and beautiful, but he holds himself the wrong way. The design's gone completely to naught because he always looks just utterly pathetic. The particulars come from his attitude to himself rather than any inherent design. As far as his design is concerned, he looks a very sleek, high-tech robot.'[15]

Meanwhile, there was a second novel to deal with. Douglas wrote *The Restaurant at the End of the Universe* during the first half of 1980 and it was published by Pan in October of that year: 'I had x amount of time to write it and I'd put it off, put it off, put it off – all sorts of other things were going on at the time: the stage show, TV, etc. – so I was given extension after extension. Eventually the MD of Pan said, "We've given you all these extensions and now we have to have it: sudden death or else. We have to have it in four weeks. How far have you got with it?" I didn't like to tell him I hadn't started it. It seemed unfair on the poor chap's heart, and so my then-girlfriend rented a house and locked me away so nobody could possibly reach or find me. I led a completely monastic experience and at the end of that month it was done. Extraordinary. It was one of those times you really go mad.'[16]

Douglas' girlfriend had a double interest in seeing the book delivered on time – she was Jacqui Graham, Press Officer at Pan Books – and she established a precedent. From now on, every single book of Douglas' (except *The Meaning of Liff*) would be written after the deadline in a state of panic and isolation.

The first novel had simply taken the first four radio episodes and expanded the story, adding more detail and some additional expository scenes. The second book, though ostensibly based on the remaining eight episodes, completely rewrote the story, so that some parts of it were emphasised, some were barely mentioned, and many were in a different order: 'The second book actually was written backwards. I got very stuck because I knew how it ended but couldn't work out how to begin it. In the end I thought, "Oh well. Sod it. I'll just go with the end." So I wrote the end and then wrote the chapter before that then the one before that and the one before that. I eventually got all the way back and said, "Ah, that must be the beginning then."'[17]

Trying to recapture the magic that made *The Hitchhiker's Guide to the Galaxy* so successful as a novel caused Douglas a certain amount of worry. He now had expectations to live up to which had not troubled him when he was working on the first book: 'The first time, it was my little world, whereas the second time was like running down the High Street naked. I find the whole business of writing appalling – it's not an occupation for a healthy, growing lad!'[18]

'Douglas' moods were always up and down like a yo-yo (well, usually something a good deal less clichéd than a yo-yo, being Douglas),' says John Lloyd. 'He was hugely bonhomous and optimistic after each book turned out to be a smash hit, increasingly gloomy and anxious as new deadlines loomed.'[19]

'When I was writing *Restaurant* and when I'd finished it, I didn't like it at all,' said Douglas, 'I was very unhappy with it and I had to write it under a lot of pressure, and then when it was all done and I really just wanted to wash my hands of it, people wrote in and said, "It's much better than the last one," and I said, "This is nonsense, this is ridiculous." But when I went back to read it again after a certain amount of time, I actually liked it a great deal more than I had when I wrote it, and I thought, "Well, maybe it was okay."'[20]

It became a recurring feature of Douglas' career that he was dissatisfied with each book as it was published, but then revised his opinion and liked it again by the time the next one appeared (with which, of course, he was dissatisfied). By 2000, eight years after he had written the fifth and final *Hitchhiker's* volume, he was able to look back with an entirely objective judgement, and say: 'My favourite *Hitchhiker* book is *Restaurant at the End of the Universe*.'[21]

Douglas in his Brentwood School days.

Douglas and friends in their Brentwood dormitory in 1968 – note the Beatles album. (*left to right*) Alan Peters, Andrew Grieve, Douglas, Peter Goodwin; (*front*) Chris Robertson; (*rear*) Stephen Schick (with Persil), Paul Neil Milne Johnstone (with squash racket).

Detective Inspector Derek Wyatt of Essex Police demonstrates the use and abuse of drugs to Brentwood pupils on 22 January 1970. Seventeen-year-old D.N. Adams (*right*) towers above his classmates in this previously unpublished photo. Charles Thomson is in the middle of the photo with glasses and centre parting. 'The lesson,' reported the *Daily Express*, 'was in a language none of the class misunderstood: "Beware, man, if you go to a freakout at a drum."'

Will Adams (knee-britches), Martin Smith (umbrella) and Douglas at Cambridge Railway Station on 15 May 1973, publicising the first Adams-Smith-Adams revue, *Several Poor Players Strutting and Fretting*. Douglas had worn this turkey costume for the *Norman Ruins* film in 1972 and it inspired part of the *Ringo Starr Show* script.

—Lady Margaret Players/J.T./Adams, Smith, Adams Presents a Revue in the School of Pythagoras 11pm June 14th, 15th, 16th. Tickets 30p From St. John's College Porters Lodge and at door. Cheap day return 50p

Several Poor Players Strutting and Fretting

lady margaret/SPP/presents/ another Hour Upon The Stage strutting & fretting   with adams~smith~adams   in the school of Pythagoras 10:30pm Nov 15.16.17 -Tickets 30p ~on sale from St John's College Porters

THE PATTER OF TINY MINDS
a revue

Will (potato), Martin (briefcase) and Douglas (suit) - three burgeoning comedians out standing in their field. A publicity photo for the second Adams-Smith-Adams revue, *The Patter of Tiny Minds*, in November 1973.

Douglas in 1976, when he directed the Cambridge Footlights revue *A Kick in the Stalls*, with Chris Keightley, Footlights President and co-author of the legendary 'Kamikaze' sketch.

The cast and director of *A Kick in the Stalls* provide the *Cambridge Evening News* with the traditional wacky photo opportunity. (*left to right*) Douglas, Michael Landymore, Jeremy Thomas, Jimmy Mulville, Andrew Greenhalgh, Penelope Johnson.

Recording the Christmas episode ('Fit the Seventh') of the *Hitchhiker's Guide* radio series on 20 November 1978. (*left to right*) Studio manager Lisa Braun, Douglas, studio manager Colin Duff, programme secretary Anne Ling, producer Geoffrey Perkins, studio manager Alick Hale Munro. Braun and Perkins are now married.

Douglas with the cast of the *Hitchhiker's Guide* radio series in the Paris Studio, Lower Regent Street on 20 November 1978. (*left to right*) David Tate (various roles), Alan Ford (Roosta), Geoff McGivern (Ford), Douglas, Mark Wing-Davey (Zaphod), Simon Jones (Arthur). Stephen Moore (Marvin) is probably in a cupboard.

DOUGLAS ADAMS
CREATOR OF "THE HITCH-HIKER'S GUIDE TO THE GALAXY"

ORIGINAL RECORDS
38 Long Acre
London WC2
01-836 5220/5259

One of Douglas' first ever publicity headshots was this one used to promote the LPs of *Hitchhiker's Guide*. Twenty-seven-year-old Douglas looks happy enough here, but his relationship with Original Records would end acrimoniously three years later.

Douglas with Nick Landau, owner of science fiction store Forbidden Planet, on 13 October 1979, the day he signed more than 900 books (but didn't have any trouble getting to the shop).

On 12 January 1984, Simon Master (MD of Pan Books) presented Douglas with a Golden Pan award for selling one million copies of *The Hitchhiker's Guide to the Galaxy*. His second and third novels also received the award.

On the beach in Exmoor National Park in May 1984. It was here that Douglas and Steve Meretzky thought up the solution to the Infocom *Hitchhiker's Guide* computer game.

One job that fell to Douglas on the set of the *Hitchhiker's Guide* TV series was decorating this wall with different variants of '42' - it is seen briefly during one of the narration sequences.

The only known photograph from *Hyperland*, the 1990 TV documentary on communication technology which Douglas wrote and presented. He is seen here with Tom Baker, filming the opening sequence at Ealing Studios.

Douglas' friend and occasional co-writer John Lloyd (*back centre*) with a small army of ushers for his wedding on 2 December 1989. (*left to right*) Harry Enfield, Philip Pope, Andre Ptaszynski, Piers Fletcher, Richard Curtis, Howard Goodall; (*front left to right*) Peter Bennett-Jones, Jon Canter, Douglas.

Agreed in December 1997, the film deal with Disney was finally drawn up and signed in August 1998. Hopes were high but, when Douglas died three and a half years later, the film was no closer to production.

On location for the *Hitchhiker's Guide* TV series in September 1980, in a china clay pit near St Austell, Cornwall which was used for the desolate surface of Magrathea. Douglas was far more involved with the series than a writer would normally be, but was never happy with the finished show.

INTERLUDE - **CONVENTIONS**

OVER THE WEEKEND of 26–28 September 1980, Douglas left the *Hitchhiker's* film unit briefly to fly up to Glasgow to be Guest of Honour at Hitchercon 1, the first ever *Hitchhiker's Guide to the Galaxy* convention. About 150–200 fans attended and were treated to a preview of the first TV episode and, for those with a tolerance for bad drama and worse picture quality, a bootleg video of the Rainbow production.

Douglas gave a speech on the Saturday night, judged the masquerade and Vogon poetry competition, and did the *Guardian* crossword during discussion panels. He summed up his feelings in *The Meaning of Liff* by defining 'glasgow' as 'the feeling of infinite sadness engendered when walking through a place full of happy people fifteen years younger than yourself'.

'On the few occasions I accepted invitations to go to conventions I felt like such a goldfish in a bowl,' said Douglas. 'I really couldn't deal with it. That may be a personality flaw, and I know I caused some resentment by not being more available, but I just feel very, very odd about it. Normally speaking, one of the things writers have is a certain amount of anonymity. I used to find that if I went to a science fiction convention I'd be so aware of people's eyes on me I'd forget how to walk. I found that very hard to deal with, which is why I stopped going to them. Anyway, as far as I can see most science fiction writers go to conventions to get laid, don't they?'[1]

It was generally believed that this was Douglas' first taste of science fiction convention life, apart from his brief appearance at Seacon the previous year. In fact he spent the weekend prior to Hitchercon in Leeds at a *Star Trek* convention, Terracon '80, presumably so as to have some idea what to expect in Glasgow (hence, in *The Deeper Meaning of Liff*: 'absecon: an annual conference held at the Dragonara Hotel, Leeds, for people who haven't got any other conferences to go to'). He also attended a London *Doctor Who* convention, PanoptiCon III, the weekend before the Brighton Worldcon, and was scheduled to appear at the Marvel Comics Film and Fantasy Convention in 1980.

Douglas' final convention appearance was another Worldcon, Chicon IV in Chicago over 2–6 September 1982, to promote *Life, the Universe and Everything*. Prior to that he attended one other *Hitchhiker's* event, Slartibartday in London on 8 August 1981. Asked by a friend why he was going, he replied that it was because he 'might get laid'.[2]

CHAPTER **22**

IN NOVEMBER 1980, while doing the rounds of publicity for *Restaurant . . .*, Douglas gave a talk at St Andrews University alongside a writer named Sally Emerson. An Oxford graduate, and former editor of *books and bookmen* magazine, Emerson's debut novel *Second Sight* had been published to laudatory reviews a couple of months previously.

'Douglas was attractive, I thought, though I didn't think much about it at the time,' she recalls. 'He was also rather insecure and perhaps talked too much about himself. He was serious and imaginative rather than uproariously funny. In memory I see him sprawled there on a chair, legs and arms all over the place. There was a kind of magic then, when we spoke, but I was going through a difficult time and everything seemed more alive and awake and disturbing than usual.'[1]

The 'difficult time' had encompassed the collapse of *books and bookmen*, the suicide of its proprietor, Emerson's mentor Philip Dosse, and marriage to her boyfriend since university, journalist Peter Stothard (coincidentally a former Brentwood boy). At St Andrews, Douglas and Sally chatted all evening, discovering that they had mutual friends and lived near each other, though neither had read the other's work: 'In the morning I saw him rambling along a path and he looked sort of lost and sad and slightly confused.'[2] They became good friends, sometimes meeting for lunch, although other people could spot that Douglas was actually very taken with Sally.

Despite his success, Douglas was still living in a 'grim little flat'[3] in Highbury New Park with Jon Canter. 'Douglas seemed far too big for it,' says Emerson. 'I persuaded him to buy a good flat for himself in Upper Street, Islington, and also suggested he change agents to Ed Victor. I knew that Ed would be right for him.'[4]

In February 1981 Emerson visited New York to promote *Second Sight*, staying with an old schoolfriend, the actress Jane Seymour. Douglas was in New York at that time too, meeting with TV and publishing executives, and it was there they fell in love.

Douglas had enjoyed a string of relationships,* going right back to Helen Cutler at Brentwood. He had certainly never been short of a date. He took sound engineer Lisa Braun to see *Star Wars*, and actress Lalla Ward to see *The Empire Strikes Back*, and there were undoubtedly many others. (In the late 1970s, when Douglas still had Footlights connections, he had a crush on Emma Thompson.)

Despite this, Douglas freely professed no deep understanding of women: 'Everyone always asked me, "Why is Trillian such a cypher of a character?" It's because I didn't really know anything about her. And I find women completely mysterious anyway. I never know what they want. And I always get nervous about writing one as I always think I'll do something terribly wrong.'[5]

Though he may not have been conventionally handsome, Douglas was tall, strong, considerate, generous, well-read, very intelligent, sensitive, erudite, witty, endearingly uncoordinated and clearly something of a romantic. And none of that changed when he became wealthy and successful. He always had plenty of female friends, largely because he always had plenty of friends. And some of them had been more than friends. (There had been misjudgements too, such as Douglas' attempt to bed Gail Renard after a writing session, which led to the two not speaking for months, even while performing *So You Think You Feel Haddocky* ... together: 'He apologised charmingly to me years later.'[6]) But this overwhelming, passionate love was something new and it swept Douglas away.

---

* In researching this book I was told, off the record, of a science fiction convention organiser, a freelance publicist and the cousin of a close friend, all of whom apparently had 'flings' with him.

'Douglas wrote in April 1981 that from the beginning he felt that here was someone he could spend his life with,' recalls Emerson, 'but then added that that was ridiculous because you can't literally fall in love with someone purely instinctively like that. He said he wished he could travel back in time to when we first met and make sure he was treating me right. One reason he was attractive was that he was a force of nature. He was obsessive and compulsive. Having him in love with me was like being carried off by a tornado.

'It is a bit of a cliché as far as Douglas is concerned, but he wasn't quite on this planet. Certainly in these early days he hadn't learnt to conform and to see things as other people see them, and this freshness gave him the source of much of his humour. It was as though he'd just come from another galaxy and was looking at the world for the first time, and noting its absurdities and inconsistencies, all the things that over time we take for granted. But in a way this made him seem an outsider. Although he had plenty of friends, he didn't quite seem to belong anywhere, and he was often very lonely, but he and I seemed to belong together, to understand each other well, to share the same vision of the world, the same kind of dark imagination.'[7]

Douglas' family and friends seemed to approve of the relationship; Emerson was bringing some stability to his life. She got on well with Douglas' younger sister Jane: 'It was partly his sweetness to her that convinced me he was someone worth breaking up my life for. She was quite young and worshipped Douglas. This is a good man, I thought.'[8] As for Douglas himself, he had absolutely no qualms about a relationship with a married woman, and didn't care who saw them together, or that the relationship made it into the press ('Strapping Douglas Adams, whose manly charms have wrought havoc in many a female breast, has made a new conquest,' trumpeted the *Evening Standard*.[9])

'Douglas was twice stopped by the police for kissing me while driving,' recalls Emerson. 'The first time he was rather sweet about it, and shamefaced, and then he did it again. There was a recklessness about Douglas, which made him take risks in his life and his work. It was like having an affair with a hurricane, only a rather gossipy hurricane, as very soon he told everyone about it.'[10]

Douglas wrote very long, very passionate love letters to Sally. They read nothing like any of his published work, except for some of the passages in *So Long, and Thanks for All the Fish,* which is not coincidental as she was the inspiration for Fenchurch (cf. the description in Chapter 11: 'She was tallish with dark hair which fell in waves . . . it disconcerted Arthur like hell.') 'Douglas' letters would mix passion and seriousness, be wildly romantic, then go into comic fantasies. He wrote at the end of one tour de force that if he ever did have enough money that he didn't have to write again he would happily sit and write all day, but it would be only for me to read.'[11] (In researching his book *Wish You Were Here,* Nick Webb discovered that Douglas had carefully filed Emerson's letters in chronological order and had stapled to each one a carbon copy of his own reply – although the collection is incomplete, as some of Douglas' letters were handwritten or typed on both sides. 'I find it slightly chilling that Douglas kept my letters and his replies so neatly,' comments Emerson. 'Perhaps it was because he knew from the beginning how much our love mattered, and would always matter, to him. I suppose in some way it was a way, for him, of our relationship still existing: the heated letters and their replies, paperclipped together.')

However, *So Long . . .* was still three years away; in 1981, Douglas was working on *Life, the Universe and Everything.* Ed Victor nego-tiated the contract with Pan and Douglas signed it on 10 July, but there was, as usual, plenty to distract him. Not least that in September 1981 the relationship with Sally Emerson went a stage further – indeed further than any previous relationship – when she left her husband and moved into Douglas' new flat. 'It was his dream flat, with a magical roof garden reached up a spiral staircase. Very film starry, on two floors, with a bar; the bathrooms were spectacular.'[12] And still the love letters continued, though considerably shorter: 'Douglas' verbal skills at wooing were not at all bad. When I was living with him he'd leave me little handwritten notes outside where I was working. I remember one I found mid-afternoon after we'd separated to work after lunch: "I already love you more than when I last saw you at quarter to three."'[13]

Life, the Universe and Everything was the first Douglas Adams novel not adapted from the *Hitchhiker's* radio scripts. 'I've now written two books which are based on something I'd already written,' he said. 'That's not quite kosher. I want to write a book from scratch to prove that I can do it.'[14] But he didn't. Instead, he turned to the old 'Krikkitmen' story which had already been considered for three *Doctor Who* projects and the abandoned second TV series of *Hitchhiker's*. The idea behind the Krikkit Warriors, Douglas later said, was inspired by thinking about the Nazis and how most of the German nation weren't actually evil, though they might have appeared to be.

The opening chapter went through (according to Douglas) twenty drafts, eventually ending up as the book's first two lines. Intriguingly, at one stage Douglas was planning to open the story not at Lord's Cricket Ground but in the Garden of Eden. 'He felt that it all became very heavily symbolic and didactic,' recalls Sally Emerson, 'so he thought it was going to have to revert to Lord's again, where the balance might work out a bit better. He noted that when the setting is silly you can write it terribly seriously, and that works, but when your actual setting and idea is serious you find yourself adopting a rather flip or facetious tone in order to achieve a counterbalance, and that wasn't the writing he cared to read.'[15]

This is the same argument which Douglas had advanced regarding *Doctor Who*, especially the mishandling (in his view) of 'The Pirate Planet'. But why cricket? After all, he had not exactly shone at the sport. 'I am not a great cricket fan,' he explained. 'I just came across an article about the history of the Ashes – a cricket stump which was burnt in Melbourne in 1882. I happened to read it in a daydreamy mood and it went from there. There was no deep significance to it.'[16] (Another – unacknowledged – inspiration went right back to his days at Brentwood. 'One of my sermons was this,' recalls former Brentwood Chaplain Tom Gardiner. 'If visitors from Mars came down on the First XI cricket pitch, how would you go up and deal with them?'[17])

'As far as his work was concerned, I think I was a help,' says Emerson, 'because we were on the same wavelength, and indeed

I suggested an idea for *Life* . . . of another planet being jealous of the rest of the universe for existing. It was a small thing, but was an idea I'd had in a notebook. He was very stuck at the time, and distressed, so by giving him that it set him off again.'[18]

Emerson was effectively fulfilling the same function that various publishers would take on subsequent books, and which Geoffrey Perkins had instigated back in 1978. Douglas simply wrote better, or at least wrote more, or certainly wrote, when somebody else was there to keep an eye on him: 'Douglas was constantly being told by me to get on with his work. He needed the encouragement. Because he loved me, he did work but it was an uphill battle to make him do it. We both spent much of the day writing, but often I would leave and go and work in my old house in Stavordale Road (later bought by the Blairs) as I could work better there. When I got back I would cross-question him on what he'd done.'[19]

Douglas had dreams of a divorce, a marriage and a house in the country, possibly because his mother's second marriage and move to Dorset had proved so successful. He certainly wanted to have children. But the affair was perhaps too passionate to become permanent, and Emerson left Douglas just before Christmas to move back in with Stothard: 'Douglas put posters of his books all over the flat and my mother remembers this as a sign that it wouldn't work between us – it looked a bit too much of a shrine to him.'[20] Douglas was completely devastated.

'An awful lot of 1981 got consumed by a little emotional episode that year, which I'm not going to go into in any detail,' said Douglas later, when reminded that he had commented on how *Life* . . . had been written under conditions in which he wouldn't have wanted to build a bookcase, let alone write a book. The first draft was delivered just after Christmas, at which point Douglas suddenly had to leave for an American promotional tour: 'I had to phone up my publisher and say, "Look, it's not finished yet. I'm going to have to rewrite it but I have to go now." So I went away and did this tour, feeling terrible at the situation I'd left behind. I came back and sat down and wrote – I think I spent another six weeks on it – and threw out virtually every word of the first draft.'[21]

Eventually Douglas delivered his manuscript in mid-1982,

approximately one year late. Ironically, one of the few parts of the first draft to survive was the dedication, which was to Sally Emerson: 'It meant a great deal to me that Douglas dedicated *Life, the Universe and Everything* to me. He told me he had intended to dedicate it "to Sally, whom I love above the title" which would have been a typically good Douglas joke, puzzling one moment, then dazzling with its largesse. But then when I left him he couldn't make the full dedication that, obviously, so just put the shortened version. The book is a memory of a strange and extraordinary year, which had far-reaching effects on both our lives.'[22]

Life, the Universe and Everything was another bestseller and for the first time Douglas received some serious promotion from Pan Books, including the first of many *Hitchhiker*'s gimmicks, 'cans of everything' which were given away to critics and to the first hundred people in the queue at the now traditional Forbidden Planet signing session. Inside each can was a strip of paper offering fabulous prizes in a lottery with a number which . . . unfortunately was printed in an ink which dissolved on contact with oxygen.

'I've been extraordinarily surprised because I assumed, doing this third book, that by now possibly interest might have begun to slope off a bit,' said Douglas as he travelled around the country promoting the novel. 'But believe me, this book has absolutely astonished me, selling much better than the first two, which was something I really wasn't prepared for. After I wrote the second book I was utterly, completely determined that this was it – there would not be another *Hitchhiker* book. And this *is* it. After the second one I said I'm not going to do another one, after the third one I also say I'm not going to do another one.'[23]

That was a comment which would be repeated more than once before the *Hitchhiker* saga was finally played out.

CHAPTER 23

WHEN SALLY EMERSON left him, Douglas was distraught: 'It knocked me for six and I couldn't think of anything funny to save my life. I was at a point where I wanted to leap off cliffs and things like that.'[1] However, he was later able to at least find some humour in the situation: 'She went off with this bloke on, to me, the spurious grounds that he was her husband.'[2] When an interviewer asked whether the break-up was reflected in Trillian leaving a manically depressed Zaphod in *Life, the Universe and Everything*, Douglas seemed untypically rattled and confused: 'Ah, that was based on . . . er . . . It was actually based on a combination of all sorts of different things, partly my own experience, partly someone else's . . . er, a guy I know.'[3]

His friends rallied round and it was Mary Allen who came to his aid. Mary knew Sally so she understood better than most people the complex relationship they had had; she had also shared a flat with Douglas in the mid-1970s so she knew what he was like to live with: 'a very entertaining living companion, a terrific raconteur and talker, extremely untidy.'[4]

'Douglas was a man who occasionally had bouts of depression,' she recalls. 'During this particular bout of depression, he rang his friends a great deal, almost daily, and I was one of those. I'd say that there was a time when he was talking to me about an hour a day, and I was delighted to talk to Douglas, but an hour a day was getting a bit much, I had other things I wanted to do with my life. So I said, "Douglas, do you think you might be a bit lonely? You just bought this large flat and, living in it by yourself, maybe you should share it with somebody?" And he said, "Yes, great idea. Who?" So we both got out our address books and drew up this list of three people.'5

The three candidates were Geoffrey Perkins, a friend called Rosie Reid and an Oxford-educated trainee barrister named Jane Belson, then living with her parents. 'So we went through the three, did a list of pros and cons, and he said, "Well, I think the barrister sounds interesting, can you check it out?" So I phoned up Jane and said, "There's this man, he needs a flatmate, very nice." And she said, "Sounds good." So I phoned Douglas back and said, "Yes, I think Jane's interested, should we go for Jane?" He said yes. So Jane moved in and it was just under ten years later that they got married. That was a complex relationship as well.'6

Jane had in fact already met Douglas at a dinner party, and there was no denying that they went well together. A few months older than Douglas, she had been born in London to Australian parents and educated in London and Massachusetts before reading History and Economics at St Hilda's College. Called to the bar in 1978, after a brief spell working for the Treasury, she specialised in matrimonial law. The affair with Sally Emerson had possibly been too passionate to last but Jane provided stability. It helped that she wasn't a writer. 'I'm a man of obsessive enthusiasms, great bursts of energy followed by two days in bed,' explained Douglas. 'Jane is totally different which is why we complement each other so well.'7

Jonny Brock had been at school with Jane and at university with Douglas, and he could certainly see the compatibility: 'They were both very tall, and they were both very clever, and they were both very stubborn and strongwilled. I think they were a very good couple. Douglas always behaved impeccably towards her, but Jane was remarkably tolerant in that in the end she would always defer to him in terms of what they were doing. So if he wanted to buy a house in the South of France, that's what they would do, and if he wanted to go and live in America, that's where they'd go. Jane is a barrister and she found it jolly difficult to keep the practice going because in the end everything revolved around Douglas.'8

Jane was also, as Emerson had been – and Mary Allen, John Lloyd, Jon Canter *et al* before her – a sounding board for Douglas' ideas, to whom he could read his latest few paragraphs in his constant need for confidence-building feedback: 'I measure the corners of her mouth with a micrometer, to see which bits she's reacting to.'[9]

So that was one big change in Douglas' life around this time, and it did him the power of good: 'I haven't been depressed for the last year or so. It's Jane, that's what it is.'[10] The other big change was that he discovered computers. This was prompted as much as anything by his time in LA working on the film script, although he had made his first, tentative steps into word processing a few months earlier: 'It was a standalone word processor called a Nexus, which was horrendously expensive by today's standards and probably less powerful than the free calculator you'd get in a Christmas cracker.'[11]

Douglas had first considered a word processor in late 1979, when the sudden success of the *Hitchhiker* novel led to the disappearance of his overdraft and the appearance of his Porsche. He went to a computer show, wondering if such technology might be of use to him, but had been put off by, 'the impenetrable barrier of jargon. Words were flying backwards and forwards without concepts riding on their backs.'[12] By 1982, he had succumbed and bought the Nexus, which was followed in 1983, on his move to LA, with a DEC Rainbow: 'This was on the cusp of the change from 8- to 16-bit and the big thing about the DEC Rainbow was that it was both an 8-bit and a 16-bit computer. It ran CP/M. I then went home to England and got an Apricot which ran MS-DOS.'[13]

Something clicked in Douglas' brain at this point: he had clearly broken through 'the impenetrable barrier of jargon' and he realised that there was much more to computers than just word-processing. The Apricot was as different from the Nexus as the Nexus had been from his old typewriter, and as different as that typewriter had been from a ballpoint pen: 'Although the word processor is geared to a very simple task you begin to get glimpses into precisely what it is doing. The conceptual pictures you build up in your mind when you try and understand what it is doing are really fascinating.'[14]

The Apricot and Rainbow were swiftly followed by a BBC Micro and a Tandy 100. Douglas' life would never be the same. Nor would his office. Nor his bank balance: 'The first time I saw a computer I thought of it as a glorified adding machine, but I got the first twinge of something that would give a whole new meaning to the phrase "disposable income".'[15]

Early computer enthusiasts had found much to delight them in *Hitchhiker's Guide*. And it wasn't Eddie the shipboard computer, who was after all just another in a long line of talking boxes going back to HAL 9000. It was the *Guide* itself, a handheld portable data resource which was more like a real computer than anything that anybody had previously seen in science fiction, for two reasons: it didn't think, and it displayed text on a screen.

By 1978, anybody working with computers knew that the only practical user interface was a qwerty keyboard and a TV screen. Certainly by January 1981 when the TV series debuted, by which time every schoolchild had (or knew someone who had) a Sinclair ZX80 or ZX81, or even an Acorn Atom or a Commodore Pet, this was common knowledge, and earlier, far more primitive interfaces, such as punched or marked cards, were all but extinct. Yet in science fiction, computers still communicated by means of ticker tape or speech – just like Eddie. There was of course a practical reason for this: on film or television, expecting the audience to read from a screen was a bit much to ask. On radio, forget it. Then the *Hitchhiker's Guide* came along, and suddenly here was something which did not receive voice commands and which displayed the text you wanted on a screen.

The *Guide* was not an artificial intelligence, it was an electronic book. It couldn't work things out, it couldn't calculate, it couldn't think. But it could find the information you were looking for in its vast database and it could cross-refer you to other 'pages' which might also be of interest. Before the phrase was coined, the fictional *Hitchhiker's Guide to the Galaxy* was information technology.

Douglas didn't realise it at the time, but he had come up with something amazing, and in an amazing way. He certainly didn't invent the idea of a searchable and cross-referenced electronic database. Other people were working on that in the 1970s. But he had come up with the idea independently, while completely ignorant of anything to do with computers, purely as a (literal) narrative device. What is more he had presented it to the public and had thereby completely changed people's perception of computers. They were no longer giant, talking, thinking machines, they were tools whereby you typed some information in and you got other information out on a screen. 'As far as I was concerned, the *Guide* was completely imaginary,' said Douglas in 1985. 'I didn't even become computer literate until about a year ago, whereupon it suddenly swept over me like a tidal wave.'[16]

But Douglas' delight on discovering computers was as nothing to his delight when he discovered the computer that he would ever after evangelise – the Apple Macintosh: 'I had several computers before the Mac actually, but the Mac was the first to make me think, "Ah, this is the future."'[17] Douglas' first encounter with a Macintosh was in Cambridge, Massachusetts at Infocom, where he was discussing plans for the *Hitchhiker's Guide* computer game. 'They said, "We've got this little thing we think you might like to see. We've just been seeded with it." So we went into this side room and there was this box: the original 128k Mac. I sat down to play with it and just fell instantly in love with it right there and then.'[18]

Douglas claimed to be the first person in Britain to own an Apple Mac, although so did Stephen Fry. 'I've never quite resolved the argument,' says Richard Harris, Chief Technical Officer at The Digital Village and owner of the sixth or seventh Macintosh in Britain. 'This would be September '84 or thereabouts. I thought that Stephen had his before Douglas did, but I'm not sure whether they got them from Apple or brought them in themselves.'[19] Fry has since slightly revised his story, saying that Douglas bought the first two Macs in Britain and he purchased the third.

By 1985, when Douglas was profiled in *MacWorld* magazine, his study had, 'a collection of three Macintoshes, plus mice, keyboards, disk drives, a 90-megabyte Sunol hard disk, a DEC Rainbow, and a couple of printers. Timelessly, an old Hermes manual typewriter remains amidst the electronic gadgets. "I use it when I get stuck," he pointed out. "There's something wonderfully fundamental about hitting the keys and watching them strike the page, something a word-processor will never entirely replace."'[20]

The Sunol, recalled Douglas, was: 'a network hard drive that sat on LocalTalk. It was as big as some printers and it held 100 megabytes. It was hugely costly and both myself and my secretary shared it over the network. Of course, it was terribly slow. Desperately slow. So then I got a Mac Plus, the SE, then the SE/30. I even had a luggable at one point. I had a Mac II obviously and a IIfx, a IIci, a cx, and a this and a that and God knows what.'[21]

Such was Douglas' fascination with Macs, and such the enthusiasm with which he bought each new model the moment it was available that he was always eager to list his current equipment, just to show how up to date he was. In March 1987, for example, he owned: 'five Macintoshes, and as soon as I can get hold of a Mac II, it'll be six. In my workroom at home I have two Mac+s and an SE, and my secretary and my girlfriend share another Mac.'[22]

By 1999, all this hardware was antiquated and had long since been swept away (or at least put in a cupboard). Douglas had just bought himself the brand new G4: 'From taking it out of its box to being on my network with a fast ISDN connection to the internet took about fifteen minutes. It is blazingly fast, all the software I could possibly need runs on it like a dream, and after all these years I still want to hug it. Currently I have on my desk at home a new Power Macintosh and in my briefcase a PowerBook G3. My Quadra 950 runs my MIDI music system, and various elderly SEs and IIs run routers and servers around the house. I have always had lots of Macs and am devoted to almost all of them.

'I hadn't realised,' he added, 'quite how sad this was till I just wrote it down.'[23]

CHAPTER 24

'IT'S VERY IMPORTANT for me at the moment to do something different because I don't want to be indelibly stained with *Hitchhiker* in my entire career,' said Douglas prophetically in 1982. 'I probably am already, but I would like to prove to the world out there that there are other things I can do as well. I would like to write a novel which wasn't science fiction, I want to write a stage play, and the next thing I'm about to do, in fact, is, in a way, a slightly small thing. A friend and I are going off to write a sort of dictionary.'[1]

The Meaning of Liff was co-written with John Lloyd. It was extremely funny and it was a long time in development. 'While Douglas was writing the first *Hitchhiker* book on Corfu in 1978, I was sitting in the taverna down on the beach working my way through the island's supply of retsina,' recalls Lloyd (which contradicts Mary Allen's memories of the holiday). 'Every so often Douglas would slope down the hill to take a break from writing, and have lunch, and we'd play word games to while away the afternoons.'[2]

'When I was twelve, my English teacher gave everybody in the class the name of a place and said, "Okay, I want you to see what kind of word you might think it would mean,"' explained Douglas. 'I thought that was great, I loved that. In Greece, to begin with, we were playing charades. After a while, because of the amount of retsina we'd drunk, we needed to find another game that didn't involve so much standing up. So I suddenly remembered this thing I'd been given to do at school, and both Johnny and I had always shared a great fascination with words. So we started making some up.'[3]

By the time they returned to the UK, Lloyd had a list of about thirty of what would become known later as Liff-words, including ely, kettering, woking and wembley.* Lloyd subsequently produced *Not the Nine O'Clock News* and BBC files show that Douglas was offered the chance to write for the series, at £25 per minute, on 21 March 1979. Though he never submitted anything, he did make an appearance of sorts as John Lloyd recalls: 'We had a sketch in that first show with an enormously fat actor sitting in a strange room surrounded by gorgeous pouting gyrating totty dancers, over which we ran a series of captions speculating on who this lucky bastard might be. One of the captions read: "Douglas Adams and some of his accountants?"'[4]

Douglas received a writing credit in three of the five spin-off books, *Not The Nine O'Clock News* (1980), *Not 1982* (1981) and *Not 1983* (1982), though this was simply Lloyd covering his back as the sheer amount of gags created over the years by the Footlights crowd meant that assigning original authorship was often tricky. (One can see a similar thing in *Hitchhiker's*. Douglas acknowledged that 'Life, don't talk to me about life' was Jon Canter's, although he disputed Clive Anderson's claim on 'I really wish I'd listened to what my mother told me . . .') 'If you come from nowhere and you suddenly find yourself with a huge hit television series and a book that has to be written under intense pressure in two or three months – everything goes in,' says Lloyd. 'You just pile in whatever you've got and then you sort it out later and hope people won't mind. From time to time one got desperate under these terrible pressures and shoved in something that you hadn't asked for. Clive got frightfully annoyed about us using his, "I've been sucking a fisherman's friend all day," in a moment of panic.'[5]

* *The Meaning of Liff* defines an ely as 'the first, tiniest inkling you get that something, somewhere, has gone terribly wrong' and a wembley as 'the hideous moment of confirmation that the disaster presaged in the ely has actually struck'. This may become relevant later.

However, there was one part of *Not 1982* which was indisputably Adams, or at least Adams-Lloyd, and that was a series of definitions applied to town names, each listed as 'Today's new word from the *Oxtail English Dictionary*'. 'The 'Liff' snippets were bunged in by me as a last desperate measure to fill up this huge tome of gags,' explains Lloyd. 'I'd added a lot of stuff to what I'd written down in Corfu, Laurie Rowley wrote more and there were smatterings from other people. The MD of Faber, Matthew Evans, thought the definitions were the best thing in the book and suggested I turn it into a spin-off of a spin-off. To my astonishment, I had a rather fierce telegram out of the blue from Douglas saying, "Do nothing till you speak to me." He'd heard of it and wanted to be involved. But the fierceness was quite unnecessary. I was delighted: I'd assumed he'd be beyond all that.

'I readily agreed a 50–50 split, and, on the eve of my thirtieth birthday, Ed Victor and Douglas and I had dinner at Langan's and sealed the deal. It was one of the happier moments of my life. When it came to titling the book, though, I wanted *The Oxnard Eglish Dictionary* (Oxnard and Eglish being two place names) and Douglas argued strongly for *The Meaning of Liff*. His reason was that we would benefit from spoofing the name of the Python movie *The Meaning of Life*. My view was that we had something fresh which didn't need to trade on anyone else's marketing, and that *The Meaning of Liff* was confusing, derivative and meaningless. I lost that one. The other title I urged on Douglas was *The Hitchhiker's Guide to the World* which seemed to be perfectly apt given the geographical bent of the whole thing, and potentially stood to make us a great deal more money.'[6]

That wasn't how Douglas remembered it, of course: 'It was an awkward coincidence. We'd spent ages, Johnny and I, trying to find the right title for this, and we finally came up with *The Meaning of Liff* – I don't know that it's a great title, I quite like it – and it was very shortly after this that the Pythons decided to call their movie *The Meaning of Life*. I thought, "Oh, shit! It's all going to get confused." We just couldn't think of a better title, so we just stayed there.'[7]

The last time that Douglas and John Lloyd had collaborated, on the first series of *Hitchhiker's*, they had been working in Alex Catto's parents' converted garage. Things had changed and in the summer of 1982 Douglas rented Donna Summer's beach house in Malibu so that they could work on *The Meaning of Liff* while he negotiated a deal for the *Hitchhiker's Guide* movie. It also meant that Douglas could go shopping on Rodeo Drive.

'I used to sit on the deck, typing out *Meaning of Liff* and Douglas would come back, usually with armloads of equipment and flowers and clothes, and beaming from ear to ear,' recalls Lloyd. 'He would say, "Anything interesting happened today?" and of course absolutely fuck all had, usually. I just sat and looked at the sea. But one day he came back from the shopping trip and said, "Anything interesting happened today, Johnny?" "Yes, a plane crashed into the sea just over there." And indeed it had. And everybody all along the Malibu colony all rushed out of their houses and didn't know what to do including, of all people, Larry Hagman. It was a wild time.'[8]

Lloyd would pick likely-sounding names from a gazetteer and write them on index cards, splitting the pile between himself and Douglas; when each had come up with what definitions he could, they would swap. After the book's text was completed, Douglas left Lloyd to editorial duties such as compiling what must surely be the funniest index ever published and working with graphic designer Trevor Bounford on the accompanying maps. 'The original editor, Robert McCrum, made only one contribution to speak of that I can remember,' says Lloyd. 'He struck out all the definitions which contained the word "bus". It was perfectly obvious to me that this was because he'd never actually been on such a conveyance, so that none of the observations or jokes meant anything to him. I put them all back in again. "Fair enough," he said. "If you say so." Very nice chap, Robert.

'The physical appearance of the book was the result of a number of discussions between me, Douglas, Robert, Sonny Mehta and Matthew Evans. A lot of thought went into it, and that simple rather biblical style is I think one of the reasons the book still sells to this day. What Douglas and I always liked about the design was: (a) the fact that nowhere on the book does it say that it's meant to be funny; (b) it fitted perfectly into the outside top pocket of a jacket.'[9]

The publicity for *The Meaning of Liff* was extensive, with John and Douglas even making a short film for Granada TV: 'We literally went out for a day and wandered round Altrincham pointing out examples of Liffs from real life. A bit of a brave punt really but it worked absolutely brilliantly because there they were! We saw a hodnet, a botley, a piddletrenthide, a saffron walden and a kibblesworth!'[10]

It wasn't just the prospect of sitting in the sun and writing *The Meaning of Liff* which had attracted Douglas to California in 1982. He was also there to meet with Hollywood moguls about a feature film version of *The Hitchhiker's Guide to the Galaxy*. Three possible deals had already received serious consideration: the lady whose cheque had not been returned, an American who offered £50,000 for the rights ('I began to feel we were talking about different things and he wanted to make *Star Wars* with jokes. I suddenly realised that the only reason I was going ahead with it was the money'[11]), and Terry Jones. 'I think we hit on the basic problem of making a film out of *Hitchhiker*,' says Jones. 'That is that Arthur Dent doesn't really have much character and there really isn't a lot of character-development in the story. In fact there really isn't a story in terms of a ninety-minute film. It's a wonderful wander through space with lots of interesting and funny and thought-provoking things happening – but not narrative exactly. No beginning, middle and end – which I know I shouldn't be interested in as a Python, but they sort of count when it comes to ninety minutes in a cinema.'[12]

All those deals were discussed in Britain; Douglas was now in California, among the movers and shakers of Hollywood. 'Douglas was off scooting into town the whole time, having lunch,' recalls John Lloyd. 'I seem to remember at one point his back went. He was unable to walk about so he had to lie down on this chaise longue and there were these Hollywood moguls who would have to literally kneel beside him for the interview. It was very funny. He met some pretty colourful characters. He was taken out to lunch by one toad-like, cigar-toting mogul who growled, "OK, Duggie, we're gonna talk a little about money and directors and stuff and den – we're gonna talk about what kinda animal ya like ter sleep with . . ." This gentleman didn't get the contract, needless to say. It was a mad month really.'[13]

The men who did get the contract were Joe Medjuck and Michael Gross, who had worked with Ivan Reitman on the animated science fiction film *Heavy Metal*. They were now looking for another SF property to film. 'Having gone to all this trouble to make an animated movie and basically learnt how to do it, we felt that we should make another one, learning from our mistakes,' says Medjuck. 'I wandered into a science fiction bookstore on Ventura Boulevard and I don't know whether the guy there suggested the *Hitchhiker's Guide* to me or whether I just saw it and picked it up. It hadn't taken off yet, by the way – I give myself some credit here. It was there and it had a cult following but it was still a small cult as compared to a large cult. I liked the title, I got it right away. I read the book and I just loved it actually. This guy knew what was funny. As well as being obviously very smart.

'So I gave it to Mike and Ivan to read and they read it and said, "Yes, this would make a great animated film." I phoned his publisher and said, "Who would I talk to about the rights to this book?" And they gave me the name of his agent, who said, "Yes, the rights are available." I remember going and sitting on his balcony in Malibu and the first thing he said was, "I don't want to make an animated film."'[14]

Gross had come across *Hitchhiker's* by a different route, his work on *Heavy Metal* having taken him to London for a period: 'I found myself going to the sci-fi stores, where *Hitchhiker's* was well into its swing at that point, though I was unaware of it in America. So I started listening to it; very cool stuff. I still hadn't read the book but I'd heard the radio show.'[15]

'Here's what we discovered,' says Medjuck. 'A very charming, obviously smart, very funny guy with interesting comments. But the first words out of his mouth were that he wasn't interested in an animated film. He was being very protective, as he could afford to because he didn't need the money. So I went back and said to Ivan, "We still haven't found an animated film, but this is a really good idea for a movie." At that time I was much younger and much more on the cutting edge of things. I knew when things were going to get big and I said, "I predict that this is going to be really big because this is really good." I eventually was proven right. I don't make those claims any more, by the way! Ivan read the books, and said, "This is picaresque," – which is not something he's a fan of – "but it is really funny. There's something here. We could make something of this." So we basically went back and said, "Okay, we would like to buy the rights to this and we won't do it animated."'[16]

'Joe and Douglas got along beautifully,' remembers Gross. 'They just chimed at a certain level. But Douglas really didn't want to go forward with Ivan Reitman because at that point all he knew from Ivan was *Animal House* and *Stripes*. And he didn't see *Hitchhiker's* at the same level. Neither did we, but I think Ivan's point was he saw the commerciality in it. Joe and I saw the – if you'll forgive the word – intellectual side of it. We connected with the material more strongly. I took a long walk on the beach with Douglas and kind of sold him on it.'[17]

Douglas was persuaded and Ivan Reitman bought the film rights to the *Hitchhiker* saga for £200,000, then sold them to Columbia Pictures, while continuing to develop the film as producer (at no point did Reitman consider directing the film himself). The deal, as negotiated by Ed Victor, was reported in the London *Evening Standard* on 20 December 1982 ('I have been knocking my head against that wall in Hollywood for a year and a half,'[18] said Ed). Douglas' star was now very definitely rising in the west. A couple of weeks earlier the BBC TV series made its American debut, and on 26 December Douglas achieved the remarkable feat of having three books in the *New York Times* bestseller list at the same time. The hardback of *Life* . . . had been published in October, while the *Restaurant* . . . hardback and the *Hitchhiker's Guide* paperback were still selling strongly. Douglas cut out the list and framed it. 'As far as I know,' he said, 'the last British writer to have three on the lists at the same time was Ian Fleming. What does that say about the quality of my books?'[19]

But Douglas was a scriptwriter too. He had written the radio scripts, he had written the TV scripts, he saw no reason why he shouldn't write the film script. The contract included three drafts of the screenplay to be written by the author, and Joe Medjuck for one had no problem with this: 'Douglas wanted to write the screenplay. It was his baby and he obviously knew how to write radio shows, and as I say, he knew what was funny. So Douglas was in a nice situation. It's the sort of thing that can happen in Hollywood: he'd gotten a lot of money for the rights, he was being paid to write a screenplay, and his expenses were being paid. I remember his idea was he'd live here for maybe six months, work on the screenplay, and we'd go make a movie.'[20]

CHAPTER 25

AT COLUMBIA'S EXPENSE, Douglas moved into a house near Coldwater Canyon and set to writing the *Hitchhiker's* screenplay. Jane came out to stay with him (Joe Medjuck: 'I think Douglas had just taken up with Jane and he talked about a woman he had just broken up with.'[1]) and Terry Jones was also living nearby. Everything was looking rosy – until Douglas delivered his first draft.

'He was notoriously slow, but I can't remember if he delivered it late. Given his problems writing things – probably,' says Medjuck. 'My memory is that he basically took the book and turned it into a screenplay, period. Point by point. I have a vague memory that he may have written a 200-page screenplay that basically was the book. If I get a script that long, I just think the guy's an amateur. We said, "It can't just be the book. Firstly, it has to be shorter."'[2]

'Douglas wrote a 275-page long screenplay,' recalls Ed Victor. 'No-one had bothered to tell him that it had to be 125 pages, so he wrote this immense screenplay. When they saw it, they were horrified.'[3] Estimates of precisely how long Douglas' first draft was vary enormously, but it was clearly far too long to make. So he wrote another draft, more liberally adapted from the novels and the radio scripts. But still it wasn't right. Which should have been no surprise because most movies go through numerous drafts before anybody will even consider producing them.

Douglas' main problem was that he simply did not understand

how movies are structured, especially commercial films like *Hitch-hiker's Guide*. Writing spec *Doctor Who* treatments and new dialogue for Ringo Starr vanity projects was not real screenwriting and he was entirely unprepared for the requirements of Hollywood. The three-act structure, the hero's journey and similar Hollywood ideas are essential to a screenplay (independent art films excepted, which *Hitchhiker's* obviously was not) and the basic story, certainly as told in the novel, had neither a three-act structure nor a hero's journey. Ivan Reitman suggested some changes which, as producer, was his job.

And this is where Douglas' version of history really diverges from what actually happened. That second script coverage meeting with Reitman became one of the core anecdotes in his battery of stories. The fairly definitive version is the one he told on *Clive Anderson Talks Back* in 1991: 'The producer who bought it had never actually read the book. I mean it's 156 pages long and these are busy guys in Hollywood. Eventually he called me in and said, "Well the script's quite interesting, I like some of it and there's other bits I'd like to talk to you about. For instance, you do this bit where we're going to find out the answer to this thing you call the ultimate question to life, the universe and whatever it is. I mean that's great, that's terrific, people want to know that sort of stuff, particularly here in California. And then what do you do? You just say it's 42. Well, I think the audience is going to feel really jerked off by that." So I thought, "Here is a guy who's just bought two gallons of chocolate chip ice-cream and he's complaining about all the little black lumps in it."'[4]

It was a great story. It got plenty of laughs. It reinforced people's perception of Hollywood as a place where idiot film-makers change everything that made the book a success in the first place. But . . .

'That's not the way Ivan talks,' points out Medjuck. '"That's great, that's terrific . . . particularly here in California" – that's something he would never say. We're Canadians, not Californians! That's a funny joke but it's definitely not true that he would say that. It's also not true that he hadn't read the book.

'And we did not want a different answer. What we wanted was that the answer not be the climax of the movie. We wanted to build to some sort of climax and the climax shouldn't be as anticlimactic as that, which is fine when you're reading the book and quite funny in the radio programme, but we didn't want the ending to be anticlimactic. "The meaning of life is 42" was fine. It wasn't that we wanted another answer to the meaning of life. What we did want was that, after meandering a bit, which we didn't mind it doing, that it came to some sort of resolution. Which is what most movies do.'[5]

'One of the problems, the reason it never got made by us,' adds Gross, 'is Ivan is a structurally conservative film-maker. He really believes in the three acts, he really believes in motivation, a ticking clock, characters that develop. That's not what the *Hitchhiker's Guide* is, period. He got the humour, he loved the characters, he loved the robot, he loved the interaction, he just loved so much about it. But structurally, it wasn't right.'[6]

'Douglas' attitude – and he had good reason for feeling this,' says Medjuck, 'was that every time he changed from one medium to another medium, the people in the new medium thought they knew better than he did about how his story should go. This is what he didn't like about the TV shows. His attitude, which he'd earned, was that this was his baby and it didn't matter what medium it was in, he knew what its essence was. Which is not an unreasonable thing. And our attitude was: "Yes, this is true, but we don't think this translates into a medium where people go and sit in a theatre and have an experience. They usually need some sort of classic narrative form." Books don't have to work quite that way and anything that's serialised doesn't have to work that way, because you have different expectations, obviously.'[7]

Curiously, Douglas actually did understand that it was the story's lack of a climax that was the problem, yet he kept repeating his 'the audience will feel really jerked off by that' story, with its chocolate chip ice-cream punchline. And apparently he never connected the two. For example, on 12 October 1992 on Radio 2, he said: 'There's a certain structural problem that I haven't quite solved. Normally, any movie has its big climax at the end. So when you have a movie that starts with the Earth being blown up it's hard to work out exactly how you end that movie. Of course on the radio and television you don't need to end it. It just carried on and on and on. With a movie you've got to have a climactic ending, and finding a climactic ending to a movie that starts with the Earth blowing up is very hard to do.'[8]

And yet, only the day before, on Radio 5, he recounted the same story he had given Clive Anderson, almost word for word. Did he genuinely believe that was what Reitman wanted? There were at least seven further drafts of the script while Reitman was producer, in none of which was the Answer anything other than 42, and we know that Douglas had read at least one of those. But it's difficult to believe that Douglas was repeatedly telling a potentially libellous story which he knew to be untrue, even if it was funny. Douglas understood that there was a problem with the Deep Thought sequence, and had somehow convinced himself that it was the Answer which needed changing when in fact Reitman's objection was to the scene's position in the story. It was that same false memory trick which he acknowledged in the radio scripts book regarding the field in Innsbruck. Except that here he somehow retained the original memory as well and allowed both real and false memories of the same meeting to co-exist in his mind. It's a damning indictment of how badly Hollywood can screw you up if you're not prepared for it.

It didn't help matters that there was genuinely no love lost between Reitman and Douglas, as Mike Gross remembers: 'They were further apart than was ever possible to make out. Joe and I kept thinking we saw some sort of compromise situation because we just understood both sides of it, but in fact they never really reconciled. Douglas would meet with Joe and I, and we really got along as friends and we were sympathetic to each other's needs. And we got along with Ivan, we understood how Ivan worked, we understood his vision. But Ivan would speak Ivan-speak, which was a very blunt, singular, focused point of view, which at its core was not Douglas'. He had a hard time being in a room with Ivan, and Ivan had a hard time being in a room with him. Ivan did not have a great history of working with the English. Gerry Potterton who did *Heavy Metal* – he and Ivan didn't get along. I remember Ivan said at one point, "I just don't see what the English see. I may be

Canadian but I'm quintessentially American – and these people are too English."

'And the real problem for Douglas at that time was: he was *Hitchhiker's Guide*-ed out. I mean, he'd had it. It was just too much already. It was driving all the fame, but it was enough. Already ABC had tried to do something, already it was a radio show, already it was a book, already it was recorded. For him to sit down and do a draft, he was in pain, regardless of who was with him. He struggled so hard with it, he tried so hard, and he just hated the whole process. I'm amazed that Ivan kept going with it, actually.'[9]

'The major change we wanted to make in the story, which Douglas didn't mind, is we wanted to make Ford American,' remembers Medjuck. 'We didn't mind it being set in England, we didn't mind it having mainly English actors. Once we got into outer space, we figured they could be from any country. We wanted one of the major characters played by an American actor and Douglas had no problem with that. But he did have a problem with trying to force a more traditional narrative format on it. Now, I cannot remember how long this went on, but I know when it ended. We did want this to be our next movie and we thought that for Ford we could get either Bill Murray or Dan Aykroyd. And then Danny sent us a script called *Ghostbusters*.'[10]

Reitman found that he could work better with Aykroyd, a fellow Canadian who understood how Hollywood worked. Douglas was working on his third draft but it swiftly became apparent that *Ghostbusters* was a 'go' project and Douglas' screenplay was a mere contractual obligation. 'I can't remember whether he'd done his contractual work on the script or not, to be honest,' says Medjuck. 'But probably at that point we were saying, "Go do what you want – we're going to go and make this movie. You go finish writing your script." We went off and made *Ghostbusters*, which took a lot of time, and he was writing on his own, probably just to fulfil his contract. When he did his third draft, we must have given it to Columbia to get him paid, but I don't remember any comments from them to be honest. I think around then we said, "Look, it's time to get someone else working on this who's not as au fait with the original material as Douglas is."'[11]

Douglas spent seven months in LA working on the screenplay. He may have enjoyed living in Malibu putting *The Meaning of Liff* together with John Lloyd, but he grew to hate Tinseltown when it apparently didn't understand his masterpiece: 'You know all the things that happen to people in Hollywood and you think, because you know about them, they won't happen to you. You go and you sit there and day after day goes by – and everything that happens to people who go to Hollywood, happens to you. I got very, very miserable there. There are two things you basically miss if you're English, living in Hollywood. One is irony and the other is oxygen, and you need both of them. I eventually gave up. Myself and the producer, we never could quite agree about how it was going to go, and every time I rewrote it, it got worse from both our points of view.'[12]

Columbia still believed in the property however and renewed the option in the summer of 1985. 'I've had enough of writing that script,' grumbled Douglas. 'I've done several different versions. They've got another writer who's going through my versions at the moment, trying to come up with one that makes the whole thing work, then they're going to give it back to me again. I will have a lot of say, but say doesn't necessarily translate into listen.'[13]

Which was of course what he had said about the TV series.

CHAPTER **26**

ON 1 NOVEMBER 1983, Douglas and Ed Victor signed with Pan for 'the fourth volume in the increasingly inaccurately named *Hitchhiker's* trilogy', called *So Long, and Thanks for All the Fish.* (Douglas referred to the book at least once by Ed Victor's suggested title of *God's Final Message to His Creation*, but the US publisher preferred *So Long . . .* as did Douglas himself – he considered *God's Final . . .* to be 'too gallumphing'.[1]) At the time, it was reported in the SF news-sheet *Ansible* that Pan had paid £100,000 for it, and that Pocket Books had coughed up $400,000, although *Don't Panic* gives the US advance as $750,000.

When the book finally appeared, exactly a year later, it was very different from the previous three: it was in hardback, and it was a noticeably slim volume. Computers were to blame. 'One of my books was notably a lot shorter than all the others,' admitted Douglas, 'and the reason was that I tried to write it on a 128k Mac, with all the floppy swapping.'[2]

'I wasn't going to do a third one and then I wasn't going to do the fourth one. There were actually several reasons for doing the fourth, some better than others. The thing I was most sorry I wasn't able to get into the other books was God's final message to His creation. Very often in the juggle of ideas, a major one doesn't actually fit. It was just nagging me that I hadn't fit it in and I couldn't put it in any other book; in the end, it had to be in *Hitchhiker's*. Another reason – that is perhaps less of a good one – was having been very disoriented after living in Los Angeles, I was anxious to be home, in an environment that I knew very well.'[3]

One of the reasons Pan was so keen to publish another *Hitchhiker* book was that the first three continued to sell like hot cakes. At some point in 1983, the millionth copy of *The Hitchhiker's Guide to the Galaxy* was sold and Douglas became eligible for a Golden Pan award. A specially designed invitation was sent out, a silver 'thumbing hand'-shaped card, for the award ceremony, held at the exclusive Roof Garden club in Kensington on 12 January 1984. Members of TV cast and crew were in attendance; Graham Chapman, Terry Jones, Griff Rhys Jones and others were helping themselves to champagne and caviar; and seventeen-year-old Jane Thrift was swooning over the Guest of Honour: 'Isn't he lovely? I'd really want to marry him if he wasn't my brother . . .'[4] *Restaurant* and *Life* . . . would both go on to win Golden Pans.

By the summer of 1984, very little progress had been made on *So Long* . . . so Douglas decided to put the distractions of London behind him and head for the West Country. He booked himself into Huntsham Court, a small Victorian hotel in Devon owned by Andrea and Mogens Bolwig.

'"Can you do a cheap rate for a friendly impoverished writer," came the request over the telephone,' remembers Andrea, which was a rather cheeky request from a man whose combined advances for his latest novel came to a third of a million pounds. 'And so, Douglas Adams arrived at our door. The latest four-door Saab was laden with books, files, and computers. We had never seen a computer, let alone touched one! It took us two hours to unload his car.'[5] Douglas spent ten weeks at Huntsham Court, doing almost everything one can do at a nice Devon hotel except write a book. Perhaps it hadn't occurred to him that the countryside has as many distractions as London, especially the bits of the countryside with nice wine cellars.

Douglas had always had a liking for champagne and had been buying jeroboams of the stuff at dinners and parties since he first became successful. But at Huntsham Court, Mogens Bolwig introduced him to the concept that not all champagnes are the same. 'From then on, it was comparing "tastes" from various supermarkets and comparable prices, all of which had to be less than five pounds a bottle,' says Andrea. 'One sun soaked Saturday, he and Mogens began in-depth comparisons at 11.00 a.m. to accompany a full English breakfast in the garden. By 4.00 p.m. they lay spread-eagled out on the lawn, both completely and utterly blotto uttering some strange language indecipherable between Danish and English.'[6]

Douglas was enjoying himself, undoubtedly. The Bolwigs became good friends and Douglas would return to Huntsham Court numerous times and even invested in the business. But what he just could not manage in that glorious summer of 1984 was to write a novel. Part of the problem may have been that he had never actually written one before. His first two books were adapted from radio scripts and his third from an unmade film treatment. Now he was expected to create an entire novel from scratch and it was not something he found easy. Another problem was that being away from home did not make him inaccessible.

At one point, a call from America offered Douglas £50,000 to write a *Hitchhiker's Guide to the Galaxy* calendar. A few weeks later, having done absolutely nothing towards the calendar at all, Douglas received another call: the deal had fallen through so he was to be paid off with 50 per cent of his fee. A stunned Douglas put the phone down, realised that he had just earned £25,000 for doing nothing, and asked the Bolwigs to crack open the biggest champagne bottle in their cellar.

At the end of the summer, Douglas returned to Islington. The book was no nearer completion. Sonny Mehta knew that it had to be out when they had promised because a major marketing campaign had been prepared. Advertising space had been booked, press interviews were set up, the printers' schedule was arranged. There had to be a book, and there had to be one by the deadline. 'Douglas was going to miss the deadline and he asked me to call Sonny Mehta to tell him that he wasn't going to deliver the book,' recalls Ed Victor. 'Sonny said, "That's impossible," and I said, "Well, you know, he's not going to do it." And he said, "He has to do it."'[7]

Mehta decided that his only option was to sit over Douglas and make him write the book, preferably in a central London hotel. It had to be near Hyde Park so that Douglas could be let out occasionally to go jogging, and it had to have a Betamax video recorder so that Mehta could watch movies while keeping Douglas in his peripheral vision. 'Sonny said, "I'm going to take a suite at the Berkeley Hotel and Douglas is going to move in there and I won't let him go till he finishes,"' says Victor. 'So I called Douglas and I told him what was going on, and Douglas moved into this vast suite at the Berkeley and two weeks later he emerged with Sonny, a little bleary, with the manuscript. Many years later, I said to Douglas, "How did that work?" And he said, "Oh, it was very simple. I sat at the desk and typed and Sonny sat in an armchair by the desk and glowered."'[8]

So that was another reason why the book was much shorter than the previous three, and frankly not as good. Douglas had always said that the secret of his success was putting a lot of work into his writing, really caring about every sentence, every word. That clearly wasn't going to happen in a fortnight with Sonny Mehta glowering at him.

'The reason you get to be good in the first place is that you work very, very hard at getting it right,' said Douglas, reflecting later on the book and apparently blaming himself, 'and as a result you think, "Well, therefore the world will have to listen to whatever I write." You fall into a trap, and that's when you have to work doubly hard to make sure you don't let stuff by that isn't good enough. And I'm afraid, I think, that was the fault with *So Long, and Thanks for All the Fish* – I just completely lost my way.'[9]

A major theme of *So Long* ... is Arthur falling in love with Fenchurch. Douglas himself had fallen in love twice in the past four years. Was Fenchurch based on Sally Emerson, as he told her, or was she based on Jane Belson, to whom the book is dedicated? Or a combination of the two? At the time he claimed that: 'She's not based on any particular person, she's based on a number of different thoughts or observations of people or incidents. The idea of Arthur falling in love with her was really going very much into adolescent memories.'[10] Was Fenchurch partially based on Helen Cutler perhaps?

However, Douglas did admit in other interviews that, despite Arthur not being based on himself when he created that character, there were autobiographical elements in this book: 'It's always difficult bringing the biographical element in, because the connections are never that obvious. I suppose my life was a bit more stable at that point, but on the other hand it was rendered unstable by trying to write that book. Basically whenever I have a book to write, it always precipitates all kinds of major crises in my life. It's an insanely difficult thing to do, or at least I find it so.'[11]

There are two scenes which definitely are autobiographical. The intrusive woman selling raffle tickets in Chapter 12 who asks Arthur and Fenchurch, 'I say, you're not ... in love, are you?' was based on a waitress at Denny's in New York who had commented to Douglas and Sally, just before they started their affair, that she had never seen two people so in love. And there's the biscuit story, in which Arthur believes another man is stealing half the biscuits from the packet he has just bought, but subsequently discovers that he has been stealing half the biscuits from a stranger's packet. This happened to Douglas at Cambridge railway station in 1976. Allegedly.

'I put the biscuit story in there, as much as anything else, because I hoped that once it was printed people would stop asking me to tell it,' he said. 'I told it on English radio in 1978 and I've told it an awful lot since then. It's become one of those apocryphal stories that always was supposed to have happened to somebody's sister- or brother-in-law. And I just wanted to get it down on record – well actually it's Arthur saying it – that I was the one it happened to.'[12]

This has caused enormous debate, with many people convinced that Douglas appropriated an existing urban myth and claimed it actually happened to him. The story is now so legendary that it has been used in at least three films, and various other novels and TV shows. The debate over its origin came to a head with an e-mail exchange in November 1993 between Douglas and someone named Peter van der Linden, after which Douglas apparently decided not to bother arguing any more. Ironically, whereas many of Douglas' interview stories were mistaken (the crowds at the signing session,

Ivan Reitman and 42, etc) the biscuit story – the one which has been most doubted – seems to be true. We know that Douglas was in Cambridge in summer 1976 and we know that he was in a particularly distracted state. And the one thing this story requires is an enormous amount of stereotypically English diffidence, which Douglas undoubtedly had in spades.

But it didn't save *So Long, and Thanks for All the Fish* from being noticeably inferior to its predecessors. 'To be honest, I really shouldn't have written the fourth *Hitchhiker* book,' admitted Douglas, 'and I felt that when I was writing it. I did the best I could, but it wasn't really from the heart. It was a real trial and struggle to write it.'[13]

Nevertheless, *So Long . . .* was yet another bestseller on both sides of the Atlantic.

INTERLUDE - **JOHNSTONE**

TIME OUT **MAGAZINE**, probably unaware that they had inspired Megadodo Publications, ran an extract from *So Long, and Thanks for All the Fish* in the 15 November 1984 issue, accompanied by an interview with Douglas. And a figure from his past emerged to haunt him once again. 'Apropos of nothing,' wrote journalist Steve Grant, 'he proceeds to recount his long legal battle with an old school acquaintance called Paul Neil Milne Johnstone who took umbrage at some comments in *Hitchhiker's Guide* about universally awful verse.'[1]

'This character used to share a room with me at school,' Douglas told Grant. 'Kept me awake all night scratching this awful poetry about swans and stuff. When it was on radio, there was a section about Vogon poetry, which was the third worst in the universe. And somebody asked me what the first worst was, and I couldn't think and I said, "Well, it's Milne Johnstone, isn't it?" He ignored it for a while and then when the book and the album appeared, he started to wax litigious. We ended up getting this bloody letter and it turned out that although he hadn't published anything, he had gone on to edit all these poetry mags and organise various festivals. The letter ended up in the wrong department – somebody at Pan thought he was applying for a job and threw it in the bin!'[2]

Three weeks later, *Time Out* carried a letter from Johnstone himself, the only time he has spoken publicly about this affair: 'Unfortunate that, five years on, Douglas Adams should choose to reopen a minor incident; that it remains of such consequence to him indicates a certain envy, if not paranoia. Manifest that Adams is being base-minded and mean-spirited, but it is surely unnecessary for Steve Grant to act as a servile conduit for this pettiness. For the record, the "long legal battle" was simply a request to Pan to remove one sentence from the Adams script, a request to which they complied readily.'[3]

Johnstone's name was replaced with 'Paula Nancy Millstone Jennings of Greenbridge' in the novel and TV script and an indecipherable garble on the record (sticking the cut-up master tape together in the wrong order was cheaper than paying Peter Jones to record six words). However, it remained constant in repeats and CD/cassette releases of the radio series, and even in the book of radio scripts, thus negating the point of – in fact highlighting – the book/record alteration.

'He's famous as a humourless person,' said Douglas. 'Which is why I wanted to tease him, because humourless people are always the ones you most want to tease. Unfortunately he responded in a humourless way as well. If I'd been him and so publicly identified as the worst poet in the universe I think I would have rushed around to a publisher saying, "Can I do a volume please, called *The Worst Poet in the Universe*?".'[4]

A great irony is that Charles Thomson, a Brentwood contemporary of both men who is now a professional poet and founder of the 'stuckist' art movement, has no memory of Johnstone at all and, until I spoke to him, proudly assumed that 'Johnstone'/'Jennings' was a reference to himself. He was almost as aggrieved to find that he *wasn't* 'the worst poet in the universe' as Johnstone was to learn that he, apparently, was.

The last word should go to Douglas, from his *Time Out* interview: 'When the show went on at the ICA, we purposely put a reference in about Johnstone because he had been a press officer at the place and wasn't liked much there either.'[5]

CHAPTER **27**

AFTER SIGNING THE contract for *So Long . . .*, but before the couple of weeks he spent writing it, Douglas worked on the computer game of *The Hitchhiker's Guide to the Galaxy*. This was a text-only adventure, released by a company called Infocom who were far and away the market leaders in the field of 'interactive fiction' because their games combined interesting puzzles with witty writing and text parsers which could provide a reasonably sensible answer to anything the player cared to type. 'I had just thought computer games were about zapping aliens but then I discovered Infocom adventure games and I suddenly felt at home,' said Douglas. 'There was some real wit and intelligence involved.'[1]

'Douglas had already played a few Infocom games, so it was just a matter of making the introduction,' recalls Steve Meretzky, who co-authored the *Hitchhiker's* game. 'The initial contact, probably sometime in the latter half of 1983, was made through a mutual acquaintance of Douglas and Infocom, Christopher Cerf.'[2] Writer/editor Cerf worked at the Jim Henson Company and also worked with Douglas on an unmade 1986 TV special, *The Muppet Institute of Technology*. Cerf may have effected the actual introduction, but there was more to the bringing together of Infocom and Adams than the company at first realised.

'We learned only much later what had really happened,' remembers Mike Dornbrook, Infocom's Head of Marketing. 'From our point of view, Simon and Schuster had expressed interest in potentially purchasing us and started pointing out all the wonderful things that they could do for us. They were part of Gulf and Western which also owned Paramount Pictures who had all the rights to *Star Trek*. They were saying, "Hey, we could let you do *Star Trek* games. And we also have Douglas Adams." We were interested in both of those things, and we had actually a fairly intense internal debate because we didn't think we could do both at once.'[3]

Douglas had been talking with a senior executive of Simon and Schuster (his US publishers) on a plane and had mentioned that the one games company he respected was Infocom. However, when he subsequently discovered that the publishers had taken that snippet of information and used it to dangle him like a carrot in front of Infocom, he was not happy, as Dornbrook later discovered: 'Rather than have an unhappy author on their hands, they backed out. That's when I started negotiating directly with Ed Victor. Douglas would often be at the meetings but he would certainly defer to Ed on any business-related discussions. He was just working on – well, he was supposed to be working on! – *So Long, and Thanks for All the Fish*, and that was supposed to be coming out about the same time as our game, Christmas of '84.'[4]

The Infocom contract was for six games, two based on each of the published *Hitchhiker* books. With the contract signed, the next question was: who would Douglas collaborate with? Douglas and Ed were hoping for either Marc Blank, VP of Development, who had created the company's first big hit *Zork*, or Mike Berlin, whose game *Suspended* had first interested Douglas in the company. But neither of them wanted to collaborate with anybody, not even Douglas Adams.

'I'd finished my previous game *Sorcerer* in early February just as the *Hitchhiker's* game was ready to start,' recalls Meretzky. 'So partly it was a matter of timing, and partly it was Marc's feeling that I'd be a good match for *Hitchhiker's*; among the Infocom game authors. I was known for humour, and my first game *Planetfall* was considered very *Hitchhiker's*-like. I'd never heard/read/seen *Hitchhiker's* when I wrote *Planetfall*, but as folks began playtesting the game, so many of them said, "This reminds me of *Hitchhiker's Guide*," that I borrowed a set of tapes of the radio show from a friend and listened to them. I loved it, of course.'[5]

'I thought Steve and Douglas would actually be a good pairing,' says Dornbrook. 'Although I think Douglas was a little peeved that we put this junior guy on the game with him, as opposed to one of the senior people.'[6]

'Douglas' overall take on the game was a fairly direct adaptation of the existing storyline,' remembers Meretzky. 'Where he really had a flood of ideas was on some of the more incidental stuff, playing with the medium of interactivity and text adventures. Things like having an inventory object called "no tea", having the game lie to you, having an object called "the thing your aunt gave you which you don't know what it is" which keeps coming back to you even if you get rid of it, and so on.'[7]

Meretzky shared the writing with Douglas, of which there was a great deal because each puzzle required not just a response to the correct solution but also a wide variety of other responses to cover all conceivable wrong solutions: 'I was gratified when, in the final days before the game shipped, Douglas remarked that in many cases he couldn't tell which bits he'd written and which bits I'd written.'[8]

Development began in late February 1984 with Douglas spending a week in Cambridge, Massachusetts, after which the two kept in touch via phone and a very early version of e-mail. ('This is way before the days of widespread e-mail,' points out Meretzky. 'In terms of reliability and ease of use it was perhaps half a step ahead of signal fires.'[9]) In order to hit the Christmas market, Infocom wanted the game in the shops by the beginning of November, which meant finishing the writing and programming by October. Meretzky swiftly realised that this probably wasn't going to happen: 'Douglas certainly raised procrastination to an art form. We had a really tight schedule for the game, and he fell behind schedule almost immediately and kept falling further and further behind.

'Meanwhile, he was even further behind on finishing *So Long, and Thanks for All the Fish*. Although he was a horrible procrastinator when it came to working on the game, my impression was he was an even more horrible procrastinator when it came to writing his novels.'[10]

In May, while Douglas was at Huntsham Court not writing his novel, Meretzky came over for a few days to get the game finished: 'My orders were not to leave until the design of the game was done. While I was there, he stayed pretty focused on the game (when he wasn't showing me around Devon, or when we weren't enjoying the opulent cuisine of Huntsham Court). The last full day I was there, we were trying to come up with the ending of the game, that would be the game's ultimate puzzle, and would tie up all the loose ends of the story and would also use all the various items that we had introduced into the game. We were totally blocked and not getting anywhere. So Douglas suggested we drive out to Exmoor National Park. And there, sitting on driftwood on the beach, surrounded by sheep, we came up with the ending of the game.'[11]

Meretzky hurried back to Cambridge and worked feverishly on the game for three weeks so that it could have a reasonable testing period. In September, Douglas visited Infocom to finish off the last few details, and the game finally went into technical production, ready for its November on-sale date.

Douglas enjoyed working on the game for many reasons. One was that it was a displacement activity from writing his novel. Another was the opportunity it gave him to rapidly expand his computer knowledge. On their first day working together, Douglas proudly showed Meretzky a 3D crossword puzzle which he had created in BASIC on his DEC Rainbow, and his initial ideas for the game were done as a branching tree structure on his Rainbow in a programme called Brainstorm (which he had bought to try and organise his ideas for *So Long . . .*). Meretzky implemented the game in ZIL, a version of MDL or 'Muddle'.

'After a while it became too complicated to hold in Brainstorm,' said Douglas, 'so I just did word processing files and elaborately explained how you'd get from one bit to another and what the connections would be, which is rather a long-winded way of doing it. Steve was doing the coding and was also filling in a lot of the gaps, because when you're designing the way I was, there's an awful lot that you simply don't foresee and doesn't become apparent until somebody starts playing it. We did think, very briefly, was it worth my learning to write in Muddle, but the pressure of time being what it was, you didn't want a complete novice writing a major piece of code.'[12]

With the game almost ready to ship, Marc Blank and Mike Dornbrook flew to London for nine days in October to discuss marketing strategies with Douglas. Dornbrook remembers an amazing week of dinner parties and sightseeing tours: 'I figured: maybe we'll see Douglas a few times for an hour or two of meetings. We'll just squeeze into his schedule when we can. I didn't know Douglas! We spent most of our waking hours with him while we were there. He and Jane gave us an incredible tour of London. Jane was such an incredible person: incredibly intelligent, incredibly beautiful, a fantastic cook. She was, at the time, the youngest female barrister in England, he told us.

'Douglas was driving us around London on this beautiful October Sunday. He had four or five cars at the time and we were in a Volkswagen convertible. We'd drive past a building and he would start telling a story. Now he knew a lot about English history – but the thing was, Jane knew a lot more! Douglas tended to know the commonly accepted story but she would know what the latest interpretation on that was. Just driving around the city and hearing all this history and, in a very classy, intellectual way, arguing over the history – it was just amazing.'[13]

One of the dinner parties which Douglas and Jane held for the visitors was also attended by Terry Jones and his wife and by Sir Clive Sinclair. Dornbrook was astounded to find himself sitting opposite his Monty Python idol, but it was not Jones who was to make the evening so memorable:

'We got there a little bit early – Marc and I were the first to arrive. Douglas was great at serving wonderful wines; there was never a lack of very, very good alcohol at any meal with Douglas. We had had a good part of a bottle of wine before the other guests even started arriving. We had the before-dinner wine, and we had the appetiser wine, and we had the main course wine, and we had the dessert wine – at least a bottle of wine per person over the course of that evening.'[14]

Douglas had, that very day, received from Pan a copy of *So Long . . .*, the first copy off the press. It was later reported that Sir Clive had bought it from him for a donation to charity and this was regarded as an example of the entrepeneur's largesse. Dornbrook offers the fascinating inside track on what really happened: 'Douglas was very proudly showing this to everyone: copy number one. Well, Sir Clive arrived and he saw this, and he said, "Oh, I need a birthday present for my son. That would be perfect." Douglas cringed: how do I get out of this? How do I discreetly tell this person that no, no, no, there's no way I'm going to part with this. He said, "Well, I'd be happy to give him another copy and I'd be happy to sign it over to him but this one is very special to me. This is . . ." And Sir Clive just interrupted him, and said, "A thousand pounds to the charity of your choice!"

'You could just tell that Douglas didn't know what to do at that point. So he said Greenpeace – he picked a charity that he knew Sir Clive would never normally give money to! But he did graciously write a beautiful one-page special dedication to Sir Clive's son and handed it over. And Sir Clive wrote the cheque and handed it over. Well, in a sense that set the tone. It led to, later in the evening, just the most ridiculous argument.

'Towards the end of dinner, Sir Clive made some very strong statement about evolution: that it's impossible to explain evolution, that there has to be something guiding it or there has to be something in the genes that pushes for mutations because things change too quickly. As it turns out, over time more and more people are coming around to that view, but the way he said it at the time, he didn't have enough knowledge. Now, Marc and I were both biology students at MIT. We both had studied evolution fairly deeply, and we just very nicely said to him, "Well, you could actually explain that in the following way . . ."

'Eventually Marc and Sir Clive really started going at it – and it literally went on for two or three hours, this raging argument. I felt so sorry for everybody else there because they were kind of on the sidelines and this took over the evening. Douglas and Jane were politely wishing this would all end and we could move onto something else. We ended up going back to our hotel and Sir Clive actually shared the cab with us. I remember him and Marc sitting in the back of the cab, just in stony silence, staring at each other, ready to tear each other's eyes out almost.'[15]

This is a fascinating story, and not just because of what it says about how tolerant Douglas was of some of his friends. Douglas later became passionately interested in evolution, prompted to some extent by his travels around the world for *Last Chance to See* (from 1985), and his friendship with Richard Dawkins (from 1987). This evening in October 1984 pre-dates both of those and really seems to be the spark which ignited Douglas' interest. He heard detailed, reasoned arguments about current evolutionary thinking including plenty of references to Dawkins' work and it certainly seems very likely that it was this argument which set Douglas on the path to being a knowledgeable and passionate Darwinist. Had a similar argument developed a few years later, at a party where Douglas did not have to be mindful of his duties as host, he would undoubtedly have joined in with gusto.

CHAPTER 28

SHORTLY AFTER DORNBROOK and Blank flew back to the United States, Douglas followed them to help launch the *Hitch-hiker's* game at the end of October 1984. It was Infocom's first press conference, held at the Rockefeller Center in New York, and the level of interest – the first indication of how successful the game would be – surprised everyone involved.

'There were ninety-five to one hundred members of the press from all the top publications in New York,' recalls Dornbrook. 'We had *Playboy* there, we had the *New York Times* and the *Wall Street Journal*. It was just phenomenal, the turn-out we got. Partly I think because we were an interesting story in terms of this whole new computer games industry that was getting going, but also obviously to a great extent, people were fascinated with Douglas and what he had written and wanted to meet him.

'One of the things I announced that really struck a chord in the crowd – and with Douglas – was I had got in touch with WGBH, the premiere public television and radio station in the US, and said, "Hey, the original *Hitchhiker's* was a radio series and you ran it years ago. What's the possibility of bringing that back?" Now, I was used to spending millions on marketing; placing a two-page ad in a computer magazine could easily run $10,000 each time you put it in. They got back to me and they were obviously accustomed to very, very different numbers because they said, "Well, this is going to be very expensive because we have to license this from the BBC.

And we also have to pay for satellite time to distribute it to all the radio stations around the US. I hate to say this, but we'll have to charge you $18,000. Because $6,000 has to go to the BBC." I said, "$6,000 for the entire series?" All over the US, a year-long exclusive – I couldn't believe it. I said, "Sign me up!"

'So we sponsored that twelve-part series and ninety-nine PBS radio stations across the US picked it up. When I announced that I got an "Oooh!" from the crowd, and these are grizzled reporters in New York City – you don't expect a reaction like that! Douglas himself was just totally blown away. He came up to me and said, "I can't believe you're doing this. Simon and Schuster never did that for any of the books. No-one's ever done this before. This is so wonderful!" I never told him how little it cost!'[1]

The New York press conference was followed by more publicity across the country, including the Comdex trade fair in Las Vegas, many more press interviews and an appearance on *Letterman*. 'Douglas was also publicising *So Long . . .* at the same time,' says Steve Meretzky, 'so the TV appearances were more oriented toward that, with hopefully a quick mention of the game thrown in. My strongest memory of those interviews was that Douglas used the same story to break the ice with each interview – the "biscuit story". It's certainly a terrific story, but after the fiftieth time I heard it I wanted to scream!'[2]

The Hitchhiker's Guide to the Galaxy turned out to be a massive hit, selling over 400,000 copies and remaining on top of the game sales charts for most of the following year. The game was packaged, as Infocom games always were, with some impressive-looking but actually very cheap gimmicks. Douglas and Meretzky were both keen that the pack should include demolition orders for Arthur's house (in English) and the Earth (in Vogon). Douglas also suggested the inclusion of some pocket fluff. The one thing that Douglas wasn't happy with was the cover image, a laughing green sphere with a wide mouth and stick-like arms which had been used on all the American book covers. Known informally as the Cosmic Cutie in the States and as Jeremy Pac-Man by British fans, it was an attempt by Simon and Schuster to provide some degree of graphic linkage between all their covers, presumably because printing 'Douglas Adams' in large letters was too vague. Douglas loathed it.

'He told us from day one that he really wanted to avoid that if possible,' remembers Dornbrook, 'that he much preferred the British cover, that he just hated that laughing planet. I discussed it with the ad agency and that's how the vast majority of the books were sold – with that on the cover. It was such a distinctive logo and it so clearly said "humorous science fiction" that we just said to ourselves, "We would be crazy to change it." Douglas grudgingly went along with this.'[3]

With *Hitchhiker* a massive success, the next logical step was a sequel – but there was a problem. Douglas had enjoyed co-writing the *Hitchhiker's* game but had not enjoyed writing *So Long . . .* and so the last thing he wanted to work on next was *The Hitchhiker's Guide to the Galaxy II*: 'I really feel the need to branch out into fresh areas and clear my head from *Hitchhiker*. I certainly have enjoyed working with Infocom and would very much like to do another adventure game, but on a different topic.'[4]

'Douglas felt like he was in a rut,' recalls Dornbrook, 'That the more *Hitchhiker's* he did, the more he was viewed by everyone as "the *Hitchhiker's* guy" and the more he was stuck doing just *Hitchhiker's*. He wanted to break out of that. So he was pushing to do something different.'[5] That different thing would be a game called *Bureaucracy*.

The *Hitchhiker's* game was launched in the UK in May 1985. Eugen Beer of Beer Davies PR was responsible for publicising it, having already worked with Douglas on *The Meaning of Liff* and *So Long . . .*: 'One of my abiding memories is how much he loathed book signings. It's always a scary time for an author when you actually meet your fans, and Douglas had some of the ugliest and certainly some of the most boring people I've ever met in the whole of my life. They would come up to him to get their book signed and say, "I notice on page 45 you refer to . . ." and Douglas would say, "I haven't got a clue what they're talking about." He was incredibly tolerant, in fact patient beyond anything I would have been. But hey, he was selling books. To be honest I think he was embarrassed by *So Long . . .* because I think he knew it wasn't very good.

'People would always ask him the same thing: "So how did you come up with the idea of *The Hitchhiker's Guide to the Galaxy*?" He'd say, "Well, I was lying drunk in a field in Innsbruck ..." He'd go onto autopilot and you do feel quite sorry for people at that point. It is that thing that all authors have to do; you've got to be funny, you've got to entertain your public, because you've got to make them go out and buy the book. But then he couldn't wait to get the hell out of there. Douglas did like the sound of his own voice but even he, I think, got to the point of just being so bored with telling the story.'[6]

It was during the promotional tour for *So Long . . .* that Douglas told Beer how he had been approached, back in 1979, by somebody with the idea of selling a *Hitchhiker's Guide* towel. Douglas had liked the idea but Marks and Spencer had turned it down and so it came to naught, with the prototype towel languishing on a shelf somewhere. 'I've not really pursued the merchandise thing very strenuously because I'm basically a writer, I'm not in the T-shirt business,' said Douglas. 'On the other hand, if someone comes along with something and it's a nice idea I say, "Fine" – but it would have to be something reasonably good. The one thing I wanted to do ages ago was a towel, but everybody said, "Oh, it won't sell." But I wasn't really worried: I was told, "The book won't sell," I was told, "The record won't sell" – particularly by the BBC.'[7]

'All Douglas knew was that somebody in Marks and Spencer actually had a prototype,' recalls Beer. 'So I said, "Well, I'll try and track it down." Eventually I found the person who had the towel and he sent it to me. They'd taken the section where it says, "A towel is . . ." and just printed it on this big beach towel. I was completely taken with it. I just thought, "No-one's ever done a funny towel." So we said, "Look, can we do it? We'd like to manufacture them." We did a deal with Douglas and Ed Victor and went into the towel business.'[8]

Beer Davies licensed world towel rights, almost certainly a unique deal in publishing history, then placed adverts in magazines: 'I think we ended up selling a couple of thousand. If we'd done it around the time of the second or third book then it would have been fine.

But we'd missed it, everything had gone off the boil. There's only a limited number of people who want to fork out £14.95 for a sodding great towel. It had a bigger audience in the States but we couldn't physically get the towels over there.'[9]

Maggie Philips, who oversaw many of Douglas' contracts at Ed Victor Ltd, remembers numerous other attempts to license *Hitchhiker's Guide* merchandise, most of them less successful and understandably so: 'We had lots of submissions of books and board games – people saying they wanted to do a board game based on the characters in *Hitchhiker's Guide to the Galaxy,* who had not yet got a deal with Waddingtons but would contact them if we gave them permission. Lots of people tried to cash in. I always just wrote back and said, "These books are Douglas Adams' own idea. Why don't you have your own idea?" I never had a reply.

'Somebody wanted to do a mobile phone called a Babel Fish. That sort of thing happened all the time – every few days, something came in. Quite often people had progressed quite a long way with the development of these projects and were then horrified when we said, "Sorry, you can't do this. This is Douglas Adams' copyright." This happened with Douglas more than any other client we have. He was the one that everybody wanted a piece of, and who inspired lots of other ideas which people thought they could then use, and found out usually that they couldn't.'[10]

The towel was launched in 1985, a year which also saw the publication in book form of the twelve original radio scripts. This had actually started life as a proposal entitled *H2G2* – a name that would reappear many years later – incorporating radio and TV scripts together with the TV graphics and many other *Hitchhiker's*-related items. 'I think I was unemployed at the time, although I wasn't particularly unhappy,' recalls Geoffrey Perkins, who edited the book, 'but I think Douglas thought that this was the sort of thing he could give back to me to get me involved in doing things. I think it just became too difficult to get a handle on how you involved all the different bits, so it came down to doing a radio script book. It's quite a good book – relatively accurate!'[11]

CHAPTER 29

'INFOCOM WAS ALWAYS very keen to do another *Hitch-hiker* game,' recalled Douglas, 'but my feeling was that I was suffering from "sequelitis" by that time. I seem to remember that we laid plans to do another one, but it hadn't really got very far.'[1]

'Douglas wanted to do *Bureaucracy* first, because he was so sick of writing in the *Hitchhiker's* universe,' remembers Steve Meretzky. 'Contractually, we could have written five more *Hitchhiker's* games without Douglas' involvement, but we of course preferred to have him involved, both for PR purposes and because he contributed so much great stuff to the first game. So we agreed to do *Bureaucracy* first, and then that dragged on so long, by the time work started on the *Restaurant at the End of the Universe* game, text adventures were already a dying breed.'[2]

Bureaucracy had no connection with *Hitchhiker's Guide*, nor was it even science fiction. It involved, 'being thrown out of aeroplanes and being chased through jungles – a bit like Indiana Jones only a great deal more absurd,'[3] with the ultimate objective being to get your bank to acknowledge a change-of-address card. This idea, which Douglas had been mulling over for some time, had inspired an unused scene in *Life, the Universe and Everything* (a planet teeters on the brink of nuclear holocaust, finally tipping over the edge when a change-of-address card fouls up a computer; eventually it was reduced to a one-line gag about 'recreational impossibilities') and Douglas had suggested it as a game idea to Steve Meretzky at Huntsham Court in May 1984.

It was based on real life (or so Douglas claimed). When he moved from Highbury New Park to Islington and told his bank his new address, the bank acknowledged that they had changed his files and were now aware that he lived in Upper Street, Islington. And they sent this acknowledgement to Highbury New Park. So Douglas wrote again, pointing out this amusing mistake, and the bank wrote back to him, apologising, and once again the letter was sent to Highbury New Park. And this happened again and again.

Or so said Douglas when discussing *Bureaucracy*. But he seems to have been exaggerating again because, in the story's first appearance, in a contemporary interview, he cited not a series of mistakes by his bank but multiple mistakes by different organisations: 'There's no way that I can drum it into the brains of the Electricity Board, the Gas Board and the Post Office that I have changed my address. And dealing with the American Express computer has been beyond Kafka's worst paranoid nightmares.'[4] Constant repetitive mistakes by a single body fitted the computer game idea better and as Douglas repeated the tale, just like the field in Innsbruck, he came to recall only the story, not the event which inspired it.

'When Douglas proposed doing *Bureaucracy*, I was concerned,' recalls Mike Dornbrook. 'The whole financial deal we had signed with him was based on a bestselling line of books that was very, very popular, very well known. To do something completely new, I didn't feel that the royalty rates and everything were necessarily appropriate. He hadn't proved himself at anything else yet, for one thing. It was a little hard telling him that, but I had to look after Infocom's business interests.'[5]

But Dornbrook came up against Ed Victor, and the final deal was not that different from the *Hitchhiker's* one. Infocom weren't happy paying so much for an unknown quantity, but they wanted to stay on good terms with Douglas: 'That project was a real nightmare for us. It stretched on for years. It was one of those ideas where the three-minute pitch is hysterically funny, but then when you tried to turn it into something that was fun to play, there were all sorts of problems. It did eventually come out, but jeez, I don't even remember how many people worked on that. We just kept having to find new people to assign to it, then we'd lose them.'[6]

'I was about the third engineer who, uh, volunteered for that project,' recalls Tim Anderson. 'Although I worked on *Bureaucracy*, I never actually met Douglas. By that time, he had delegated his part to Michael Bywater, who came up with most of what actually made it into the game. Douglas was of course involved at the beginning of the project, but the main thing I remember about the scenario was something involving a box; the problem was to be set up in such a way that it would be almost impossible to specify the box you actually wanted to open. Not having had the benefit of a design session with Douglas, I never grasped the point of it beyond that, so it wasn't in the program as shipped.'[7]

'Michael Bywater was sent over to kind of finish it off,' says Dornbrook. 'Everyone was frustrated. We were frustrated, Douglas was frustrated about how it was going and how it wasn't going. Michael came over to try to get things moving on it. If I remember correctly, he was here on the order of two months. I think it was a frustrating process for him too.'[8]

Steve Meretzky didn't work on *Bureaucracy* but was able to see what was happening with it: 'Douglas' procrastination seemed much worse than it was with *Hitchhiker's*. That seems odd, because he did the first game only grudgingly, since he had already done *Hitchhiker's* for several different media, but *Bureaucracy* was what he most wanted to do. Perhaps the newness and excitement of working in interactive fiction had worn off; perhaps he had more distractions in his life at that point; perhaps it was that the succession of people who had my role in *Bureaucracy* didn't stay with the project for more than a portion of its development cycle and therefore never became a well-integrated creative unit with Douglas; perhaps it was that, lacking the immovable Christmas deadline that *Hitchhiker's* had, it was easier to let the game just keep slipping and slipping.'[9]

Bureaucracy eventually emerged onto shelves in 1987, three years after *Hitchhiker's* and at a time when text adventures were no longer the flavour of the month. Douglas' name on the packaging was small and barely noticeable. *Hitchhiker's Guide* had sold 400,000 units; *Bureaucracy* barely managed 40,000. After *Bureaucracy* was finished, or at least after Douglas had dropped off the project and passed the writing side over to his old friend humorist Michael Bywater, work started on a *Restaurant at the End of the Universe* game.

'The thing is, the *Hitchhiker* game was based very, very loosely on the book,' said Douglas, 'and deliberately so, because I didn't want to just do a trot through the book. I've seen some games where it's just like the original book only you get to do the typing, which I think is really not a good way of doing it. So I wanted to write a game that would have the same starting point and the same kind of feel as *Hitchhiker*, the same kind of logic to it, but would go where the game wanted to go. And in doing *Restaurant* I don't want to pick up the story where it left off and simply carry on doing the same thing. That would be boring.'[10]

Stu Galley was assigned to collaborate with Douglas and a certain amount of work was done – Steve Meretzky still has the designs – but by 1993 Douglas was confidently telling fans who enquired: 'No, the game was never started.'[11]

What has remained unknown till now is that Douglas worked on another computer game in between *Hitchhiker's* and *Bureaucracy*, and it wasn't for Infocom. It was called *Labyrinth* and it was an Activision/LucasArts co-production based on the 1986 film of the same name. Douglas knew three people connected with the film: screenwriter Terry Jones, director Jim Henson, and Henson's associate Christopher Cerf.

'It was decided that a group of us would all fly to London for a week of brainstorming on the design with Douglas Adams,' remembers Lucasfilm Games designer/project leader David Fox. 'The sessions were very stimulating and Douglas had a good many ideas, many of which made their way into the final game. It was Douglas' suggestion that the game open as a typical text adventure and then, when the player gets into the movie theatre playing the film *Labyrinth*, the screen fills with David Bowie's image, and from that point on, it's a graphic adventure.'[12]

In the opening text portion of the game, the player has a choice of two films: *Labyrinth* starring David Bowie, or *The Elephant Movie* starring Adam Braite. Assuming one doesn't choose the latter ('A herd of elephants sweep majestically across the plain'), the player finds themself in a cinema watching *Labyrinth* and trying to chat up a cute girl (or boy – the game asks what sex you are at the start) while being pestered by a geek (or geekette for female players). Rather than typing, the player could make commands by picking a verb and a noun from two menus. 'Adam Braite' turns out to be a pun. 'Douglas really liked the word "adumbrate", meaning "to prefigure indistinctly or foreshadow", so it ended up on the verb list,' remembers Fox. 'If I remember right, this obscure word was used in an even more obscure puzzle at one point in the game. You had to "adumbrate the elephant" when you were stuck in a prison, and an elephant would come and break a hole in the wall, freeing you. Definitely one of those things that was far funnier in the brainstorming session than in the game.'[13]

'While we were in London, Douglas had a great party to which he invited Jim Henson,' recalls Brenda Laurel, another member of the creative team. 'As Jim was leaving, he presented Douglas with a very large smoked salmon. Douglas just stared at it. Finally Jim said, "Say it, Douglas." Getting it at last, Douglas said, "So long, and thanks for all the fish."'[14]

December 1986 saw the publication of *The Utterly Utterly Merry Comic Relief Christmas Book,* co-edited by, and featuring several contributions from, Douglas. Comic Relief had been officially launched on Christmas Day 1985 and in April 1986 had staged a comedy gala in London for three nights. On Saturday 5 April the event was promoted on Radio 4's *Loose Ends* and, with most of the charity's 'name' supporters sleeping off the previous night's show, it fell to Douglas to go on the radio, where he said that a record and video of the show would be forthcoming. He also announced a book to be published in December, compiled from all new material by Britain's best comedians and comedy writers.

'I was in the shower at the time,' recalls Eugen Beer. 'I rang him up and said, "Douglas, we'll do the PR for free. We'll make sure there are no costs, get everything sponsored." Douglas was ostensibly, I think, supposedly trying to be one of the editors. In true Douglas fashion, of course, he never did anything, though he went round with Terry Jones, doing interviews. It was phenomenally successful, it sold about 350,000 copies. I have to say it also was, and still is, a very funny book. It was Richard Curtis did most of it, I think, in the end, and Peter Fincham.'[15]

The book was credited as 'edited by Douglas Adams and Peter Fincham' although there was no mention of this on the cover, and it included not only supplemental *Liff* entries but also the only three short stories which Douglas ever wrote. 'The Private Life of Genghis Khan' was a fairly literal adaptation of the old *Out of the Trees* sketch, but culminating in an appearance by Wowbagger the Infinitely Prolonged, the immortal alien from *Life, the Universe and Everything*. 'A Christmas Fairly Story' (*sic*) was a collaboration with Terry Jones, a surreal story of a future where coal falls from the sky, which reads much more like Terry than Douglas. ('I think I wrote something and then Douglas improved on it,' says Jones. 'I don't know why it's never been reprinted.'[16])

Then there was 'Young Zaphod Plays It Safe', a prequel to the *Hitchhiker's* saga which showed that short stories were as unsuited to Douglas' style as short sketches. The story ends with the escape to Earth of a very dangerous alien being; this was meant to be Ronald Reagan but any satirical point was lost in the vague phrasing and for years afterwards many *Hitchhiker's* fans believed it to be Jesus.

With Eugen Beer's comments in mind, it's impossible to say how much work on the book was done by Douglas, how much by Fincham (executive producer of many hit TV comedy shows of the '80s and '90s) and how much by the tireless, uncredited Richard Curtis. In late 1986 Douglas sent a 'thank you' letter out to the many contributors: 'Astonishingly, utterly astonishingly, the *Utterly Utterly Merry Comic Relief Christmas Book* is now finished. It has all been written, designed, typeset, everything. All that remains to be done is a few lunches, and that will be it. It is, I believe, the first comedy book ever to be finished less than three months late, and has therefore already stolen a considerable march on all the other Christmas books, most of which are now known to be over four months late already.'

'We sold 500,000 copies pretty fast,' recalled Douglas, many years later, 'and then we were attacked by the Church for one item about the Nativity, told from the point of view of one of the sheep. They threatened to sue us for blasphemy. Which is a pity – we could have sold many more copies and relieved a lot more famine if it hadn't been for the Church.'[17]

INTERLUDE - **MONEY**

IT WAS 26 September 1986 and Douglas Adams was a guest on *Wogan* on BBC1, discussing one of his projects which never happened: 'London to New York the Silly Way.' Fed up with flying across the Atlantic, Douglas had realised that it was possible to get there by a circuitous surface route: ferry to Calais (this was pre-Channel Tunnel), then connecting trains across Europe, Russia and the USA, interrupted only by a hike of twenty miles or so across the frozen Bering Strait.

Terry Wogan looked rather nonplussed and asked about *Hitch-hiker's Guide*: 'Douglas, the book was very successful, made an enormous amount of money.' 'I'm told, yes,' replied Douglas. 'I'm not quite certain where I put it.'[1]

Douglas did know where he put it. He gave it – well, £375,000 of it (maybe £342,000, exact figures vary) – to his accountant to put in a bank account until the end of the tax year, at which point it could be retrieved and paid to the Inland Revenue. The accountant had other ideas, and Douglas was simply too busy to notice.

'I'd been going backwards and forwards between England and the States relentlessly for a long time,' he said. 'I just got fed up with living in airplanes, which is very much like living in a vacuum cleaner: it's a long tube, and it's very noisy, and it smells stale inside, and you get treated like dirt. So I decided I'd stay put and renew my contacts with my friends and family, and I discovered all kinds of interesting things, like my accountant having stolen half a million dollars from me – because I was completely out of control – and that caught my interest.'[2]

Douglas sued and would have won his money back plus damages, except that the accountant promptly committed suicide. This made Douglas feel even worse: not just the betrayal by, then tragic death of, someone he knew and trusted, but also the fact that the accountant's death made the money unrecoverable: 'The shock was indescribable. I thought I was rich and the next moment I thought I was bankrupt. I don't understand money at all, I just understand shopping.'[3]

'Douglas was hopeless with money, and loved spending it,' says Sally Emerson. 'I remember cross-questioning him about his accountant, because he just handed everything to him – bills, receipts, etc. – and let him do all the accounts, without Douglas checking anything.'[4]

'I used to discuss things with Douglas to do with financial affairs sometimes,' recalls Jonny Brock. 'I was quite heavily involved with the disaster with his accountant, which was a very difficult time for him, about which he was extremely good. He lost a lot of money and had to get it all back in order to pay off the Revenue. I remember when he was singing the praises of this flash accountant he had who drove a Rolls-Royce. I vividly remember saying to him, "You know, that's not necessarily a very good thing." That was a scrape he got into but it wasn't his fault and he got out of it by working jolly hard.'[5]

'With this appalling thing with my accountant, it means I'm actually working for my living again, as opposed to, you know, earning money I don't actually need,' mused Douglas philosophically. 'I've always known that I was going to have to earn a lot of money one way or another simply because I have no idea how money works, and therefore I just don't keep hold of it very well – and I can never quite work out why.'[6]

CHAPTER **30**

DOUGLAS WAS A major author, with millions of copies in print and all five of his books (including *The Meaning of Liff*) had been bestsellers. Ed Victor was determined to make sure that Douglas got what he was worth, especially as there was that little matter of the outstanding tax return. So his next novel *Dirk Gently's Holistic Detective Agency*, and its then-untitled sequel were sold by auction to the highest bidder. William Heinemann bought UK hardback rights to both books on 3 December 1985 for £575,000, and on 10 January 1986, a deal was signed with Simon and Schuster for the US rights. The advance was a staggering $2.27 million.

All Douglas had to do now was write them: 'They will be recognisably me but radically different – at least from my point of view. The story is based on here and now but the explanation turns out to be science fiction.'[1]

To nobody's surprise, Douglas then totally failed to write the books. Hoping that a trip out of London might help (it hadn't with *So Long, and Thanks for All the Fish*, but there was no harm in trying again), Douglas set off for Shropshire: 'Halfway down the A40 I thought, "I seem to have spent my bloody life driving this road." So I turned round and ended up in Florence. It was a very liberating experience.'[2] And typically Douglas.

Around this time, Douglas also bought an apartment in New York, overlooking Central Park (the same building that Simon Jones and his wife lived in). 'He thought he could write anywhere

231

and he liked New York,' recalls Jones. 'It was ideal for him to be near us.'[3] It was also ideal for the Joneses who were able to move into Douglas' apartment when their own was flooded.

The first *Dirk Gently* book was set for delivery in December 1986 and publication in April 1987 (later revised to June): 'I'm starting it right now,' claimed Douglas after signing the contract. 'What I would like to do is write this book and then immediately write the second one and see if I can get them both done within a year.'[4] When the deadline rolled around, however, Douglas' editor Sue Freestone discovered that he had written precisely one sentence. It was a very good sentence; it was "High on a rocky promontory sat an Electric Monk on a bored horse," and it would eventually kick off Chapter Two of the novel. But it was all that Douglas had to show for over a year's work and a combined advance of about two million pounds.

'I addressed myself to writing something completely new,' recalled Douglas. 'I spent a year thinking about it, worrying that I couldn't do it and getting into a bit of a panic. And then finally I'd got enough of the ideas assembled, and from the moment I passed the deadline, I sat down, wrote it, and finished it in a matter of two or three weeks. It's certainly the book I've enjoyed writing the most for ages, and I feel that I've now got a new lease on life, because I was getting so bloody bored with *Hitchhiker's*. It had been ruling my life for the best part of ten years – and I just didn't have anything more to say in that context.'[5]

It was another case of locking Douglas up until the book was finished. Douglas had, Freestone observed, turned novel writing into a spectator sport.

Dirk Gently's Holistic Detective Agency was not *Hitchhiker's*, it was something completely new. It was partially set in St Cedd's College, Cambridge, featured a time-travelling don named Professor Chronotis, and centred around an attempt to prevent (or ensure) a spaceship explosion aeons ago. So in fact it wasn't something completely new at all: it was 'Shada' mixed with bits of 'City of Death' and given a good shake-up. At this time, Douglas believed that nobody apart from hardcore *Doctor Who* fans would ever know the story of 'Shada' so it was safe to use, and hadn't a *Doctor Who* story that nobody had seen saved him before?

Douglas' three *Doctor Who* adventures are among the very few never officially published in book form. Back in 1978 Douglas had considered novelising his original, longer version of 'The Pirate Planet' but events had rather overtaken him: 'Target Books has said to me many times, "Can we get someone to novelise your stories?" and I have always said, "No, if they're going to be done, I'd rather do them myself." To which they respond, "Oh, well, we'd be very pleased if you did them. We have our standard deal. We pay you £600." To which I say, "Well, I don't want to be embarrassing about this but I do have a tendency to be a bestselling author." Unfortunately they then say, "Oh yes, well anyway £600 is our standard offer." Those are the rules and that's their offer. It's terribly Vogonian thinking!'[6]

At a later date, the *Doctor Who* novelisation rights passed to Virgin, who spotted the gap in the catalogue and rang up Douglas to discuss possible novelisations: 'Amazingly, they pretty much repeated the offer – and logic – of the Target people. Bloody-mindedness, that's what it is!'[7]

It was an impossible situation. Clearly neither Target nor Virgin could establish a precedent of paying their *Doctor Who* authors according to their standing in the industry, even assuming that they could afford the sort of advance that Douglas would require. Equally clearly, there was no way that Ed Victor was going to let a Douglas Adams novel of any sort go for less than the current value, which was about a million pounds. So Douglas was free to re-use plot elements from the stories, provided he didn't use any BBC copyright characters. This was no problem for Douglas, who had always found characters interchangeable anyway.

Douglas' recent trip to Madagascar* featured briefly in *Dirk Gently's . . .*, transplanted to Mauritius so that the book could feature dodos, although there is a reference to Madagascar just to show that Douglas had actually been there. There is also, as with *So Long . . .*, a female cellist (inspired by an early girlfriend). Music was

* See Chapter 32

enormously important to Douglas' writing. In the previous novel it had been the Dire Straits album *Making Movies*; in this book it was Bach.

'Whenever I'm writing there will tend to be some piece of music that I will play over and over again in the background, almost like a mantra,' he explained. 'It'll drive anybody else in the house absolutely mad, so I usually have to go away to write. When I was writing *Dirk Gently's Holistic Detective Agency*, the Bach *Schubler Chorale Number Five* was the piece of music that I was playing incessantly in the background. And in fact it worked its way into the plot of the book, though I never actually say what the music was.'[8]

That explanation came from Douglas' appearance on *Desert Island Discs* in 1994. His other chosen records were the Shadows' 'Man of Mystery', the Beatles' 'Drive My Car', Ligeti's *Requiem* (from *2001*), Paul Simon's 'Hearts and Bones' and a recording of 'All of Me' by Ella Fitzgerald which was so rare that the BBC didn't even have a copy and had to borrow Douglas' – plus three pieces by Bach: the *Schubler Chorale Number Five*, the *B Minor Mass*, and the *Italian Concerto*. Douglas later wrote the inlay notes for two CDs of Bach music.

And so, with help from Sue Freestone, J.S. Bach and Doctor Who, the first *Dirk Gently* novel was somehow finished, two or three weeks after the deadline. The way Douglas got round this was by typesetting the book on his Macintosh at home and presenting it to Heinemann as a camera-ready manuscript. It was an original and clever, if slightly worrying, solution to what was by now a stereotypical Douglas Adams problem. But Douglas saw it merely as an innovation and made great play out of it in interviews, even listing the technical details of how it was done in an author's note at the start of the book: 'It was a fascinating and therapeutic way of working. Usually, finishing a book is a terrible anti-climax. Immediately going back to the book, with several days of very hard work, was an ideal wind-down.'[9]

Dirk Gently's Holistic Detective Agency was published in June 1987 and well received by critics. No-one seemed to spot that it was a rehashing of ideas from two old *Doctor Who* stories, and Douglas certainly wasn't going to tell them: 'Quite often people have said to me, particularly when I was doing the *Dirk Gently* books, "Aren't you essentially still doing the same stuff?" I remember one interview I did on breakfast television for the first *Dirk* novel, and the interviewer said in a rather peremptory way, "This book is like all your other books, isn't it? It's just a lot of ideas." I was stumped by that.'[10]

CHAPTER 31

DOUGLAS FOLLOWED *DIRK Gently's Holistic Detective Agency* with a second adventure for the character, who was based loosely on Michael Bywater. However, the late delivery of the first novel meant that there was no way he was going to make the November 1987 deadline for the second, even if he did his own typesetting again. Heinemann were, somewhat naively, hoping to hit the summer market again with a June 1988 publication.

Douglas had always passed his deadlines, right since the days of the first *Hitchhiker's* radio series. He was famously quoted as saying: 'I love deadlines. I love the whooshing noise they make as they go by.'[1] But *The Long, Dark Tea-Time of the Soul* was the start of a slippery slope for Douglas; it was the first time that not only his deadline but his publication date came and went without a finished manuscript. Heinemann, conscious that (a) they had paid a lot of money for this book, and (b) Douglas was a cash-cow who would sell enormous amounts whenever he was published, rescheduled publication for October to hit the Christmas market instead.

In October, Douglas was back on *Wogan,* explaining what had happened to an increasingly bemused Irish talk-show host: 'I was meant to be on an author tour of Australia, going round telling the Australians to buy my books. I was very late with this book. It was getting to the middle of July; I should have delivered it in November. So they said, "You've got to be on such-and-such a plane," and I basically wasn't. I hadn't finished the book. So faxes and telexes were rushing backwards and forwards across the world. The courier arrived, took away my British Airways ticket, came back with a Qantas ticket for the next flight.

'I sat and was pounding away and pounding away and it got to the next flight and I still hadn't finished. So more faxes and telexes – a lot of tension building around the world at this moment. Courier arrived again, took away my Qantas ticket, went away, brought back the British Airways ticket for the next flight. My publishers phoned me up at this point and said, "We have 350 paying guests who have paid a lot of money to have dinner and hear you speak. It's in Perth and we would like you to be there. The taxi will be there at seven o'clock this evening. Please be in it." So 6.59 arrived and I still hadn't finished the book. Luckily, a minute later I had! The taxi arrived, I was bundled into the taxi. I hadn't actually been to bed for three nights. My sleep was replaced by the odd stint of eight minutes twenty-three seconds on the exercise bicycle in the basement.'[2]

The exercise bicycle sessions were that long because that was the length of the third movement of Mozart's *Piano Concerto in A Major*, which was Douglas' piece of music for this particular novel. The interesting thing about Douglas' music/writing obsession was that he could not actually write while music was playing, and so would break off occasionally to play Mozart or Bach or Paul Simon, then return invigorated to his writing. It was an odd, obsessively compulsive way of writing books, but at least it got them written. Eventually.

What was more worrying, in hindsight, was that Douglas was alternating between stressful writing and frenetic pedalling on his exercise bicycle. That was not healthy.

Terry Wogan had by this point realised that he was not going to get a word in edgeways. Douglas was off on one of his anecdotes, barely pausing for breath. At least it was a new story and not the field in Innsbruck or Andrew Marshall being rude in pubs. Wogan restricted himself to arching the occasional sardonic eyebrow at the audience.

Douglas continued in full flow: how he had flown to Singapore, hot and sweaty and in a state of nervous tension, and phoned corrections to the last chapter through from Singapore airport; how he had arrived in Perth at four in the morning to be collected by some long-suffering Pan Books employee ('It's okay. There's a happy ending. Don't look so worried,'[3] he told Wogan); how he slept for eight hours then woke up convinced that the book needed another 500-word passage, but was dissuaded by Sue Freestone who enjoined him to go out and have a good time; what a good time he had that evening, drinking in Fremantle with Ben Elton; the message from Freestone on his answering machine when he returned, the worse for wear, saying, 'Yes, you're right. It does need another 500 words'; how the hotel could not provide a computer or a manual typewriter, only an electric typewriter, the workings of which he could not fathom; how he wrote the passage out by hand, dictated it to Freestone's answering machine, then corrected the pages that were faxed out to him in Australia.

'It's different than Tolstoy, isn't it?' he concluded. 'But the strange thing is, under those circumstances you actually come up with all the best stuff. Stuff you couldn't have written any other way. It's very strange.'[4]

It wasn't an interview, it was a monologue by Douglas, and not a terribly interesting one either. Most of the audience's enjoyment came from Terry Wogan's bemused expression as he sat and patiently waited for his guest to finish.

Dirk Gently would not see print again until the posthumous publication of part of *The Salmon of Doubt* in 2002, but he did re-emerge onto the stage in 1995 in a student production in Oxford, simply titled *Dirk*. Douglas came to see the play on the last night (3 June) and was delighted: 'They managed to solve the problem of how you deal with lots of complexities and contradictions of plot by simply ignoring them. It was wonderful!'[5]

'He seemed to be oddly charmed,' recalls James Goss, who co-wrote the play with director Arvind David. 'He seemed surprised that anyone had tried to adapt it, and even more surprised that it worked so well. I remember sitting up in the eaves watching this terribly tall man squeezed into a tiny seat with his incredibly long legs splayed out across the aisles. I spent all of that performance just watching him laughing. It was incredible.'[6]

Dirk was revived by the Oxford University Dramatic Society at the Oxford Playhouse over 5–8 November 1997, a production funded by former OUDS member Rowan Atkinson, and once again Douglas was in the audience: 'It was funny watching it on stage, because I suddenly began to think about it again, and think, "Well, they did this well, but what they should have done was this, and they should've done that." It starts the whole ball rolling in your head. I suddenly thought, "I would love to see this happen as a film," because I can now see, having thought about it freshly in this context, what kind of a movie it could be, and it could be great.'[7]

In fact the film rights to *Dirk Gently* had been first sold back in 1990 and a US TV series was under consideration in 1992, on both of which projects Douglas decided to keep a back seat, in contrast to his close involvement with the *Hitchhiker* movie. By 1997 the TV rights had been acquired by a British company, Wall to Wall Television, who signed Michael Marshall Smith to write a pilot script. Smith had come from Footlights and won numerous awards for his SF and fantasy novels; Douglas met with him on 3 November 1997 to discuss Smith's first rough outline.

'I got as far as producing some detailed adaptation notes and even a rough breakdown of how the plot would progress,' recalls Smith. 'There are obviously a lot of issues involved in adapting a book like that – not least bringing the flavour along with the action, and getting some of the material out of the internal dialogues – but I think we'd pretty much cracked them. But I seem to recall that our vision for the way the story should be done was somewhat different to Wall to Wall's. After a while we started to see it more as a movie; Wall to Wall were seeing it as a series, and only had TV rights. I was very busy at the time, and so was Douglas, and I think in the end we just agreed to put it on a back burner for a while, until these issues could be resolved.'[8]

The possibility of a *Dirk Gently* film continued to be touched on. Douglas announced in August 2000 that he had written the first five pages of a screenplay and that Michael Nesmith was attached to the project; he also promised Simon Jones an unspecified role in the film. But like the mooted *Starship Titanic* film, it was abundantly clear that nothing would happen so long as the *Hitchhiker's Guide* movie remained in Development Hell.

INTERLUDE - **GOD**

IN 1998, DOUGLAS gave an interview to a publication called *American Atheist*, in which he explained his views on religion and his position as a radical atheist in detail. To quote extensively from that interview here would be redundant – it is on the web and in *The Salmon of Doubt* – but it only demonstrates Douglas' view at age forty-six.

At school, Douglas had been a thoroughly committed Christian. 'Many years ago, I was extremely religious,' he admitted. 'My parents belonged to a Christian community, which had quite a strong effect on my growing up, and all the way through school I took Christianity very seriously.'[1]

'He was always a great sermon-taster,' remembers Brentwood Chaplain Tom Gardiner. 'He used to listen very carefully and he would give me comments about things, which I used to enjoy. He had a Christian training, he was brought up in the Christian tradition and he had a great deal of sympathy for it.'[2]

Douglas certainly seems to have remained a committed Christian until he left Brentwood, but somewhere between school and university he apparently had a moment of revelation when he listened to a street-corner evangelist and realised that religious dogma flew in the face of the reasoned arguments he had been taught to apply in history, science and other subjects. Though there had been no overt sign of this at Brentwood, Tom Gardiner (who also marked some of Douglas' English work) could see how it developed: 'I felt that in his writing he showed that he was a martyr to epistemology, having a great struggle with what words actually meant. How are we to employ them? To what extent are words serviceable? And this was his problem in religion as well.'[3]

'I'm very firmly agnostic,' said Douglas in 1984. 'I have terrible rows with my girlfriend who is a convinced atheist. This seems to me irrational. There's no evidence either way.'[4] But though Jane couldn't convince him, Richard Dawkins could. Dawkins e-mailed Douglas a fan letter in 1987 after reading *Dirk Gently's Holistic Detective Agency* and discovered that Douglas was equally enamoured of his books. The two became a mutual appreciation society, with Dawkins seemingly usurping John Cleese' position as Douglas' idol. ('He told me of an instance when John Cleese had been quite brusque with him, not going out of his way to put him at his ease when he could quite easily have done so,' remembers Mark Lewisohn, which may have some bearing on the matter.[5])

Thereafter, Douglas was quite outspoken on religious matters (though never as much as Dawkins) yet was quite happy to continue in his admiration of Bach and other religious music, a contradiction which bothered Douglas not in the slightest. He even briefly considered writing a whole book on atheism.

'I think this radical atheism that he professed was a pretty late development,' says Jonny Brock, who had known Douglas since Cambridge. 'I may be being unkind but I think it was very much driven by Richard Dawkins who as you know is completely obsessed with atheism, far more than Douglas ever was. I think it was partly Douglas trying to please the scientific establishment and particularly Richard Dawkins who he was rather foolishly, I think, in awe of. I'm not saying he would have become Christian again, or Buddhist or anything else, but I think it was a transitional phase.'[6]

Tom Gardiner agrees to some extent: 'It's more or less a Marxist pattern: there's a thesis which is the Christian one, then the antithesis which is Dawkins, then there would follow a synthesis, which would be his knowledge from having lived in both worlds – a world with God and a world without God. Though I'm not saying for a moment, as some would say, that if he had lived he would have "come back to the true faith".[7]

'If it turned out that there was a God, I would feel I'd been the victim of a monumental confidence trick,' said Douglas. 'I'd feel that the universe was playing silly buggers. I'll wait and see but I won't lose any sleep over it.'[8]

CHAPTER **32**

BETWEEN JULY 1988 and April 1989, Douglas travelled around the world, accompanied by a zoologist and a BBC recording engineer. The result was *Last Chance to See* – not only Douglas' favourite of all his books but undoubtedly the single best piece of work he ever created. As described in the book's opening chapter, the idea came to Douglas back in April 1985 when he and Jane had spent several days living in the jungles of Madagascar.

The reason for this was that the World Wildlife Fund were sending well-known authors to out-of-the-way places to write articles for the *Observer* magazine and thereby raise awareness of ecological issues. In interviews Douglas liked to give the impression that the offer of the Madagascar trip had come out of the blue and taken him somewhat aback, but in fact he had been actively seeking such an opportunity for several years.

Back in 1979, when he was preparing to give his talk at the World Science Fiction Convention, Douglas had met Dr Jack Cohen, a respected evolutionary biologist with a sideline in helping SF authors to devise viable ecosystems for their fictional planets. After some initial confusion (Cohen was dismantling a slide projector which he had used and Douglas assumed that he was merely a technician) the two got to discussing science. Two or three years later, Cohen received a call from Douglas who was going through one of his bouts of depression and wanted to now how he could become actively involved in biology as an escape from writing novels.

'I had recently been working on a BBC nature series called *The*

Trials of Life' recalls Cohen, 'and I said to Douglas, "You do understand, don't you, that this sort of thing is extremely dull to make? These cameramen spend a week sitting in the jungle just to get that one brief shot." And he said, "Yes, that's it – I want to spend a week sitting in the jungle."'

Cohen put Douglas in touch with biologist and author Colin Tudge who contacted the WWF and, after an earlier plan to explore coral reefs in the Red Sea was dropped, ultimately came the invitation to visit Madagascar. Douglas typically decided that all this preamble was not as amusing a story as nearly dropping the phone in surprise at the 'unexpected' invitation and wondering whether they had called the wrong person, and that became the standard interview tale.

Alain le Garsmeur was the freelance photographer assigned to the WWF/*Observer* project. Before meeting Douglas however, his first task was an expedition to the Mongolian desert with Gore Vidal and his male assistant named Austin.

'There was no wildlife there!' chortles le Garsmeur. 'But it worked out quite well because he wrote about the wildlife which we didn't see. The second one was Douglas in Madagascar. I'd never met Douglas before, so the *Observer* said to me, "He's a very big man, very tall. You won't fail to recognise him." We got to Paris airport to get the flight to Madagascar and he was travelling first class. He said, "You can't be travelling in the back. Come first class." I said, "Well, are you going to pay for the ticket?" He says, "No." So I did travel first class but I had to put it on my expenses!'[1]

In Madagascar, Douglas, Jane and le Garsmeur were met by WWF zoologist Mark Carwardine, who also had never met Douglas before but recognised him instantly. 'Tall, very tired, more than a little confused,' were his first impressions, 'but also eager to please, game for anything, and friendly.'[2] What they were searching for was the aye-aye, an extremely rare and bizarre species of lemur. 'The aye-aye is the kind of weird and wonderful creature that a writer of humorous science fiction might concoct on a really good day,' explains Carwardine. 'We thought Douglas might be interested to know that it already exists.'[3]

Whether this quartet would actually see an aye-aye was debatable, especially as no-one else had seen one for quite some time and there were believed to be only about fifteen left, living on the tiny island of Nosy Mangabé. Just in case, le Garsmeur photographed Douglas with a stuffed one: 'You know what it's like for us photographers – we like to make sure we come back with something. Douglas was very, very keen on photography – I think that's why we got on well. The aye-aye was on this little island, so we had to get a boat across, and his new Nikon was suddenly covered in sea water! He looked a rather sad figure. We took the mickey out of him very much, though we didn't gang up on him.'[4]

Douglas, Jane, Mark and Alain stayed three or four nights on Nosy Mangabé, sleeping in a hut with a concrete floor. It was a long, long way from Islington in every sense. Douglas may have spent the 1970s hitchhiking round Europe and sleeping on friends' sofas, but he had long since become used to the good life of first-class airline travel and top hotels. 'Mark was definitely more used to roughing it,' recalls le Garsmeur. 'He's a zoologist and he knows his way round things. I was a bit like Douglas, a bit out of our depth really, to be honest, in this jungle. And I think Jane found it more difficult than he did. They were very loving towards each other; it was rather nice. She helped him tremendously to get through it all. Because he could get a bit fed up, being asked to do these things. But he's a good trouper.'[5]

The group actually spotted an aye-aye on the first night and le Garsmeur got off three frames on his motor drive: 'We went out for two other nights and we never saw it again!'[6] Nevertheless, Douglas was delighted with the trip: 'The whole expedition was the most tremendous experience. I'd just done a promotional tour of the USA before this and was convinced I was turning into a room-service bore. This really sorted me out.'[7]

'The best way to tell if you get on with someone is to be thrown together for a couple of hard weeks' travelling and spend every night sleeping on a wet concrete floor in the middle of a jungle,' says Carwardine. 'We found that we got on extremely well and enjoyed travelling together in Madagascar immensely. For Douglas, it opened his eyes to a whole new world and, I think, changed his life quite dramatically.'[8]

And so the idea of *Last Chance to See* was hatched. Mark and

Douglas would travel the world for a year, seeking out species on the brink of extinction (le Garsmeur declined the chance to join them, confident that Douglas would take all the pictures required). The project would result in a book and a radio series, and would raise both specific and general concerns about the environment. A publishing deal was secured with Heinemann, with Douglas insisting on splitting everything 50–50 with Carwardine. Ed Victor protested, but Douglas stood firm. The next stage was to approach the BBC.

'It was very much my deliberate intention to do it for radio rather than television,' said Douglas. 'It basically means that you travel the same way that everybody else does, you're not encumbered by equipment, and not only that but people's reactions to you are not modified by the fact that you're pointing a bloody great television camera at them. If you take a film crew, basically you have to organise it like a military operation, and that would have fundamentally changed the nature of what we were doing.'[9]

'Douglas was particularly keen for our travels to be genuine adventures, with radio tagging along for the ride, rather than more clinical TV productions,' confirms Carwardine, 'The BBC went along with this. The producer and two studio managers shared the travelling between them and, amazingly, Douglas and I paid for all the travel costs ourselves – out of the advance for the book.'[10]

There was one slight misstep in preparation, when Douglas made another of his less-than-tactful phone calls to Geoffrey Perkins: 'Douglas phoned me up and said, "I'm doing this thing. I'm basically going in search of animals that might become extinct. I'm going to go round jungles and places and record them all and it's going to be a great show. I wondered whether you were interested in doing it." I thought: this is brilliant. I said, "Yes, I'm completely free. I'd love to. So we would go out and record these things?" He said, "No, no, I'll be there and I'll just talk into a tape recorder and send you the tapes back, and you put them into a programme."'[11]

Needless to say, Perkins politely declined. Eventually, with all the publishing and broadcasting arrangements in place, Douglas and Mark just had to decide where they were going and what they would be looking for. There was – sadly – a wide choice.

'We spent many evenings talking late into the night,' recalls

Carwardine. 'I'd turn up with a list of possible endangered species, then we'd pore over a world map and talk about where we'd both like to go. Among the animals we considered were the kouprey, a kind of forest ox living on some minefields in Vietnam; the northern hairy-nosed wombat in Australia (because Douglas liked its name), and the no-eyed big-eyed wolf spider in Hawaii (for similar reasons!) In the end, we went for a good geographical spread and a mix of mammals, birds and reptiles.'[12]

A proposal document dated 1986 suggests travelling to Australia in February 1987 to look for the kakapo and the Tasmanian tiger, to Asia in May to search out the kouprey and the Komodo dragon, and to South America in November on the trail of the quetzal and the golden lion tamarin. Of these, the Tasmanian tiger was the most ambitious as it was declared extinct in 1936, although the proposal contends that one had been photographed the previous year, 'by a man out walking his dog'.

The final list was: Komodo dragon (July/August 1988), Rodrigues fruitbat (September), baiji dolphin (October), Juan Fernandez fur seal (November/December), mountain gorilla and northern white rhinoceros (February 1989), kakapo (a flightless New Zealand parrot which was undoubtedly the book's 'star', February/March) and Amazonian manatee (March/April). Carwardine then set to the task of battling through all the bureaucracy in the way of actually getting to each of the places where these animals lived.

It is not this biography's job to recount the adventures which Mark and Douglas experienced while researching *Last Chance to See*, as they recounted them magically in the book. But the book only touches on the trip's highlights. For every day when the team saw and recorded exotic wildlife, there were many more when they were getting there, getting home, or were there but just not finding anything.

'There was a lot of boring travelling, long flights, etc.,' remembers Carwardine, 'and lots of waiting around for a mixture of bureaucrats and animals. Both Douglas and I have very low boredom thresholds. We spent an inordinate amount of time talking about everything under the sun. Funnily enough, Douglas didn't read much while we were travelling. I don't think he could concentrate on something so different and far-removed from the situation in hand. But the first thing he did on getting back to civilisation was to buy books and read solidly for hours.

'When we got back to Sydney after our visit to Komodo, he went to his hotel room and disappeared for an hour – shaving, showering, etc. – and then went off to find a bookshop. He bought at least twenty books on an incredible variety of subjects and then went back to bed for three solid days and nights to read the whole lot in one sitting. His other great thing on returning to civilisation was the phone – he made loads of phone calls. The thing about Douglas was that he thoroughly enjoyed roughing it and living life in the wilds for a week or so, but then he pined for the comforts of civilisation. He only enjoyed the tough bit in short bursts, which is completely understandable of course.'13

The final expedition complete, Mark and Douglas retired to Douglas' villa in the South of France to write the book (in Douglas' case, for tax reasons). Between them they had many fantastic memories, helped by all the BBC recordings and hundreds of photographs. Douglas had made copious notes in the field using his latest toy, a Z88 electronic notebook, but he sat on it in Chile and lost everything. ('I discovered that the business of writing a travel book is actually very closely akin to fiction,' he said, 'because mostly when you get back you can't remember what happened and you have to make it up.'14) Nevertheless, the two co-authors had plenty to work on in Juan les Pins. Unfortunately, they also had plenty of things to distract them from working on any of it.

'Every day, we would get up fairly late and start talking about how we must knuckle down and start the book,' recalls Carwardine. 'We'd decide to go for a stroll along the front and maybe have a coffee while we talked through the structure of the first chapter. Then coffee would merge into lunch and we'd agree to enjoy one last leisurely lunch before heading straight back to the villa to write for the rest of the day. Lunch finished around late afternoon and, having failed miserably to mention the book at all, we agreed that the day was going to be hopeless for writing so we might as well enjoy it. We usually went out to eat in the evenings, sometimes driving all the way to Monte Carlo "for one last good evening before the hard work begins". Then we followed the same routine the following day . . . After four solid months in the villa we emerged with one page written – and even that didn't make it into the book. After that, we returned to London and were locked in Douglas' house in Islington until it was finished.'[15]

Douglas always gave the impression that writing *Last Chance to See* had been significantly easier, or at least more pleasurable, than writing his novels, but clearly this was not the case. One page was better than the one sentence he'd written for *Dirk Gently's Holistic Detective Agency*, but it must still have been massively frustrating for Carwardine (nice meals in Monte Carlo notwithstanding) as he prepared all the information and Douglas sat at the computer keyboard, completely failing to write the book.

In a move startlingly reminiscent of 'finish the page you're on', Heinemann eventually decided that enough was enough and published the book with only six of the eight expeditions included, which is why the fur seal and the manatee are not mentioned (and the final chapter is considerably shorter than the others) although both species were covered in the radio series. That wasn't how Douglas remembered it, however. When asked why the fur seal wasn't included in the book, he replied: 'There were altogether too many of them. They were thought to be extinct, but then a colony of 200 were discovered and there are now up to 2,000.'[16]

The radio series went slightly more smoothly, the only problem being that the Komodo dragon recordings were somehow lost. 'We insisted that everything that went out on the radio, other than something that was obviously a commentary done back in the studio, would be absolutely live,' said Douglas. 'We wouldn't fiddle with anything at all. Now, we actually went down into the gully where these things were all feeding on a goat and it was the most repulsive and extraordinary experience I've ever been through. I was standing there almost vomiting, trying to describe it. But there was something wrong with the tape. So then, weeks and weeks later, I had to go into a studio in Broadcasting House and relive it, just in front of a microphone. I just imagined it and acted it – and it ended up on *Pick of the Week!*'[17]

Last Chance to See is a fantastic book, and many of Douglas' friends, colleagues and fans cite it as their favourite. Unfortunately, in the manner of these things, it was his poorest selling title. Douglas was frustrated by the lack of interest in what he perceived (quite correctly) as his best and most important work.

'*Last Chance to See* was a book I really wanted to promote as much as I could,' he lamented, 'because the Earth's endangered species is a huge topic to talk about. The thing I don't like about doing promotion usually is that you have to sit there and whinge on about yourself. But here was a big issue I really wanted to talk about and I was expecting to do the normal round of press, TV and radio. But nobody was interested. They just said, "It isn't what he normally does so we'll pass on this, thank you very much." As a result the book didn't do very well. I had spent two years and a hundred and fifty thousand pounds of my own money doing it. I thought it was the most important thing I'd ever done and I could not get anyone to pay any attention.'[18]

Nevertheless, travelling the world and writing the book (eventually) was a very positive experience for Douglas. It matured him and turned him from a writer into a thinker: 'I think one of the reasons I was very interested in doing this is, when I was doing *Hitchhiker* I was always trying to find different perspectives on everyday things so that we would see them afresh. And I suddenly realised that the animals in the world, because they all have completely different perceptual systems, the world we see is only specific to us, and from every other animal's point of view it's a completely different place.'[19]

'I also discovered that because I had an external and important subject to deal with I didn't feel any kind of compulsion to be funny the whole time – and oddly enough a lot of people have said it's the funniest book I've written.'[20]

Unfortunately for those who enjoyed *Last Chance . . .*, Douglas never wrote another non-fiction book, though he did discuss another wildlife project with photographer Jody Boyman, whom he met in 1993: 'Douglas and I bandied around the idea of expanding on *Last Chance to See*, coming up with a coffee-table version brimming with photos of the animals he so insightfully and hilariously described. Although the project never got underway, I did end up travelling to Botswana and Zimbabwe for a month with his beloved younger sister Jane, and we had an absolutely wonderful time.'[21]

CHAPTER 33

ON 25 OCTOBER 1988, William Heinemann Ltd signed a deal with Serious Productions Ltd for a novel called *Starship Titanic* and another simply listed as 'Untitled Book 2'. The first book would appear four years later under a different title,* and the second would never be written and the contract would eventually be cancelled. (Douglas had founded Serious Productions as a holding company in 1981: 'Most people I know with companies had silly names for them, so I decided I was going to have a Serious name.'[1] In 1993 it became Completely Unexpected Productions Ltd, but there was no significant difference.)

'I did the deal to do these next two books and I hadn't quite decided what the first one was going to be,' explained Douglas. 'I hadn't decided if it was going to be a *Hitchhiker* book but I had decided it was going to be a science fiction one, and they said, "Well you've got to give us a title for the contract, it doesn't matter what the book is or what the eventual title is, it just makes everyone feel more secure and calm because there's actually a title on the contract." And *Starship Titanic* was an idea I'd had knocking around from years ago, and my agent always said, "Oh you must do this, you must do this," and I wasn't overkeen, but I eventually agreed to use that title as a place holder.'[2]

* A book actually called *Starship Titanic* would follow six years after that.

Nineteen eighty-eight had already been a relatively busy year. As well as *Last Chance . . .* trips to Komodo, Mauritius and China, Douglas had been touring Britain to promote *The Long, Dark Tea-Time of the Soul.* It was also a busy time for Douglas' fans, with plenty of exciting new things to buy including Neil Gaiman's *Don't Panic,* the first in-depth look at the whole *Hitchhiker's Guide* phenomenon, and the *Hitchhiker's* radio series finally available on cassette and CD (the first ever BBC radio programme on the new format). The corporation somehow managed to clear all the background music, as well as the Eagles' main theme. The one thing they couldn't clear, necessitating a brief edit in 'Fit the Third', was Marvin humming the Pink Floyd song 'Shine On You Crazy Diamond', which was ironic as Douglas was by then good friends with both David Gilmour and Nick Mason.

'The BBC Clearing the Use of Seventies Rock Music in Comedy Science Fiction Stories Department tried to clear the use of this snatch of music,' explained Douglas. 'They didn't ask me about it and had no idea that I knew any of the band. In fact there's no reason why they should ask me – if I had every detail of every obscure copyright negotiation referred back to me it would be a full-time job. The BBC department in question would have been dealing with Pink Floyd's lawyers, and exactly the same applies. So we were all locked in a legal battle without any of the principals having the remotest idea. Another point is that I think that the actual piece was probably copyrighted at least in part to Roger Waters, whom I don't know at all. In fact, being a friend of Dave and Nick would probably have weighed against me in that case . . .'[3]

Another matter for the lawyers was an advertising campaign for the *Daily Telegraph,* using graphics modelled on those of the TV series (though not by Pearce Studios), a Peter Jones soundalike voice-over ('I was abroad, so they got someone to imitate me'[4]) and the slogan 'The Earth-dweller's guide to life, the universe and everything'. It was either a staggeringly bare-faced attempt to infringe on somebody else's intellectual property, or an indication of how entrenched in the public consciousness *Hitchhiker's* had now become.

'It was a newspaper that was very much associated with middle age trying to appeal to a younger audience,' recalls Maggie Philips. 'They had this whole campaign that an advertising agency had done, then somebody said, "Hold on, this is the title of a Douglas Adams book." It was a total rip-off. They came to see us when it was well-established; they had space booked and television time and everything. Luckily for them, Douglas was okay about it, but they had to pay us quite a lot of money.'[5]

There was, however, still no sign of a new novel.

Foreign editions of Douglas' books continued to proliferate and keeping track of them all was almost a full-time job. The first had been *Per Anhalter Durch Die Galaxis* (*Hitchhiker's Guide* in German) in 1981 and the books had since been translated into French (*Guide du Routard Galactique*), Dutch (*Het Transgalactisch Liftershandboek*), Finnish (*Linnunradan Kasikirja Liftareille*), Spanish (*Guia del Autoestopista Galactico*), Hebrew (*Madrih Hatrempist Lagalaktiza*), Swedish (*Liftarens Guide till Galaxen*) and almost every other language in which books were printed.

'I went through an Italian translation, just looking for any passage I might vaguely recognise,' said Douglas, 'and came across the Italian for "don't panic", and in Italian it was "*non fatebi pranderi del panico*", which doesn't have the same kind of bite, does it? I think that rhythm is a very important part of the way humour works, and obviously that's very hard to translate, and when the Japanese edition came I couldn't even tell you which bit was my name.'[6]

'Douglas has very enthusiastic long-term publishers in Germany and some other territories as well,' says Maggie Philips. 'People were generally queuing up to buy Douglas' books. The contract always gives us control of the title, because sometimes titles mean something completely different if you translate them literally.'[7] 'The German editions do sell well,' agreed Douglas. 'I like to think that the sort of ideas and characters I'm dealing with in *Hitchhiker*, even if there's an English perspective on it, are sufficiently universal that anyone would enjoy it.'[8]

Douglas himself was not multilingual, which was odd for someone who travelled around the world so much and was so enamoured of language. Apart from school lessons in French and Greek, he only once attempted to learn a foreign tongue, shortly after he had split up with Graham Chapman and there seemed to be nothing else to do: 'When I was in this state of depression, I kept trying to find activities that would stop my brain going round and round and round. One day I decided I was going to learn German, and went and got a pile of "Teach Yourself German" books, and spent every single waking instant poring over those books. And by a curious coincidence, at the end of a month, I happened to wander out into the garden, and there was a strange woman looking for someone who used to live in the flat and she was a German. So I sat and talked in German with her, and discovered I'd actually done incredibly well. But since then I've never spoken German, and I don't think I can remember a word.'[9]

So popular was Douglas in Germany that a German composer of avant-garde jazz, Klaus König, actually wrote and recorded a suite based on the *Hitchhiker* books, called *At the End of the Universe – Hommage A Douglas Adams*. Douglas was faintly embarrassed by this but kindly agreed to sanction the recording and pick some appropriate quotes from his novels for the CD booklet. And still there was no sign of a new Douglas Adams novel.

The Meaning of Liff was revised and expanded, at the publisher's suggestion, into *The Deeper Meaning of Liff* over Christmas 1988 although for some reason it wasn't published until 1990 (possibly to avoid clashing with the paperback of *Long, Dark Tea-Time*). 'We'd enjoyed the first experience, and several years had elapsed, so I suppose we thought we might manage a few new ideas,' recalls John Lloyd. 'Douglas found a window in his tumultuous schedule, and this time he announced that he had taken a residence not in Malibu but in Palm Beach, Sydney, Australia. He also announced that as it was a roomy house he'd taken the precaution of inviting half a dozen other friends along as well. So it was exceptionally jolly. We all spent Christmas there together in the middle of the most tremendous monsoon.

'Douglas then went into a bit of a decline because he'd briefly split up with Jane and was regretting it, but Jon Canter manfully stepped in and wrote some of the best jokes in the book while

Douglas was getting over it. In due course Douglas got out of bed and, being a genius – and of course because there was now an undeniable deadline – did more than his share in a single week.'[10]

There was even talk of a *Liff* TV series: 'We are in the very, very early stages of putting together a series of short television programmes based on it, presented by Rowan Atkinson, which should be fun,' confided Douglas. 'The only fly in the ointment being as soon as Lloydie and I sit down to discuss the structure of the television programme we just begin to argue!'[11]

All these things happened before Douglas wrote the first word of his new novel.

Oh, and he got married.

Jane and Douglas had, as mentioned above, split up in 1988, ironically just as Douglas was setting off on the publicity rounds for *The Long, Dark Tea-Time of the Soul*, which he had dedicated to her (an unfortunate repetition of the situation with *Life, the Universe and Everything* and Sally Emerson). This was not their first break-up, and it would not be their last. Douglas was always difficult to live with and Jane estimated that, of the nine years they spent together before marrying, they actually spent three years apart. On 12 October 1988, Douglas was a guest on the LBC programme *The Night Is Young* when, after cheerfully discussing his schooldays, his work-rate, J.S. Bach, Eric Clapton and the aye-aye, the interviewer innocently asked him about the latest book's dedication.

There was an anguished pause. Douglas very rarely discussed his home life. He had always been more discreet about his relationship with Jane than he had about Sally Emerson. Not that he was secretive, but he always had more interesting and exciting things to talk about. 'Erm, actually that's an unfortunate question at the moment,' stuttered Douglas eventually, 'because Jane and I have just split up. So this was for her, sadly.'[12]

Things might have been easier if Douglas had just said 'No comment,' or 'Next question please,' but he was simply too polite to do that. The poor interviewer didn't know about his love-life – no reason why she should – and asking the identity of a book's dedi-catee was a legitimate question. Unsure whether Douglas wanted to talk about this or not, she enquired sympathetically: 'Is it someone you've been with a long time?'

'Yes, yes,' said Douglas, ruefully. 'In fact, my being away all this year is quite good from that point of view. But it's a very sad thing at the moment. So this was a sort of present for her.'[13]

'Me and my big mouth,' whispered the interviewer – Douglas gave a little laugh of relief – and she tried gainfully to change the subject. Unfortunately, she changed it exactly the wrong way. Perhaps it was the next question on her list. She said: 'I don't think you have children – did you ever think having children would be a good idea?'

She wasn't to know that the very reason why Douglas and Jane had split up was because one partner desperately wanted children and the other didn't. There was another agonising pause; Douglas was always so utterly good-natured that he really seemed to be sorrier for the poor interviewer – suddenly finding herself in an emotional quagmire when a few moments ago she was hearing well-rehearsed jokes about aye-ayes and Eric Clapton – than he did for himself, opening his heart on late-night radio across the capital.

Another interviewee might have just gestured to quickly move onto the next question or play a record, but Douglas did his best to answer. The poor woman was only doing her job after all. 'Yes. Yes. Erm, this is quite a difficult one actually. I would love to have children. It still seems to be a way off, I guess. So I shall see what sort of state my life is in at the end of this year. Well, a year from now.'[14]

It was an unusual moment in an otherwise normal interview, and a very rare public glimpse deep into the private Douglas Adams. By 1991, Douglas and Jane would be back together.

On 7 January 1991, Douglas, Ed Victor and representatives from Heinemann met to discuss the book for which Douglas had signed a contract more than two years previously. There were a lot of reasons for the book's non-appearance, not least that Douglas had been researching *Last Chance to See* until April 1989 – the whole planet was now one big displacement activity to him – and had then spent several months in the South of France not writing that book either. The situation would not be helped by the death, shortly after that meeting, of Douglas' stepfather Ron Thrift, to whom he had been close (Douglas' own father had passed away in June 1985).

But the main reason that there was no book was simply that no-one had yet sat Douglas down and glowered at him.

In fact, not only had Douglas not written the novel, he hadn't even written the title. 'They said, "We must have a title by the end of this week," so it's quite tricky,' he told the secretary of the Official *Hitchhiker's Guide* Appreciation Society. 'As you may have noticed, other than *Dirk Gently*, all the titles that I've used have been quotes from previous books and I would like to be able to do that again. I keep on going through the books looking for the phrase that's right, that describes what happens in the book, and I haven't found it yet. If I don't get it this week I'm going to have to invent a title.'[15]

The title he settled on was *Mostly Harmless*, which was rather disconcerting for the appreciation society, as their quarterly newsletter had been called that for the past twenty years. Also agreed with Heinemann was a publication date – 17 October 1991: 'providing of course that I get it finished in time.'[16]

As usual, Douglas had a vague idea what the book was going to be about. In the last book Arthur Dent had fallen in love; in this one he would acquire a daughter. Not with Fenchurch, who disappeared from the saga as swiftly as Trillian had, but with, surprisingly, Trillian: 'A lot of people didn't know that Arthur Dent had a daughter, including – I might add – Arthur Dent. It comes as a tremendous surprise to him, as it also comes as a considerable surprise discovering how it was he fathered this child. Actually it was meant to centre around the story of Random but in fact she only comes in for about the last quarter of the book. It's funny how often that happens – that the main thing that starts you off on a book actually comes in just at the end, while you've been fiddling around.'[17]

There was by now a strange dichotomy between the ongoing *Hitchhiker's* story and the public perception of the franchise. To most people, *The Hitchhiker's Guide to the Galaxy* was the wacky outer space adventures of Arthur Dent, Ford Prefect, Zaphod Beeblebrox, Trillian and Marvin the Paranoid Android – as it had been in the radio series, the TV series, the first three books, the stage plays and the computer game.

But *So Long . . .* had dispensed with Zaphod and Trillian (and Slartibartfast and the Heart of Gold and many of the other iconic elements . . .) and had only resurrected Marvin briefly. To Douglas, *Hitchhiker's* was the personal odyssey of Arthur Dent. When asked if any of the established *Hitchhiker's* characters would be in the new book, he responded with one word: 'Arthur.'[18]

Probably realising that this was not entirely what the fans wanted to hear, he swiftly qualified this: 'I suspect Marvin will probably make a brief appearance. Ford is a sort of off-stage presence. I haven't made my mind up about Zaphod because I see Zaphod now as being an irredeemably seventies character, a guy who's perpetually stuck in flares.'[19]

By October, there was no sign of *Mostly Harmless*, and publication was put back to January 1992; Heinemann were confident that a new Douglas Adams book would fly off the shelves whatever it was and whenever it came out.

Douglas and Jane were married in front of witnesses at Finsbury Town Hall on 25 November 1991; she did not take his name. The news was sprung on friends, family and colleagues later that day at a party at the Groucho Club which was ostensibly to celebrate both the paperback publication of *Last Chance to See* and the award of a third Golden Pan for *Life, the Universe and Everything*. The *Daily Mail* reported: 'So secretive was Adams that he only told his esteemed literary agent, Ed Victor, in a telephone call after the ceremony.'[20] This may be true, although the same report stated that Douglas' home in Duncan Terrace, Islington had: 'a basement swimming pool, a snooker room and two fishponds on the roof.' This last idea amused Douglas greatly: 'They are wrong by two, which isn't a very big number, but relatively speaking it's actually quite a large number.'[21]

CHAPTER 34

ONE OF THE things which Douglas found to distract himself from writing *Mostly Harmless* was an edition of *The South Bank Show* which Melvyn Bragg decided to make about him. The original plan had been to film a documentary about the process of writing a Douglas Adams novel – except of course that Douglas hadn't written one. Douglas suggested instead a documentary about his legendary inability to write novels, his so-called writer's block, and the result was an extraordinary blend of drama and documentary, mixing characters from the *Hitchhiker's* series (Simon Jones, David Dixon and Stephen Moore reprised their TV roles) and the *Dirk Gently* books (Michael Bywater played the character which had been based on himself) with interviews with Douglas, Sue Freestone and Richard Dawkins.

The great thing about this, from Douglas' point of view, was that writing the script for *The South Bank Show* gave him a legitimate excuse to halt whatever work he had done – which was nothing at all – on *Mostly Harmless*. The irony was staggering: he was not writing his contracted novel because he had decided instead to write a semi-fictionalised documentary about the problems he was having that prevented him from writing the novel; he was creating a new story for his *Hitchhiker's* characters in which they discussed how difficult Douglas found it to come up with new stories for his *Hitchhiker's* characters. As with *So Long* . . . and the computer game, the one thing that could encourage him to work on a project was the threat that if he didn't he might have to work on a different project.

And Douglas really put effort into *The South Bank Show* script, possibly because nobody outside *The South Bank Show* production team would ever read it and so there was no pressure. 'Hold shot for quite a long time,' said one camera direction, 'but not as long as Stanley Kubrick would.' The programme was scheduled for early the following year to tie in with the hardback publication of *Mostly Harmless*. It was broadcast on 5 January 1992.

There was still no sign of the book.

By this stage in his career Douglas was something of a media personality, cropping up on TV and radio fairly regularly, often on chat shows, sometimes on panel games. He even made a surprise guest appearance in the 1991 Royal Society Christmas Lectures for Young People, presented by Richard Dawkins. Unlike many authors, Douglas relished interviews, which were not only a chance for him to trot out the old anecdotes ('So tell me, where did the idea for *Hitchhiker's Guide to the Galaxy* come from?') but were also handy displacement activities.

'I have this strange relationship with publishers, whereby they give me a lot of money to write a book and I, erm, don't,' commented Douglas on *Clive Anderson Talks Back* when he should have been publicising the new *Hitchhiker's* novel but talked about *Last Chance to See* instead because he still didn't have a novel to publicise. 'And I can't understand. As far as I'm concerned once they've paid me that seems to be the deal.'[1]

Douglas' 'media career' had begun in April 1980 when Nigel Rees (formerly of *The Burkiss Way*) invited him onto the Radio 4 quiz *Quote . . . Unquote*. Rees was pleased with Douglas' contribution and called on him again on 16 October 1981 when a contracted panelist failed to show. Studio Manager Lisa Braun (who had worked on *Hitchhiker's*) had Douglas' telephone number and he was called on at half an hour's notice. 'We rang him up and guess where he was? In the bath,'[2] recalls Rees.

Despite this, Douglas was not invited back onto the show again. 'He just became such a phenomenon,' explains Rees. 'Also, although I admired his writing enormously, as a performer he had a reputation as being a bit of a bore. For example he appeared on *Wogan* and he talked non-stop for twenty minutes. I think I was possibly slightly reluctant to have him on that basis: that he was now so much into his own way that he perhaps wouldn't have fitted into *Quote . . . Unquote.*'[3]

One of Douglas' final such appearances was on *Have I Got News For You* on 11 December 1992, partnering Paul Merton (Angus Deayton was Douglas' next-door neighbour). He seemed uneasy and made very few contributions to the programme, a situation exacerbated by the natural dominance of Ian Hislop's guest, Peter Cook. 'He always said he would rather die than do anything like that again,' recalls his PA Sophie Astin, 'probably because you're on the spot.'[4]

What is interesting, and rather sad, is that alongside Douglas' increased media exposure – as himself, rather than just An Author with A Book To Plug – came an intermittent but insidious decrease in the attendances at Douglas' public appearances. Twelve years previously he could command queues of a thousand or more at a signing session. In October 1992 he spoke at the Oxford Union and barely twenty people turned up to hear him. Some of the dates on his later UK tours, for *The Illustrated Hitchhiker's Guide* in 1994 and the *Starship Titanic* game four years later, could barely scrape attendances in double figures. This was not necessarily Douglas' fault – some astoundingly complacent publicity must certainly share the blame – but there had been very little publicity for that first signing at Forbidden Planet and it had still drawn a thousand people. There would be no deluge of fans twenty minutes into the session when he toured in the 1990s.

Douglas' one and only TV programme of his own, apart from the *Hitchhiker's* series, was a documentary called *Hyperland*, commissioned at the end of 1989 and broadcast on 20 September 1990. This was a look at the future of communication technology which was in equal parts amazingly prescient and amusingly wide of the mark. It was also, of course, yet another displacement activity from the new novel. Douglas played (a version of) himself, frustrated at his television which he threw onto a huge pile of old sets, built in a tank at Ealing Studios. Tom Baker played a 'software agent' ('Do you know what that means?' 'You want fifteen per cent?') and the programme included interviews with many people at the cutting edge of interactive technology. The whole was presented in a linear facsimile of an interactive programme.

Hyperland was developed as a collaboration between Apple's Multimedia Lab and the BBC's Interactive Television Group, as the first of a projected series of six programmes entitled *Future Worlds*. 'The idea was that we would find six people each of whom had a unique vision of what the future might be like, and ask each of them to make a fairly personal film,' explains producer Max Whitby. 'Douglas was the first person we thought of to make a film, particularly about the future of television. The whole conception behind *Hyperland* was that we would use the tricks of television to invent the future and to bring alive ideas that may not be practical in 1990, but as we've all seen rather hilariously in the intervening years, rapidly became commonplace.'[5]

Whitby knew enough about Douglas' working methods to realise that, left to his own devices, he would never actually write a script: 'The only way to extract the script from him was for me to go round and write it with him. We probably wrote the *Hyperland* script in about five or six sessions, each of which took three or four hours. I would sit at the keys and he would have ideas. Basically the pressure was that unless he did enough, I wasn't going to go away. He wasn't allowed to play his guitars or do anything else for the period that we wrote the script.'[6]

Though the other *Future Worlds* programmes never appeared, *Hyperland* became the first of a loose trilogy of programmes produced by Whitby (who also worked with Douglas on a CD-ROM version of *Last Chance to See*). *Horizon: Colonising Cyberspace* was broadcast a year later and *Equinox: School's Out* followed in 1992. Though Douglas didn't write or appear in either programme, Whitby used him as a consultant on both. *Hyperland* was never repeated, never shown abroad (there were clearance problems with some of the clips used) and never released on video, though Douglas would often send tapes to friends and sometimes showed it at conferences.

While *Hyperland* was in production, Douglas was invited to join a California-based think tank called the Vivarium, set up at Apple in the mid-1980s, where his role was to provide 'unseriosity'. 'I thought that was delightfully silly,' recalls Larry Yaeger, who had joined the Vivarium a couple of years earlier. 'We always had this image that, because Douglas had done a lot of thinking about what computers might look like, he might have some actual genuine insight into what computers ought to look like. Specifically the Vivarium programme, as a theme, always had a goal of producing a user interface that was so simple that children could use it and yet was complex enough to present the underpinnings of a computational ecology.'[7]

Douglas knew Yaeger from the latter's approach, a few years earlier, about the possibility of creating the *Hitchhiker's Guide* for real (on the Apple II+!). Other Vivarium advisors included Richard Dawkins, Alan Kay (both friends of Douglas) and even Koko the gorilla. 'Alan Kay tended to make advisors to the Vivarium programme anyone who was an interesting person, a good thinker and someone he'd like to have dinner with,' laughs Yaeger. 'So Alan brought Douglas in on that kind of arrangement: let's see if we can pick your brains any way it works out. And one of the ways it worked out was that Douglas and I hooked up and chatted a bit about these user interfaces and stuff, but it wasn't a major pursuit. We never got around to developing a user interface specifically geared towards our discussions with Douglas.'[8]

Though his direct involvement with the Vivarium was limited, it was an important step in Douglas' progression from Author to Thinker. It also built on his new-found passion for ecology and, through the use of test groups of six- to twelve-year-olds, gave him a useful insight into the American education system which would become relevant ten years later.

And it was yet another excuse for not having written *Mostly Harmless.*

Heinemann revised their schedule yet again as the third anniversary of the original contract sailed past in late 1991, naively hoping that Douglas might deliver a manuscript in January 1992 which they could then rush through the publication process to have the book in the shops by March. As January wore on and no manuscript was forthcoming, Heinemann shuffled publication back yet again, this time to a vague June/July slot. All this was costing the publisher money but they were determined to get a book somehow. The second half of the contract had been cancelled and Douglas had announced that his next book after this one would be published by Jonathan Cape. Heinemann wanted to milk their cash cow while he was there.

Finally, in March, Douglas was once again locked in a hotel room for two weeks, this time with Sue Freestone and Michael Bywater. It had worked with *So Long . . .* – not that the result had been very good, but at least it was a collection of words just long enough to be called a novel – and it was worth trying again. But Douglas was by now wise to the ways of publishers and persuaded Freestone to let him out of the hotel to give a speech at a conference in America and no sooner had he been reinstalled in his hotel than he was granted leave again for his fortieth birthday. Douglas was almost like a schoolboy finding new ways to get out of doing prep.

'I'm the absolute archetype of the sort of writer who does the last ninety per cent of the work in the last ten per cent of the time,' he said. 'That applied to *Mostly Harmless*, and in fact it's always been the case. It becomes a sort of zen problem, because there has to be a deadline that everybody believes, including myself, and having broken so many previous ones, you never quite believe in whatever the current one is. The zen-like problem is trying to see which is the real one. I spend about a year in a state of panic. I do all sorts of outlines that instantly get abandoned because they don't work. But I'm determined to crack the schematics problem because I know that if I could work to a detailed plot I'd write better books.'[9]

'I was there for the terrible mad rush to finish the book,' recalled Bywater. 'The atmosphere in the place was like I imagine a kind of eighteenth-century loony bin with this mad giant crashing about the place shouting. The only way we could actually persuade Douglas to finish *Mostly Harmless* was offer him several convincing scenarios by which he could blow up not only this Earth but all Earths that may possibly exist in parallel universes.'[10]

That was no way to get a good book out of a perfectionist writer whose skill lay in poring over every comic phrase. Nevertheless, a manuscript of *Mostly Harmless* was received by Heinemann in July and the book was published in October 1992 in both the UK and USA. It was to be the last book Douglas would ever complete.

'Douglas Adams had a writer's block as big as the Ritz,' said Ed Victor. 'He had it on the first book he wrote, he had it on the last book he wrote.'[11] But the strange thing is that this patently isn't the case: writer's block is a blank mind, an inability to think of anything to write. It's a lack of ideas, and Douglas never had that. ('I used to tell people that I got all of my ideas from my dog,' he said. 'If they pointed out that I didn't have a dog, I'd say, "No, he's off thinking up more ideas."')[12]

'I think it's been greatly exaggerated, this "writer's block",' says Jonny Brock. 'There's an awful lot of *schadenfreude* about it. It's inevitable: you avoid things until the last moment because that's the way intelligent people do things; they need that urgency to really drive them. In Douglas' case, it was exaggerated. But it wasn't writer's block. It was partly that he was the master of displacement activities – sharpening pencils and making tea – which I think everyone does. It was also partly boredom: he became frustrated with the *Hitchhiker* idea, he then became frustrated with the *Dirk Gently* idea.'[13]

'People talk about him not getting on with his work, and he certainly made a monumental fuss about it,' says Sally Emerson. 'But it was partly because he was a perfectionist and creatively very ambitious. Douglas was trying to describe what hadn't been described before, and doing so in a new way.'[14]

Rather than a shortage of ideas, Douglas had too many and simply could not finish (or often could not start) one thing before wanting to get on with the next one. But the biggest contributing factor to the myth of his writer's block was the ridiculous degree of freedom which he was given by his editors. It reached a stage where Douglas simply would not bother to do any writing unless locked away. Every single thing he ever wrote in any medium after the original *Hitchhiker's* pilot was written in a short time in a state of panic, usually with somebody else watching over him (with the exception of *The Meaning of Liff* which was a collection of unconnected jokes).

Given the chance to ignore a deadline, Douglas would – because he could. Jill Foster knew that writers need bullying, but all those connected with Douglas' later works seemed to forget this and were apparently surprised at his repeated non-delivery. That was not writer's block. That was Douglas being weak-willed and easily distracted (which is perhaps forgivable). It was also either laziness or sheer naivety on the part of those whose job it was to ensure that he delivered the books for which he had already been paid enormous amounts. It did a terrible disservice to the publishers and booksellers who had made plans for these books, to the fans who wanted to read them, and to Douglas himself. Like most creative people, he needed strict guidance to achieve his best. That is what agents, editors and publishers are for, and their disinclination to give Douglas such guidance, except in short, concentrated bursts at the last possible moment, is mystifying.

Douglas' entire literary career spanned fourteen years, and his output of seven novels and two other co-authored books was actually quite a reasonable work rate, even if four of the novels had been adapted from existing scripts. But the period between signing a contract and delivering the novel had been growing with each successive book: he had been 'writing' *Mostly Harmless* for four of those fourteen years. The longest P.G. Wodehouse ever took to write a novel was only three years and the result was *Joy in the Morning*, arguably his finest book. *Mostly Harmless* was far from Douglas' best work; it wasn't as bad as *So Long . . .* but it was for the most part a thoroughly unmemorable novel.

This ending to Douglas' career could only be seen retrospectively and posthumously, of course. For the last nine years of his life, Douglas would maintain the illusion that he was writing another book, but the time that he spent on not writing each novel seemed to increase exponentially, so nothing was seriously expected from him before the late 1990s.

Fortunately for Douglas, but unfortunately for his readers, he was never again locked in a hotel room.

Mostly Harmless sold well on both sides of the Atlantic. Douglas' fans were many and loyal and they loved him for what he had created in the late 1970s and early 1980s. He had shown them that he could still cut the mustard with the *Dirk Gently* novels and they were prepared to forgive him for *So Long . . .* Douglas would actually have preferred to forget that volume altogether: 'I almost like to regard this as a fourth book,' he said of *Mostly Harmless*, 'because I hate – I did not like the fourth *Hitchhiker's* book.'[15] ('Hardly alone there, is he?' commented the ZZ9 Plural Z Alpha newsletter.)

That said, five years down the line he was able to look back at *Mostly Harmless* with some objectivity and decide that he didn't like that either: 'I didn't enjoy writing it very much because I had a lousy year, for all sorts of personal reasons I won't go into, but writing a funny book against the background of a lousy year is quite tricky.'[16]

INTERLUDE - **PARTIES**

AFTER 'TALL', THE word most frequently associated with Douglas was 'party'. He was legendary for his fabulous parties, but they didn't start when he became fabulously wealthy. He threw great parties at Cambridge and had even done so back in his Brentwood days. 'He would have the most magnificent parties round at his grandmother's house,' recalls David Wakeling. 'Friends would be invited and we would have to share the house with all those animals. Invariably they would get let out and we'd end up chasing around after them.'[1]

Jane also had a history of great parties. 'At Oxford and subsequently, Jane gave the best parties of anyone I have ever known in my life,' says her friend Juliana Abell. 'She didn't give them often, but every one was memorable.'[2] Between the two of them they established a reputation at Upper Street and Duncan Terrace as host and hostess *par excellence*.

'The parties took place throughout the house,' remembers Abell. 'My abiding memory is of Douglas struggling with an unfeasibly huge bottle of champagne – he was the only person with the height to get to grips with it. There was an entire bathtub filled with ice and bottles. There was great conversation and fizz and I'm sure there was dancing and food. It was completely informal. I suppose what made Jane's parties such winners was the simple combination of decent booze, reasonable food and a lot of seriously interesting and bubbly people who would be likely to enjoy themselves. Jane never imposed herself on her parties, just enjoyed them too.'[3]

Jane and Douglas also held dinner parties and an annual Christmas carol party, which Douglas took very seriously, in spite of his atheist ideas. Only those friends with good singing voices were invited to the carol parties. But the apotheosis of Douglas' parties were the Partially Plugged events, at which 200 or more people would cram into Douglas' front room to enjoy a performance by his musician friends. The band included David Gilmour, Nick Mason, Gary Brooker, Robbie McIntosh, Wix and Margo Buchanan; as for the audience . . .

'That was special,' recalled Buchanan. 'The audience was more famous than the band. I remember one night trying to see a face I didn't recognise in the audience. There was Melvyn Bragg sitting cross-legged next to Salman Rushdie. Paul Allen the Microsoft guy was sitting next to Lenny Henry. Then I saw Angus Deayton passing a bottle of wine to Terry Gilliam who was next to Terry Jones. And right at the back was George Martin. Incredible.'[4]

'Douglas was the consummate music party host,' says Jody Boyman. 'I attended Partially Plugged 2 and 3 at his home in Islington, and I don't think I've ever seen Douglas more in his element.'[5] 'It reminded me of Victorian musical soirées where people would have their friends round and you'd invite someone to sing some *Lieder* or something at the piano,' says Eugen Beer. 'I remember one night, I found myself sitting on a windowsill and the window was open. I was looking at the people squatting, cross-legged on the floor in front of me. I suddenly realised that sitting there, grooving in the way that makes people squirm, that sort of horrible, affected, swinging of the head and body and clicking of the fingers – was Salman Rushdie. I suddenly realised I was right in the line of bloody fire! I said to my girlfriend, "I'm not taking a bullet in the back for him."'[6]

Though the parties were packed – who wouldn't want to see a private performance by the combined highlights of Pink Floyd, Procol Harum and Paul McCartney's backing band? – not everyone enjoyed them completely. 'They were very interesting, but in a way they were a bit pretentious,' says Beer. 'It was all fine, but there was a reverence to the whole thing. I think everyone else had a great time but I found them slightly dysfunctional. But the champagne would flow and the food was magnificent, everyone had a jolly good time.'[7]

'Douglas' parties got too grand for me,' admits Terry Jones. 'There was a sense in which Douglas seemed to get stuck in star-worship. He seemed to become very impressed with the incredibly famous people he'd got to know – and that was a little disappointing, since it somehow diminished himself.'[8]

CHAPTER 35

TWO INTERESTING VERSIONS of *Hitchhiker's Guide* appeared around this time, both of which were illustrated variants of the first novel. Douglas met Byron Preiss at a trade convention in 1991 and signed a deal with him to handle a DC Comics adaptation of *Hitchhiker's*. Douglas never seemed terribly au fait with comics as a medium, although his love of the *Eagle* was well-known, and he claimed in later years not even to be sure which of his books had been adapted to the format (it was the first three *Hitchhiker* novels).

But Douglas could be a dark horse and in 1987, as a guest on *Start the Week*, he revealed a remarkable knowledge. The conversation had turned to comics and BBC weatherman Ian McCaskill commented how much they had changed since his day: 'The last Justice League of America I remember was Spider-Man and people like that, and now they're totally different . . .'

'Spider-Man wasn't in the Justice League of America,' said Douglas, cutting off McCaskill in a voice which betrayed stunned amazement at such a basic error. 'Spider-Man was Marvel. Justice League of America was Superman, Batman, Flash, Green Lantern, Wonder Woman . . .'[1] The list just rolled off his tongue and the other guests hooted with laughter as Douglas professed to having a huge collection of comics as a child, of which *The Flash* was his favourite. Not once before or since did Douglas give any indication that he had ever read American superhero comics.

Howard Zimmerman was editor and project director on the *Hitchhiker's* comics and liaison with Douglas was part of his job. He also selected the artist, Steve Leialoha, and the writer, John Carnell. 'Douglas's involvement was major at the beginning, minimal thereafter,' he remembers. 'He wanted to make sure we were doing it "right". His contract with us gave him sign-off on the scripts and character concepts. He made Leialoha do about a dozen different versions of Marvin, each time having him make the android more shapeless and faceless.'[2]

When the comics appeared in October 1993 *Hitchhiker's* fans were disappointed to find that, rather than giving free rein to the story and adapting it to the medium's strengths as had happened with the transition from radio to novel, to TV (albeit less effectively) and then to computer game, it was simply a literal, abridged, illustrated edition of the novel. The comics could have given *Hitchhiker's* the vast visual splendour that Hollywood clearly wasn't going to. On the other hand, the fans had no idea how close the comics came to replicating another of Hollywood's tricks.

'Our marching orders came from Douglas, who wanted to see a straightforward adaptation of the existing work,' explains Zimmerman. 'I wanted to update and Americanise various aspects of the story to give it broader appeal to our main audience – American readers. I sent the first book's script to Douglas for approval. In it, I had changed the famous bit about "digital watches" to "cellphones" as an update, and Americanised the spellings. Well, I got a two-page, single-spaced, typewritten letter from Douglas in the mail as a response. Most of it was about *not* changing digital watches to cellphones or changing very much of anything else for that matter. He expressed his clear desire to see the book material faithfully adapted, not Americanised to any great degree, and not updated at all.'[3]

Douglas' revisions to script and artwork delayed the comics by a year. The first set sold about 25,000 copies per issue, which was on the low side, but Byron Preiss/DC had licensed *Restaurant* . . . and *Life* . . . as well, and they subsequently appeared in similar format. 'Douglas was quite happy with the first book,' recalls Zimmerman. 'His involvement kind of waned after that, because he was satisfied that we were not killing, mutating, or otherwise doing serious harm to his first born.'[4]

'How closely did you work with John Carnell and Steve Leialoha for the DC Comics adaption of *Hitchhiker's*,' Douglas was asked in a 1998 webchat, 'and did the *Restaurant . . .* comic ever get produced?' 'Not at all,' replied Douglas, adding: 'I think the *Restaurant . . .* one got done, I'm not sure.'[5]

In terms of both the illustrations themselves and Douglas' involvement, the comics could not hold a candle to the oversize, silver-jacketed book which was published in 1994 as *The Illustrated Hitchhiker's Guide to the Galaxy*. Whereas the comics had met a mixed reception from the fans and been largely ignored by everyone else, the *Illustrated Hitchhiker's Guide* was adored by fans, and by critics, and was a massive commercial failure. Such are the ways of publishing.

The idea first cropped up in July 1993 in meetings between Douglas and Emma Way, Editorial Director at Weidenfeld and Nicolson: a lavish coffee-table book, using state-of-the-art computer technology to combine photographs of actors and props and create imagery such as had never been seen before (and was not likely to be seen anytime soon unless Hollywood pulled its finger out). Douglas recommended Kevin Davies to oversee the project.

Davies had recently directed a documentary video for BBC Worldwide, *The Making of the Hitchhiker's Guide to the Galaxy*, combining behind-the-scenes video from the set of the TV series with new interviews and narrative material about Arthur Dent returning home. Simon Jones, David Dixon and Vogon Guard Mike Cule reprised their roles. Davies met with Douglas on 26 June 1992 to discuss both the video and a proposed animation series based on the *Hitchhiker's Guide* readout graphics which sadly never happened. 'An option we would seriously consider if we get the film rights back is actually doing more *Hitchhiker* on television, adapting *Life, the Universe and Everything*,' said Douglas. 'It would seem therefore a good idea to see how these things can be made to dovetail or relate to each other in some way.'[6]

Douglas was interviewed in his office on 11 October and the video was released in March 1993. Pleased with Davies' work, Douglas had no hesitation in recommending him for the Weidenfeld and Nicolson job. Douglas himself was considerably more involved than he had been with the comics, where his role was simply to say no to any changes which the editor wanted to make.

'What basically happened is that we had a series of meetings when we discussed what the images should be,' he explained, 'and I was suggesting certain things that I thought we should have pictures of which were not the obvious ones. I wanted to steer as much as possible away from doing just straightforward depictions of key events, and I wanted to do stuff like the donkey that has had all four legs talked off it, which is nice and tasteful. I thought there was a much more interesting story to be found in the tiny lines here and there. But there is one I did entirely myself because it was getting right to the end of the process. The design team were running out of time, money and ideas and they phoned me up in a panic and said, "Have you got ideas what we can do for the number 42?" So I did it on my computer as a puzzle.'[7]

This arrangement of coloured spheres was a source of much debate, largely because Douglas never revealed the full answer, although various interpretations of 42 could be read by viewing the puzzle through different coloured filters. Douglas was very proud of the image and particularly pleased when he was able to have it included in the cover designs of new American paperbacks of all five *Hitchhiker's* novels – which also meant the removal of the irritating green thing.

'The point of the puzzle was this,' he later explained. 'Everybody was looking for hidden meanings and puzzles and significances in what I had written. So I thought that just for a change I would actually construct a puzzle and see how many people solved it. Of course, nobody paid it any attention. I think that's terribly significant.'[8]

Douglas was very, very pleased with the resulting book, as well he should have been. He even appeared in it: one of the photographs showed galactic cops Shooty and Bang Bang relaxing in a 'seedy space rangers bar' with Ed Victor as Bang Bang (agonising to his girlfriend) and Douglas as Shooty (writing a novel in crayon). This was shot in Stringfellows nightclub, which nineteen years earlier had been the Little Theatre, venue for *So You Think You Feel Haddocky* . . . 'I'm really pleased with a lot of the way this has worked, but eventually at the end of doing a project like this you now have a much, much better idea of how to do it. There's a bit of me that thinks, "Ah well, having learned from this, let's go and approach another one in a completely other way." What I would do, just because the technology has eminently changed again in the last twenty minutes, is create all the elements actually in the computer and create a three-dimensional set which you can then photograph from any angle. Nobody has tried that.'[9]

The Illustrated Hitchhiker's Guide wasn't the only thing Douglas was very, very pleased with in 1994. On 22 June, Polly Jane Rocket Adams was born; friends and fans startled by the sci-fi name were assured that it was because Jane had eaten so much rocket lettuce during her pregnancy.

Douglas was a devoted father. He had waited a long time for this – 'I regret not having started a family earlier'[10] – and he doted on Polly. From the moment she was born, she was surrounded by technology. Decorating her room, Jane suggested removing the ethernet port, but Douglas insisted that it stay. 'She'll be needing that soon,' he told a reporter. 'I'm just trying to work out what computer to get her.'[11] Of course, he got her a Macintosh. When she was three.

In 2000, Douglas was using the iVideo package on the iMac as part of an Apple promotional event: he videoed Polly miming to the song '(I Wanna Be A) Rock Star' by his friend Margo Buchanan and edited the footage together (with a brief cut-away to John Cleese, who was also there). Ever after, any enquiry about Polly led to Douglas whipping out his laptop and running the video; other fathers would just have shown a photograph in a wallet. In fact, Douglas was so proud of Polly that occasionally Jane had to rein his enthusiasm in, using a code-word so as not to dent their daughter's confidence. If Douglas gushed too much about Polly, Jane would whisper 'Dodag', which stood for: 'Darling, our daughter's a genius.'

Ever the amateur scientist, Douglas studied his daughter's growth, not in a clinical, dispassionate way but as a microcosm of his own journey of discovery in the world: 'Apart from being a source of enormous joy and pleasure, it's just fascinating watching somebody beginning to make their sense of the world, and seeing those models beginning to erect themselves in her head.'[12] Douglas and Jane were keen to have more children, but complications stemming from an ectopic pregnancy made this impossible.

Ironically, having spent years playing down the number's significance, Douglas became a father at 42. His forty-second birthday in March 1994 had been a lavish affair and he had been showered with gifts, so that he barely noticed the piece of paper which David Gilmour handed him. It was only later that Douglas realised that it was a certificate entitling the bearer to perform on stage with Pink Floyd. Douglas was to achieve his great ambition and become – for a brief moment – a rock star.

Pink Floyd featured large in Douglas' history. The Disaster Area stuntship was an allusion to 'Set the Controls for the Heart of the Sun' and Marvin had performed a snatch of 'Shine On You Crazy Diamond' in one radio episode. Douglas had subsequently befriended drummer Nick Mason and then guitarist Gilmour. His moment of fame came on 28 October 1994 when he played guitar on 'Brain Damage' and 'Eclipse' from *Dark Side of the Moon* at Earl's Court: 'The bit I played was that little guitar figure that any seventeen-year-old guitarist can play. But the difficult thing, I discovered, is not being able to play something like that, but being able to play it slowly enough, and that was pretty neat. It was interesting realising how much of the power and effect of Floyd actually comes from playing very slowly and how difficult to do that is.'[13]

Bizarrely, this was actually the second time that Douglas had shared a stage with Pink Floyd. On 5 July 1975 Graham Chapman added a comedy element to the second Knebworth Rock Festival and Douglas was one of several friends persuaded to support him, dressed as Python 'Gumbies'. (According to Chryssie Lytton Cobold's account, *Knebworth Rock Festivals*, Chapman, 'was given a hard time by the punters and eventually shouted off the stage'.)

Several months before the concert, Douglas had suggested the title for the band's new album. That happened on 16 February 1994 after a talk by Douglas to raise money for the Environmental

Investigation Agency; a group of his friends, including Mason and Gilmour, went for dinner afterwards and it transpired that the record label needed an album title the following morning, with the band still undecided. Douglas' favourite track was 'High Hopes' which, having heard it on an unlabelled DAT, he thought was called 'The Division Bell' – and he suggested that as the title. In return, Gilmour donated £10,000 to the EIA.

Douglas met another of his musical heroes, Gary Brooker of Procol Harum, through his friend Paul 'Wix' Wickens, a top session musician who was Paul McCartney's keyboard player. Though he never actually played guitar with Procol Harum, Douglas did introduce them occasionally and recited a spoken part of one song at the band's thirtieth anniversary concert on 19 July 1997.

Douglas' other musical accomplishments were more modest: he played rhythm guitar on the TV theme single and he composed some music for the *Starship Titanic* CD-ROM. However, he did retain serious musical ambitions and had plans to record an album with the help of producer Glyn Johns: 'It will basically be something very similar to *Sergeant Pepper*, I should think,'[14] he announced in 1994.

From that early boxy guitar, Douglas had amassed what was confidently believed to be the largest collection of left-handed guitars in the world. Accounts of exactly how many vary; twenty-seven is a widely believed figure but in a letter to Scott Jennings, owner of Route 66 Guitars in Hollywood, Jane Belson mentioned moving back to London, 'with three cats and thirty-five guitars in tow'.[15]

'I believe from the records I've found that I sold him fifteen of those instruments between 1992 and 1995,' says Jennings. 'Douglas said he came by every time he came to LA, although there were occasions when he called to say he was only passing through town and wanted to see if I had added anything to my personal collection that he could come by and talk me out of. This became something of a pattern for us. Early on he figured out that he only wanted to know about the instruments I didn't want to sell.'[16]

In 1992 Kathi Goldmark was a media escort, driving authors around on the San Francisco leg of signing tours. Realising how many writers had musical aspirations she brought together a band called the Rock Bottom Remainders, featuring among others Stephen King, Amy Tan and Dave Barry. At that year's American Booksellers' Association Conference in Miami, the band gave their first public performance and the support act was an acoustic duo, the Hard Covers. This was Douglas and Ken Follett.

'Ken really wanted to be in the band but of course we already had a bass player,' recalls Goldmark. 'I thought it would be really swell if I got the two of them together to be an opening act. So they got together and practised some songs. Douglas did "The Boxer" – I did some harmony with him, practising the harmonies on long-distance wires from London to San Francisco. All of us in these groups secretly take the music a little bit more seriously than we would ever admit.'[17] Douglas opened for the Rock Bottom Remainders on another occasion as a solo act. Together with his lectures, this helped to satisfy his craving to be a writer-performer. In 2001 he started discussing a musical collaboration with Chris Difford of Squeeze, but that was never to be.

'The thing with Douglas was that he was very good with harmony but not so good with rhythm,' observed Follett. 'I remember on one occasion he did a guitar solo – perfectly in tune – of a Paul McCartney song, in which he finished half a bar before the rest of us.'[18]

Though Douglas' personal life and musical career were making strides in 1994, *The Illustrated Hitchhiker's Guide* wasn't so successful. Tentative plans for *The Illustrated Restaurant at the End of the Universe*, or even a softback edition of the first book fell through when it was massively remaindered. The flaw was simply that it was too expensive, about twice the price of an average hardback, also impractically large – and in any case, everyone who bought it already owned the paperback anyway. Many copies were sold to remainder shops where fans bought them at a greatly reduced price. Many others were bought by Douglas himself.

'This particular edition was lavishly and rather expensively produced (not at my instigation, incidentally) and was therefore rather highly priced and didn't sell as well as it might have done,' said Douglas. 'It ended up being remaindered. At the same time, I was being asked on a fairly regular basis where it was possible to find a copy. The simplest answer was to buy the last copies from the publishers and sell them via the website. As a way of making money, it's probably up there with selling pencils from a cup.'[19]

The book had been published on 2 September 1994. Six months later, the remaindered copies were cluttering up Douglas' office – a picture of him surrounded by them accompanied an interview in the *Observer* of 10 March 1995. It was an inglorious end to a fantastically ambitious project.

Meanwhile, Ed Victor was approached by anthologist Peter Haining about including 'Young Zaphod Plays It Safe' in an anthology of comic SF and fantasy, *The Wizards of Odd*. Douglas, when tracked down, asked to be allowed to revise it and after some considerable delay eventually delivered, as Haining's deadline loomed, a version which included twelve additional words in the final sentence: 'to the effect that the missing escape capsule contained a "Reagan" and.' This finally settled the argument, but as Reagan had long since left office and was by now diagnosed with Alzheimer's disease, the satire was not only pointless but slightly tasteless.

Though unavailable in the UK for a decade, 'Young Zaphod . . .' had been included in an American omnibus, *The More Than Complete Hitchhiker's Guide*, since 1989. Why hadn't he made this revision then, when it would have had both topical and geographical relevance? Possibly he simply didn't know that the book existed. As could be seen from the 'Shada' video debacle, Douglas was quite happy to sign anything presented to him, confident that Ed (or whoever) had okayed it. Hence also his uncertainty over which of his novels had been adapted into comic books.

Douglas was similarly unaware that *Mostly Harmless* was published as a trade paperback by a British book club, staring in amazement when a copy was presented to him to sign. American subscription publisher Easton Press issued all five *Hitchhiker's* books in leather-bound, hand-tooled, gold-stamped editions, and despite having signed the contract in December 1998 and actually signed all the books himself, Douglas professed amazement when a fan mentioned the $300 set on his website forum less than nine months later: 'Are you sure you've got the decimal point in the right place? The most expensive edition I'm aware of was the big silver one.'[20]

This can't have just been Douglas' poor memory. It was increasingly clear, as the 1990s progressed, that he had less and less interest not only in writing but also in what happened to the books he had already written, happy to devolve such responsibility to Ed Victor.

CHAPTER 36

SUE ANSTRUTHER WAS the Head of Spoken Word Publishing at BBC Worldwide (formerly BBC Enterprises). In 1993 she noticed that the tapes and CDs of *Hitchhiker's* had sold 75,000 units, and she came up with the idea of returning *Hitchhiker's Guide* to its original home on Radio 4 with a third radio series. (This may be the source of the urban myth that someone at the BBC approached Douglas in late 1992 asking whether he had ever considered adapting *Hitchhiker's Guide* for radio. Or perhaps that's true; stranger things have happened at the BBC.) Anstruther put her suggestion to Jonathan James-Moore, Head of Light Entertainment, who put the idea to Douglas, who agreed that perhaps it was time.

'They have been after me for years to do a third radio series,' said Douglas, which wasn't strictly true, 'and I said, "It would be great and I'd love to do it but only if I was doing it myself and as heavily involved as in the previous one. And I don't see when I'm going to have time for that." And then I turned forty and I began to realise that I wasn't going to have time to do all the things I wanted to do. And everyone wanted a third radio series so I actually thought I should give in to them, so I said okay.'[1]

Douglas suggested as producer Dirk Maggs, who was experienced in both comedy and science fiction, producing acclaimed dramatisations of *Superman* and *Batman*. Maggs had started at the BBC in 1978 and recalls tapes of *Hitchhiker* being kept in the radio news room at Bush House for producers and presenters to enjoy when things were quiet on the news front: 'I went to Duncan Terrace one Spring day to talk to Douglas. I didn't know quite what to expect because my understanding was that he was going to make a film, even at that time. Douglas was just so warm and welcoming immediately that any nerves I might have had dissipated right away. And the first thing he said was, "I've really been enjoying your comic book adaptations on radio." I said, "Oh, thank you very much." He said, "In fact, that's what gave me the idea of doing a third series of *Hitchhiker*."'[2]

If Douglas did say this, then he was taking credit for Sue Anstruther's idea. Perhaps he came up with the idea simultaneously and coincidentally, but didn't he also say (see above) that the starting point was his fortieth birthday in March 1992, after mulling the idea over for years? Whatever the reality behind the conflicting reports of its birth, a new radio series of *The Hitchhiker's Guide to the Galaxy* (dubbed 'The Tertiary Phase' by Douglas) was in development in 1993, thirteen years after the last episode was broadcast.

Actually, that's not strictly true. In a sense, it was only eleven years. In August 1982 Sheila Steafel (who had been in Douglas' anguished *Week Ending* cast) starred in a one-off show on Radio 4 called *Steafel Plus* with writing credits that were a mini-*Who's Who* of British comedy: Ray Galton, Johnny Speight, Peter Tinniswood, Barry Cryer, Andy Hamilton and Douglas Adams. Jonathan James-Moore was the producer. Douglas' contribution was a short chat-show sketch in which Steafel interviewed Arthur Dent, played by Simon Jones. Arthur was bewildered to find himself being interviewed (in the Paris Studio, ironically) because he had just spent several years living in a cave on prehistoric Earth. Sadly for him, it transpired that he was still there, dreaming.

Forgotten for twenty years, this sketch was rediscovered in 2002 and accepted into the *Hitchhiker's* canon as a sort of 'Fit the Six-and-a-halfth'. In 2003 the script was published in a '25th Anniversary Edition' of *The Hitchhiker's Guide to the Galaxy: The Original Radio Scripts*. (Intriguingly, there was very nearly another mini-episode in October 1982 when Arthur Dent – Simon Jones in the original dressing gown – and Marvin – Stephen Moore on tape plus a hapless BBC employee inside the TV costume – appeared on *The Light Entertainment Show*, a live Radio 2 extravaganza to celebrate the corporation's sixtieth anniversary. Compered by former Max Quordlepleen Roy Hudd, this was a fast-paced series of newly written sketches based on classic BBC comedy shows. Producer Jonathan James-Moore commissioned a *Hitchhiker's Guide* script from Douglas but, unsurprisingly, nothing had arrived by the deadline. Instead, a short, pun-filled routine between Arthur, Marvin and Hudd was quickly put together by staff writers Tony Hare and Pete Hickey.)

Slightly over ten years later, Douglas was meeting to discuss the new radio series with Maggs and James-Moore. For some reason, Ed Victor was represented by Stephen Durbridge (who has no memory of the meeting, although he recalls acting on Victor's behalf on the proposed *Dirk Gently* TV series).

'I think the seeds of disaster were sown at this meeting and if I'd thought ahead a bit more, maybe I could have done something to avert it,' says Maggs, ruefully. 'But it's too late now. On the way there, I said to Jonathan, "Have you thought who should adapt this for the radio?" He said, "No, I feel we'd be better off with who he'd prefer." I said, "That's fine. But if Douglas has no preference, I'd really like to put my hand up for it, even if Douglas takes the credit, and fully with Douglas looking over my shoulder. I feel that I could do a good job." When it came to the meeting, which was all very pleasant, Douglas said, "Well, I'd do it myself but to be honest with you, I've written it twice and that's enough for me. So I would get an adaptor in." In the end they turned to Stephen Durbridge and did he have someone he could suggest who he also represented? And so the name Alick Rowe came up.'[3]

Rowe was an award-winning radio writer with a deftly humorous touch and on paper should have been ideal. The plan was that he would adapt *Life, the Universe and Everything* in eight episodes. Maggs telephoned Rowe, who was not completely familiar with *Hitchhiker's* but was keen to give it a shot. A few weeks later, he delivered his script for Episode One. 'It was a nicely written piece of work but it didn't read like the book,' remembers Maggs, tactfully. 'In retrospect maybe what I should have done was sent it back to

Alick, but I sent it straight to Douglas. About three days later I got a phone call from Douglas, sounding quite distressed, feeling that this absolutely was not what he had in mind. A case in point: Alick had given a dinosaur dialogue. Well, Alick's a fine writer but if Douglas didn't write a dinosaur with dialogue, there was a very good reason for it. Douglas pointed this out in fairly forthright language, which I absolutely agreed with.'[4]

'I just said, "This is dreadful, this is absolutely dreadful, this is appalling,"' recalled Douglas. 'Then there was a bit of argy-bargy and shenanigans and so on and basically I pulled the plug on it.'[5]

Douglas hated Rowe's script; Rowe felt that he had adapted the story perfectly well; Maggs was caught in the middle. Douglas was very supportive throughout the whole affair, he remembers, but cracks were starting to appear in what should have been a relatively straightforward project.

While the writing was going on, Maggs had contacted all the original radio cast and had asked Brian Johnstone and Fred Trueman to play the cricket commentators: 'Johnners had heard of *Hitchhiker's* but didn't really know what it was. But he said, "It sounds like a jolly good laugh."'[6] He even had plans to record the series in Dolby Prologic Surround Sound and had been arguing the viability of this with the BBC who seemed as entrenched and conservative as they had been back in 1977 (when one executive had objected to the idea of a comedy series in stereo because the listeners would not know which speaker the next joke was coming from). Meanwhile, BBC Worldwide had pencilled in a release date for a four-cassette pack and a four-CD tin box.

When Maggs hadn't heard anything further from Douglas, he rang and was invited over: 'As I walked in, Douglas' PA said, "Oh, he's just writing an episode." My heart leapt within me! I thought, "This is good news!" So I went down to his little study in the basement and there he was on an Apple PowerBook, the first one I'd seen. And he had written up the first ten minutes of Episode One – as he would like it. Immediately, the difference between Alick's adaptation and what Douglas wanted was quite apparent, you could see how it should work.

'But he said, "The trouble is I just don't have the time to do this.

I've been doing this today because I wanted you to see how good it could be." I said, "You know, I'd quite happily do it myself if you don't mind. You can take the credit." He said, "Well, let me think about it. Now it's with the agent, I'm not quite sure . . ." He certainly wasn't against the idea but I think it had just gone slightly out of our hands. Everybody had a finger in the damn pie by then. Something happened between the nexus of Light Entertainment, BBC Worldwide and Stephen Durbridge. The next thing I heard – it was off. That was it. And it was just horrible because I had to ring everybody and tell them. We could have done a great finishing chapter to the whole of the saga on radio. But something went wrong and I think it was more than the sum of its parts.'[7]

Douglas had been delighted that the original cast were all back on board and even had plans to play Agrajag himself, but The Tertiary Phase just gradually faded away. It was said to be 'on hold' in April 1994 and still 'under discussion' three months later, but was never heard from again. The idea was briefly resurrected in 1998 but almost immediately halted by a new film deal. 'My impression was that Douglas and I were both trying to find a way to make it happen, and there were factors beyond our – or Jonathan's – control,' reflects Maggs. 'I suspect we're talking the legal/agent area of things. Douglas and I were in the hands of the people with the contracts. If it happened now I'd know better, but I'd only know better because of this awful experience.'[8]

'The Tertiary Phase was a case of my letting the marketing people tell me what to do, which is never really a good idea,' said Douglas. 'I made it clear that I would want to approve the scripts and the writer changed too much in adapting it. It wasn't just the dialogue shuffled around with the narrative bits turned into passages from the book. I said, "I'm sorry, but I can't approve this." And the BBC said, "Well, you've got to approve it. We start recording next week." I said, "I don't think you've quite got the hang of what 'script approval' actually means."'[9]

There was another way in which Douglas nearly returned to radio in 1993 – with his own station. A number of new licences in London became available and among the forty-eight applications was a proposal for a station mixing music with comedy. It was called Radio Barking and it was Eugen Beer's idea: 'The first person I pulled in on it was John Lloyd as the great comedy guru. I'd stayed closer to John after *The Meaning of Liff* than I had to Douglas because he was spending a lot of time up in Birmingham, doing *Spitting Image*. I remember taking John out for dinner and explaining the idea and he was incredibly sceptical. But then he got it and said, "I think we should get Douglas involved." So we went to see Douglas and he got it. We literally got everyone who was anyone in British comedy to support it.'[10]

Though Douglas wasn't financially involved in the bid, he hosted meetings at his home and spent a weekend editing the submission document which Beer and Lloyd put together. Laid out like pages of the *Radio Times*, it was said to be one of the best submissions ever made to the Radio Authority and attracted a degree of media interest. (One programme suggestion which smacks of Douglas was *The God Slot*: readings from, and discussions about, P.G. Wodehouse.) But it didn't win a licence. 'To be honest, the Radio Authority just didn't believe that it was feasible,' recalls Beer. 'Beer Davies actually underwrote that whole exercise. We were a bit disappointed that some of the people who were much wealthier than us, who stood to gain from it if it happened, didn't put their hands in their pockets. But such is life.'[11]

Returning to his roots seemed to be a theme in Douglas' life in the early 1990s. In July 1992 he was a guest at the Brentwood Prep School Speech Day, where he was delighted to see Frank Halford, with whom he would remain in contact until the end of his life. This was also an opportunity to visit his beloved grandmother, Mrs Donovan, who sadly passed away very shortly afterwards. Douglas maintained his links with the school, attending a fund-raising dinner later that year.

In retrospect, Douglas Adams' adult life breaks down into decades. In the 1970s he developed his writing skills and eventually, after a lot of hard work and plenty of false starts, achieved a spectacular breakthrough. He spent the 1980s writing books, or rather not writing them. In the 1990s, Douglas put all that behind him, though he maintained the increasingly transparent pretence that he was working on a new novel, and transformed himself from 'Douglas Adams, humorous sci-fi author' to 'Douglas Adams, information technology guru'.

The bedrock of this new Douglas was The Digital Village (TDV), the company he founded with Robbie Stamp and Richard Creasey in 1996. It was an idea that came to Stamp, a producer at Central TV, two years earlier: 'I was one of a then young group of executives looking at the effects of digital technology on traditional media businesses. I felt there were some exciting possibilities opening up in terms of people who could understand what it would mean to develop an idea or a brand across a variety of different platforms and channels.'[12]

Douglas realised that it was not radio per se but the collaborative experience which it offered that he missed: 'When I started out I worked on radio, I worked on TV, I worked on stage. I enjoyed and experimented with different media, working with people and, wherever possible, fiddling with bits of equipment. Then I accidentally wrote a best-selling novel and the consequence was that I had to write another and then another. After a decade or so of this I became a little crazed at the thought of spending my entire working life sitting in a room by myself typing. Hence The Digital Village.'[13]

Creasey, Stamp's boss, had known Douglas since they appeared together on a panel at the Edinburgh Television Festival in the mid-1980s. With Stamp and a few others he set up a Special Projects Group at Central to investigate how the company could take advantage of 'new media' and when that folded, following a take-over by Carlton TV, Stamp had the idea for The Digital Village. 'I suppose, had we set up a New Media Department at Central, it would have been TDV,' says Creasey. 'I would have tried to work Douglas into the department – but it didn't work out that way.'[14]

Stamp met Douglas when he and Creasey visited Duncan Terrace with writer/producer Paul Springer, who was developing a movie called *Subculture*. 'Paul at that stage was hoping that Douglas would help him with the writing of the film that he was trying to get off the ground,' remembers Stamp. 'Which, knowing what I now know, looked like a slightly forlorn hope.'[15]

Robbie and Douglas struck up an immediate friendship and discussed plans for a TV series about evolution to be written and presented by Douglas. In 1996, Douglas said that TDV's first project would be: '*Life, the Universe and Evolution* – a series of science documentaries that I will write and present.'[16] This idea had certainly been around since 1992 and was described in 1994 as: 'A big science series for television which I would write and present, *The Universe – a Personal View*. I would love to use the title *Life, the Universe and Everything* but I think it would confuse things rather. It would largely be on the subject of computing and evolution.'[17]

'I think Douglas would have done a fabulous job because he had that capacity to make complex ideas accessible,' reflects Stamp. 'But the notion of Douglas as a presenter wasn't very firmly established and sadly that never came to pass. We did indeed try, in the early stages of The Digital Village, to get a big series on evolution off the ground at the BBC and we just couldn't make it fly.'[18]

In fact, Douglas' only TV presenting job came in June 1998 when he provided new introductory and concluding segments for the twenty-fifth anniversary broadcast of Jacob Bronowski's *The Ascent of Man* on the BBC Horizons satellite channel. 'I'm full of admiration for people who make intelligent science available to the intelligent layperson,' he enthused at the time, while despairing of, 'programmes that dolly it up with silliness. Understanding what you didn't before, to me, is one of the greatest thrills.'[19]

CHAPTER **37**

ROBBIE STAMP WASN'T actually looking for a business partner when he broached the subject of TDV to Douglas: 'I was talking about it in his front room in Islington and he said, "What would it cost to buy a stake in the company?" I came up with a figure off the top of my head and he said, "I'm in." That was it.'[1] So it was decided: Stamp was to be CEO, Creasey a non-executive director, and Douglas decided to call himself 'Chief Fantasist'. 'Douglas' role was very much to go into a space where he would be able to work on things other than books,' explains Stamp. 'It would be a place into which he could put some of his own projects, and a place where hopefully we were going to nurse other people's projects as well. He was very, very committed at the beginning. I don't think I'm fooling myself there.'[2]

One reason for Douglas' commitment may have been that he was dissatisfied with an earlier attempt to ride the information technology revolution. On 5 March 1995 he was appointed to a Government committee, the Department of National Heritage's newly created Library and Information Commission. 'I will be advocating a strong I.T. policy,' he announced. 'In the long term I look forward to the point when all our written records are digitally accessible. Other people on the Commission say the book is sovereign. I'm not sure I see the seeds of a consensus. But the I.T. move is afoot, and not before time.'[3] Presumably a consensus was never reached, because Douglas resigned six months later. 'Much as I love books, especially with the name P.G. Wodehouse stamped on them, I'm not sentimental about them,' he explained. 'If digital technology was to improve to such an extent that it would be possible to have a palmtop computer that you could comfortably read a novel from, then I would be very happy to do so.'[4]

Meanwhile, more directors were joining the fledgling company: Ian Charles Stewart had helped to launch *Wired* magazine (Douglas had been a contributing editor to the ill-fated UK edition); Mary Glanville had a television background; Ed Victor knew publishing; Richard Harris knew technology. TDV set up an office upstairs from Ed Victor Ltd in Bailey Street, London and set about raising finance. The first serious piece of investment was finalised on 19 December 1995 and came, with Ed Victor's help, from Alex Catto, who had provided writing space for Douglas and John Lloyd seventeen years previously. The Digital Village then moved to offices in Camden (they would later relocate to Maiden Lane, Covent Garden) and began developing projects.

'This has taken up quite a lot of my time and energy in the last few months,' explained Douglas in July 1995, in the first of many TDV-related interviews. 'It probably won't be up and functioning until sometime next year. It's a multimedia company that consists of me and a bunch of friends mostly from British TV and we are aiming to do TV programmes, also CD-ROMs, and most importantly, as far as I'm concerned, on-line publishing. Which I think is the most exciting new area to be working in. It's rather like being in the film industry in about 1905, when the whole industry is actually being invented around you, and every idea you have is a new one.'[5]

One problem which gradually became apparent was that the press and public perceived TDV as 'Douglas Adams' company' and it was very difficult to develop any projects which didn't originate with Douglas or at least carry his branding. 'There was a real area of confusion there,' admits Creasey. 'On the one hand, I think we were all very happy for it to be Douglas' company because he was so inspiring. On the other hand, we had lots of dreams in the early days that it would do other work as well. We were going to be involved in documentaries, feature films – and the internet. And bit by bit they all went away to being a company which was by and large concerned with what Douglas did because it was so predominantly important. Bit by bit we went down one avenue which was, in the nicest possible way, a disaster.'[6]

'Douglas hadn't yet found a way to be a creative godfather to other people's projects,' says Stamp. 'My experience is that when you get people writing books, they're primary creatives – I think they find it quite hard to nurse other people's work. What they tend to need is a team around them that will help them to build their work and their ideas, but I don't think they're desperately good at godfathering other people's.'[7]

At all times, Douglas was particularly keen to stress that TDV was a 'multiple media', not 'multimedia,' company: 'We're producing CD-ROMs and other digital and on-line projects, but we're also committed to working in traditional forms of the media. Our first CD-ROM, written and scripted by myself, is going to be called *Starship Titanic*. And on the internet front, our designers and programmers are working to produce an electronic index which we hope will entice surfers away from rivals like Yahoo and Netscape. Ours will be more user-friendly, and we'll call it *The Hitchhiker's Guide to the Internet*, which is not a bad piece of branding if I do say so myself.'[8]

'Multimedia's whatever you care to make it, usually bad animation and crap movies all lumped together in one badly designed screen,' explains Richard Harris. 'The whole idea behind the "multiple media" company – overly ambitious as it ultimately turned out to be – was that we would be able to casually re-purpose content for whatever medium we wanted to deliver it in, using the best features and the appropriate interface for each thing we wanted to deliver. Unfortunately we got stuck on *Starship Titanic* and that became our albatross, it took over our plan before we could start the other stuff.'[9]

'We were offered a lot of money to build the CD-ROM game of *Starship Titanic*,' recalls Creasey. 'Simon and Schuster put the money in and that led us down one route that we didn't expect to go. We hadn't really thought of getting into games particularly. Douglas threw himself into it, and it became a huge project: much, much bigger than any of us envisaged, especially as it was an area about which we knew nothing and Douglas was pushing the barriers. It became clear about a year into it that it was massively out of control.'[10]

Starship Titanic was a one-paragraph joke from *Life, the Universe and Everything.* Ed Victor loved the image it created and had encouraged Douglas to explore the idea, although up to this point it had merely been the working title on the contract for *Mostly Harmless.* However, the idea had a life even earlier than that. Shortly after the radio series, Douglas was approached by a commercial TV company to create a science fiction series in the vein of, but unconnected with, *Hitchhiker's* – and though it never came to anything, *Starship Titanic* was the result. By 1991 Douglas was considering *Starship Titanic* as a film script, but was worried that it would affect the still-in-limbo *Hitchhiker's* movie.

By June 1997, the idea had very definitely solidified into a CD-ROM game: 'I think that CD-ROM itself is a very interesting medium in and of its own right. It's not well-served by just taking something from another medium – essentially, the linear medium of the book – and just moving that to CD-ROM. Yes, it's a fair enough exercise, and there are all sorts of instances where it can work very well. But it's worth doing for its own sake and on its own terms, and not just dragging a book into it with all the linearity that comes with it.'[11]

Was Douglas here referring to his one previous excursion into CD-ROM territory, *Last Chance to See*, which was released in 1995 through the Voyager company (founded by Joe Medjuck, onetime producer of the *Hitchhiker's* movie)? The *Last Chance . . .* disc had the book's full text, much of the radio series, a recording of Douglas reading the book and several hundred photographs – but it was hardly interactive. Voyager also released the first four *Hitchhiker's* books as a searchable text CD-ROM, but the long-standing idea of a fully interactive version of *Hitchhiker* (which even predated CD-ROMs – in the late 1980s Douglas could be found enthusing about a possible 'interactive video disc') never came to pass.

'So I thought, "Let's take this idea, *Starship Titanic*, and actually start it as a CD-ROM,"' said Douglas. 'I'm not in a position to make any sort of formal announcement, but I very much hope that it will have a future as a movie as well. But we shall see about that. I very specifically didn't want to have the inevitability of then having to sit down and write a book based on it as well. I just wanted to be freer than that.'12 That was a prophetic statement: the story behind the book – *Douglas Adams's Starship Titanic: A Novel by Terry Jones* – is a saga in itself, a series of problems almost entirely unconnected to those afflicting the game.

'I was working on the game,' explained Douglas, 'and out of it emerged a storyline, and I wrote a film treatment. And then suddenly I said, "Oh, I've got to get a book out of this as well." And the publishers needed it immediately. Terry was doing a voice part on the game, playing a semi-deranged parrot – a part that many people feel he was born to play. He saw the graphics and said, "My god! This is wonderful! Is there anything else I can do?" And I said, "Do you want to write a novel?" So I gave him a twenty-page story outline, and in three weeks, he came back with it. So essentially, I did the outline, and then Terry did what we call "the actual words".'13

As usual, Douglas wasn't telling the whole truth, although on this occasion there was a good reason: he was being tactful about one of his heroes. What actually happened was that he commissioned Robert Sheckley to novelise *Starship Titanic*, but Sheckley's novel, for whatever reason, was rejected by the publishers (nor was Douglas happy with it*). 'The novel's an interesting story,' says

---

* A similar situation occurred in 2000 when Douglas persuaded Pan Books to commission artwork for new paperback editions of the *Hitchhiker's* novels from Pink Floyd album cover artist Storm Thorgerson. Douglas was a fan of Thorgerson's work and had provided text for a softback collection of the artist's pictures, but when the cover designs arrived in early 2001 he was disappointed with them and asked the publisher not to use them. Facsimiles of the original covers were hastily devised instead for the paperbacks which were scheduled for June 2001 and consequently amended to become 'Memorial Editions' at the last moment. Having paid Thorgerson for his designs (and with Douglas' personal feelings sadly no longer a factor) Pan eventually used them on B-format editions published by their subsidiary imprint Picador in 2002.

Robbie Stamp, 'because from a long time ago, Douglas said, "The last thing I want to do is write a novel." But what Robert Sheckley turned in wasn't great, and Random House just went, "We can't publish this." Douglas was pretty unhappy about the idea. The publisher was insistent that the book should come out the same time as the game. So he said, "I want to write the book," and they said, "Great." Of course then it didn't quite happen, so we had to get somebody else to write it.'[14]

'The treatment had all the characters – or at least all the names – and most of the plot,' recalls Terry Jones. 'Douglas owed Simon and Schuster a book and they were going to publish the Robert Sheckley version with Douglas' name on it if he didn't come up with an alternative by 5 June. I'd read the treatment and made some comments on it – and Douglas rang up and asked if I'd be prepared to write the book. I loved the idea of just stopping everything else and concentrating on that. It was great fun to do because as far as I was concerned all the really hard work had been done. Douglas had the whole structure and world and ideas there – all I had to do was fill it in. Every time I got stuck I just had to refer back to the treatment and off I'd go again.'[15]

But there were wheels within wheels and fires within fires in this story. The person who had been confidently expecting to write the book was another friend of Douglas', Michael Bywater. Bywater had already worked extensively on the game, and had written much of the text on the accompanying website. It's not clear whether Bywater took exception to Sheckley being offered the job, or to Jones being offered it when Sheckley's work proved unsuitable. (It is also known that Douglas rang Michael Marshall Smith about the adaptation, but he was on holiday.) Whatever, the *Starship Titanic* novel was a source of bad blood between Douglas and Bywater, one of his oldest friends.

For all that he was universally acclaimed by friends and colleagues as a warm, friendly, generous man, Douglas had his share of fallings-out. He fell out massively with Sir Clive Sinclair in the wake of the dinner party evolution argument. John Lloyd was very unhappy after Douglas decided to write the novel solo: 'When *Hitchhiker* first came out I became a bit obnoxious,' said Douglas, 'and when *Not the Nine O'Clock News* was a success he became a bit obnoxious, so we weren't quite such good friends.'[16] Jonny Brock recalls Douglas falling out with Mark Carwardine over some technicality regarding *Last Chance to See*, and indeed had his own argument with him when Douglas declined to recommend him as an investor in TDV. There are many other examples.

'It's to Douglas' great credit that although inevitably he fell out with people, he managed to consistently remain friends with them,' says Brock. 'I was often astonished to find, at his parties, reams of people that I knew he'd fallen out with catastrophically. I mean, really, really badly. Because they'd let him down or they'd ripped him off or they'd broken promises or they'd really behaved badly. But he just couldn't bring himself to ostracise people and that was greatly to his credit. Although he would be offended by this, it was very Christian of him. He just couldn't help forgiving people. Partly because he wanted people to love him and he wanted people round him and he loved giving parties and he loved being the centre of attention, of course. But I think also he had a very forgiving nature.

'There were people who'd done horrible things to him, and Jane found that very, very difficult. She was wonderfully loyal to him always and never complained but there were quite a lot of times over the last ten years when I think if one had asked Jane she would have said, "I just don't want to have these people around because I don't like what they did to Douglas and I don't like them anyway." But Douglas was a very trusting and forgiving person.'[17]

Douglas and Bywater apparently made their peace later, but there were at least two other long-time, close friends and colleagues of Douglas' with whom he was rumoured to be still on bad terms at the time of his death – which of course drew a line under any outstanding disputes. The incident with Bywater was evidently not an isolated one. Quite what happened in the wake of that initial falling-out is something about which nobody is prepared to speak on the record, but it seems to have involved allegations and counter-allegations, and possibly even lawyers.

Whatever happened, it was a mess. And though Douglas' for-giving nature would ultimately restore harmony to his social life, the incident with Bywater was just one more hassle for TDV. And still the problems with the novel weren't over. There was, at one stage, some debate over who should be publishing it, based on whether it counted as 'the next Douglas Adams book' or not. In the end it appeared as a paperback original from Pan, the first 'Douglas Adams book' not to debut in hardback for fifteen years.

In America, the novel was published in hardback by Harmony Books and Terry and Douglas embarked on an extensive signing tour across the country. Ironically, this caused further problems for Pan Books who were waiting to get the proofs approved. The British paperback, set for 21 November, emerged in December 1997, a few weeks after its minimal advertising. It was greeted by negative reviews and public indifference.

'I'd agreed to do the signing tour because I really hadn't had the chance to spend time with Douglas for – I don't know – ten or fifteen years,' says Terry Jones. 'It was like returning to the early days of our friendship. We'd forgotten how well we got on together and what fun we had. It was a magic time and one of my very best recollections of Douglas. There was some talk of doing more books, but I think the initial negative responses to this one put a damper on the idea. I personally blame the publishers. I think it was a stupid idea to call it "*Douglas Adams's Starship Titanic – A Novel by Terry Jones*". They were so anxious to push it as a Douglas Adams book that some of his fans felt they'd been cheated. If they'd simply put "*Starship Titanic* by Douglas Adams and Terry Jones" there wouldn't have been the problem.'[18]

The final indignity forced onto the *Starship Titanic* novel was that, in their rush to get it into shops, Pan somehow missed a huge formatting error which spread Douglas' four-page introduction over 11 pages. On the plus side, TDV took great delight in publishing the entire novel on the web: every single word of it, in alphabetical order.

But that was just the spin-off novel.

The problems that were happening with the game itself were of a different order of magnitude ...

INTERLUDE - **NET**

ON 4 OCTOBER 1993, the following message appeared on the internet newsgroup alt.fan.douglas-adams: 'Hi, I've finally managed to get a convenient connection to the Internet. I opened an account at the Santa Fe Institute earlier in the year, but it was slow and complicated using it from London so I gave up on it. I know there is a ton of accumulated mail on my Santa Fe account, which I will try and get to. I'll try and post news here from time to time if it seems like it might interest people.'[1] From then on, Douglas was a constant lurker, and a regular poster, on the newsgroup devoted to his work.

Though Douglas quite definitely did not invent the internet, the internet seemed to have been invented for Douglas Adams. It allowed him to interact with his fans without actually having to meet them, and he was quite happy for his e-mail address to be widely publicised (though usually his inbox was checked for him by Sophie Astin): 'I'm happy to be available by e-mail because it's much easier and quicker to answer than regular snail mail – which tends to pile up in huge backlogs which I then have to get a secretary to deal with. I guard my home address and phone number because I have my privacy, my family, my friends and security to think about. But cyberspace is – or can be – a good, friendly and egalitarian place to meet.'[2]

Douglas first went on-line in 1983 using an American-based service called The Source through which he was able to communicate

– at great trouble and expense – with colleagues such as Steve Meretzky. Shortly afterwards he started also using a British system, Telecom Gold, and he enjoyed reporting on the *Hitchhiker's* game's progress on various computer bulletin boards. In 1985 Douglas did his first on-line chat on Micronet Celebrity Chatline; he would do many more over the next sixteen years.

As the internet developed, Douglas found it massively useful, and he could be found joining in discussions in newsgroups dedicated to music ('Someone told me recently they thought there was now a source of lefty thumb picks. Anyone know of it?'[3]), computers ('I've just got a Duo 270c, which seems like a pretty good bit of kit, but it comes with the Apple Express Modem. Does anyone know the initialisation string for use with Versaterm?'[4]) and scuba diving ('I thought we were going to St Croix after Christmas. Now my wife tells me it might be Puerto Vallarta. What's the diving like in Puerto Vallarta?'[5]). He was also able to ask specific questions when researching his late 1990s radio shows: 'Can anyone please recommend a good book on the history of the plate tectonic theory?'[6], 'Can anybody tell me what tribes of Native Americans originally inhabited California, particularly Southern California?'[7] and 'Is Marshall McLuhan still alive?'[8]

In November 1998 a forum was established on www.douglas-adams.com which allowed Douglas' fans to discuss him and his works and allowed Douglas to make occasional announcements about what was or was not happening. Another advantage was that Douglas' posts were clearly and unequivocally identified as such: 'I enjoy corresponding with people in completely different areas of the net that have nothing to do with who I am, but are just about things I'm interested in,' he said. 'I get the occasional "Excuse me for asking, but are you the DA who wrote . . . ?" etc , which is fine, but I really like to leave it behind if I can. What I don't enjoy is being picked on by smartasses. I guess it comes with the territory, but I still don't like it, and this is me saying so. If you have some involved reason for thinking that I am not me, then please sort it out for yourself and don't bother me with it. I know who I am, and if you have a problem with that, then it stays your problem.'[9]

CHAPTER 38

AS RICHARD CREASEY observed, when the *Starship Titanic* project had been going for only a year it was already 'massively out of control'.[1] He was swiftly appointed Editor-in-Chief at TDV and took an active part in sorting out the problems. But from the fans' point of view, Douglas was still enthusing massively about the game: 'The most fabulous, beautiful, most technologically advanced, gorgeously outfitted, gorgeously designed starship, a cruise liner called the *Starship Titanic*, has been built in the middle of a galactic civilisation of which we know nothing. It's the most advanced ship ever built. Technologically, it cannot possibly go wrong, and on its maiden voyage, it crashes into hyperspace and disappears. And where does it land? It crashes into your house. So, you find your way up into this ship, or not if you want to play a two-minute version of the game, and you find yourself in this environment which is a cross between the *Queen Mary*, the Chrysler building, Tutenkahmun's tomb and Venice.'[2]

But for all that this game had Douglas' name above the title, he had much less involvement in it than he had with the *Hitchhiker's* game; the *Starship Titanic* credits listed more than fifty people. 'One person, or in this case two people, was the usual way of doing a game at Infocom,' explained Douglas. 'In the case of *Starship Titanic*, you have enormous additional levels of complexity: you have the graphics, the animation, the sound, all this stuff, and it's dozens of people working on it, over a period of two years.

It starts out as me saying, "This is how the game is going to go, this is what I've decided," but really, from the first moment that code starts hitting silicon, we're off into territory where everybody who is working on the project is having a fundamental creative influence on the game.'[3]

'One of the things which Douglas found slightly frustrating about the process,' recalls Robbie Stamp, 'was that his previous experience of working on a computer game was him and Steve Meretzky. Certainly at the beginning of *Starship Titanic*, Douglas was very enthusiastic about being able to get his hands on the building blocks, the tools with which you can make a game, himself. And actually that's a quite dangerous path because we chose some tools for the game which were woefully inadequate, in the end, for what he wanted to do. Then we had to write our own tools.'[4]

'Originally, we were going to construct the game in an off-the-shelf authoring system,' explained Douglas in one of his more technical interviews, 'and the one that was chosen was Metropolis, a Macintosh program with a run-time version of Windows. It's a highly object-oriented authoring system that was specifically designed to enable a high-level language where the author would actually be able to get in there and make things happen and adjust things. The problem is, it turned out that Metropolis couldn't do all the stuff we needed it to do because this is going to be a very, very heavyweight program. So we were going to wait for Metropolis 2.0 and then began to get a little insecure about how soon that was coming. And as it turned out, Metropolis 2.0 finally arrived about three weeks ago, along with the announcement that it was being discontinued.'[5]

Having to construct from scratch a new bespoke authoring system was just one of the problems besetting *Starship Titanic*. There was a finite amount of money (although the project was refinanced at least once) and a finite amount of time (though the release date was put back several times) and a limited amount of work that Douglas himself could do on the game.

'I think that it was a harsh reality, even by the time we started The Digital Village,' says Stamp, 'that Douglas hadn't been seen to figure big financially by anyone, publishers included, for a little while. So there wasn't tons of money slopping around and there was always that "Will he deliver? Won't he deliver?" worry knocking around at the back of people's minds. I think he found the *Starship Titanic* process fabulous at one level, but also a bit frustrating as he felt it slipping out of his hands, and in the end I think he felt quite distanced from it.'[6]

For all its publicity and high-profile names, TDV was a fairly small company, with a limited amount of resources. The founders had not planned to start the company off with a groundbreaking CD-ROM game; they were expecting to make a TV series, which was where most of them had expertise, with perhaps some sort of multimedia spin-off. They couldn't turn down *Starship Titanic*, but they had no real experience of that sort of project, or the amount of time, money and effort it would take to produce. 'I don't think anybody is ever quite prepared for the amount of work required to do a title like that,' says Eitan Arrusi, who was called in as a games consultant. 'Having done one, I know that it just knocks you on your arse. There's just no way to comprehend it until you've done it.'[7]

'It was under-budgeted in terms of time and resources and, brutally, experience,' admits Stamp with laudable honesty. 'I think Simon and Schuster maybe should have been tougher with us in the early stages, but they wanted it out. What it means is that, looking back on it, we were never going to make a game of that complexity, from a standing start, in what was effectively fifteen months. They didn't give us our first money until May 1996, but it was due to be out in September 1997. There's just no way that that was a realistic proposition.

'Those problems in the end, I believe, were less important than the fact that the product was eighty to eighty-five per cent good, but that crucial thing which really turns something into a big hit just wasn't there. And that was because by the time we had a handle on the gameplay, it was too late to do anything about it. The team were working round the clock to get the thing finished and shipped. We'd gone out on an absolute limb to get this thing finished and done and there just was no more money or time. I would have liked nothing more than to be able say, "This is fantastic. If we spend summer testing it and launch it this autumn, it'll probably be great." But we didn't have that possibility.'[8]

'The problem with interactive titles of any sort is that it takes so long for you to see anything,' says Arrusi, the man behind the hit game *Burncycle*. 'If you've got a two-year cycle, it might be twelve or fourteen months before you even have the code ready and another two months before you've got crude things wandering around on the screen. The amount of time that you have then to go back and modify and alter and see whether that bit works is rapidly shortening because you've spent two-thirds of your time just trying to get something onto the screen.'[9]

Starship Titanic was officially launched at the E3 games conference in June 1997, with the expectation that it would be in the shops in time for Christmas. It wasn't, but it would certainly ship in January 1998, although Douglas said that it could be February or March. (This was when he was promoting the novel which the publishers had been so keen to launch simultaneously with the game: 'After all the furore to get the book done in time to release it with the game, the game has done what every single piece of software in the history of multimedia has done, which is turn out to be six months late.'[10]) The game eventually appeared in April 1998, by which time everyone had forgotten about the launch and the industry was getting excited about what they might see at the next E3. And that was just the PC version. The Macintosh game, much to Douglas' chagrin, did not appear until March 1999. 'The temptation with a project is to say it's never ready,' admitted Douglas. 'Saying, "We could do this, we could do that, we can improve it here, we can improve it there." But there comes a point where you have to let go and move on to the next thing.'[11]

TDV let go way too late. Magazines have deadlines and the game simply wasn't available for review until a few days before it was in the shops, a situation not helped by somebody discovering a quicker way of getting the discs pressed which shaved a few more days off the delivery deadline. A fantastically good game could have survived such an ineptly marketed launch, but *Starship Titanic* was not a fantastically good game. It looked gorgeous, thanks to Oscar-winning designers Isabel Molina and Oscar Chichoni, and the press had sung its praises in advance, based on their designs and Douglas' reputation. But when it came to actual gameplay, *Starship Titanic* was found wanting. Puzzles were dull, solutions were often arbitrary, and the characters were forgettable.

Nor was the much-hyped interactivity a great boon. Harking back to his Infocom days, Douglas wanted the game to have a 'conversation engine', so one was specially written by Linda Watson of the Virtus Corporation. It was called *TrueTalk* but even that hit a problem: the name had already been used and so it was changed to *Velocitext* ('Which sounds to me like a 1950s typewriter,'[12] commented Douglas). *Starship Titanic* did not feature text-to-speech capability – the technology simply wasn't there – so sixteen hours of dialogue was recorded by Jones, John Cleese (as 'Kim Bread'), Philip Pope and others. This required three discs, which further reduced the game's playability.

And for all the hype, the 'conversations' with the characters were still totally unnatural: the on-screen character would prattle away for a couple of minutes, then the player would type: 'G E T P A R R O T.' It was a very one-sided conversation, and it rapidly became irritating.

The tie-in novel had come and gone, largely unnoticed. Magazine reviews didn't appear until the game had been in the shops for a month or two, and many were far from favourable. 'I think actually Douglas was quite proud of the game,' says Stamp. 'He felt that it was genuinely good and he always loved the way it looked. Oscar and Isabel had done a fantastic job on that; they really had a conceptual grip on this thing which, although at times it sent the team a bit up the wall, was one of the strongest elements of the game.'[13]

Starship Titanic was not a flop, but it was far from the hit that TDV and Simon and Schuster had hoped for. One irony was that it came out the same year as James Cameron's film *Titanic*, expected to be a flop but actually the most successful film of all time. Some people even saw *Starship Titanic* as a cash-in on the film. (Douglas knew Cameron and a year or so later the two of them went on a white-water rafting expedition, when Cameron commented to Douglas how odd it was that two people who had worked on *Titanic* projects were trying to keep a boat afloat.)

The Digital Village was set up to produce a wide range of products in numerous media, but apart from *Starship Titanic* and *h2g2** very little else appeared under the TDV branding. There were two series on Radio 4, written and presented by Douglas: *The Internet: The Last Battleground of the Twentieth Century* and *The Hitchhiker's Guide to the Future with Douglas Adams*. There was a video of Douglas reading extracts from the *Hitchhiker* novels, recorded at the Almeida Theatre, Islington on 21 August 1995. There was *Unsung*, a CD of music by Douglas' friend Robbie McIntosh with liner notes by Douglas: 'Robbie McIntosh is one of the world's best guitar players, and also one of its most incompetent human beings, as anyone who has watched him trying to buy a shirt will tell you.'

That was it.

There were plans for so much more.

'We were in a bar somewhere in Camden, talking about creative things for the company,' recalls Stamp, 'and I said I thought one of the things we ought to have a stab at would be a long-running, serious science fiction series. So Douglas came up with one.'[14] This was *The Secret Empire*, an alternative history where space exploration had been privatised after the near-disaster of *Apollo 13* and a range of companies had established bases on the Moon, 'like the East India Company in space'.[15] Technology was breaking new ground and seven people were overseeing new developments that would push humanity forward and outward.

'We had ideas for how you could keep the same seven characters but each time round move the action on maybe a hundred years or so,' says Stamp. 'You would always be working at that point which Douglas was interested in, the moment when technology was being tried out for the first time. It progressed to a full treatment with ideas for one or two of the episodes. Douglas wanted to have a sort of Gene Roddenberry relationship with it; he very much wanted to be the progenitor and creator.

* see Chapter 40

'The last conversation I had with him before he died, he was talking about a TV series called *The Oracle at Delphixus*, which was an idea that he and I talked about many years ago. It was pretty much as you'd imagine: an oracle planet and a different story each week. Different groups of pilgrims come with their story and they're given an insight into their world and their lives.'[16]

And then there was the book. Or books. Douglas had by now lost touch – or rather, been allowed to lose touch by lax publishers – with what writing a novel involved: sitting down at the computer on a regular basis. 'I'm actually very busy right now. I'm working on four fiction works in the coming year – so, yes, I'm still writing!'[17] he said in May 1998. Douglas hadn't written a book for six years, and had been unable to do so then without constant supervision: what made him think he could write four in the foreseeable future?

One of these four was *The Different Engineer*: 'That's a story I've been working on for a while,' he said in December 1997, 'but that is the third working title and there's no saying that it's the last. I want to get it done if possible during the early part of next year.'[18] By March, the title had definitely changed, though Douglas wasn't sure to what, because it had been pointed out to him that William Gibson and Bruce Sterling had written a novel called *The Difference Engine*. (SF fans and critics had assumed that *The Different Engineer* was a pun on the Sterling/Gibson book – but of course Douglas wasn't sufficiently SF-literate to have heard of it.)

Another literary project was *The Waterboatmen*. Unlike *The Different Engineer*, Douglas never mentioned this in interviews, but Robbie Stamp remembers it fondly: 'I always thought it was a lovely title. It was very different from all those smart, English, ironic comedy titles. It's got mythical connotations of the River Styx and wise men carrying us along, and it was an extension of this idea that had been knocking around for a long time, *The Jobber*, about somebody who is unemployed but a brilliant fixer. You'd bring in your clock, your radio, your video and he'd fix it for you for a tenner or whatever it is. And one day this guy appears and gives him a piece of equipment and says, "Can you do anything with this?" He fixes it and the guy is from outer space and he's done him a big favour. He gets involved in this huge galactic battle between two empires, one of which has this empress like Ursula Andress in *She*. The people who he befriends are in fact the baddies, and that only becomes clear at the end of Act One.'[19]

On top of these, Douglas was supposedly working on the *Hitchhiker's Guide* and *Dirk Gently* movies and several other books all called, at one time or another, *The Salmon of Doubt*. 'What intrigued me was that Douglas was an exceptionally fast writer,' observed Richard Creasey (whose father John Creasey wrote several hundred books). 'He would say to me, "Here's this great idea I've got in my head," and I would say, "Douglas, can you shove it down on paper so we can actually see it?" And the next day would come three, four, ten sides of paper explaining this great idea. But it seemed to me that once you attached money to that writing, inhibitions came in: "Is every single word I've written worth this number of hundred dollars?" Probably not.'[20]

One non-Adams project which was fairly well advanced was a TV series called *Avatar* written by Eitan Arrusi and Mike Jay (which became *Avatar Forest*, probably because James Cameron was developing a movie called *Avatar*). 'It was a kind of cyber-thriller, a more mainstream version of *Max Headroom* perhaps,' remembers Jay. 'We were commissioned, and paid, to write a couple of drafts of a pilot episode.'[21]

Mary Glanville had set up a deal with ABC to produce low-cost drama in the UK for the US market. Initially the idea was a series based on the thriller novels of John Creasey, to which TDV had purchased the rights. When that fell through, *Avatar* was invented. Douglas had no direct connection with the series but would have been executive producer had it ever gone into production. 'The brief was that it should be an adult-orientated show using technology – and obviously The Digital Village were a technology-based company – but beyond that it was more or less left up to me and Mike,' remembers Arrusi. 'I think the idea was to do it cheaply, a low-budget show coming out of the UK which was potentially going to capture the old *Doctor Who* market except more adult.'[22]

'We didn't have, in the end, the wherewithal in-house to develop good enough scripts,' says Stamp, 'and it was beginning to get difficult at the same time that *Starship Titanic* was beginning to get difficult. Had we got *Secret Empire* off the ground, I think that would have worked because it was Douglas' original conception. But with *Avatar Forest* it was a little bit more difficult. He could never quite get his hands around it.'[23]

Ideas were one thing that Douglas was never short of, and there is a raft of projects which he started but which never came to fruition. With *The Salmon of Doubt* published posthumously and development continuing on the *Hitchhiker's* movie, could any of his TDV-developed projects resurface? Robbie Stamp thinks it's possible: 'Two or three of the ideas which Douglas had were more than sufficiently advanced to be able to see if we couldn't make them happen one day.'[24]

CHAPTER 39

WHILE ALL THIS was going on, what was happening with the *Hitchhiker's* film?

After Douglas dropped off the project in the mid-1980s, producers Ivan Reitman, Joe Medjuck and Michael Gross hired a screenwriter named Abbie Bernstein. 'I tried to preserve as much of the original material intact as I possibly could,' she says. 'There were just certain things that they felt they wanted, to make it resemble a more linear commercial film, and that was my job. I worked on it for two years and seven drafts.'[1]

By the third Bernstein draft, Rocky Morton and Annabel Jankel, directors of the original *Max Headroom* pilot, had become attached to the project. They had their own views on how the film should be made and the process dragged on for several years. 'I remember a lot of meetings that were funny in that you had six people in the room and no two people would agree with each other on various story points,' says Bernstein. 'Even if somebody did manage to change somebody else's mind, it wouldn't help because by the end of the meeting the other person would have changed their mind so you'd still have six different opinions!'[2]

When Douglas eventually saw the screenplay that was credited to 'Douglas Adams and Abbie Bernstein' he was horrified. Bernstein never met Adams but did later apologise to him via their mutual friend Neil Gaiman. 'That screenplay was absolutely nothing to do with me,' said Douglas. 'I didn't know it was being written, never met Abbie Bernstein and when, quite a long time afterward, I happened to see the script, I was horrified beyond belief. I was even more horrified when I discovered that that script was sitting in public view in a script library on the internet. I'm appalled to think how much harm that script may have done my reputation over the years.'[3] (Douglas certainly did know the script was being written. Hadn't he said, 'They've got another writer who's going through my versions at the moment,'[4] back in 1985?)

David Puttnam became attached to the project in 1987, although his exact connection is unclear and he certainly never spoke with Douglas. The movie was promptly put 'into turnaround', which meant that Columbia still owned the rights but had no intention of making it, and it was up for sale if another studio wanted to buy it off them. By October 1992 Douglas was pragmatic about the whole affair: 'I've given up worrying about it. There came a point where I was actually on the brink of buying back the rights myself until I suddenly came to my senses in the middle of the night and thought, "That is a hell of a lot of money." I would have to mortgage the house.'[5]

In fact, Douglas had lawyers working on this for nearly a year, before 'coming to his senses'. But still the idea nagged at him. True, he would have to pay Columbia £200,000 (plus ten years' interest if the film went into production), but his book advances were big enough that he could actually afford it without mortgaging his house and he was also receiving offers of £100,000 or more for the computer rights from Sony and Warner Brothers, 'so the thing was almost self-financing'.[6] Negotiations stalled as the recession bit, but in 1993 a deal was signed, money was handed over, and the feature film rights to *The Hitchhiker's Guide to the Galaxy* rested once more with its creator.

By then, two possible directors had already been discussed. On 26 June 1992, after several months of negotiations through Ed Victor, Douglas met up with his old friend John Lloyd, by then a successful commercials director: 'Johnny at the moment is very keen on directing it. We haven't gone out to raise money yet on that basis, but because a lot of people are waiting for him to make a movie, I think it would be absolutely no problem whatsoever.'[7]

Ironically, only a week before the meeting with Lloyd, another far more experienced director threw his hat into the ring: 'The other possibility is somebody who has expressed interest in it many times in the past and suddenly is in a position to do what the fuck he wants – which is Jim Cameron.'[8] Both sets of talks came to nothing and neither was ever openly mentioned but the possibility of a film directed by someone as sympathetic to the material as John Lloyd, or as powerful as James Cameron (fresh from *Terminator 2*), is tantalising indeed.

Douglas regained the rights sometime between 2 January 1993 ('It's a vast sum and it's not something I'd want to hand over to buy back something I thought of in the first place'[9]) and 31 October ('I have re-acquired the film rights at mind-grilling expense, and am working in close contact with the producer, who is Michael Nesmith'[10]). Nesmith and Douglas had a lot in common, not least that both their careers were overshadowed by their first, enormous successes: *Hitchhiker's* and the Monkees. Nesmith subsequently invented MTV, rode the domestic video boom, founded Pacific Arts and recorded more than a dozen albums. Possibly his strangest work was the Council on Ideas, an annual event begun in 1990 whereby he would fly five leading global thinkers to his Santa Fe ranch and pay them to identify the most pressing problem in the world. Douglas never took part, though he was staying with Nesmith when the 2000 Council met.

Introduced by Ed Victor, Douglas and Nesmith worked on the *Hitchhiker's* film on and off throughout most of 1994 and 1995 with the extraordinary idea of shooting it in IMAX, but by August 1996, with no financial backing having appeared, the project faltered: 'My agent and I have changed directions completely on that one. Mike Nesmith is no longer in the running, although we parted very amicably and are still the best of friends. But it's in the hands of someone completely different who plans something very radical and exciting. However, because negotiations are at a delicate stage, I still can't, unfortunately, give anything away.'[11]

Serious negotiations started in Hollywood in the second half of 1997, and a new film deal was agreed on Christmas Eve – with Disney. 'I remember going home for that Christmas thinking,

"The deal's been done. How nice,"' says Robbie Stamp, who was executive producer. 'Because God, we worked hard on that.'[12] The spark that reignited Hollywood's interest in *Hitchhiker's* was the success of *Men in Black*, which showed that intergalactic, effects-filled sci-fi comedy on the big screen was not only possible but profitable.

'Hollywood went "Comedy science fiction works. What else is there? Has anybody ever done *Hitchhiker's*?",' recalls Stamp, 'and suddenly it's one of those properties that's floating round. The agent at CAA was Bob Bookman, who then started talking to studios. It was bought by an executive called David Vogel when Joe Roth was there, who founded Spyglass – although they weren't Spyglass at that stage, they were Caravan. Caravan had been set up by Roger Birnbaum and Joe Roth. Joe Roth had then gone into Disney, Roger had stayed with Caravan. Then Caravan metamorphosed into Spyglass with a guy called Harry Barber who came from Morgan Creek. We also then met Jay Roach.'[13]

Roach met Douglas in the summer of 1997, just as his feature directing debut, *Austin Powers: International Man of Mystery*, was opening. 'Douglas and Jay got on extremely well,' says Stamp. 'Jay was keen to do it, Douglas was keen that Jay should do it, Disney were happy – he was one of their up-and-coming stars.'[14] Most importantly for Douglas, he was going to write the screenplay himself.

'If I said I wasn't highly delighted about this, I would, of course, be a lying bastard,' he said in a piece he wrote for *SFX* magazine. 'Although it's been a long, long wait since the idea was first mooted, now is a much, much better time to make it than then. However, I do want to be cautious. Announcing an agreement to do a deal is a very different thing from announcing the release of a movie, and we have a lot of hurdles to cross.'[15]

The screenplay which Douglas had worked on with Nesmith was rewritten into a new draft and Vogel, executive producer at Disney, responded with notes in October 1998. By that time *Starship Titanic* was past and The Digital Village was developing 'a brand new *Hitchhiker* game for home computers and consoles, which is currently being described as, "an action-adventure game involving cricket, tea, petunias and very long lunches." Both the film and game are scheduled to appear in summer 2000.'[16]

Douglas submitted another draft, based on Vogel's suggestions; more notes came back in April 1999. By now Douglas was becoming slightly annoyed that he wasn't more involved. On 14 April, while flying back from LA, he wrote Vogel a letter which was subsequently published in *The Salmon of Doubt* (one of the highlights in a curate's egg of a book). Douglas complained, very politely, about, 'a one-way traffic of written "notes" interspersed with long, dreadful silences' – did he not realise that this is standard operating procedure on Hollywood screenplays, or was he expecting special treatment? – and offered to meet Vogel in Hollywood the following week. He then appended thirty-two different phone and fax numbers at which he could be reached, including 'Angus Deayton and Lise Meyer (next-door neighbours who can take a message)' and the Islington branch of Sainsbury's ('they can always page me').

An editor's note in *Salmon* observes that the letter resulted in 'a productive meeting that pushed the movie forward'. Where it actually pushed the movie was away from Douglas: Vogel wanted the next draft to be written by someone else, someone with Hollywood experience.

'It wasn't planned in advance, and of course that was very painful to Douglas,' recalls Robbie Stamp. 'I remember the agony of talking about what it meant and should it happen. But David Vogel persuaded Douglas. Very bluntly put: it ain't going to go. I think he used the image of cathedral building: "You don't put in all the buttresses yourself. We need somebody who's a craftsman now to come in and do it."'[17] The writer assigned was Josh Friedman (*Chain Reaction*) who understood and liked *Hitchhiker*. He read Douglas' most recent draft and then, starting from scratch, wrote his own.

By the time that Friedman's draft was handed in (March 2000 – a copy was promptly leaked to the internet), David Vogel had moved on, replaced by Peter Schneider and Nina Jacobson, who were less enthusiastic. By October 2000, the movie was in turnaround and Jay Roach was telling journalists, '*Hitchhiker's* is quirky and expensive and it's hard to sell. It's a risk, but *Austin Powers* was rejected at every studio before New Line took it.'[18] Roach and Douglas announced that they would explain precisely what was happening with the film in a big joint webcast interview. But, like the film itself, that webcast never actually happened.

But hadn't Douglas said back in June: 'I finished and delivered this new draft last week, and it's suddenly really working in a way that no previous version really did. It's a very hard circle to square but I think we've finally got there, after all these years.'[19] Indeed he had, and he acknowledged the existence of the Friedman script too, without explaining how it had come about: 'There was a bit of a commotion on the web last month about a version of the screenplay that got leaked, and which people didn't like very much. There is a whole story to be told about that script and the role it played in the politics of the development process, but now is not the time and maybe there won't ever be a time. But it wasn't my script and bears very little relation to any script of mine. The new script is my script and I'm extremely pleased with it.'[20]

Behind these calming words was desperation. Douglas had indeed delivered another draft of the script, but not one that he had been paid for. 'Douglas, pretty much off his own back, without a deal, wrote another draft,' confirms Stamp. 'He read Friedman's script and said, "I hate this. I'm going to go and write another draft. This is nuts."'[21]

Roach and his business partner Shauna Robertson were by then looking for another writer to have a go, working from Friedman's script (among others, they approached Ted Elliott and Terry Rossio, who had done uncredited work on *Men in Black*). Although Roach liked Douglas' unpaid, spec script, the movie still wasn't happening and Disney started considering other options. 'It wasn't even turnaround,' says Stamp. 'They said, "Well, okay, quietly: you can shop this around. If somebody else says they'll take it then maybe we'll consider letting it go." It was a slightly messy period. I don't know how many people actually read the script, but people were just passing on it.'[22]

When the contract had been agreed on Christmas Eve 1997, the putative release date was summer 2000. That had now come and gone. What made this delay even more galling for Douglas was that in 1999 he had moved, with Jane and Polly in tow, to California. They rented out Duncan Terrace and found a fantastic house in Santa Barbara, close enough to LA for Douglas to attend business meetings, but far enough away to be very definitely somewhere else. Also, John Cleese lived there.

Douglas was fed up with all the transatlantic commuting he was doing; what little interest he maintained in TDV could be handled by phone or e-mail, and he simply wanted to spend more time with his daughter. Some of his friends were concerned at the effect the upheaval might have on five-year-old Polly, but they found a good school in Santa Barbara and she bloomed. 'I love the sense of space and the "can do" attitude of Americans,' exclaimed Douglas. 'It's a good place to bring up children, and even the state schools are considered of excellent quality. Living in Islington, we would probably have had to move to get Polly into a good school anyway. That or send her across town.'[23]

'When Polly left with Douglas and Jane to go to America, she was a relatively diffident child who hadn't got much confidence,' says Richard Creasey. 'When I went to see Douglas in Santa Barbara, Polly had blossomed into a fantastic child. She had all these huge advantages that, in these early years of growing up, America had given her.'[24]

Jane was initially opposed to the move, having bad memories of their previous time in LA – 'Jane said it was hateful,' recalls Juliana Abell. 'She told me it was horribly like Jackie Collins' *Hollywood Wives*'[25] – but eventually acquiesced. Douglas was so enthusiastic about the move that it took him several months to even notice that Jane had any qualms about it.

'Going off to America was a big, big sacrifice for Jane,' recalls Jonny Brock. 'Although she did qualify for counsel in the States – which is remarkable – she never practised there and that did affect her career. But she was loyal to Douglas and if he was going to live in America she'd go with him. I was very worried when they went to Santa Barbara, but Jane made it work and in fact she enjoyed it much more than I thought she would, although I think they would have come back eventually.'[26]

CHAPTER **40**

THE DIGITAL VILLAGE had been set up as a multiple media company, but it didn't take too long to become, quite against its founders' wishes, a single medium company, even a single project company. 'I think it evolved pretty quickly that *Starship Titanic* was about to take up every single ounce of management ability that we had,' says Richard Creasey. 'The budget and the schedule were both looking pretty difficult in every single way. We were always aware that Douglas was so interested in the absolute detail being right, in getting a dream that no-one else had done there. It didn't occur to us until really quite late in the day that we had a major headache on our hands.'[1]

'For better or worse, we had to finish that game and get it out,' says Robbie Stamp. 'Because without it, there definitely wasn't going to be a company. That was very difficult. We just managed to keep some development and some thinking ideas around what became *h2g2*, but *Starship Titanic* became like a black hole. Its gravitational pull sucked everything inside: financial resource, time resource, management resource. In the end, pragmatically, I had to say, "We've just got to get this game done." Then it's a very difficult message because you're saying, "We want to be this multiple media company. But we're just doing a game." It's quite a difficult thing when you're talking to investors: "So you're a games company?" "No, no, we're not a games company." "But you're doing a game."'[2]

There had been hopes – serious, genuine hopes – that *Starship Titanic* would become an all-conquering, multiple media franchise. Overtures had been made to Granada and LWT about a possible TV version. But then the game was released and it very rapidly became apparent that it was not going to be a smash hit. 'We went through all the errors of thinking, "This is going to be the one which absolutely cracks it, we've got another *Hitchhiker's Guide* on our hands,"' recalls Creasey. 'And I suppose that was always possible until the day it was released, and suddenly it didn't quite take off. It did well by comparison with other complicated CD-ROM PC games. But it didn't fly. And the reality is: it was never going to fly when it wasn't on one of the great consoles. It was conceived as a CD-ROM project and was very much stuck in what was then becoming a slightly outdated format.'[3]

And so The Digital Village turned its attention to the web project which Douglas had been talking about for so long, '*The Hitchhiker's Guide to the Internet*'. Creasey believes that, rather than being Douglas' Plan B, the project simply had to wait those extra couple of years for the internet to be ready: 'It was delayed until technology caught up and enabled us to do it, but by that time it was probably too late, because we'd chewed through a whole lot of money for different reasons. If I look back with 20/20 vision, it's what we should have done from the minute we set up TDV. I never saw it as a Plan B; it was always a Plan A which was delayed by *Starship Titanic*.

'Douglas' fight had gone out of him. He'd spent so much time on *Starship Titanic* that he didn't want to put that amount of time and energy into something which didn't bring huge profits back. His mind had gone off to Hollywood anyway. And Robbie and I realised that we aren't at heart games people. Therefore, if you're left in charge of "what do we do next?", you look to your greatest asset, which undoubtedly was Douglas, then you look at your own key strengths and they were undoubtedly working on something which is mainly factual.'[4]

And so was created *h2g2*, a constantly growing and evolving encyclopaedia of knowledge from around the world, collected by thousands of individuals, fully accessible and fully cross-referenced.

It was, to all intents and purposes, the Earth edition of *The Hitchhiker's Guide to the Galaxy*.

'When I invented *The Hitchhiker's Guide to the Galaxy*, some twenty-odd years ago now, I didn't think of myself as being a predictive science fiction writer,' said Douglas. 'But I kept returning to the *Guide* as a good idea – something that, instead of being compiled by an editor, everyone could work on together. But there were two things that needed to be in place. One is the web, which lets people share everything. But there's a limitation on the web in terms of creating a real-time, on-the-fly collaborative guide – people log in at their desks.

'The real change takes place when the second shoe falls, which is mobile computing, and that is beginning to arrive now. We're beginning to get internet access on mobile phones and personal digital assistants. That creates a sea change, because suddenly people will be able to get information that is appropriate to where they are and who they are – standing outside the cinema or a restaurant or waiting for a bus or plane. Or sitting having a cup of coffee at a café. With *h2g2*, you can look up where you are at that moment to see what it says, and if the information you need is not there you add it in yourself. For example, a remark about the coffee you're drinking or a comment that the waiter is very rude.'[5]

Jim Lynn was technical lead on the project from the start: 'Part of the problem was, we were told: "We need to build a *Hitchhiker's Guide to the Galaxy*." But the question is: "Well, what the hell is that?" So we had a few brainstorming ideas. There were a few wrong avenues taken. The original producer on it, Emma Westecott, wanted it very much to be driven by fiction, by characters that she'd developed.'[6]

When the site was launched, it had about 200 entries, mostly humorous, some entirely fictional, written by freelancers. Not only was that not what the site was meant to be, but some of the freelancers had clearly never read *Hitchhiker's Guide* and went as far as removing *Hitchhiker's* references from the material that the technical team contributed. Animations were included, based around supposedly humorous characters who were 'guide researchers', most of whom had no connection with Douglas Adams. Douglas was distracted anyway by attempts to shore up the faltering *Starship Titanic* and ongoing events in Hollywood. The fact that his original idea for a web resource was being turned into a bunch of cartoons based around someone else's characters was something he could do without.

'I had a great deal of input at the beginning, which was setting the thing up,' he explained. 'I also have input concerning my ideas about where it should go in the future. But the day-to-day development of the website at this point, I don't have so much involvement with.'[7]

'Douglas hated confrontations of any kind,' says site editor Mark Moxon. 'If you showed him something that he really didn't like, he would tend to avoid the issue rather than criticising. As far as I remember, he liked the technology, the implementation and the way the website ran, but he hated the content that was put on there. All the characters, the animation, pastiches of his writing style written by other people: I think he looked at it and thought, "That's not what I thought *The Hitchhiker's Guide to the Galaxy* was about." The underlying technology was good, but it was completely hidden under this veneer of misdirected editorial stuff.

'Gradually, over the next couple of years, I put quite a lot of time into trying to persuade him that the quality of the stuff that's being written now was totally different: "Look, we've got rid of the cartoons. Now people are writing great stuff that has nothing to do with your style, but they're inspired by what you did." I don't know if he ever got into it in a big way, but certainly he was a lot more complimentary about it when he was coming back in the last summer of TDV, than he was when I first joined, when he was quite dismissive of it.'[8]

Douglas himself only contributed occasionally to *h2g2*, and then it was mostly material written for his occasional column in the *Independent on Sunday*. (Another of those columns, written after the death of Peter Jones, was recycled into a half-hour Radio 4 tribute programme presented by Douglas in July 2000.) 'He'd written an article for us about tea, and it was an excellent short article,' recalls Lynn. 'It had every element that you'd want for a text from Douglas. Then Emma said, "That's lovely but we'll have to rewrite it so that it's one of the characters speaking." None of the rest of us could quite believe that she thought that was a good idea. I think Douglas was very ticked off by the fact that somebody was suggesting that we rewrite his copy. Otherwise why have Douglas Adams at all? We were in a position where, quite frankly, if he'd given us a shopping list, we'd have put it up on site! And people would have looked it it – because it would have been interesting.'[9]

Douglas launched the site on an internet-themed edition of *Tomorrow's World* broadcast live from the British Library on 28 April 1999. When Douglas mentioned h2g2.com, the site received about 400 simultaneous hits, crashing the servers. But the most amazing thing about *h2g2* was that it was launched with no editorial team, partly because TDV couldn't really afford one. After a few weeks, Moxon was taken on and did his best to maximise the community and information aspects of the site, gradually fading out the embarrassing fiction and cartoons. He found that there was a backlog of nearly 2,000 entries waiting to be looked at, edited and added to the site.

'The few of us who had a modicum of writing skills, when we weren't actually busy doing the coding, would look at the queue and try and find something that was worth editing,' recalls Lynn. 'But because we had a queue, we had to go through an awful lot of tosh. The number of people who put, "The answer to the ultimate question of life, the universe and everything is 42." Or, "Earth: mostly harmless." Yes, haha. It was unmaintainable in that sense.'[10]

Nobody at that point really knew what *h2g2* was or what it was for. Douglas was moving to the USA, and Stamp and Creasey were trying to reconfigure the company's future plans in the wake of *Starship Titanic*'s underperformance. 'There was nothing on the site really about what people were supposed to do there,' recalls Moxon. 'That was the reason why people were writing "42" all the time. There were an awful lot of documents kicking around TDV from the previous two years. There was an eighty-two-page document that was probably very interesting for somebody at university somewhere but as a practical implementation plan it was a load of bollocks. So I ignored all that and basically sat down with the tech team and we knocked out a plan.'[11]

One thing that distracted Douglas from *h2g2* was that he was increasingly in demand as a conference speaker, but hand in hand with this acceptance into the academic/commercial community came an increasing abandonment of the fans who had made his name in the first place. Douglas did not attend the 20th Anniversary *Hitchhiker's Guide to the Galaxy* Convention organised by ZZ9 Plural Z Alpha in May 1998 – he didn't even send a good luck message. Though he made the occasional generous exception, Douglas was now simply too expensive for most colleges or literary festivals to book as a speaker, and in any case he wanted to expound his views on information technology and ecology, not discuss his latest book or computer game.

Which is not to take away the impressive achievement that was a man, educated in science no higher than O-level, giving keynote speeches at international scientific conferences. If anything, it was Douglas' refreshingly undogmatic and open-minded approach – and of course his humour – which endeared him to other great minds. And Douglas was amused to discover that his new peers were so far ahead of the game that they sometimes forgot basic ideas.

'He was on a kick for a while of, "It's the axial tilt, stupid",' recalls Larry Yaeger. 'He had asked a lot of people, including a lot of very smart people, about why we have winter and summer. He found it astonishing that even some very intelligent people couldn't tell him why this was the case. The answer of course is the axial tilt of the Earth. I saw him do a talk at the Apple Worldwide Development Conference, where one of his electronic slides had the phrase, "It's the axial tilt, stupid." The inference was: why not make bumper stickers of these things?'[12]

It was at Digital Biota 2 in Cambridge over 10–13 September 1998 that Douglas gave what would be hailed as the greatest speech of his career. 'It was a great, great conference about the evolution of artificial life,' recalls Richard Harris, one of the organisers. 'At one of the evening sessions, after Richard Dawkins had spoken,

Douglas was asked to stand up and give a talk. He'd been trying to avoid doing anything because he felt that all these people who knew infinitely more about the subject than he did were there. But he launched into a largely extemporised speech which turned into a rant on digital theology and how artificial life systems could probe the non-existence of God. I knew I'd heard most of the ideas in there before but as far as I'm aware Douglas putting them together into what turned into that very coherent, beautifully presented speech was almost entirely off the cuff.'[13]

A transcript of 'Is There an Artificial God?' quickly made its way to the web and was published in *The Salmon of Doubt*. It wobbles a little at the beginning as Douglas finds his rhythm, there are a few elements recognisable to those who have heard other Douglas speeches, such as the puddle analogy, and having announced that he would explain 'the four ages of sand' he had to be reminded towards the end that he had only covered three. But by anybody's standards, it's an astounding speech.

Douglas had three standard speeches memorised and he would constantly hone them, like a comedian honing a stand-up routine. 'He would spend hours and hours and hours perfecting the lectures,' remembers Sophie Astin. 'He'd spend a day, and at the end of it he would change one sentence. Douglas' speeches had a tendency to start losing the plot halfway through, then suddenly pick up again and finish brilliantly, but the middle bit got a bit lost occasionally. Towards the very end of his life he started using notes again.'[14]

The key to Douglas' success as a public speaker was that he was still, at heart, a frustrated writer-performer: 'What remains of the urge to perform I use up by occasionally going and doing dramatic readings from the books around American colleges and that kind of thing.'[15] 'I asked him once if he got nervous before doing it,' says Astin, 'and he said he was absolutely cacking himself before going on stage, but as soon as he got there it was fantastic.'[16]

CHAPTER **41**

'**ROBBIE WAS A** pretty unique CEO who enabled a very creative company to be built,' recalls Mark Moxon. 'Douglas was a very inspiring person who would talk about things and you would see, "Yes, that could happen. It won't happen yet, but it's very interesting and wouldn't it be great to be working on a project that could do that." I think gradually this kind of vibe bashed into the reality of the finance officer saying, "We've got no money," and all of a sudden it started falling apart. It was a bit of a shame to see. We weren't going out blowing money on champagne and stuff. It wasn't that sort of dot.com.'[1]

On 20 September 1999, TDV announced that it had received new investment from three venture capital companies. This went some way to patching the cracks in the company which had begun to show when the release date for *Starship Titanic* started slipping and had been exacerbated by turning down what could have been crucial investment earlier in the company's history. TDV also changed its name to h2g2 Ltd, partly because it was clear by then that there would be no other projects, but mostly because TV companies wouldn't advertise external websites and the only way round that was to make the URL the company name. 'My role is simply to have the wild ideas,' commented Douglas. 'Other people get to figure out how to make money with it.'[2]

'We were supposed to make money the way that everybody building content sites on the internet thought that they were going to make money,' reflects Robbie Stamp. 'It was going to be a combination of advertising, maybe a subscription element to parts of the site, then we would be moving on to mobiles. One of the things that killed a lot of the first generation of mobile content companies was the mobile operators' refusal to share any revenue.'[3]

h2g2 Ltd did actually make a WAP version of *h2g2* available, launched on 17 December 1999, with exactly a fortnight of the millennium left (Douglas had no time for millennial pedants). A deal with Vodafone was signed the following month, but as with all WAP deals, the phone companies were happy to carry the data and completely refused to pay any sort of royalty for it.

That was another nail in the coffin of the company formerly known as TDV. 'We were actually getting very good, long sessions,' remembers Stamp. 'Even with all the bad press that WAP got, people were spending eight, nine, ten minutes on *h2g2*, but we weren't getting a penny for that. If we made misjudgements, we were not alone in making misjudgements. We were not uniquely, in retrospect, wrong about the hope that if you created content that people were interested in, you would be able to make money from it.'[4]

Another possible revenue source was e-commerce. That September 1999 press release contained the first and last mention of 'tradingpost.h2g2.com, the e-commerce wing of *h2g2*, guiding members to a range of imaginative products for the Christmas Season'.

'A lot of money went into that, tens of thousands of pounds,' recalls Jim Lynn. 'Not a bad idea, but we didn't have any products! It was like buying a shop, painting it up, putting all the shelves up, putting in the cash registers, and then thinking: "What shall we sell in here?" You've got to start with a product line. I didn't want anything to do with it because it wasn't what the company should have been about; I was quite adamant that it was a very, very bad idea and I kept telling everybody. But they got an outside contractor to come in and do the designs, and they talked to a company about the commerce side of it. The end result, when people saw the mock-up of the website that was done by the designers – everybody hated it. It wasn't even very well designed, so luckily that killed it.'[5]

Ideas were flowing thick and fast by this point, as the company desperately sought some kind of income while other dot.coms crashed and burned spectacularly. It was suggested that regular contributors to *h2g2* could be 'paid' in Altairian Dollars, to be redeemed against stock at tradingpost.h2g2.com, but of course that would only work if the trading post had anything to sell. In reality, the Altairian Dollars would have been more like Flainian Pobble Beads.

Then there was Milliways, a Planet Hollywood-style chain of restaurants with a sci-fi theme and with internet portals and webcams at every table, allowing people to meet each other for lunch in different countries. That idea actually attracted some investment interest from, bizarrely, an Arabian princess. 'It was genuinely a possibility that they would license this idea,' remembers Lynn. 'And maybe they would have live events that were hosted in the restaurant but also people could view via webcams and join in as paying events on the internet – so another revenue stream. But in the end, the princess' advisors stopped answering phone calls, and I think that was about the time that the theme restaurant bubble burst and people realised that it wasn't a licence to print money.'[6]

When the dot.com crash came, it came quickly, and even a relatively small company like h2g2 Ltd was in trouble. The company had been aiming for a stock market launch, which suddenly wasn't going to happen. That meant that the pot of money from venture capital investment would gradually leak away, with nothing to replace it. In March 2000, the management announced a financial freeze: no new staff, no new equipment, no pay-rises. That was an ely, and it was time to start thinking seriously about solutions to the problem.

The technical and editorial teams found themselves receiving some extraordinary requests which smacked of simple desperation, like breaking text up into small chunks spread over several pages to generate more hits. In desperation, the company even turned to one of the professions which Douglas had specifically included on the Golgafrinchan 'B'-Ark: marketing executives.

'The really, really, really, really stupid requests,' emphasises Moxon, 'and they were fucking stupid, let's not make any bones about it, came from the marketing people, who were just appalling. Their requests would be so fundamentally impossible, given either current or the-way-we-did-things technology, that you'd think,

"That's quite an easy no." But they wouldn't really take no for an answer. I'd say, "No, that's not technically possible." And they'd go, "Why not?" And I'd go, "Well, what do you know about PERL?" Eventually they'd give up and try something else, but I found myself thinking, "You don't know shit about this website, do you? It's quite obvious you just don't get it." Although I should point out that you can't blame the marketing people for the fact that the company ran out of money.'[7]

Over the summer, as hoped-for financial deals fell apart, the directors sought new investors, keeping the staff up to date with regular meetings. Douglas would attend if he was in the country. 'It was very open,' says Moxon. 'It got more and more open as things got worse and worse, as I think you have to. Certainly in the summer it probably was not evident to most people in my team that there were issues. They knew that money was tight but they believed that there was a buyer out there. Things were okay and they'd get through it. The management were really trying very hard and they were as confounded by the state of the financial markets as anybody in the company. But probably by September people thought, "We're going down the pan here."'[8]

One good thing came out of the company's increasing financial crisis: the marketing executives were jettisoned. The wembley came at the end of November: the directors, who didn't pay themselves for November, announced that there would be no money to pay anybody in December. Anyone who wanted to was given the chance to leave but the staff were loyal and stayed, working for nothing.

Help arrived in the unlikely shape of the BBC, and it was Douglas who, indirectly, saved the company. Several months previously, Richard Creasey had been approached by radio producer Mark Rickards who wanted Douglas to present a series called *The Hitchhiker's Guide to the Future*. Through Rickards, Creasey was able to introduce Douglas to Ashley Highfield, BBC Director of New Media, where it transpired that *h2g2* was one of Highfield's favourite websites. 'Ashley said to Douglas, "How can I help?",' recalls Creasey, 'Douglas said, "Meet up with my two guys who are in charge, Richard and Robbie." Ashley invited us to lunch. I said, "Hey, cancel the lunch. I don't need to drink to the success of the BBC and say how great it is. We need a forty-five-minute meeting with Ashley and his financial director to work out how they can buy *h2g2*."

'It started out as a million-to-one shot and it zeroed into one in which it suddenly dawned on us that we might just make this. Douglas' reaction was two-fold. On the one hand, deeply relieved as a director of h2g2 Ltd that he wouldn't end up with a company which went completely broke. On the other hand, had it gone completely broke, he would have been free and able to write, so that was quite enticing. He was being offered nothing by the BBC, nor indeed was anybody else, but the BBC was a natural harbour to continue the dream that he, Robbie and I had had.'[9]

Three months of agonising waiting ensued as BBC legal and technical people debated the viability of a transfer. The BBC couldn't buy up a private company, but they could purchase the *h2g2* site and all its effects, including jobs for all staff who wanted them, leaving h2g2 Ltd as a company with no assets (the development work on the new *Hitchhiker's Guide* game had already been established as a separate company). What is more, the *h2g2* site did not use proprietary software, but was a specially written C++ programme. However, every single word of content would need checking (eventually) and the BBC would have to revise its policy of not allowing links to external websites.

On 29 January 2001, *h2g2* closed; the BBC now owned it but it did not yet meet their criteria. Ironically, the sudden, unexplained cessation of activities persuaded many observers that the site was dead. The *h2g2* staff were paid for December and January and prepared to move into Bush House. The announcement that what was once h2g2.com would now be bbc.co.uk/h2g2 came on 21 February and the site went back on-line on 12 March. On 10 April, Douglas gave a talk at Embedded Systems in San Francisco. 'I just lost my brilliant dot.com company,' he announced, 'which, like everybody else's brilliant dot.com company, was based on the idea that if you multiply zero by a sufficiently large number it will suddenly turn into something.'[10]

The Hitchhiker's Guide to the Future was repeated on Radio 4 over Easter. The final part went out on 5 May. Six days later, Douglas Adams died.

INTERLUDE - **SALMON**

- 1991: Douglas is countenancing the idea of a third *Dirk Gently* story: 'I'm still very fond of the character and of the set-up, so I'm perfectly happy with the idea that one day, I'll go and do some more. I just don't have any planned at the moment.'[1]

- 1992: With *Mostly Harmless* completed, he muses on the other half of that 1988 two-book deal: 'I've got several different notions juggling with each other at the moment. I'm trying to work out if it will be one book or two books. Or three books. I'm trying to find which threads come together. It might well be a *Dirk Gently* book. Or it might be yet a third thing. I'm sitting here playing around with plot strands and seeing what emerges.'[2]

- 1993: His next book will be a *Dirk Gently* novel called *A Spoon Too Short*: 'Also, much to my surprise, I find I have a whole lot of new *Hitchhiker* ideas.'[3]

- 1994: The book is retitled *The Salmon of Doubt*, a title designed solely to irritate his editor which remains constant as the book morphs from one idea to another, being equally irrelevant to all versions: 'It is not finished. It is way, way behind as everyone reminds me because this year has been interrupted by two major events: (a) my going off and spending a long time writing the screenplay, and (b) the baby. I have to get it finished by the end of this year because it's been so long now it's beginning to become a burden rather than a pleasure, so I have to get the thing bloody well finished and out of the way because there is so much else I want to do.'[4]*

- 1995: By March the book is postponed indefinitely, then shortly afterwards reannounced for October, but it is no longer a *Dirk Gently* novel. In September, the trade journal *Locus* reproduces a dust jacket for *The Salmon of Doubt: A Dirk Gently Novel*, to be published spring 1996 – this is wrong in every important respect.

- 1996: 'We want to know what *The Salmon of Doubt* is about.' 'So would I!' 'When is it due?' 'When it's ready!' 'Why was Dirk Gently written out of it?' 'Wrong fit!'[5] In December, the book is rescheduled for summer 1997, after which it drifts into publishing limbo.

- 1997: *The Salmon of Doubt* will be a sixth *Hitchhiker's* book, using ideas from the second radio series, but won't be published for at least two years: 'It is now several projects away. It started out as a *Dirk Gently* book, but it wouldn't work. I then wrote Dirk out of it and I still couldn't get it to work. At that point I just got bored and cross and started to think about other things.'[6] Five months later, Douglas is far less certain that it's a *Hitchhiker* book.

- 1998: Douglas is still talking about revamping ideas from the *Dirk Gently* book, of which he claims he wrote about a third, into *Hitchhiker's Guide Vol. 6*: 'And, for old time's sake, I may call it *Salmon of Doubt*, I may call it – well, who knows?'[7] Only a month later he says: 'There is very much in the wind at the moment the strong possibility of a new *Dirk Gently*. It's a few years since I've written a novel and I think we're moving from a position of a publisher having a contract with me to having a contract *on* me. So that's something I'd better turn my attention to pretty damn pronto.'[8]

- 1999: 'I am writing a new novel right at the moment but I am trying to stick by a policy of not saying anything in public about what is in the novel until it is finished, but it is not a *Hitchhiker* novel or a *Dirk Gently* novel. It's something entirely new.'[9]

- 2000: 'It's now several years since I've written a book, as my publishers, agent and bank manager keep reminding me! But the great thing about not having written a book for several years is that I've built up an enormous backlog of ideas, where previously I'd felt I'd run out of them. It's now a question of one of those old writer's bugbears, which is time and application to get them done.'[10] The main character was called Harry, but this has been changed for obvious reasons.

- 2001: 'I abandoned *The Salmon of Doubt* about halfway through because I just thought it was getting too dull. Since then, I've now got lots and lots of different story lines waiting for me to turn them into books. One of them I shall apply the title *Salmon of Doubt* to, but I don't know which one yet.'[11]

After abandoning that partly written *Dirk Gently* book in 1995, Douglas' claims to be working on a new novel were increasingly unbelievable. Those who knew him well in the 1990s have no memory of any actual work in that direction. 'I never heard Douglas say, "I've written a chapter,"' observes Richard Creasey. 'Although I was with Douglas when he was thinking things through, and one day it may have just happily come out in a wild rush.'[12] 'There was no evidence of a new book that I saw,' agrees Sophie Astin, 'and I would have noticed. I think it made him panic every time he thought about it.'[13]

- 2002: Eleven not entirely connected chapters, mostly from the original *Dirk Gently* version of *The Salmon of Doubt*, are published on the anniversary of Douglas' death in a collection of articles and stories confusingly called *The Salmon of Doubt: Hitchhiking the Galaxy One Last Time.* The novel fragment is a sad and unnecessary inclusion in a book which some people consider to have been rushed out with unseemly haste.

* I am indebted to David Honigmann, whose review of *Hitchhiker* in the *Financial Times* explained the relevance of this title: '*The Salmon of Doubt* is a riff on the Irish legend of the Salmon of Certainty, which grants whoever eats it all the knowledge in the world. The seer Fionn labours for seven years to catch it, but when he does he leaves someone else to cook it while he gathers firewood. The other man – who turns out to be Fionn, son of Uail, son of Baiscne – consumes three drops of oil from the fish, and he gets the knowledge, not Fionn the seer. In other words, what turned out to be Adams' last project was named for the story of someone who procrastinates for seven years over a project to gain the secrets of life, the universe and everything, only to have the prize snatched away from him at the last minute. He would have appreciated the irony.'

CHAPTER 42

JOE MEDJUCK HAD worked with Douglas on the *Hitchhiker's* film in the 1980s, but hadn't seen him since 1995, when the CD-ROM of *Last Chance to See* was released. A couple of years later he moved to Santa Barbara, and in late March 2001 he discovered that Douglas Adams was due to give a talk at the local university the following week. Medjuck was busy on 5 April, but he read that Douglas now lived in Santa Barbara too. He made contact through www.douglasadams.com, and Douglas was delighted to hear from him.

A week or two later, Medjuck was at a local bistro with his wife and son when, quite by chance, he spotted that Douglas and Polly were there too. Douglas always loved to see old faces from the past and the two spent some time catching up. When they parted, Douglas and Joe agreed to arrange a proper get-together soon. Back home, Medjuck gave his son a copy of *The Hitchhiker's Guide to the Galaxy* to read.

On Wednesday 9 May, he bumped into Douglas again: 'I was going to drive into Los Angeles and I was going for coffee in my local place here, and Douglas was there in his gym outfit. He explained that he'd been quite busy because his mother was in town but: let's get together and have a meal together the next week. A friend of mine phoned me Saturday morning and said, "I don't know if you've heard . . . ?"'[1]

Douglas had been back to the gym on Friday, accompanied by his friend and neighbour Chris Ogle. While exercising, Douglas Adams had suffered a fatal heart attack.

Douglas had no history of heart trouble but he had been to see a doctor only a few days earlier who found an arrhythmic heartbeat – usually nothing to worry about. And he had never really enjoyed good health. His nose, which he famously broke on his own knee during his first rugby match at Brentwood, had not worked properly since then, which compounded the childhood asthma that originated from his grandmother's menagerie. The slightest action could put his back out, leaving him prone and in pain for several days. Over the years he had suffered acute appendicitis, bordering on peritonitis, and a hernia; and his eardrum once burst in New York.

His love of good wine can't have been beneficial, and he had smoked heavily for more than two decades. And then there was his sheer size: 'A body like this – six foot five inches and seventeen stone – is a huge thing to heave around the place and sometimes I become almost paralysed with tiredness. So once a month I decide, "OK, today's the day!" and crash out for twenty-four hours. And when I get up I'm ready to knock buildings down.'[2]

Or he could pedal frantically for eight minutes and twenty-three seconds on an exercise bicycle.

The first that anybody outside Douglas' immediate circle knew was when Stephen Fry posted a brief, heartfelt message on www.douglasadams.com: 'Douglas, you left the party far too soon. All your friends, even those who never met you, will miss you.'[3]

Everyone felt shock; some people felt regret too. Others may even have felt a strange kind of relief. Were there people he had fallen out with who would never now make amends with him? Almost certainly, but on the other hand one of his close friends was heard to comment that Douglas' passing 'cleared the slate'. That he was loved – genuinely adored – by friends and colleagues and especially fans was beyond doubt. That he had a few non-friends – enemies is far too strong a word – was not widely publicised. That he could be as difficult and infuriating as he was warm, generous and brilliant was something which was, out of sensitivity for his family, temporarily forgotten. And rightly so.

'Douglas knew tons of people and his circle, as we know, was very wide,' says Robbie Stamp. 'But his friend-friends – the people he could turn to, his personal friends – was I think a much smaller number of people. I was glad to be one of those friends, part of a group to whom he could turn with things as well as all the work stuff and all the ideas. When you lead the kind of life that he did, I think it's all too easy to lose touch with people. But he was a kind and generous friend. He was, for example, immensely concerned the night my father died.'[4]

Certainly, not all of Douglas' circle got on with each other. Here is one of his close friends talking about another: 'I have a very low opinion of him. I don't like him as a person, I don't like the way he behaves, I don't like the way he expresses himself, I don't like the way he bullies people – in fact I don't like him at all.' Douglas could bring people together – he desperately wanted to be loved and he *was* loved – but he couldn't make them like each other.

And just how well off was Douglas at the end? It was thirteen years since he last received a book advance. Yes, he had royalties, but on only nine books, two of which were co-written. Santa Barbara is an absurdly expensive place to live, and he was still jetting around the world first class on a regular basis. TDV had gone down the drain with all his investment. Douglas, ever the optimist, had subsequently invested in a company researching molecular computers; he wasn't going to see a return on that anytime soon. He made good money from his talks at conferences and corporate events, but he only did one a month and Jane was no longer working. Douglas was still very, very good at spending money. And he always left the accounting to someone else.

The film deal with Disney was worth a huge amount, and Douglas had received a very large payment from the company when the deal was signed at the end of 1997; a very large sum indeed, considerably more than might normally be paid for such an option, reflecting Disney's interest and faith in *Hitchhiker's* as a property. But that was more than three years previously and he would only receive the rest of the money – another very considerable sum – if the film was actually made, which was looking less and less likely.

If the *Hitchhiker's* movie had gone into production, if just one piece of film had run through a camera, Douglas would have been paid a very large amount of money. But it hadn't, and he wasn't. In the last few months of his life Douglas was in a strange and uncomfortable situation. He had moved to the USA, with family in tow and at considerable expense, specifically to get the movie of *Hitchhiker's Guide* made, and now that looked as if it might not happen anytime soon. In any case, Douglas and Jane had already made plans to return to London in July 2002. Ostensibly this was because they were unhappy about George W. Bush and the farrago of the 2000 Presidential Election, but there must have been other considerations.

What it came down to, ultimately, was pride. Douglas had spent most of his adult life trying to get a feature film of *Hitchhiker's* off the ground; it almost became an obsession. And if anything contributed to his death, it was a realisation that he might ultimately lose his twenty-year battle with Hollywood.

Because Douglas was massively successful at almost everything else. Success sometimes came through good fortune, but mostly it came through very, very hard work and determination. Douglas simply wasn't a quitter. It all went back to the days of Adams-Smith-Adams: Will and Martin spent a few years writing comedy as a second career, devoting most of their time to publishing and advertising. They ended up with nice houses and nice cars. Douglas was the one who took only such odd jobs as were needed to keep his overdraft down, while sleeping on people's floors and sofas, and he became an internationally fêted millionaire.

What Douglas wanted, Douglas eventually got. Always. He was an *Eagle* reader who got his name in the *Eagle*. He was a *Doctor Who* fan who wrote for the show and then became the series' script editor. He was a *Monty Python* fan who wrote and performed with the Pythons. He was a Beatles fan who was invited to Paul McCartney's Christmas party. He was a Procol Harum fan who invited his friends round to hear Gary Brooker perform in his living room. He was a Pink Floyd fan who played on stage with Pink Floyd. He was a Richard Dawkins fan who became one of Richard Dawkins' best friends.

Douglas wanted the *Hitchhiker's* radio series to sound like a rock album – and it did. He wanted to turn the series into a novel – he did so and it was an instant bestseller. He wanted to create a *Hitchhiker's* computer game with Infocom – the company welcomed him with open arms and the game topped the charts. He wanted to prove that he could write something other than *Hitchhiker* – the *Dirk Gently* books showed he could do just that.

He had a stunning home in one of California's most desirable communities. He had a fantastic wife and a beautiful daughter. His address book included many of the biggest names in science, literature, comedy, computing and rock music. His name was enough to open almost any door, to set up almost any meeting. His parties were legendary. He had lots of fast cars, state-of-the-art Apple Macintoshes, and the world's largest collection of left-handed guitars.

He was fêted, he was adored, he was rich, he was successful. He was happy.

Except for that damned, niggling *Hitchhiker* movie which Hollywood had been playing silly buggers with for twenty years.

'For four years, Douglas Adams and I pitched *Hitchhiker's* the movie to every studio in Hollywood – twice,' lamented Jay Roach. 'Each executive said the same: "Too quirky for too big a budget." Douglas would just respond, "That's ridiculous," and we kept going.'[5]

But Roach had his own career and other films that needed making: a third *Austin Powers* movie, a sequel to *Meet the Parents*. At the end of April 2001, Roach admitted to Douglas that he was giving up on *Hitchhiker's*, but giving up was not something that Douglas knew how to do.

'I think he had a strong sense that somehow the material was so good, people had loved it so much that they were bloody well going to take it on his terms or that was it,' reflects Robbie Stamp. 'There was that sense of conquering Hollywood. For a lot of people it still sits at the pinnacle of the entertainment business and they want a crack at it. And Douglas desperately wanted that. But he found that, in Hollywood's terms, although everyone was prepared to be decent and we were going to get meetings and so on – Hollywood is about money.

'And he hadn't made anybody any money in Hollywood terms.

He hadn't even made his publishers much money recently. So I think that there was a slight sense of disappointment that the fanfare when he arrived wasn't quite as loud maybe as he wanted it to be. The party he had before he left was a Hollywood party: "That's it, I'm off. I'm going. I'm going to make it." He was an immensely stubborn man, immensely stubborn. And he just dug his heels in.'[6]

Or, as John Lloyd described Douglas' attitude from their Footlights days: 'Whatever he did, he did it big, and he was always perfectly certain that whatever it was would come to pass. He wasn't the kind of person who would take, "No. Definitely not. Bugger off," for an answer.'[7]

Douglas had weathered failure before, and he had seen ideas briefly considered which came to nothing, but to put this amount of effort into a project and then see it crash and burn could only have been agonising. More to the point, there was the looming spectre of money. Was Douglas basing his financial future on that second, very large payment from Disney that was dependent on the film actually being made? Did he think he would receive it in 2000? In 2001? There was still no agreement on the script, and without Roach attached, any possibility of production was receding further and further and further away.

Did that mean he would have to write another book? Even assuming that a publisher was prepared to pay him (of course they would, but could he see that?), could he face the anguish that each novel caused him, an anguish which he thought had ended nine years previously?

On 10 May, still despairing about the film project that had dominated his life for more than twenty years, Douglas rang Jay Roach and told him, 'Hollywood is full of Vogons who think they're poets.'[8] Unsure where to turn, and held back by his immensely placid nature, Douglas worked out his frustration in the only way he knew how.

In the gym.

Douglas Adams' funeral was held on 16 May 2001 in Santa Barbara. Mary Allen, Simon Jones, Terry Jones, Michael Nesmith and Chris

Ogle all spoke. The service opened with the *Schubler Chorales* and closed with 'Hey Jude', 'Drive My Car' and 'Paperback Writer'. Jane and Polly moved back to London almost immediately; there was no longer any reason to stay in California (and American inheritance tax would have been punitive). A memorial service was held in September – broadcast over the web by the BBC – and Douglas' ashes were finally laid to rest in Highgate Cemetery in June 2002.

In the cruellest of ironies, the *Hitchhiker's Guide* movie went back into development. A new scriptwriter was assigned and there was no longer an author around to complain about his story being mistreated.

Quite apart from his books, computer games and radio and TV series – plus a huge circle of friends and millions of devoted fans – Douglas left two subtle yet extraordinary legacies. One was *h2g2*, safely ensconced at the BBC. The software which TDV had developed to run the site was adopted for other bbc.co.uk communities, and because of the way the programme seemed to replicate itself within the corporation it was called DNA, but that wasn't the only reason.

And somewhere out in space, acting perhaps as a hyperspace junction where intergalactic hitchhikers can swap tales and compare towels or just stick out their hopeful thumbs and hold scraps of cardboard reading 'Alpha Centauri', is an asteroid officially designated – on 10 May 2001 – as 'Arthurdent'.

AUTHOR'S AFTERWORD

WHEN I STARTED writing this book, I wanted to be as accurate as possible about the life and career of Douglas Adams. I also wanted to solve some discrepancies, such as the one about what exactly happened at that first signing session at Forbidden Planet in 1979. As I investigated further, speaking or corresponding with more than ninety of Douglas' family, friends and colleagues, I found that other stories accepted as truth were also shaky. Gradually it became clear that many of the well-known anecdotes told about – and by – Douglas were wrong in very significant ways.

The danger now was that I would look like I was criticising Douglas himself. This was not, is not, and never has been my intention; I only want to present the most accurate account possible of the life of a man whom I admired for more than twenty years and who influenced my life immeasurably, and believing without question everything he said in interviews is not the way to do it. Let me reiterate from the start of this book: Douglas Adams was not a liar. Nor do I think that establishing the truth in these instances makes his life and career less remarkable or his achievements less laudable or his early passing less tragic.

A few weeks before my deadline, as I added the final few paragraphs to the book, quite by chance I met Gail Renard who recalled Douglas saying, 'I wonder what it would be like to hitchhike around the galaxy?'[1] after a Greek holiday. Gail did not know Douglas in 1971. I wondered: could the most famous story of them all, 'lying drunk in a field in Innsbruck', also be inaccurate?

Quite improbably, two weeks later Martin Smith contacted Gail for the first time in many years, and she put Martin in contact with me. I asked him when he first heard about the idea of intergalactic hitchhiking and he told me: 'To Will and I it was first broached just after Douglas returned from Greece in, I am fairly certain, the summer of 1973. He had bought *A Hitchhiker's Guide to Europe* and, whilst relaxing post-coitally (as he explained it, she was a Dutch girl), looking at the stars from a rock on the north side of Santorini, he thought it would be a pretty neat idea if there were an intergalactic version of the *Hitchhiker's Guide!*'[2]

There is the final piece of the puzzle. Douglas Adams did not think up the idea for *The Hitchhiker's Guide to the Galaxy* in an Austrian field in 1971. Every book, magazine and newspaper which repeated that story is, it seems, wrong. He was lying on a Greek rock in 1973. Perhaps he changed the story out of courtesy to his unknown Dutch companion – who knows?

That's something for future biographers to discover.

M.J. Simpson
Leicester
www.mjsimpson.co.uk
November 2002

FURTHER READING

AN EXCELLENT, ALBEIT less detailed, account of Douglas Adams' life is Neil Gaiman's *Don't Panic: Douglas Adams and the Hitchhiker's Guide to the Galaxy* (Titan, 1988), updated by David K. Dickson in 1993, and by myself in 2002. Where appropriate I have avoided in this book duplicating anecdotes from *Don't Panic*. A concise examination of Douglas' career is my own *The Pocket Essential Hitchhiker's Guide* (Pocket Essentials, 2001) while Nick Webb's *Wish You Were Here: The Official Biography of Douglas Adams* (Headline, 2003) is a more personal memoir.

A comprehensive bibliography of Douglas' work was published in issue 115 of the British magazine *Book and Magazine Collector* in October 1993; an updated version appeared in issue 228 of the magazine in March 2003. The *Hitchhiker's Guide* TV series was covered in staggering detail by Kevin Davies and Andrew Pixley in *Time Screen* issue 20 in Spring 1994, though this is now very hard to find.

The DVD of *Hitchhiker's Guide* includes Kevin Davies' superb documentary *The Making of the Hitchhiker's Guide to the Galaxy* and extremely informative on-screen production notes, also by Kevin. The American DVD also includes the BBC documentary *Omnibus: Douglas Adams – The Man Who Blew Up the Earth*. An excellent authorised biographical documentary is Joel Greengrass and Rick Mueller's *Life, the Universe and Douglas Adams*, available through www.douglasadams.com.

The entire radio series is available on CD, including a twentieth anniversary documentary and a lengthy interview with Douglas; the story of the radio series is told in *The Hitchhiker's Guide to the Galaxy: The Original Radio Scripts* (Pan Books, 1985, reprinted 2003).

On the web, the primary sources of information are the BBC site **www.bbc.co.uk/cult/hitchhikers**, the official site **www.douglas adams.com**, and the newsgroup **alt.fan.douglas-adams**. The author's own site, *Magrathea*, can be found at **http://homepage.ntlworld. com/mjs2000** and is the only constantly updated site on the web for Douglas Adams/*Hitchhiker's Guide* news. There are also useful fansites at **www.floor42.com**, **www.douglasadams.se** and **www.guidegalactique.fr.st**, the last in French but with some content in English.

All the above notwithstanding, the best source for news and information on the legacy of Douglas Adams remains ZZ9 Plural Z Alpha, the Official *Hitchhiker's Guide to the Galaxy* Appreciation Society, and its quarterly magazine *Mostly Harmless,* which publishes full transcripts of many of the interviews conducted for this book. For more details send an SAE to: ZZ9 Plural Z Alpha, 4 The Sycamores, Hadfield, Glossop, Derbyshire SK13 2BS, U.K. or go to **www.zz9.org**

REFERENCES

All articles are interviews with Douglas Adams unless stated.
M.J.S. = M.J. Simpson, D.N.A. = Douglas Noël Adams.

Prelude – Forbidden Planet
1. Harriett Rubin, Fast Company/*LA Times*, July 1997
2. Iain Johnstone, *Sydney Morning Herald*, May 2001
3. Memories of D.N.A. by Stan Nicholls, www.thealienonline.com, May 2001
4. Interview with M.J.S., February 2002
5. Correspondence with M.J.S., February 2002
6. As 4
7. As 5
8. Post by D.N.A. on www.douglasadams.com, 14 July 1999
9. *The Hitchhiker's Guide to the Galaxy: The Original Radio Scripts*, Pan Books, 1985
10. Ibid.
11. Interview with M.J.S., March 2002

Chapter 1
1. Kate Bassett, *Cambridge Alumni Magazine*, Lent Term 1996
2. Graham Bridgstock, London *Evening Standard*, 16 November 1990
3. Danny Danziger, *Independent*, 11 March 1991

4. Interview with Neil Gaiman for *Don't Panic*, date unknown (from transcript)
5. Post by Adams on www.douglasadams.com, 17 March 2000
6. Jonathan Webster, *Live Wire/20:20*, 1996
7. Claire Smith, www.virgin.net, September 1999
8. Interview with M.J.S., April 2002
9. Brendan Bolles, www.bmug.org, 1998
10. Frank Halford interviewed by Andrew Wilson, *Mail on Sunday*, 7 March 1998
11. Andrew Wilson, *Mail on Sunday*, 7 March 1998
12. As 10
13. Nicholas Wroe, *Guardian*, 3 June 2000
14. Frank Halford interviewed by Rick Mueller and Joel Greengrass for *Life, the Universe and Douglas Adams*, 2002 (from transcript)
15. As 8
16. Interview with M.J.S., March 2002
17. As 8
18. Meirion Jones, *Your Computer*, October 1982

Chapter 2
1. Interview with M.J.S., April 2002
2. Article by D.N.A. in *The Best of Days? – Memories of Brentwood School*, 1999
3. D.N.A. interviewed by Sue Lawley on *Desert Island Discs*, BBC Radio 4, 6 February 1994
4. Nicholas Wroe, *Guardian*, 3 June 2000
5. As 3
6. As 1
7. As 3
8. Interview with M.J.S., May 2002
9. Correspondence with M.J.S., May 2002
10. As 1
11. As 4
12. As 1
13. As 2
14. As 1

15. Interview with Kevin Davies, Gavin French and Paul Mark Tams for *Tardis*, October 1978 (from transcript)
16. Frank Halford interviewed by Andrew Wilson, *Mail on Sunday*, 7 March 1998
17. Brendan Bolles, www.bmug.org, 1998
18. As 1
19. As 4
20. As 9

Chapter 3
1. Interview with M.J.S., March 2002
2. D.N.A. interviewed by Sue Lawley on *Desert Island Discs*, BBC Radio 4, 6 February 1994
3. As 1
4. Interview with M.J.S., June 2002
5. Interview with M.J.S., April 2002
6. As 4
7. D.N.A. interviewed by Iain Johnstone on cassette of *Douglas Adams' Guide to the Hitchhiker's Guide to the Galaxy*, BBC Radio Collection, 1999
8. As 1
9. As 4
10. Interview with M.J.S., May 2002
11. Ibid.
12. As 5
13. David Sexton, *Sunday Telegraph*, 7 July 1987
14. David Howe and Owen Tudor *Beka/Oracle*, 1978
15. Interview with M.J.S., April 2002
16. As 5
17. Interview with Neil Gaiman for *Don't Panic*, date unknown (from transcript)
18. David Morgan, *Monty Python Speaks!*, Fourth Estate, 1999
19. Ibid.
20. As 1

Interlude – Europe
1. Claire Smith, www.virgin.net, September 1999
2. Harriett Rubin, Fast Company/*LA Times*, July 1997
3. As 1

Chapter 4
1. Interview with Neil Gaiman for *Don't Panic*, date unknown (from transcript)
2. Meirion Jones, *Your Computer*, October 1982
3. Nicholas Wroe, *Guardian*, 3 June 2000
4. Unidentified cutting in Neil Gaiman's files for *Don't Panic*
5. Interview with M.J.S., April 2002
6. Interview with M.J.S., April 2002
7. Interview with M.J.S., April 2002
8. D.N.A. interviewed by Iain Johnstone on cassette of *Douglas Adams' Guide to the Hitchhiker's Guide to the Galaxy*, BBC Radio Collection, 1999
9. As 5
10. Interview with M.J.S., April 2002
11. As 8
12. Interview with M.J.S., January 1998
13. As 10
14. As 5
15. Interview with M.J.S., published in *Mostly Harmless*, July 1994
16. As 7
17. As 10
18. Correspondence with M.J.S., May 2002
19. As 12

Chapter 5
1. Interview with M.J.S., April 2002
2. Ibid.
3. Interview with M.J.S., April 2002
4. Johnny Brock at D.N.A.'s memorial service, September 2001
5. As 1
6. Interview with M.J.S., April 2002
7. Ibid.

8. Ibid.
9. Interview with M.J.S., March 2002
10. Interview with M.J.S., published in *Mostly Harmless*, July 1994
11. Interview with M.J.S., April 2002
12. As 10
13. Ibid.
14. Ibid.
15. David Morgan, *Monty Python Speaks!*, Fourth Estate, 1999
16. Nicholas Wroe, *Guardian*, 3 June 2000
17. D.N.A. interviewed by James Naughtie on *Book Club*, BBC Radio 4, 2 January 2000
18. Jon Canter interviewed by Rick Mueller and Joel Greengrass for *Life, the Universe and Douglas Adams*, 2002 (from transcript)
19. As 11

Chapter 6
1. Neil Gaiman, *Don't Panic*, Titan, 1988
2. Correspondence with M.J.S., May 2002
3. Mary Allen interviewed by Rick Mueller and Joel Greengrass for *Life, the Universe and Douglas Adams*, 2002 (from transcript)
4. Correspondence with M.J.S., April 2002
5. Interview with M.J.S., April 2002
6. Unidentified author, *Blitz*, Spring 1981
7. Interview with M.J.S., published in *Mostly Harmless*, July 1994
8. As 5
9. Ibid.
10. D.N.A. interviewed by Iain Johnstone on cassette of *Douglas Adams' Guide to the Hitchhiker's Guide to the Galaxy*, BBC Radio Collection, 1999
11. Listing in *Radio Times*, 28 August 1974
12. Interview with M.J.S., published in *Mostly Harmless*, August 1995
13. As 5

Chapter 7

1. Interview with M.J.S., April 2002
2. Interview with M.J.S., May 2002
3. Danny Danziger, *Independent*, 11 March 1991
4. Interview with M.J.S., June 2002
5. Interview with M.J.S., March 2002
6. Interview with M.J.S., June 2002
7. Ibid.
8. Webchat, www.barnesandnoble.com, 19 November 1997
9. Interview with M.J.S., March 2002
10. Gregg Pearlman, Antic Publishing Inc/eeeeeegp.com, 27 March 1987
11. Claire Brialey and Noel Collyer, *Mostly Harmless*, 1991
12. David Morgan, *Monty Python Speaks!*, Fourth Estate, 1999
13. Ron Hogan, www.beatrice.com, 1997

Chapter 8

1. Interview with M.J.S., May 2002
2. Interview with M.J.S., April 2002
3. Interview with Kevin Davies, Gavin French and Paul Mark Tams for *Tardis*, October 1978 (from transcript)
4. David Morgan, *Monty Python Speaks!*, Fourth Estate, 1999
5. Tape recording of meeting with Kevin Davies, 26 June 1992
6. As 3
7. As 4
8. Quoted in *Graham Crackers: Fuzzy Memories, Silly Bits and Outright Lies* by Graham Chapman, Career Press, 1997
9. As 3
10. Post by D.N.A. on www.douglasadams.com, 1 September 2000

Interlude – Beatles

1. Gregg Pearlman, Antic Publishing Inc/eeeeeegp.com, 27 March 1987
2. Interview with M.J.S., May 2002

3. Telephone conversation with Mark Lewisohn, 4 August 1994, quoted in interview with M.J.S., May 2002

Chapter 9
1. Ringo Starr quoted on www.harrynilsson.com, originally in *Q* magazine, 1998
2. David Morgan, *Monty Python Speaks!*, Fourth Estate, 1999
3. *Ten Years of Terror: British Horror Films of the 1970s*, ed. Harvey Fenton and David Flint, FAB Press, 2001
4. Ringo Starr quoted on www.harrynilsson.com, original source unknown
5. David Howe and Owen Tudor, *Beka/Oracle*, 1978
6. John Fleming, *Starburst*, 1981
7. Interview with M.J.S., July 2002
8. As 5
9. Danny Danziger, *Independent*, 11 March 1991
10. As 2
11. Correspondence with M.J.S., July 2002
12. Interview with M.J.S., April 2002
13. John Fleming, *Starburst*, 1981
14. Interview with M.J.S., April 2002

Chapter 10
1. David Morgan, *Monty Python Speaks!*, Fourth Estate, 1999
2. Interview with M.J.S., February 2002
3. Interview with M.J.S., April 2002
4. Interview with M.J.S., April 2002
5. Ibid.
6. Ibid.
7. Interview with M.J.S., April 2002
8. As 4
9. Ibid.
10. Interview with Kevin Davies, Gavin French and Paul Mark Tams for *Tardis*, October 1978 (from transcript)
11. As 4
12. Ibid.
13. Ibid.

14. Interview with Neil Gaiman for *Don't Panic*, date unknown (from transcript)
15. Interview with M.J.S., July 2002
16. As 10

Chapter 11

1. Interview with M.J.S., May 2002
2. Interview with M.J.S., published in *Mostly Harmless*, August 1995
3. Interview with M.J.S., April 2002
4. Interview with Kevin Davies, Gavin French and Paul Mark Tams for *Tardis*, October 1978 (from transcript)
5. As 2
6. Interview with M.J.S., June 2002
7. As 1
8. As 3
9. Interview with M.J.S., January 1998, published in *Mostly Harmless*, April 1999
10. *Omnibus: Douglas Adams – The Man Who Blew Up the Earth*, BBC 2, 4 August 2001
11. Gregg Pearlman, Antic Publishing Inc/eeeeeegp.com, 27 March 1987
12. Ibid.
13. Interview with M.J.S., February 2002
14. As 2

Interlude – Precedent

1. D.N.A. interviewed by James Naughtie on *Book Club*, BBC Radio 4, 2 January 2000
2. Interview with M.J.S., April 2002

Chapter 12

1. Interview with M.J.S., published in *Mostly Harmless*, August 1995
2. Interview with M.J.S., January 1998
3. Robert Greenberger, *Starlog*, January 1986
4. David Howe and Owen Tudor, *Beka/Oracle*, 1978

5. Claire Brialey and Noel Collyer, *Mostly Harmless*, 1991
6. Interview with M.J.S., January 1998
7. Simon Brett interviewed by Rick Mueller and Joel Greengrass for *Life, the Universe and Douglas Adams*, 2002 (from transcript)
8. Interview with Kevin Davies, Gavin French and Paul Mark Tams for *Tardis*, October 1978 (from transcript)
9. Unidentified author, *Blitz*, Spring 1981
10. As 4
11. D.N.A. interviewed by James Naughtie on *Book Club*, BBC Radio 4, 2 January 2000
12. As 8
13. Anthony Read interviewed by Marcus Hearn in *Doctor Who Magazine*, December 1990
14. Nigel Griffiths, *Graham Williams – A Tribute*, December 1990
15. Roger Birchall, *Starburst*, October 1985

Chapter 13

1. Interview with Kevin Davies, Gavin French and Paul Mark Tams for *Tardis*, October 1978 (from transcript)
2. David Howe and Owen Tudor, *Beka/Oracle*, 1978
3. Webchat, www.bbc.co.uk, 21 March 2000
4. Mark Wing-Davey interviewed by Pat Ottewell in *Images*, 1982
5. D.N.A. interviewed by Simon Fanshawe and Mariella Frostrup on *Sunday Brunch*, BBC Radio 5, 11 October 1992
6. Interview with M.J.S., January 1998
7. As 5
8. Correspondence with M.J.S., April 2002
9. Interview with M.J.S., February 1998
10. Claire Brialey and Noel Collyer, *Mostly Harmless*, 1991
11. Interview with M.J.S., January 1998, published in *Mostly Harmless*, April 1999
12. Keith Phipps, www.theavclub.com, February 1998
13. As 11
14. Iain Johnstone, *Sydney Morning Herald*, May 2001

15. Interview with M.J.S., April 2002
16. *The Hitchhiker's Guide to the Galaxy: The Original Radio Scripts*, Pan Books, 1985
17. Interview with M.J.S., April 2002
18. Ibid.
19. Ibid.
20. Correspondence with M.J.S., 1994
21. Interview with M.J.S., January 1998
22. Interview with M.J.S., February 1998
23. *Omnibus: Douglas Adams – The Man Who Blew Up the Earth*, BBC 2, 4 August 2001
24. Ibid.
25. Nicholas Wroe, *Guardian*, 3 June 2000

Interlude – Answer
1. Ken Bussanmas, *Fantastic Films*, March 1984
2. Post by D.N.A. on alt.fan.douglas-adams, 2 November 1993
3. Iain Johnstone, *Sydney Morning Herald*, May 2001
4. Post by D.N.A. on www.douglasadams.com, 5 September 1999
5. Unidentified cutting in Neil Gaiman's files for *Don't Panic*

Chapter 14
1. Interview with M.J.S., January 1998
2. Interview with M.J.S., published in *Mostly Harmless*, August 1995
3. Interview with M.J.S., January 1998, published in *Mostly Harmless*, April 1999
4. David Howe and Owen Tudor, *Beka/Oracle*, 1978
5. Interview with M.J.S., April 2002
6. Interview with Neil Gaiman for *Don't Panic*, date unknown (from transcript)
7. Interview with M.J.S., April 2002
8. Ibid.
9. Interview with M.J.S., May 2002
10. As 7
11. Ibid.

12. Quoted in unpublished draft of *Don't Panic* by Richard Hollis, original source unknown
13. Interview with M.J.S., April 2002
14. As 5
15. Ibid.
16. Ibid.
17. As 4

Chapter 15
1. Nigel Griffiths, *Graham Williams – A Tribute*, December 1990
2. Interview with Kevin Davies, Gavin French and Paul Mark Tams for *Tardis*, October 1978 (from transcript)
3. Ibid.
4. Ibid.
5. Interview with M.J.S., April 2002
6. Interview with M.J.S., March 2002
7. David Howe and Owen Tudor, *Beka/Oracle*, 1978
8. Neil Gaiman, *Don't Panic*, Titan, 1988
9. Charles Martin, *Doctor Who Magazine*, 6 February 2002
10. Interview with M.J.S., April 2002
11. Roger Birchall, *Starburst*, October 1985
12. Kevin Davies, *TV Zone*, August 1992
13. As 1
14. As 9
15. Ibid.
16. Danny Danziger, *Independent*, 11 March 1991
17. Source unknown
18. Webchat, www.scifi.com, 1998

Chapter 16
1. David Boraks, unidentified North Carolina newspaper, October 1996
2. Nick Webb interviewed by Rick Mueller and Joel Greengrass for *Life, the Universe and Douglas Adams*, 2002 (from transcript)
3. Interview with M.J.S., May 2002
4. Interview with M.J.S., April 2002

5. As 2
6. D.N.A. interviewed by James Naughtie on *Book Club*, BBC Radio 4, 2 January 2000
7. Interview with M.J.S., April 2002
8. Interview with Neil Gaiman for *Don't Panic*, date unknown (from transcript)
9. As 7
10. Mary Allen interviewed by Rick Mueller and Joel Greengrass for *Life, the Universe and Douglas Adams*, 2002 (from transcript)
11. As 3
12. D.N.A. interviewed by John Dunn, BBC Radio 2, 12 October 1992
13. John Fleming, *Starburst*, 1981
14. As 7
15. Interview with M.J.S., March 2002
16. Interview with M.J.S., February 2002
17. Memories of D.N.A. by Stan Nicholls, www.thealienonline.com, May 2001
18. As 16
19. David Sexton, *Sunday Telegraph*, 7 July 1987
20. Nicholas Wroe, *Guardian*, 3 June 2000
21. As 3

Interlude – Genre

1. Nick Webb interviewed by Rick Mueller and Joel Greengrass for *Life, the Universe and Douglas Adams*, 2002 (from transcript)
2. Interview with M.J.S., April 2002
3. Interview with M.J.S., February 2002
4. Interview with M.J.S., March 2002
5. Jonathan Webster, *SFX*, August 1996
6. Ibid.
7. Quoted in unpublished draft of *Don't Panic* by Richard Hollis, original source unknown
8. Interview with Neil Gaiman for *Don't Panic*, date unknown (from transcript)

9. As 7
10. As 8
11. As 7
12. Jonathan Webster, *LiveWire/20:20*, 1996
13. As 8
14. John Fleming, *Starburst*, 1981

Chapter 17
1. Interview with M.J.S., June 2002
2. Ibid.
3. Interview with M.J.S., May 2002
4. As 1
5. Ibid.
6. Interview with M.J.S., April 2002
7. News item in *Evening News*, 15 November 1979
8. As 6
9. As 1
10. Ibid.
11. Interview with Neil Gaiman for *Don't Panic*, date unknown (from transcript)
12. As 1
13. Ed Victor interviewed by Rick Mueller and Joel Greengrass for *Life, the Universe and Douglas Adams*, 2002 (from transcript)
14. As 1
15. Ken Bussanmas, *Fantastic Films*, March 1984
16. As 1
17. Ibid.
18. As 6
19. As 1
20. Ibid.

Chapter 18
1. Interview with Kevin Davies, Gavin French and Paul Mark Tams for *Tardis*, October 1978 (from transcript)
2. Interview with M.J.S., April 2002
3. Ibid.

4. Quoted by Jonathan Cecil in interview with M.J.S., January 1998
5. As 2
6. Ibid.
7. Interview with M.J.S., March 2002
8. Interview with M.J.S., May 2002
9. As 2
10. *The Hitchhiker's Guide to the Galaxy: The Original Radio Scripts*, Pan Books, 1985
11. Iain Johnstone, *Sydney Morning Herald*, May 2001
12. Correspondence with M.J.S., April 2002
13. Interview with M.J.S., February 2002
14. Ibid.

Chapter 19
1. Unidentified author, *Blitz*, Spring 1981
2. Source unknown
3. Article by Kevin Davies in *Mostly Harmless*, January 2001
4. Interview with M.J.S., April 2002
5. Ibid.
6. D.N.A. interviewed by Ludovic Kennedy, *Paperbacks*, BBC 1, 15 April 1981
7. Interview with M.J.S., January 2002
8. Interview with M.J.S., January 2002
9. Interview with M.J.S., January 2002

Chapter 20
1. Interview with M.J.S., March 2002
2. Interview with M.J.S., April 2002
3. As 1
4. Ibid.
5. Ibid.
6. Interview with M.J.S., April 2002
7. Interview with M.J.S., January 1998, published in *Mostly Harmless*, April 1999
8. As 1
9. Ibid.

10. Ibid.
11. John Fleming, *Starburst*, 1981
12. Short article by Mike Cule in *SFX*, March 1998
13. Ibid.
14. Article by Kevin Davies in *Mostly Harmless*, January 2001
15. As 1
16. Interview with M.J.S., April 2002
17. As 6

Chapter 21
1. Interview with M.J.S., April 2002
2. D.N.A., interviewed by John Dunn, BBC Radio 2, 12 October 1992
3. Roger Birchall, *Starburst*, October 1985
4. Claire Brialey and Noel Collyer, *Mostly Harmless*, 1991
5. Thomas Kingsley Troupe, www.mndaily.com, 1998
6. Stan Nicholls, *Wordsmiths of Wonder*, Orbit, 1993
7. Interview with M.J.S., May 2002
8. Alan J.W. Bell interviewed by Neil Gaiman for *Don't Panic*, date unknown (from transcript)
9. Ibid.
10. Interview with Neil Gaiman for *Don't Panic*, date unknown (from transcript)
11. Interview with M.J.S., October 1993, published in *Mostly Harmless*, January 1994
12. Interview with M.J.S., February 1998
13. As 10
14. Robert Greenberger, *Starlog*, January 1986
15. As 10
16. Ibid.
17. D.N.A. interviewed by Simon Fanshawe and Mariella Frostrup on *Sunday Brunch*, BBC Radio 5, 11 October 1992
18. Unidentified author, *Blitz*, Spring 1981
19. Interview with M.J.S., April 2002
20. D.N.A. interviewed by Ludovic Kennedy, *Paperbacks*, BBC 1, 15 April 1981
21. Webchat, www.bbc.co.uk, 21 March 2000

Interlude – Conventions
1. Stan Nicholls, *Wordsmiths of Wonder*, Orbit, 1993
2. Sally Emerson, interview with M.J.S., June 2002

Chapter 22
1. Interview with M.J.S., June 2002
2. Ibid.
3. Ibid.
4. Ibid.
5. Interview with Neil Gaiman for *Don't Panic*, date unknown (from transcript)
6. Interview with M.J.S., June 2002
7. As 1
8. Ibid.
9. News item in London *Evening Standard*, 20 July 1981
10. As 1
11. Ibid.
12. Ibid.
13. Ibid.
14. Unidentified cutting in Neil Gaiman's files for *Don't Panic*
15. As 1
16. Meirion Jones, *Your Computer*, October 1982
17. Interview with M.J.S., May 2002
18. As 1
19. Ibid.
20. Ibid.
21. As 5
22. As 1
23. D.N.A. interviewed by Cindy Russell on *Northsound*, BBC Radio Scotland, 1982

Chapter 23
1. Interview with Neil Gaiman for *Don't Panic*, date unknown (from transcript)
2. Neil Gaiman, *Don't Panic*, Titan, 2002
3. Unidentified cutting in Neil Gaiman's files for *Don't Panic*

4. Mary Allen interviewed by Rick Mueller and Joel Greengrass for
   Life, the Universe and Douglas Adams, 2002 (from transcript)
5. Ibid.
6. Ibid.
7. Sue Heal, *Today*, 19 June 1987
8. Interview with M.J.S., April 2002
9. As 3
10. As 1
11. Ian Bursley, EEMA, 1996
12. Unknown author, *Office Systems*, January 1982
13. Brendan Bolles, www.bmug.org, 1998
14. Meirion Jones, *Your Computer*, October 1982
15. Caroline Bassett, *MacUser*, 2 October 1992
16. Sharon Darling, *Computer!*, April 1985
17. Webchat, www.bbc.co.uk, 8 November 2000
18. As 13
19. Interview with M.J.S., April 2002
20. Jeffrey S. Young, *MacWorld*, May 1985
21. As 13
22. Gregg Pearlman, Antic Publishing Inc/eeeeeegp.com, 27 March
    1987
23. Unknown author, www.apple.com, 1999

Chapter 24
1. D.N.A. interviewed by Cindy Russell on *Northsound*, BBC
   Radio Scotland, 1982
2. Interview with M.J.S., April 2002
3. Gregg Pearlman, Antic Publishing Inc/eeeeeegp.com, 27 March
   1987
4. As 2
5. Ibid.
6. Ibid.
7. As 3
8. As 2
9. Ibid.
10. Ibid.
11. John Fleming, *Starburst*, 1981

12. Interview with M.J.S., March 2002
13. As 2
14. Interview with M.J.S., April 2002
15. Interview with M.J.S., April 2002
16. As 14
17. As 15
18. News item in London *Evening Standard*, 20 December 1982
19. Jeffrey S. Young, *MacWorld*, May 1985
20. As 14

Chapter 25

1. Interview with M.J.S., April 2002
2. Ibid.
3. Ed Victor interviewed by Rick Mueller and Joel Greengrass for *Life, the Universe and Douglas Adams*, 2002 (from transcript)
4. D.N.A. interviewed by Clive Anderson on *Clive Anderson Talks Back*, Channel 4, 1 November 1991
5. As 1
6. Interview with M.J.S., April 2002
7. As 1
8. D.N.A. interviewed by John Dunn, BBC Radio 2, 12 October 1992
9. As 6
10. As 1
11. Ibid.
12. D.N.A. interviewed by Terry Wogan on *Wogan*, BBC 1, 26 September 1986
13. Roger Birchall, *Starburst*, October 1985

Chapter 26

1. Interview with Neil Gaiman for *Don't Panic*, date unknown (from transcript)
2. Brendan Bolles, www.bmug.org, 1998
3. Robert Greenberger, *Starlog*, January 1986
4. Quoted by David Learner in article in *Mostly Harmless*, March 1984
5. Correspondence with M.J.S., May 2002

6. Ibid.
7. Ed Victor interviewed by Rick Mueller and Joel Greengrass for *Life, the Universe and Douglas Adams*, 2002 (from transcript)
8. Ibid.
9. Gregg Pearlman, Antic Publishing Inc/eeeeeegp.com, 27 March 1987
10. As 1
11. As 9
12. Ibid.
13. Ibid.

Interlude – Johnstone
1. Steve Grant, *Time Out*, 15 November 1984
2. Ibid.
3. Letter in *Time Out*, 6 December 1984
4. Interview with Neil Gaiman for *Don't Panic*, date unknown (from transcript)
5. As 1

Chapter 27
1. Bryan Appleyard, *The Times*, 11 January 1986
2. Interview with M.J.S., February 2002
3. Interview with M.J.S., April 2002
4. Ibid.
5. As 2
6. As 3
7. As 2
8. Ibid.
9. Ibid.
10. Ibid.
11. Ibid.
12. Gregg Pearlman, Antic Publishing Inc/eeeeeegp.com, 27 March 1987
13. As 3
14. Ibid.
15. Ibid.

Chapter 28
1. Interview with M.J.S., April 2002
2. Interview with M.J.S., February 2002
3. As 1
4. Roe Adams, *Electronic Games*, April 1985
5. As 1
6. Interview with M.J.S., April 2002
7. Roger Birchall, *Starburst*, October 1985
8. As 6
9. Ibid.
10. Interview with M.J.S., February 2002
11. Interview with M.J.S., April 2002

Chapter 29
1. Brenda Garneau, www.pcme.com, 1997
2. Interview with M.J.S., February 2002
3. Michael Cross, *Independent*, June 1987
4. Unknown author, *Office Systems*, January 1982
5. Interview with M.J.S., April 2002
6. Ibid.
7. Correspondence with M.J.S., March 2002
8. As 5
9. As 2
10. Gregg Pearlman, Antic Publishing Inc/eeeeeegp.com, 27 March 1987
11. Post by D.N.A. on alt.fan.douglas-adams, 6 October 1993
12. Correspondence with M.J.S., May 2002
13. Ibid.
14. Correspondence with M.J.S., May 2002
15. Interview with M.J.S., April 2002
16. Interview with M.J.S., March 2002
17. Post by D.N.A. on www.douglasadams.com, 15 January 1999

Interlude – Money
1. D.N.A. interviewed by Terry Wogan on *Wogan*, BBC 1, 26 September 1986
2. Gregg Pearlman, Antic Publishing Inc/eeeeeegp.com, 27 March 1987
3. Bryan Appleyard, *The Times*, 11 January 1986
4. Interview with M.J.S., June 2002
5. Interview with M.J.S., April 2002
6. As 2

Chapter 30
1. Bryan Appleyard, *The Times*, 11 January 1986
2. Sue Heal, *Today*, 19 June 1987
3. Interview with M.J.S., April 2002
4. Interview with Neil Gaiman for *Don't Panic*, date unknown (from transcript)
5. Gregg Pearlman, Antic Publishing Inc/eeeeeegp.com, 27 March 1987
6. Charles Martin, *Doctor Who Magazine*, 6 February 2002
7. Ibid.
8. D.N.A. interviewed by Sue Lawley on *Desert Island Discs*, BBC Radio 4, 6 February 1994
9. Michael Cross, *Independent*, June 1987
10. Stan Nicholls, *Wordsmiths of Wonder*, Orbit, 1993

Chapter 31
1. Widely quoted (cf. *Life, the Universe and Douglas Adams*) but original source unknown
2. D.N.A. interviewed by Terry Wogan on *Wogan*, BBC 1, August 1988
3. Ibid.
4. Ibid.
5. Jonathan Webster, *SFX*, August 1996
6. Interview with M.J.S., April 2002
7. Keith Phipps, www.theavclub.com, February 1998
8. Interview with M.J.S., February 2002

Interlude – God
1. Stan Nicholls, *Wordsmiths of Wonder*, Orbit, 1993
2. Interview with M.J.S., May 2002
3. Ibid.
4. Steve Grant, *Time Out*, 15 November 1984
5. Interview with M.J.S., May 2002
6. Interview with M.J.S., April 2002
7. As 2
8. Piers Townley, *Loaded*, April 1998

Chapter 32
1. Interview with M.J.S., April 2002
2. Interview with M.J.S., June 2002
3. Ibid.
4. As 1
5. Ibid.
6. Ibid.
7. Sue Heal, *Today*, 19 June 1987
8. As 2
9. Claire Brialey and Noel Collyer, *Mostly Harmless*, 1991
10. As 2
11. Interview with M.J.S., April 2002
12. As 2
13. Ibid.
14. D.N.A. interviewed by Clive Anderson on *Clive Anderson Talks Back*, Channel 4, 1 November 1991
15. As 2
16. Stephen Pile, *Daily Telegraph*, 20 October 1990
17. D.N.A. interviewed by Simon Fanshawe and Mariella Frostrup on *Sunday Brunch*, BBC Radio 5, 11 October 1992
18. Stan Nicholls, *Wordsmiths of Wonder*, Orbit, 1993
19. As 17
20. As 9
21. Correspondence with M.J.S., January 2002

Chapter 33
1. John Fleming, *Starburst*, 1981
2. Claire Brialey and Noel Collyer, *Mostly Harmless*, 1991
3. Post by D.N.A. on alt.fan.douglas-adams, 29 March 1994
4. Interview with M.J.S., January 1998
5. Interview with M.J.S., February 2002
6. As 2
7. As 5
8. As 2
9. Danny Danziger, *Independent*, 11 March 1991
10. Interview with M.J.S., April 2002
11. As 2
12. D.N.A. interviewed on *The Night Is Young*, LBC, 12 October
    1988
13. Ibid.
14. Ibid.
15. As 2
16. Ibid.
17. D.N.A. interviewed by John Dunn, BBC Radio 2, 12 October
    1992
18. As 2
19. Ibid.
20. News story in the *Daily Mail*, 26 November 1991
21. D.N.A. interviewed by Simon Fanshawe and Mariella Frostrup
    on *Sunday Brunch*, BBC Radio 5, 11 October 1992

Chapter 34
1. D.N.A. interviewed by Clive Anderson on *Clive Anderson Talks
    Back*, Channel 4, 1 November 1991
2. Interview with M.J.S., May 2002
3. Ibid.
4. Interview with M.J.S., April 2002
5. Interview with M.J.S., May 2002
6. Ibid.
7. Interview with M.J.S., January 2002
8. Ibid.

9. Stan Nicholls, *Wordsmiths of Wonder*, Orbit, 1993
10. *Omnibus: Douglas Adams – The Man Who Blew Up the Earth*
    BBC 2, 4 August 2001
11. Ibid.
12. Quoted in unpublished draft of *Don't Panic* by Richard Hollis,
    original source unknown
13. Interview with M.J.S., April 2002
14. Interview with M.J.S., June 2002
15. D.N.A. interviewed on *Bookshelf*, Radio 4, January 1991
16. Anthony Brown, *Mostly Harmless*, January 1998

Interlude – Parties

1. Interview with M.J.S., April 2002
2. Correspondence with M.J.S., April 2002
3. Ibid.
4. Margo Buchanan interviewed by John Walsh, *Independent*,
   21 October 1996
5. Correspondence with M.J.S., January 2002
6. Interview with M.J.S., April 2002
7. Ibid.
8. Interview with M.J.S., March 2002

Chapter 35

1. *Start the Week*, BBC Radio 4, 15 June 1987
2. Interview with M.J.S., April 2002
3. Ibid.
4. Ibid.
5. Webchat, www.scifi.com, 1998
6. Tape recording of meeting with Kevin Davies, 26 June 1992
7. Jonathan Jones and John Campbell Rees, *Mostly Harmless*,
   January 1995
8. Post by D.N.A. on www.douglasadams.com, 10 January 1999
9. As 7
10. D.N.A. interviewed by Iain Johnstone on cassette of *Douglas
    Adams' Guide to the Hitchhiker's Guide to the Galaxy*, BBC
    Radio Collection, 1999
11. Ruth Shurman, *Guardian*, 1994

12. As 10
13. Unknown author, www.nas.com, 1996
14. Stephen Pile, *Daily Telegraph*, 20 October 1990
15. Quoted by Scott Jennings in interview with M.J.S., June 2002
16. Interview with M.J.S., June 2002
17. Interview with M.J.S., April 2002
18. News story in *The Times*, 17 May 2002
19. Post by D.N.A. on www.douglasadams.com, 19 January 2000
20. Post by D.N.A. on www.douglasdams.com, 21 September 1999

Chapter 36
1. Jonathan Jones and John Campbell Rees, *Mostly Harmless*, January 1995
2. Interview with M.J.S., March 2002
3. Ibid.
4. Ibid.
5. As 1
6. As 2
7. Ibid.
8. Ibid.
9. M.J.S., *Mostly Harmless*, September 1997
10. Interview with M.J.S., April 2002
11. Ibid.
12. Interview with M.J.S., March 2002
13. Leyal Swan, *Hindustan Times*, 4 September 1998
14. Interview with M.J.S., April 2002
15. As 12
16. Jonathan Webster, *SFX*, August 1996
17. As 1
18. As 12
19. Steve Overbury, *Satellite TV Europe*, June 1998

Chapter 37
1. Interview with M.J.S., March 2002
2. Ibid.
3. Kate Bassett, *Cambridge Alumni Magazine*, Lent Term 1996
4. Jonathan Webster, *LiveWire/20:20*, 1996

5. Webchat, www.msn.com, July 1995
6. Interview with M.J.S., April 2002
7. As 1
8. As 4
9. Interview with M.J.S., April 2002
10. As 6
11. M.J.S., *Mostly Harmless*, September 1997
12. Ibid.
13. Tim Appelo, www.amazon.com, 1998
14. As 1
15. Interview with M.J.S., March 2002
16. Interview with Neil Gaiman for *Don't Panic*, date unknown (from transcript)
17. Interview with M.J.S., April 2002
18. As 15

Interlude – Net

1. Post by D.N.A. on alt.fan.douglas-adams, 4 October 1993
2. Post by D.N.A. on alt.fan.douglas-adams, 2 December 1993
3. Post by D.N.A. on rec.music.makers.guitar.acoustic, 11 November 1993
4. Post by D.N.A. on comp.sys.mac.portables, 14 November 1993
5. Post by D.N.A. on rec.scuba, 29 November 1993
6. Post by D.N.A. on sci.geo.geology, 14 December 1993
7. Post by D.N.A. on sci.anthropology, 20 February 1994
8. Post by D.N.A. on alt.politics.media, 15 December 1994
9. Post by D.N.A. on alt.fan.douglas-adams, 2 December 1993

Chapter 38

1. Interview with M.J.S., April 2002
2. Brenda Garneau, www.pcme.com, 1997
3. Matt Newsome, *Interactive Fiction Now*, March 1998
4. Interview with M.J.S., March 2002
5. Jason MacIsaac, www.elecplay.com, 23 April 1998
6. As 4
7. Interview with M.J.S., April 2002

8. As 4
9. As 7
10. Ron Hogan, www.beatrice.com, 1997
11. Anthony Brown, *Mostly Harmless*, January 1998
12. As 2
13. As 4
14. Ibid.
15. Ibid.
16. Ibid.
17. Gordon Cameron, *Computer Graphics*, May 1998
18. As 11
19. As 4
20. Interview with M.J.S., April 2002
21. Correspondence with M.J.S., April 2002
22. As 7
23. As 4
24. Ibid.

Chapter 39

1. Interview with M.J.S., April 2002
2. Ibid.
3. Post by D.N.A. on alt.fan.douglas-adams, 16 July 1998
4. Roger Birchall, *Starburst*, October 1985
5. D.N.A. interviewed by John Dunn, BBC Radio 2, 12 October 1992
6. Tape recording of meeting with Kevin Davies, 26 June 1992
7. Ibid.
8. Ibid.
9. Gilbert Wong, *New Zealand Herald*, 2 January 1993
10. Post by D.N.A. on alt.fan.douglas-adams, 31 October 1993
11. Jonathan Webster, *SFX*, August 1996
12. Interview with M.J.S., April 2002
13. Ibid.
14. Ibid.
15. Short article by D.N.A. in *SFX*, March 1998
16. TDV press release, 15 August 1998
17. As 12

18. News story in *Entertainment Weekly*, 13 October 2000
19. Webchat, slashdot.org, 21 June 2000
20. Ibid.
21. As 12
22. Ibid.
23. Angella Johnson, unknown newspaper, 1999
24. Interview with M.J.S., April 2002
25. Correspondence with M.J.S., April 2002
26. Interview with M.J.S., April 2002

Chapter 40
1. Interview with M.J.S., April 2002
2. Interview with M.J.S., March 2002
3. As 1
4. Ibid.
5. Janelle Brown, www.salon.com, 12 June 2000
6. Interview with M.J.S., April 2002
7. Webchat, www.bbc.co.uk, 21 March 2000
8. Interview with M.J.S., April 2002
9. As 6
10. Ibid.
11. As 8
12. Interview with M.J.S., January 2002
13. Interview with M.J.S., April 2002
14. Interview with M.J.S., April 2002
15. Interview with Neil Gaiman for *Don't Panic*, date unknown (from transcript)
16. As 14

Chapter 41
1. Interview with M.J.S., April 2002
2. Janelle Brown, www.salon.com, 12 June 2000
3. Interview with M.J.S., March 2002
4. Ibid.
5. Interview with M.J.S., April 2002
6. Ibid.
7. As 1

8. Ibid.
9. Interview with M.J.S., April 2002
10. Speech at Embedded Systems Conference, San Francisco, from transcript by Greengrass Communications

Interlude – Salmon
1. Claire Brialey and Noel Collyer, *Mostly Harmless*, 1991
2. Stan Nicholls, *Wordsmiths of Wonder*, Orbit, 1993
3. Unknown author, *Bookcase*, November 1993
4. Jonathan Jones and John Campbell Rees, *Mostly Harmless*, January 1995
5. Jonathan Webster, *SFX*, August 1996
6. Quoted in *Mostly Harmless*, June 1997, original source unknown
7. Matt Newsome, *Interactive Fiction Now*, March 1998
8. Jason MacIsaac, www.elecplay.com, 23 April 1998
9. Webchat, www.worldwithoutborders.com, 8 April 1999
10. Webchat, www.bbc.co.uk, 21 March 2000
11. Brendan Buhler, *Daily Nexus* (UCSB), 5 April 2001
12. Interview with M.J.S., April 2002
13. Interview with M.J.S., April 2002

Chapter 42
1. Interview with M.J.S., April 2002
2. Graham Bridgstock, London *Evening Standard*, 16 November 1990
3. Post by Stephen Fry on www.douglasadams.com, 12 May 2001
4. Interview with M.J.S., March 2002
5. Quoted in correspondence with Joel Greengrass, August 2002
6. As 4
7. Interview with M.J.S., April 2002
8. As 5

Author's Afterword
1. Quoted by Gail Renard in interview with M.J.S., June 2002
2. Correspondence with M.J.S., July 2002

INDEX